Cisco® Networking For Dummies®

OSI Reference Model Layers

Layer	Name
7	Application
6	Presentation
5	Session
4	Transport
3	Network
2	Data Link
1	Physical

Protocols by OSI Layer

OSI Layer	Protocols, coding, conversions
Application	Telnet, FTP, SMTP
Presentation	ASCII, EBCDIC, JPEG, GIF, encryption
Session	RPC, ZIP, SCP, SQL, NFS
Transport	TCP, NBP, UDP
Network	IP, ICMP, BGP, OSPF, RIP
Data Link	MAC, LLC, Frame Relay, LAPB, PPP
Physical	Ethernet, Token Ring, HSSI, 802.3

Five steps of data encapsulation

1 User information is converted into data

2 Data is converted into segments

3 Segments are converted into packets (or datagrams)

4 Packets (or datagrams) are converted into frames

5 Frames are converted into bits

IP address classes

Class	Range	Default Subnet Mask
A	0–127	255.0.0.0
B	128–191	255.255.0.0
C	192–223	255.255.255.0

Switching types

- **Cut-through:** Reads only destination address before forwarding frame

- **Store and forward:** Reads entire frame before forwarding it on

ISDN terminal equipment types

Terminal equipment type	Description
TE1	ISDN standard terminal equipment
TE2	before ISDN standards, requires terminal adapter (TA)

ISDN reference points

Reference point	Used between
R	Non-ISDN ports and TA (terminal adapter)
S	User terminals and NT2 devices
T	NT1 and NT2 devices
U	NT1 devices and terminators

ISDN Lines

ISDN BRI: 2 B (bearer) channels at 64Kbps each and 1 D (data) channel at 16Kbps (144Kbps Total bandwidth)

ISDN PRI: 23 Bbps channels at 64Kbps each and 1 D channel at 64Kbps (1.54 Mbps)

Common Well-known Port Assignments

Port Number	Assignment
20	FTP data transfer
25	SMTP (Simple Mail Transfer Protocol)
53	DNS (Domain Name System)
80	HTTP (Hypertext Transfer Protocol)
110	POP3 (Post Office Protocol)

Cisco® Networking For Dummies®

Cheat Sheet

LAN Switching Basics

LAN Segmentation breaks up collision domains by creating more segments with fewer workstations in each segment. A LAN can be segmented with a bridge, switch, or router.

Bridges operate at the Data Link layer (Layer 2) and examine the MAC (Media Access Control) address of a frame and then forwards the frame if it is not a local address. Bridges forward multicast messages.

Routers operate at the Network layer (Layer 3) and examine the network address of a packet and forwards the packet using the best available route. Multiple active paths can exist to a destination.

VLAN (Virtual LAN) is a switch port that has been assigned to be of a different subnetwork.

Routing Protocols

Interior routing:

Distance Vector: Uses metrics (such as the number of hops) to determine the best route to a destination and knows the direction and distance to any network connection.

- **RIP** uses a 15 hop count maximum
- **IGRP** uses a 255 hop count maximum

Link State: Creates a topographical view of the network by exchanging LSP ("Hello") packets with other routers. Uses SPF (Shortest Path First) algorithm to determine route.

- **OSPF** makes routing decisions on route costs

Exterior routing:

EGP (Exterior Gateway Protocol)

BGP (Border Gateway Protocol)

Novell IPX Frame Types

Novell	Cisco
Ethernet_802.2	sap
Ethernet_802.3	novell-ether (default)
Ethernet_snap	snap
Ethernet_II	arpa

Access List Numbers

Type	Range
IP Standard	1 – 99
IP Extended	100 – 199
IPX Standard	800 – 899
IPX Extended	900 – 999
IPX SAP	1000 – 1099

Subnetting Formulas

Maximum number of subnets available on a network:

$$2^{(masked\ bits)} - 2*$$

Maximum number of hosts available on a subnet:

$$2^{(unmasked\ bits)} - 2*$$

* Two is subtracted to remove the all 1s and all 0s addresses.

For Dummies®: Bestselling Book Series for Beginners

 ™

References for the Rest of Us! ®

BESTSELLING BOOK SERIES

Are you intimidated and confused by computers? Do you find that traditional manuals are overloaded with technical details you'll never use? Do your friends and family always call you to fix simple problems on their PCs? Then the *...For Dummies*® computer book series from IDG Books Worldwide is for you.

...For Dummies books are written for those frustrated computer users who know they aren't really dumb but find that PC hardware, software, and indeed the unique vocabulary of computing make them feel helpless. *...For Dummies* books use a lighthearted approach, a down-to-earth style, and even cartoons and humorous icons to dispel computer novices' fears and build their confidence. Lighthearted but not lightweight, these books are a perfect survival guide for anyone forced to use a computer.

"I like my copy so much I told friends; now they bought copies."

— Irene C., Orwell, Ohio

"Quick, concise, nontechnical, and humorous."

— Jay A., Elburn, Illinois

"Thanks, I needed this book. Now I can sleep at night."

— Robin F., British Columbia, Canada

Already, millions of satisfied readers agree. They have made *...For Dummies* books the #1 introductory level computer book series and have written asking for more. So, if you're looking for the most fun and easy way to learn about computers, look to *...For Dummies* books to give you a helping hand.

IDG BOOKS WORLDWIDE ®

Cisco® Networking FOR DUMMIES®

by Ron Gilster and Kevin Ulstad

IDG BOOKS WORLDWIDE

IDG Books Worldwide, Inc.
An International Data Group Company

Foster City, CA ◆ Chicago, IL ◆ Indianapolis, IN ◆ New York, NY

Cisco® Networking For Dummies®

Published by
IDG Books Worldwide, Inc.
An International Data Group Company
919 E. Hillsdale Blvd.
Suite 400
Foster City, CA 94404
www.idgbooks.com (IDG Books Worldwide Web Site)
www.dummies.com (Dummies Press Web Site)

Library of Congress Control Number: 00-103398

ISBN: 0-7645-0740-0

Printed in the United States of America

10 9 8 7 6 5 4 3 2 1

1O/RU/QZ/QQ/IN

Distributed in the United States by IDG Books Worldwide, Inc.

Distributed by CDG Books Canada Inc. for Canada; by Transworld Publishers Limited in the United Kingdom; by IDG Norge Books for Norway; by IDG Sweden Books for Sweden; by IDG Books Australia Publishing Corporation Pty. Ltd. for Australia and New Zealand; by TransQuest Publishers Pte Ltd. for Singapore, Malaysia, Thailand, Indonesia, and Hong Kong; by Gotop Information Inc. for Taiwan; by ICG Muse, Inc. for Japan; by Intersoft for South Africa; by Eyrolles for France; by International Thomson Publishing for Germany, Austria and Switzerland; by Distribuidora Cuspide for Argentina; by LR International for Brazil; by Galileo Libros for Chile; by Ediciones ZETA S.C.R. Ltda. for Peru; by WS Computer Publishing Corporation, Inc., for the Philippines; by Contemporanea de Ediciones for Venezuela; by Express Computer Distributors for the Caribbean and West Indies; by Micronesia Media Distributor, Inc. for Micronesia; by Chips Computadoras S.A. de C.V. for Mexico; by Editorial Norma de Panama S.A. for Panama; by American Bookshops for Finland.

For general information on IDG Books Worldwide's books in the U.S., please call our Consumer Customer Service department at 800-762-2974. For reseller information, including discounts and premium sales, please call our Reseller Customer Service department at 800-434-3422.

For information on where to purchase IDG Books Worldwide's books outside the U.S., please contact our International Sales department at 317-572-3993 or fax 317-572-4002.

For consumer information on foreign language translations, please contact our Customer Service department at 1-800-434-3422, fax 317-572-4002, or e-mail rights@idgbooks.com.

For information on licensing foreign or domestic rights, please phone +1-650-653-7098.

For sales inquiries and special prices for bulk quantities, please contact our Order Services department at 800-434-3422 or write to the address above.

For information on using IDG Books Worldwide's books in the classroom or for ordering examination copies, please contact our Educational Sales department at 800-434-2086 or fax 317-572-4005.

For press review copies, author interviews, or other publicity information, please contact our Public Relations department at 650-653-7000 or fax 650-653-7500.

For authorization to photocopy items for corporate, personal, or educational use, please contact Copyright Clearance Center, 222 Rosewood Drive, Danvers, MA 01923, or fax 978-750-4470.

is a registered trademark under exclusive license to IDG Books Worldwide, Inc. from International Data Group, Inc.

About the Authors

Ron Gilster (CCNA, A+, Network+, i-Net+, MBA, and AAGG) has been involved with networking and internetworking since 1993 as a trainer, teacher, developer, merchant, and end-user. He has over 33 years of total computing experience, including over 13 years involved with the networking of computers. Ron is employed by HighSpeed.Com, a leading LMDS, DSL, and broadband communications company and ISP, where he is the General Manager of Internet Solutions and the external networking infrastructure of the corporation, including VPN, telephony, intranet, extranet, and Internet services operations. He is the author of *A+ Certification For Dummies*, *Network+ Certification For Dummies*, *I-Net+ For Dummies*, and *CCNA For Dummies*, plus several books on networking, the Internet, computer and information literacy, and programming.

Kevin Ulstad (CCNA, Network+, A+) is currently a regional account executive for HighSpeed.Com, responsible for LMDS, DSL, and networking solutions. His recent experience also includes stints as the LAN administrator for that company's local area networks. Kevin is the coauthor of *CCNA For Dummies*.

ABOUT IDG BOOKS WORLDWIDE

Welcome to the world of IDG Books Worldwide.

IDG Books Worldwide, Inc., is a subsidiary of International Data Group, the world's largest publisher of computer-related information and the leading global provider of information services on information technology. IDG was founded more than 30 years ago by Patrick J. McGovern and now employs more than 9,000 people worldwide. IDG publishes more than 290 computer publications in over 75 countries. More than 90 million people read one or more IDG publications each month.

Launched in 1990, IDG Books Worldwide is today the #1 publisher of best-selling computer books in the United States. We are proud to have received eight awards from the Computer Press Association in recognition of editorial excellence and three from Computer Currents' First Annual Readers' Choice Awards. Our best-selling ...For Dummies® series has more than 50 million copies in print with translations in 31 languages. IDG Books Worldwide, through a joint venture with IDG's Hi-Tech Beijing, became the first U.S. publisher to publish a computer book in the People's Republic of China. In record time, IDG Books Worldwide has become the first choice for millions of readers around the world who want to learn how to better manage their businesses.

Our mission is simple: Every one of our books is designed to bring extra value and skill-building instructions to the reader. Our books are written by experts who understand and care about our readers. The knowledge base of our editorial staff comes from years of experience in publishing, education, and journalism — experience we use to produce books to carry us into the new millennium. In short, we care about books, so we attract the best people. We devote special attention to details such as audience, interior design, use of icons, and illustrations. And because we use an efficient process of authoring, editing, and desktop publishing our books electronically, we can spend more time ensuring superior content and less time on the technicalities of making books.

You can count on our commitment to deliver high-quality books at competitive prices on topics you want to read about. At IDG Books Worldwide, we continue in the IDG tradition of delivering quality for more than 30 years. You'll find no better book on a subject than one from IDG Books Worldwide.

John Kilcullen
Chairman and CEO
IDG Books Worldwide, Inc.

IDG is the world's leading IT media, research and exposition company. Founded in 1964, IDG had 1997 revenues of $2.05 billion and has more than 9,000 employees worldwide. IDG offers the widest range of media options that reach IT buyers in 75 countries representing 95% of worldwide IT spending. IDG's diverse product and services portfolio spans six key areas including print publishing, online publishing, expositions and conferences, market research, education and training, and global marketing services. More than 90 million people read one or more of IDG's 290 magazines and newspapers, including IDG's leading global brands — Computerworld, PC World, Network World, Macworld and the Channel World family of publications. IDG Books Worldwide is one of the fastest-growing computer book publishers in the world, with more than 700 titles in 36 languages. The "...For Dummies®" series alone has more than 50 million copies in print. IDG offers online users the largest network of technology-specific Web sites around the world through IDG.net (http://www.idg.net), which comprises more than 225 targeted Web sites in 55 countries worldwide. International Data Corporation (IDC) is the world's largest provider of information technology data, analysis and consulting, with research centers in over 41 countries and more than 400 research analysts worldwide. IDG World Expo is a leading producer of more than 168 globally branded conferences and expositions in 35 countries including E3 (Electronic Entertainment Expo), Macworld Expo, ComNet, Windows World Expo, ICE (Internet Commerce Expo), Agenda, DEMO, and Spotlight. IDG's training subsidiary, ExecuTrain, is the world's largest computer training company, with more than 230 locations worldwide and 785 training courses. IDG Marketing Services helps industry-leading IT companies build international brand recognition by developing global integrated marketing programs via IDG's print, online and exposition products worldwide. Further information about the company can be found at www.idg.com.

1/26/00

Dedication

Ron Gilster:

To all of the hardworking, dedicated readers whose kind words of encouragement make all of the late nights and hard work worth it — may you achieve your goals.

And to my loving wife, Diane, and children, Jeana, Rob, Kirstie, and Mimi, thanks for all of the support.

Kevin Ulstad:

To my wife Linda and children Heather, Megan, Ashlie, and Andrew, my sincere thanks.

Authors' Acknowledgments

We would like to thank the wonderful folks at IDG Books who helped get this book published, especially Joyce Pepple, Judy Brief, Mary Corder, Nate Holdread, Tonya Maddox, Gwenette Gaddis, Angie Hunckler, and the virtual cast of tens who work behind the scenes to shield us from the cold, cruel, technical part of the process. And to Brenda Cox and the Technical Support crew for their continued support to our valued readers.

Special thanks to Ciaran Bloomer for the technical editing job he provided.

Publisher's Acknowledgments

We're proud of this book; please register your comments through our IDG Books Worldwide Online Registration Form located at http://my2cents.dummies.com.

Some of the people who helped bring this book to market include the following:

Acquisitions, Editorial, and
Media Development

Project Editors: Nate Holdread, Tonya Maddox, Darren Meiss

Acquisitions Editor: Judy Brief

Copy Editor: Gwenette Gaddis

Proof Editor: Dwight Ramsey

Technical Editor: Ciaran Bloomer

Editorial Manager: Constance Carlisle

Editorial Assistant: Sarah Shupert

Production

Project Coordinator: Nancee Reeves

Layout and Graphics: Karl Brandt, Jason Guy, Shelley Norris, Tracy K. Oliver, Jill Piscitelli, Brent Savage, Rachell Smith, Julie Trippetti,

Proofreaders: Laura Albert, Corey Bowen, Vickie Broyles, Sally Burton, York Production Services, Inc.

Indexer: York Production Services, Inc.

General and Administrative

IDG Books Worldwide, Inc.: John Kilcullen, CEO

IDG Books Technology Publishing Group: Richard Swadley, Senior Vice President and Publisher; Walter R. Bruce III, Vice President and Publisher; Joseph Wikert, Vice President and Publisher; Mary Bednarek, Vice President and Director, Product Development; Andy Cummings, Publishing Director, General User Group; Mary C. Corder, Editorial Director; Barry Pruett, Publishing Director

IDG Books Consumer Publishing Group: Roland Elgey, Senior Vice President and Publisher; Kathleen A. Welton, Vice President and Publisher; Kevin Thornton, Acquisitions Manager; Kristin A. Cocks, Editorial Director

IDG Books Internet Publishing Group: Brenda McLaughlin, Senior Vice President and Publisher; Sofia Marchant, Online Marketing Manager

IDG Books Production for Branded Press: Debbie Stailey, Director of Production; Cindy L. Phipps, Manager of Project Coordination, Production Proofreading, and Indexing; Tony Augsburger, Manager of Prepress, Reprints, and Systems; Shelley Lea, Supervisor of Graphics and Design; Debbie J. Gates, Production Systems Specialist; Steve Arany, Associate Automation Supervisor; Robert Springer, Supervisor of Proofreading; Trudy Coler, Page Layout Manager; Kathie Schutte, Senior Page Layout Supervisor; Janet Seib, Associate Page Layout Supervisor; Michael Sullivan, Production Supervisor

Packaging and Book Design: Patty Page, Manager, Promotions Marketing

◆

The publisher would like to give special thanks to Patrick J. McGovern, without whom this book would not have been possible.

◆

Contents at a Glance

Cartoons at a Glance

By Rich Tennant

page 7

page 87

"It's okay. One of the routers must have gone down and we had a brief broadcast storm."

page 371

"You the guy having trouble staying connected to the network?"

page 241

"A little harder please, Gus."

"This part of the test tells us whether you're personally suited to the job of network administrator."

page 299

"I find it so obnoxious when people use their cellular phone in public that I'm making notes about it on my HPC for a future opinion piece."

page 169

"...and Bobby here found a way to extend our data transmission an additional 3000 meters using coax cable. How'd you do that, Bobby—repeaters?"

page 401

Fax: 978-546-7747
E-mail: richtennant@the5thwave.com
World Wide Web: www.the5thwave.com

Table of Contents

XX **Cisco Networking For Dummies** _____

Introduction

*I*f you have purchased or are considering the purchase of this book, you most likely fit one of the following categories:

- ✔ You are an experienced network administrator who wishes to learn more about Cisco Systems networking and internetworking because this information is valuable to your career and advancement.
- ✔ You're wondering just what Cisco networking is all about.
- ✔ You think that reading this book may be a fun, entertaining way to learn about the networking and internetworking with Cisco Systems, Inc. routers and switches.
- ✔ You love all . . .*For Dummies* books and wait impatiently for each new one to come out.
- ✔ You're a big fan of anything Cisco and just can't get enough of it.

If you fit into one or more of these descriptions, then this is the book for you!

Why Use This Book?

So, if it is your goal to learn more about Cisco Systems' networking devices, then you are in the right place! This book is intended to provide you with a basic review of Cisco networking fundamentals and principles, as well as a brief overview of how Cisco networks are designed, installed, configured, and operated.

Learning about the market leader

Cisco Systems, Inc. is the largest manufacturer of networking systems in the world. It dominates the router and switch market to the extent that Cisco routers and switches are considered by many to set the standard for all other companies.

The reasons behind this success are the same reasons why Cisco equipment is chosen by most network administrators for their networks, big or small: reliability, scalability, flexibility, and interoperability. Yes, this does sound like a lot of abilities, but Cisco routers, switches, and other equipment keep running without problems, are readily upgraded, are easily adapted to new network configurations, and are compatible with virtually every transport or access method.

Using a . . .For Dummies reference

As with all other . . .*For Dummies* books, this book is a no-nonsense reference and study guide. It focuses on the areas you are likely to need as you begin working with Cisco networking equipment. We also include some background and foundation information to help you understand both the basic and more complex concepts and technologies.

This book presents the facts, concepts, processes, and applications a Cisco network administrator needs in step-by-step lists, tables, and figures, without long explanations. The focus is on providing you with information on the hows and whys of choosing a Cisco network and not to impress you with our obviously extensive and impressive knowledge of networking and its related technologies (nor our modesty, we might add).

In developing this book, we made two groups of assumptions:

- ✔ You have an entry-level knowledge of networking, routers, bridges, switches, and other networking components, as well as a fundamental knowledge of electronics, computers, software, protocols, and troubleshooting procedures.

- ✔ You have some experience with Cisco hardware and its integration into networking environments, but are looking for a general overall guide to Cisco networking.

And, while it is not a primary objective of the book, it should be an excellent study aid for preparing for the CCDA (Cisco Certified Design Associate) and the CCNA (Cisco Certified Networking Associate) exams. Although, you may find *CCNA For Dummies* (also published by IDG Books Worldwide) to be a more specific study guide.

Using This Book

This book is organized so you can find out more about Cisco networking in the sequence you prefer, or you can read about specific networking areas without the need to wade through stuff you already know. Each chapter gives you a list of the topics covered in it that you can use as a guide to what's in the chapter.

You'll also find that some topics may be covered in more that one place in the book, with one location providing more information than the other. This is done more for emphasis or to put a topic into context of a network concept or practice. When this happens, we provide you with a cross-reference back to where the topic was covered in detail.

The following sections tell you what we included between the covers of this book.

Part I: Networking Basics

Parts I and II of the book are intended for readers that are new to networking in general, not just Cisco networking. We tried to include a thorough overview of networking terminology, concepts, and fundamentals to provide you with the foundation in networking you need as you work with the other parts of this book. If you have a good understanding of networking principles and basics, you can most likely skip this part of the book. But, it won't hurt you to look it over, anyway.

Part II: Network Operations

This part of the book provides an overview of the standards and guidelines that define how a network interacts with its nodes and other networks. We also review the logical, virtual, and software elements used to transmit or carry data over the network. A very important part of this review deals with network addressing and network operating systems.

Part III: Cisco Networking

In this part, we finally get to the good stuff. This is the first of four parts that relate to Cisco networking and Cisco routers, switches, and other networking and internetworking devices and the roles they play in a LAN. The point of the material in this part of the book is to help you understand how a router works, how it fits into your network, and how it can best serve your needs, which is exactly the point, isn't it?

Part IV: Managing a Cisco Network

Cisco networks must be managed, which includes administration, configuration, monitoring, and in most situations, cursing, stomping, and praying. So, in this part of the book, we give you an overview of how the network administrator works with a Cisco router, including working with the command line interface, the configuration processes, providing for security, and the "s-words" — subnet, subnet mask, and subnetting. However, we leave the cursing part to other references.

Part V: LANs and WANs

As its name implies, this part of the book covers the concepts and technologies used to organize networked resources into networks in local areas as well as wide areas. Although not obvious from the name, the use of switching systems is the focus in this part of the book. A large part of Cisco networking involves the effective use of switching. This part covers the use of switches in a network and how they can be used to segment a LAN. Also covered are the link types that can be used to create a WAN.

Part VI: The Part of Tens

This part provides four lists, each of which has at least ten pieces of very valuable information. The lists in the Part of Tens are: ten really great sites for information on Cisco routers, switches, and other networking equipment; ten network design tips that will help you create a better network; ten tips for a safe and trouble-free installation; and ten things you should pay attention to when configuring a Cisco router.

Part VII: Appendixes

This book has two appendixes: one for now and one for later. The one for now is the Glossary in Appendix B, which includes most of the terms used in the book relating to networking, computing, and really technical stuff. We have provided as much of a non-technical definition as we could without using geekspeak. The one for later is a reference of common IOS commands and their options and parameters, found in Appendix A.

Icons Used in This Book

 The Technical Stuff icon highlights a technical discussion on how a concept works or is applied.

 Remember icons point out general information and subjects that you should remember for application on your network.

 Tip icons flag information that can come in extra-handy during the testing process. You may want to take notes on these tidbits!

 The Warning icon alerts you to some potentially dangerous or treacherous material. Heads up!

Feedback

We'd like to hear from you. If an area of Cisco networking isn't covered as well as it should be, or if we've provided more coverage than you think is warranted about a particular topic, please let us know. Your feedback is solicited and welcome. You can send email to us at the following email addresses:

Ron Gilster: rgilster@hscis.net

Kevin Ulstad: kulstad@highspeed.com

Part I
Networking
Basics

The 5th Wave   By Rich Tennant

Alice in WonderLAN

I wonder why she's not getting her files?

I wonder why I'm not getting my files?

I wonder why it takes so long to transfer files?

I wonder why I can't access the printer?

I wonder who's been into my memos?

I wonder why I couldn't just do this on my Macintosh?

In this part . . .

*I*f you are new to networking in general, not just Cisco networking, this part of the book is meant for you. We've tried to include a thorough overview of networking terminology, concepts, and fundamentals to provide you with the foundation in networking you'll need as you work with the other parts of this book. If you have a good understanding of networking principles and basics, you can most likely skip this part of the book. But, it can never hurt to look it over, anyway.

As a Cisco networker, you'll need an understanding of network structures, the OSI model, networking hardware, software, cabling media, and the role played by each of these components in building a network.

Chapter 1

Networking No Longer Means Passing Out Your Business Card

● ●

In This Chapter

▶ Reviewing network types and terminology

▶ Describing standard network topologies and their characteristics

▶ Knowing network topology advantages and disadvantages

● ●

*B*efore you can start building a Cisco network, you should first know and understand the concepts that are the basic building blocks of networking. As in all walks of computing life, the devil is definitely in the details. If you understand the basic concepts of networking, the common network topologies, and their usage, you can avoid the network devil and the pitfalls that await the uninformed, the foolish, and the hasty.

All Cisco networkers are expected to speak a certain language. The vocabulary of a true Cisco networker includes such basic terminology as *network, topology, peer-based, server-based, LAN, WAN, MAN,* and *fault-tolerance,* not to mention all of the really technical terms and concepts that we cover in later chapters. In addition to your ability to amaze and impress your friends with your steel-trap grasp of network-speak, you will be able to understand documentation, new product announcements, and upgrade bulletins, and be able to determine if new products are appropriate for your network.

If you are new to networking, spend the time building a strong and wide foundation of basic networking terminology and concepts. We're not sure we will make you an expert in any of the topics covered here, but we certainly will get you ready to work on a Cisco network, and isn't that why you're here?

Hardware, Software, and the Magic

We can talk forever about network topologies and technologies, but eventually it all boils down to the stuff — the hardware and software — that makes up the network, and the magic applied by the network administrator to make it all function as a network. Networks are mostly things, as in hardware, software, and administrative processes, and these things are used to build, configure, and manage a network.

The most basic elements of any network are servers, workstations and other network nodes, and cabling used to connect them:

- **Cable** — The physical medium over which information is transmitted between nodes in a network. The five main types of cable used in networking are coaxial, shielded twisted-pair (also referred to as just twisted-pair), unshielded twisted-pair, IBM, and fiber-optic. See Chapter 4 for more information on network cabling types.

- **Server** — A network computer from which workstations (clients) access and share files, printers, communications, and other services. A server can be dedicated to a single service — for examples, file servers, print servers, application servers, Web servers, and so on. See Chapter 3 for more information.

- **Node** — Any addressable network points, including workstations, peripherals, or other network devices. *Node* is commonly used interchangeably with *workstation*.

- **Workstation** — A personal computer connected to a network by a cable that is used to perform tasks using application or utility software or using data stored locally or provided by a network server. A workstation is also known as a client.

Stringing along with the cable

Chapter 4 lists more than 30 different types and uses for cable and wire in a networked environment, but in general nearly all networks being created today use cables from a very short list of cable types. Probably the most common type of cable used on networks is UTP (Unshielded Twisted-Pair) copper wire cabling. Coaxial cables are still frequently used, with fiber-optic cables gaining fast, and, although not always thought of as a network media type, wireless networking is also gaining popularity.

Workstations and nodes

A *workstation* is a computer attached to the network and a node is an addressable workstation, peripheral, or other device attached to the network. Although in general usage, *node* is commonly used to refer to a workstation, when node is used, you should consider all things that could possibly be a network node.

Let us put this another way, only those computers on which you can actually perform work that uses network resources is a workstation. It gets its name from the fact that you can perform work at this network station. A node, on the other hand, is any networkable computer, printer, scanner, fax machine, or other piece of hardware that can be attached to the network. And before you start with the "a printer can do work" business, the focus here is on you and where you can get work done.

Now that we've explained in it nauseating detail, you'll find that often the terms workstation and node are used interchangeably. But, there really is a difference.

Starting at the Beginning

We're going to start you off with the most basic of network basics:

A network is two or more computers connected by a transmission medium for the purpose of sharing resources.

Any two computers that are directly connected by some medium, such as a wire, a cable, or a wireless connection, for the purpose of sharing files, programs, or even *peripherals,* such as printers, scanners, CD towers, and so on, form a network, like the one shown in Figure 1-1. The underlying truth of networking is something that you must absolutely understand: One computer cannot be a network!

Figure 1-1 illustrates a network of the kind we're describing. Ben's computer has been connected to Jerry's so that Ben can share Jerry's nifty new laser printer. In this configuration, Ben and Jerry can also share data on each other's hard disk as well. Regardless of its simplicity, the two computers in Figure 1-1 form a network!

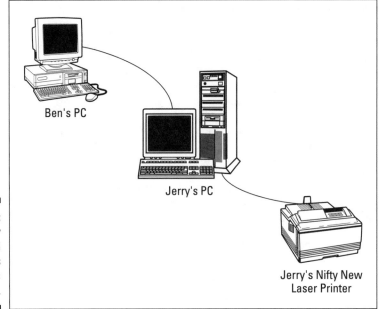

Ben's PC

Jerry's PC

Figure 1-1:
Two directly
connected
computers
form a basic
network.

Jerry's Nifty New
Laser Printer

Sharing resources (yes, data is a resource) is what networks are all about. Networks have advanced to the point that most network users now take the network for granted — which should be the objective anyway when you really think about it. Users want immediate access to the resources they need to carry out a task on their computers. Whether he needs software, data, or access to a particular piece of hardware, such as Jerry's printer, a user wants the network to make every available resource seem as if it is directly connected to his personal computer, with the network itself transparent.

Building Networks at Home and Away

Regardless of how a network is constructed internally, it is also classified by the proximity of its nodes and its intended function. Networks can be classified primarily in two standard ways. The two common designations are

- **Local area network (LAN):** A LAN connects workstations (also called nodes) in a relatively small geographical area, usually a single office, department, or building for the purpose of resource sharing.

- **Wide area network (WAN):** A WAN connects nodes and interconnects LANs located over geographically large areas, such as states, countries, and even globally, using dedicated long-distance, high-speed lines. The Internet is the WAN.

Keeping it local

The most common type of network is the local area network or LAN. As its name implies, a LAN exists to service the resource needs of a group of local workstations, usually in one geographical location. A LAN can be in one room, one building, one campus, or one city. As long as the network does not include servers or hosts from outside the family, organization, or company, and the purpose of the network remains focused on sharing local resources, the network is a LAN.

At one time, the rule of thumb was that a local area network existed on media that was totally owned by the network operators — for example, a single company or agency. In some ways, this rule still holds true, but as LANs grow larger and the line between a LAN and a WAN (wide area network) becomes less distinct, a local network may include telecommunications services from an outside provider.

Taking it wide

A wide area network (WAN) connects nodes and interconnects LANs located over geographically large areas, such as states or countries, and even globally, using dedicated (not shared) long-distance, high-speed lines. A WAN is probably more commonplace than you think. The largest and most well-known WAN around is the Internet. A WAN combines local area networks over some form of public communications service. If a company's LAN in Los Angeles is connected to their LAN in Louisiana, in other words, the LAN in L.A. is connected to the LAN in LA, over the public telephone system, it forms a WAN. In order for you to connect to the Internet from your workplace computer (strictly for business purposes, of course), your LAN must connect to the Internet WAN and must actually become a part of it. The Internet qualifies as a WAN in that it is merely a network of networks, all of which are connected over a variety of public communications lines.

Please Accept My Topologies

The layout or shape of a network generally must conform to a couple of major constraints, not counting the cost of the network. One primary consideration is the physical layout of the space into which the network is to be integrated. Another is the networking technology most desired by the network administrator. Generally, the space into which the network must go does not dictate the technology that must be used. However, size and layout considerations within each of the major networking technologies can make one network layout more functional than another.

If you could look at a network from a bird's eye view, you would get a sense of a general shape to the network. This shape and the pattern used to connect the workstations to the network, is its *topology,* or its physical layout.

Four basic topologies are used in laying out networks:

- ✓ **Bus topology:** The network's nodes are connected to a central cable, called a backbone, that runs the length of the network. The bus topology is most commonly associated with Ethernet networks, the most commonly installed form of the bus topology, although most Ethernet networks consist of star clusters attached to the bus backbone (see "Working with an Ethernet network" later in this chapter). Figure 1-2 illustrates the bus topology.

- ✓ **Ring topology:** The primary network cable (backbone) is installed as a loop, or ring, and the nodes are attached to the primary cable at points on the ring. The ring topology is the basis for the token ring network structure, the most common implementation of the Ring topology (see "Won't you wear my ring around your net?" later in this chapter). Figure 1-3 shows an illustration of the ring topology.

- ✓ **Star topology:** On networks using the star topology, each workstation is connected directly to the central server with its own cable, creating a starburst-like pattern. This topology, common to the now largely defunct ARCNet networks, is now more commonly used with Ethernet and token ring networks to cluster workstations, which are then attached to the primary network cable. Figure 1-4 shows a common use of the star topology with a bus topology network.

- ✓ **Mesh:** Using this topology, each workstation is directly connected to every other node on the network, including the server, all other workstations, and any networked peripheral devices. As it should sound, this creates a mess, er, mesh of network connections. This topology is not very common, but is used in situations where a high degree of network redundancy is required. We haven't included an illustration of a mesh topology, because it would look more like a mess topology. Just as it sounds, every node on the network is connected to every other node on the network. Draw six small circles on a piece of paper in no particular pattern. Now connect each circle to every other circle. *Voilá*, you have a mesh topology diagram.

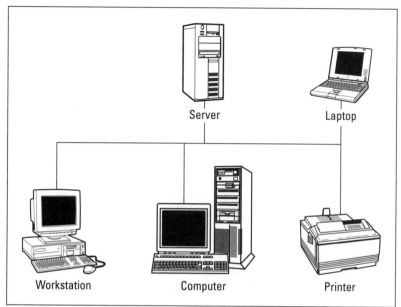

Figure 1-2:
The bus
topology.

Server   Laptop

Workstation   Computer   Printer

Let's get conceptually physical

A conceptual layout of a network is one that exists in the perfect world. In a conceptual rendering of the network, the bus topology is shown a straight line, the ring topology is round, the star toplogy looks just like a daisy, and the mesh topology is almost neat.

The conceptual network layout is intended to show the network as near to how the network will see itself. It identifies each of the nodes, assigns them an identity, and relates them to the other elements of the network.

On the other hand, the physical layout attempts to depict the network as it will actually and physically be installed. In the physical layout, the bus meanders, the ring is lopsided, the star looks like the work of a gorilla with a pencil, and the mesh is very messy. The physical layout identifies cable lengths, connection points, interconnection devices (hubs, switches, bridges, routers, etc.), and any other element, part, component, or device that must be physically installed for the network to function as designed.

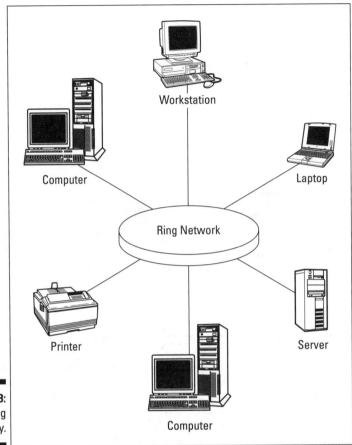

Figure 1-3:
The ring
topology.

Another term used to describe a network is *infrastructure*. This refers to all of a network's components, including its hardware, software, cabling, conceptual layout, and physical layout (see the sidebar "Let's get conceptually physical"). This term is commonly used to describe the operating elements of a network to contrast from the data carried over the network. In fact, it is accurate to say that the network infrastructure carries the network's data.

Riding the bus

In a network built on the bus topology, the nodes are connected to a backbone cable, the primary network cable that runs the length of the network. The backbone extends to a length long enough to connect every node in the network (refer to Figure 1-2). Bus topologies are defined by three unique characteristics: its signal transmission, its use of cable termination, and how it maintains continuity.

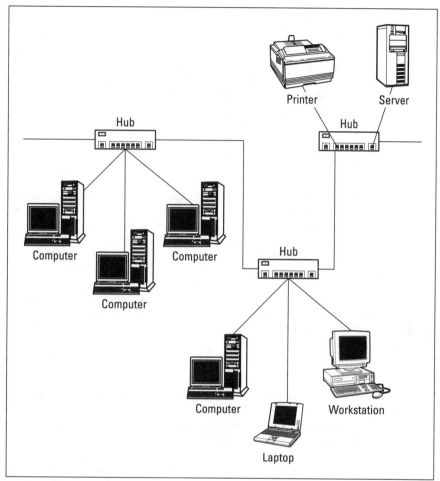

Figure 1-4:
The star
topology
used with
the bus
topology
(called a
star-bus
topology).

Signal transmission

To avoid problems, which we discuss in Chapter 2, generally only one computer can transmit a signal at a time on a bus network backbone. There are specifications around (such as the IEEE 802.4 standard) that define technologies that can be used to allow multiple signals over a bus network, but in general bus networks are limited to a single message.

Politely, when one node is "talking," the other nodes are "listening." As the signal travels down the cable, each node examines the signal to see if the signal was sent to that node. If not, the signal moves on down the cable to the next workstation, which repeats the examination. Because a bus network node only listens for messages sent to it and does not actually pass signals along by regenerating the signal, the bus topology is considered to be a *passive* network structure.

Cable termination

Unless some mechanism stops a signal from bouncing back and forth on the network backbone, a signal would bounce off the ends of the cable indefinitely. With the signal, obviously lost and without a destination on the network, occupying the backbone, all other nodes would be prevented from sending out any other signals. Remember that, by definition, only one signal can be on the backbone at a time. To prevent clogging the system, the backbone cable must be terminated at each end. The terminator, far from the movie type, is a single resistor that is placed at each end of the backbone cable to absorb any unclaimed or undelivered signals, which has the effect of clearing the cable.

A network cable can also be terminated by a connection to another network cable with a bridge, router, or other connectivity device. Each network cable in this situation is known as a network *segment.* Two computers on the same cable are on the same segment. Two computers on two different cables may be on the same network, but are on separate network segments.

You may want to refer to the Glossary included at the back of this book for definitions on any of the terms we use here. We cover such things as bridges and routers in later chapters, but the Glossary can provide you with a brief definition and help you with our meaning.

Continuity

As long as a bus network's cable is terminated at each end, the network continues to function. If one of the nodes on the network fails, the network cable is operable as long as its cable connections are intact. This doesn't mean that any problems caused by the failed node will magically disappear; it only means that the network cable is still okay.

For this reason, among others, the star-bus topology is used to connect nodes to the backbone through a clustering device, such as a hub or multistation access unit (MAU). Should the attached cluster fail, there is little or no affect on the remainder of the network.

Won't you wear my ring around your net?

Token ring networks, although not as popular as the bus or star-bus topologies, are quite common and supported by Cisco internetworking devices. IBM has developed and popularized the token ring technology that is used for virtually all ring topology networks. There are other Ring structures, such as Apple Computer's TokenTalk, but the vast majority of them are token ring. The ring topology looks like a, well, like a ring (refer to Figure 1-3). What can you say? The primary network cable forms a loop that, in effect, has no beginning or end. This eliminates any termination problems on the network.

Signals placed on the network cable travel around the ring from node to node until they reach the correct destination. In reality, a ring structure rarely is installed in a perfectly round shape, but then, you knew that.

In contrast to the bus topology, the ring topology is an *active* topology. Each node on the ring network receives the signal, examines it, and then regenerates it onto the network (if the signal was not meant for that node). As a result, when a computer on the network is unable to regenerate the signal, the entire network is affected and continuity is lost.

Passing the token

Have you ever been to a meeting in which some object is used to control who can talk? For example, suppose that at a meeting, all the participants arrange themselves in a circle and pass a pine bough around the circle. Whoever is holding the pine bough is allowed to share his or her thoughts on how to solve the group's dilemma or share their opinions on a particular topic. If everyone follows the basic sharing rules, that only the person holding the sappy stick can speak, order is maintained and everyone gets his turn. Well, as lame as it may sound for holding a group discussion, this concept works very nicely for the Ring topology. However, instead of a pine bough, the object passed around is called a *token,* which is much like an electronic hall pass. Only the node possessing the token can transmit on the network. Believe it or not, this process is called *token passing.*

Like a Bus network, only one network node can send data at a time — the node holding the token. A node proves that it has the token by embedding it in the message it sends over the Ring network. None of the other nodes can send messages to the network because they don't have the token and cannot access it. The destination node, the node to which the original message was addressed, must include the token in its response to the sending node. When it has completed its session, the sender releases the token to the network and the next node wishing to send a message over the network picks it up.

Continuity

Any breakdown on the ring network impacts its continuity. This is one reason why genuine ring networks are rarely implemented. More often than not, a ring network uses some form of mixed topology, such as a star-ring. (See the next two sections for more information on mixed topologies.)

I want to see stars!

Once upon a time, terminals were directly connected to mainframes, each with its own piece of wire resulting in a configuration that had the wires emanating from the central unit like a starburst. Ah, the good old days! This same configuration is the basis for the star topology in which network nodes are directly connected to the central server.

The star topology is a case of good news and bad news. The good news is that if one node goes down, the rest of the network won't even know about it. The bad news is that if the server goes down, the entire network goes down. Which is one of the big reasons this topology is rarely, if ever, used as the foundation topology for an entire network.

However, the star topology is used to improve the configuration and performance of both the bus and ring topologies, creating the star-bus and the star-ring topologies (see the next section for more information on these mixed topologies).

Mixed topologies

The star topology is more commonly used today to cluster workstations on bus or ring networks. This creates hybrid or mixed topologies, such as the star-bus and the star-ring:

- ✔ **Star-bus:** A hub is used as a clustering device that is attached to the network backbone (refer to Figure 1-4). This is the most common topology of Ethernet networks.

- ✔ **Star-ring:** This is also called the ringed-star (not to be confused with a Ringo Starr). A multi-station access unit (MAU) is used to group workstations into a cluster. The MAU is interconnected to the next MAU in line to complete the ring. The star-ring topology is the most common form used for ring (token ring) networks.

Applying LAN Technologies

Each of the most commonly used network topologies — bus, star, and ring (see "Please Accept My Topologies" earlier in this chapter) — are the basis for the standard LAN technologies used to define and implement local area networks. The three common LAN technologies are

- ✔ Ethernet
- ✔ Token ring
- ✔ Fiber Distributed Data Interface (FDDI)

Working with an Ethernet network

An Ethernet network, the most popular networking technology in use, is by definition built on a bus topology operating on baseband rates of 10 Mbps, 100 Mbps, or 1,000 Mbps (1 Gbps). However, in actual use, Ethernet networks are usually implemented on a star-bus topology with either 10 Mbps or 100 Mbps of bandwidth.

The advantages of Ethernets

The main advantage of building an Ethernet network is that the components needed are readily available and relatively inexpensive. This is the result of Ethernet's popularity. It may be a case of the chicken and the egg as to which came first: that Ethernet is popular because it is cheap and easy or that Ethernet is cheap and easy because it's so popular. That Ethernet is popular there is no doubt. We believe that its popularity is a result of the facts that it is easily implemented and administered; virtually all operating systems and network devices support it; and it's vendor and platform independent.

Another advantage of Ethernet is that the technology has few limitations beyond those imposed by the network cable itself (see Chapter 4). Also, its relatively simple installation, maintenance, and expansion make it a good choice.

When an Ethernet network is installed using the bus-star topology, losing one hub-based cluster has no direct affect on the rest of the network, beyond the fact that any node attached to the missing hub is now not addressable.

Broadband versus baseband

Here's a brief definition of broadband and baseband signaling:

✔ **Baseband networks** use only one channel to support digital transmissions. Most LANs are baseband networks.

✔ **Broadband networks** use analog signaling over a wide range of frequencies. This type of network is unusual, but many cable companies are now offering high-speed Internet network access over broadband systems. Broadband services include such things as LMDS (Local Multipoint Distribution Services) and DSL (Digital Subscriber Lines).

The disadvantages of Ethernets

Ethernets can be tricky to troubleshoot, especially if the network has not been built with troubleshooting in mind. Networks installed on UTP (unshielded twisted-pair) cable are limited to cable lengths of around 100 meters and are limited to the number of repeater segments that can be effectively supported on a network. A *repeater segment* is a portion of the network that is beyond a repeater placed on a network cable to extend its signal length. These limitations can be solved with Cisco switches and routers, but they can be troublesome when growing or updating a legacy network (an existing network that uses pre-existing technology).

In its simplest form, an Ethernet network is installed in a daisy-chain form, see Figure 1-5, with each node connected to the next to create the backbone. In this arrangement, common to thin coaxial cable (see the Glossary for a definition on thin coaxial cable) installations, when one node goes down, any nodes beyond the down node are now not addressable. In its purest form, the nodes connect to the backbone by tapping into it along the path, see Figure 1-6. In this arrangement, should a node fail, the other nodes are unaffected. This is one very good reason why the pure bus topology, as opposed to the daisy-chain form, is the most commonly used format on Ethernet networks.

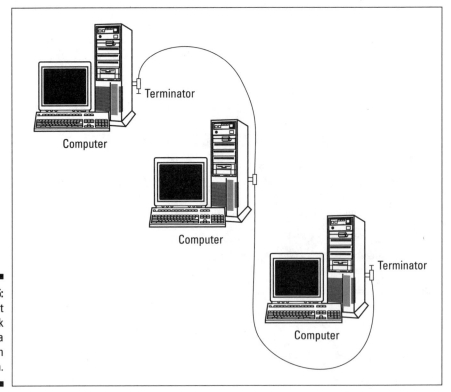

Figure 1-5:
An Ethernet network created in a daisy-chain pattern.

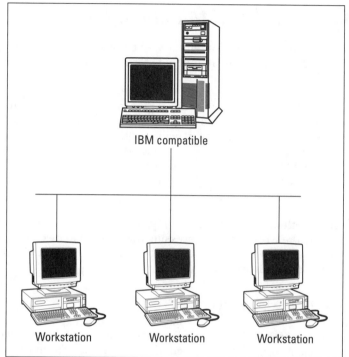

Figure 1-6:
Ethernet
nodes
attach to the
network
backbone
independent
of each
other.

IBM compatible

Workstation   Workstation   Workstation

When Ethernet networks get really busy, the network can become congested by colliding messages, despite the best attempts of CSMA/CD (see "Policing the Ethernet" in this section) to prevent it from happening. So an Ethernet network will surge and recede in waves of activity followed by periods of nodes waiting to send, and on and on. The Ethernet network administrator's life is spent figuring out ways to prevent this from happening.

Policing the Ethernet

The mechanism used on a network technology to control access to the network media and to prevent message collisions is called an *access method.* The access method used by Ethernet networks is CSMA/CD (Carrier Sense Multiple Access/Collision Detection). Under CSMA/CD, when a station wishes to send information over the network, it listens to see whether other stations are broadcasting. If the network is not in use, it sends its message. On occasion, two stations may broadcast at the same time, and a collision occurs. When this happens, each station retransmits its message using a back-off algorithm that specifies a period of time that each workstation should wait before retransmitting. Each network node examines all network traffic, looking for messages addressed to that node. If the message is addressed to a particular node, the node processes it accordingly; otherwise, the message is ignored.

Ring around the token ring network

Token ring networks operate at either 4 Mbps or 16 Mbps. Logically, token ring networks are laid out in a loop that starts and ends at the same node, forming a ring — hence its name.

In contrast to the processes used on an Ethernet network, a token ring node receives messages only from its nearest upstream neighbor (NAUN) and sends signals to its nearest downstream neighbor. (No, it is not a NAD. The downstream neighbor does not have an acronym.) Like Ethernets, though, token ring networks are implemented in a mixed star-ring topology in which each station is connected to an MAU, and MAUs are connected together to actually form the ring.

The access method used for a token ring network is token passing. In this method, only the workstation possessing the token is allowed to transmit on the network. As the workstation completes its tasks, it places the token on the network for another node to use.

The advantages of a token ring network

The largest single advantage of a token ring network, especially when created using nodes clustered on MAUs, is that when a node fails, the network is still alive and well. Another commonly cited advantage to a token ring structure is the reduced chances for message collision. The token passing access method used on ring networks greatly reduces the chances for message collisions as compared to Ethernet networks.

To speed up the network, most new implementations of token ring now support 16 Mbps (as compared to the older standard of 4 Mbps). Some now support two tokens alive on the network at the same time, to really speed things up. However, the tokens must circle the network in the same direction to avoid collisions.

The disadvantages of a token ring network

Some of the disadvantages of a token ring network are that equipment for token ring networks, because they are less popular, tends to be just a little more expensive, and that their top-end speed is 16 Mbps. Compared to 100 Mbps for Fast Ethernet, and now Gigabit speed Ethernet, the speed of the token ring network is downright slow.

FDDI is a double-ring ceremony

FDDI (Fiber Distributed Data Interface) is an ANSI (American National Standards Institute) standard that defines a dual-ring technology that operates at 100 Mbps over fiber-optic cabling. FDDI is not nearly as popular as Ethernet or token ring, but it is a particular favorite of Cisco and is included in its literature and white papers quite often.

FDDI is better suited for networks that operate over large geographic areas, in electronically hostile environments, or for networks that have large bandwidth demands, because it is implemented on fiber-optic media and uses high data-transmission rates. It employs two attached and interconnected rings that operate independently, which gives FDDI systems a built-in media redundancy (which means they have built-in backup cabling) that can be applied when one or more ring segments fail. FDDI, and its newer cousin CDDI (Copper Distributed Data Interchange), are used primarily to interconnect departmental or building LANs on a corporate or collegiate campus.

Chapter 2

The ISO OSI and Other Weird Groups of Letters

*I*n 1984, the International Standards Organization (ISO) spruced up its specifications for connecting network devices and released the "Open System Interconnection Reference Model," which goes by the nickname of "Open System Interconnect" or OSI model. The ISO OSI (easy to remember, huh?) model is the internationally accepted standard for networking. It provides the networking world with a common and standard blueprint for designing, implementing, and operating networking hardware and software. It also provides the basic operating and interconnection rules for all network operating systems, network messaging, and communications connectivity devices.

The underlying foundation of all Cisco networking is the Open Systems Interconnection Reference Model. In fact, the OSI model is the foundation to all network communications — Cisco networks, as well as all others. To succeed on the job, you really must know the OSI model and each of its layers, including each layer's scope of operations, and its relationship to the other layers.

By understanding the OSI model and its layers, you have a good general knowledge of networking. One goes with the other. A thorough understanding of the OSI model is critical to success as a Cisco network administrator. It is not enough to simply know the names of the seven layers. You need to know what each one does and understand why the communications industry uses a layered network model.

Approach the OSI model like you are building a brick wall, and study each layer, and the "mortar" that connects them, from the bottom (Physical layer) on up to the top (Application layer). Even if you are an experienced network technician or administrator and can spell ISO OSI backwards, it sure can't hurt you to review the OSI model one more time.

This chapter gives you an overview of the OSI model and all seven of its layers, with an emphasis on the four layers on which Cisco networks operate.

OSI: The Supermodel of Networking

Why bother with the OSI model? Probably the most important reason is that nearly everything Cisco (and virtually every other network equipment manufacturer) does is defined, documented, and described in terms of the OSI model layer on which it operates. This translates to the fact that you really need to learn the OSI model, its layers, what each does, and with whom it does it, if you expect to understand networking, especially internetworking.

The OSI model is not a standard in the sense that it can be implemented like an Ethernet or token ring network standard. And it is not a suite of protocols, although it defines the guidelines used by many protocols. Just what the OSI model is or isn't can become confusing because of the way it is referenced. You will read, here and in other books, that a certain activity is implemented on a particular OSI level. All this means is that the guidelines that govern that certain activity are included in the standards of that particular level on which a specific protocol or software application was based.

The difference between networking and internetworking (for those that are really interested)

Throughout this book, if you haven't noticed already, we use the terms networking and internetworking, along with network and internetwork, as if they are interchangeable. Well, on a Cisco network that includes a Cisco router or high-end Layer 2 (see "And Now for the Soft Stuff" later in the chapter) switch, your network is an internetwork. Huh? Well, bear with us.

A network without a router is just a network (see Chapter 1 for a good description of a network). However, adding a router usually makes

a network into an internetwork. This isn't automatic, of course. You could add the router just to control internal network traffic and not connect to the outside world, but a router is used primarily to connect your internal network to the external network.

So, if your router connects your network to other routers, your network is an *internetwork*. In fact, the big I internetwork — the Internet — is the granddaddy internetwork, which is where it got its name.

If you work with internetworking long enough, you will eventually think of the OSI as a working model, but only in the sense that devices begin taking on an OSI identity. For example, you may think of routers as Layer 3 functions, switching as a Layer 2 activity, and cabling as Layer 1 media. The router, switch, and cable are not OSI devices; they just perform functions defined in its standards.

The OSI model is more of a blueprint or framework for the ways in which networking devices and services should interact with one another in handling the activities involved with carrying data from one network node to another.

Betting on the lucky 7

The OSI model consists of seven layers. However, much to your sweet tooth's dismay, it is more like an onion than a cake, with each layer encompassing the preceding layer. Figure 2-1 illustrates the seven layers of the OSI model.

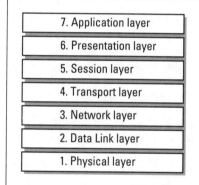

Figure 2-1:
The seven layers of the OSI model.

7. Application layer

6. Presentation layer

5. Session layer

4. Transport layer

3. Network layer

2. Data Link layer

1. Physical layer

Here is a brief overview of each OSI layer:

- **Physical layer:** This is the bottom layer for the OSI model and as its name suggests, it is concerned with the physical nature of a network, which includes cabling, connectors, network interface cards, and the processes that convert bits into signals for sending and signals into bits when receiving. See "First, the Hard Stuff" later in this chapter.

- **Data Link layer:** This layer is concerned with providing context to the Physical layer's bits by formatting them into packets, providing for error checking and correction, and avoiding transmission conflicts on the network. "Listing the Functions of Layer 2," later in this chapter, provides the details for this layer.

✔ **Network layer:** This layer handles addressing of data for delivery and converting network addresses into physical addresses. Routing messages on the network and internetwork also happens at this layer. See Chapter 5 for more information on the Network Layer.

✔ **Transport layer:** This layer of the OSI model deals with network computers communicating with each other and matching the message to the capabilities and restrictions of the network medium. It is at this layer that network messages are chopped into smaller pieces for transmission and reassembled at their destination, preferably in the correct order. See Chapter 5 for more information on the Transport Layer.

✔ **Session layer:** The Session layer manages communication "sessions," including handshaking, security, and the mechanics of an ongoing connection. *Handshaking* is the very technical term for the actions two communicating devices perform to build a connection over which a session is conducted. For quick definitions of terms like this and others, use the handy Glossary we tucked back in Appendix B.

✔ **Presentation layer:** This layer, the sixth of the OSI model, is where raw data messages are packaged in generic form so they can withstand the rigors of being transmitted over a network. Incoming messages are broken down and formatted appropriate to the receiving application.

✔ **Application layer:** This is the seventh and top layer of the OSI model. As its name suggests, it interfaces with applications wishing to gain network access. Do not confuse the Application layer with Microsoft Office, WordPerfect, or Corel Draw or end-user application software. It is applications like Windows NT Server or NetWare that operate at this layer.

The top three layers (Session, Presentation, and Application) are used primarily to support applications. We don't mean the applications on your desktop, such as Microsoft Word, Lotus 1-2-3, or Oracle. These layers include such functions as the FTP (File Transfer Protocol), HTTP (Hypertext Transfer Protocol), and data conversion, compression, and encryption, which interface with your desktop applications to get data ready for transport by the bottom four layers or after transport, to prepare the data being received for use by your desktop applications.

The bottom four layers (Physical, Data Link, Network, and Transport) are used for moving data from one network device to another.

A model of efficiency

The networking industry uses layered interconnection models for five primary reasons. A layered model takes a task, such as data communications, and breaks it into a series of tasks, activities, or components. Several layered models are in use. The Department of Defense (DoD) uses a five-layer model, on which the Internet is based. These two models are contrasted in Figure 2-2.

Cool ways to remember the layers of the OSI model

Should you wish to impress your friends or relatives by reciting the seven layers of the OSI model in sequence, either top to bottom or bottom to top, here are a number of different sayings that you can use to remember the layers of the OSI model:

"Please Do Not Throw Salami (or Sausage, if you prefer) Pizza Away" — This works for bottom to top. And it's my personal favorite: the saying and the pizza.

"APS Transport Network Data Physically" — APS refers to Application, Presentation, and Session. This one works for the layers you need for the Network+ test.

"All People Seem To Need Data Processing" — Here's another top to bottom reminder.

"Please Do Not Tell Secret Passwords Anytime" — I know, it's getting lame!

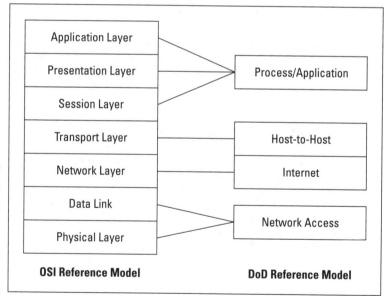

Figure 2-2: The seven-layer OSI model contrasts to the five-layer DoD model.

Five reasons a layered model is used

Actually, a layered model is used for a variety of reasons, but we think these five are probably the most important:

✔ **Standards:** Probably the most important reason for using a layered model is that it establishes a prescribed guideline for interoperability between the various vendors developing products that perform different data communications tasks. Remember, though, that layered models, including the OSI model, provide only a guideline and framework, not a rigid standard that manufacturers can use when creating their products.

✔ **Change:** When changes are made to one layer, the impact on the other layers is minimized. If the model consisted of only a single all-encompassing layer, any change would affect the entire model.

✔ **Design:** A layered model defines each layer separately. As long as the interconnections between layers remains constant, protocol designers can specialize in one area (layer) without worrying about how any new implementations will impact other layers.

✔ **Learning:** The layered approach reduces a very complex set of topics, activities, and actions into several smaller interrelated groupings. This makes learning and understanding the actions of each layer and the model on the whole much easier.

✔ **Troubleshooting:** The protocols, actions, and data contained in each layer of the model relates only to the purpose of that layer. This allows troubleshooting efforts to be pinpointed on the layer that carries out the suspected cause of the problem.

Down one side and up the other

Remember that the OSI model is never actually implemented, but the network hardware, protocols, and other software used to build a network act in a layering and unlayering fashion that is defined by the guidelines of the OSI model. As illustrated in Figure 2-3, a packet is passed down through the OSI layers from the Application layer to the Physical layer, where it is physically transmitted to the Physical layer of the receiving network. At the receiving end, it is passed back up through the layers, from Physical layer to the Application layer.

As the data passes down through the OSI layers, each layer uses the services of the layers above or below it. From the upper layers, data is encapsulated into smaller pieces that are sent down to lower layers. This process continues down to the Physical layer, by which time the original data is converted into binary form that is transmitted across the network's physical media. At the receiving end, the process is reversed and the data is passed back up until it reaches the Application layer, converted back into application data.

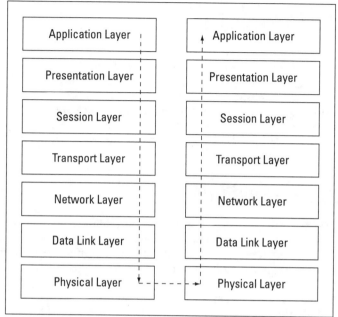

Figure 2-3:
The route
data takes
through the
OSI model's
layers.

The official OSI name for the data passed around on networks is PDU. There are several versions of what PDU stands for, including the original "protocol data unit," the easily remembered "packet data unit," and the heavyweight "payload data unit." A PDU is a unit of data that is packaged for movement from one OSI layer to another as it winds its way from its source to its destination. PDUs are also called data frames, or frames for short, when the Data Link layer passes them to the Physical layer. Commonly, PDUs are referred to interchangeably as packets, frames, and datagrams.

As shown in Figure 2-3, the PDU is passed down through the sending side layers and each layer performs its own brand of magic: Formatting it, breaking it into smaller pieces, adding error-checking tools, and more. Some of the layers also add their own headers (or trailers) to the PDU as it passes down through the layers. When transmitted by the Physical layer, the original message has picked up four headers and perhaps a trailer.

The headers added by some of the layers provide instructions to the counterpart layers at the other end. For example, the Transport layer breaks up the message into segments. The header added by the Transport layer on the sending side contains instructions for sequencing and reassembly of the segments for the receiving side Transport layer. As the packet passes up through the receiving side layers, the headers are stripped away at the appropriate layers until the original message is delivered to the destination application.

First, the Hard Stuff

The various devices that make up networks beyond your desktop computer all generally operate on one layer of the OSI model. We hate to keep nagging the point, but remember that the OSI model is a framework or blueprint for the way things should work. Some hardware strictly conforms to the standards and other hardware conforms more loosely. However, if network equipment wishes to be interoperable with other networking devices, some conformity is required. This is what the OSI model contributes.

Getting physical

The Physical layer (Layer 1 of the OSI model) defines, well, the physical parts of the network. This layer is concerned with moving bits on the physical media. Therefore, it deals only with the hardware affecting the physical movement of data from point A to point B. This includes such things as

✔ Electrical issues and standards that have been developed by various contributing organizations such as the EIA/TIA (the Electrical Industry Association/Telecommunications Industry Association), the IEEE – (pronounced "eye triple-E" and meaning the Institute of Electrical and Electronics Engineers), and UL (Underwriters Laboratories)

✔ Networking hardware, including network interface cards (NICs), network media (copper wire, glass fiber, or wireless signals), repeaters, hubs, and other devices that move the electrical impulses of binary data across the network

✔ The distance limitations of network media, and how these limitations apply in wiring closets through horizontal and intermediate cross-connects

✔ Some basic network topologies and other physical properties of a network

All of the physical hardware used to transport bits around the network is on the Physical layer. This includes network adapters, cabling, wall plugs, cross connects, hubs, repeaters, and connectors. Even wireless network media is on the Physical layer.

Could you repeat that?

There is a condition that happens in sending data over a copper line, as well as in life, called *attenuation,* when the transmitted signal begins to lose its strength due to distance and needs to be re-energized. A *repeater* is a device that is added to a network to solve attenuation problems in cable wire. A repeater cleans up the signal, gives it a little boost, and sends it on its way.

Although it may sound a little like your mom, it is actually a small device that usually has only one input connector and one output connector that can be inserted into the network anywhere the signal needs a boost. A common use for a repeater is to extend the effective range of the cabling by overcoming the distance limitations of the cable.

Just a hub of activity

Hubs are used in a star topology to provide multiport connectivity to a network. Many workstations and peripherals can be clustered to a hub that is then connected to another hub, a switch, a router, or directly to a cross connect.

Hubs are either active or passive. A passive hub merely repeats any signals it receives from one of its ports to all other ports, without re-energizing the signal. Passive hubs do not help the distance limitations of their network's cable. Active hubs, in their most basic form, also include a repeater-type feature that re-energizes the signal before sending it on to its ports. Smart active hubs intelligently direct a signal to the port on which its destination exists.

A bridge over troubled layers

The hardware that operates on the Data Link layer (Layer 2) is concerned with addressing packets on the physical network, making sure a packet is properly addressed to get to its destination. The physical network is not limited to the local physical space and can, and does, include many WAN activities (see Chapter 18). The primary Data Link layer device is a bridge. Other Layer 2 devices are switches and brouters (pronounced "browters").

A bridge is used to connect two or more network segments to form a larger individual network. Another way to look at this definition is to think that a bridge is used to divide a larger network into smaller segments. A bridge records the physical addresses of network nodes and on which of its ports an address is located. The physical address of a node is represented by the Media Access Control (MAC) address of the NIC (network interface card) of the node. By recording the MAC addresses located on its segment, a bridge can determine whether a packet should cross the bridge to reach its destination.

A switch, also called a multi-port bridge, is a smart bridge. It uses MAC addresses to determine the port on which a message should be sent and sends it only to that port. Chapter 9 provides more detail on switches and network switching.

A brouter is a cross between the Layer 2 bridge and the Layer 3 router (see the next section). It is able to perform services from either layers or just those of a bridge or a router, depending on what is needed by the network.

The MAC bridge

No, McDonald's is not in the networking business now. Bridges are commonly referred to as MAC layer bridges because they operate on the MAC sublayer of the Data Link layer. As discussed later in this section (see "Communicating on the MAC sublayer") and in Chapter 7, each network device has a unique MAC address. A bridge uses the MAC address to perform its tasks, including

- ✔ Monitoring network traffic
- ✔ Identifying the destination and source addresses of a message
- ✔ Creating a routing table that identifies MAC addresses to the network segment on which they are located
- ✔ Sending messages to only the network segment on which its destination MAC address is located

A bridge builds up its routing table by cataloging the network nodes that send out messages. A bridge examines the MAC address of a message's source or sending node. If this address is new to the bridge, the bridge adds the address to the routing table along with the network segment from which it originated. The bridge's routing table is stored in its RAM, and just like a PC's RAM, it is dynamic — when the power goes off, it goes away. When the power is restored, the bridge will rebuild the table. Because most network nodes send and received packets continuously, the complete rebuild of the routing table doesn't take long.

Bridging over troubled waters

Because a Data Link frame can effectively live forever, it is possible that a packet addressed to an unknown or non-existent MAC address could bounce around the network indefinitely. This condition is solved by allowing only a single path to be active between two segments at any time through the Spanning Tree Protocol.

The Spanning Tree Protocol designates each interface on a bridge to be either in Forwarding or Blocking state. When an interface is in Blocking state, only special packets reporting the status of other bridges on the network are allowed through. All other packets are blocked. As you can probably guess, an interface in Forwarding state allows all packets to be received and for-warded. The state of a bridge's interfaces are affected whenever a path on the network goes down and the bridges negotiate a new path, changing interface states from Blocking to Forwarding, as needed.

The normal operating mode for a bridge is called store and forward. They receive (store) and examine a whole frame before forwarding it on to the appropriate interface. The time that it takes to examine each frame increases the latency (delay) in the network. *Latency* is the amount of time that it takes a packet to travel from source to destination.

Routing over the internetwork

Hardware devices that operate on the Network layer of the OSI model are concerned with network addressing on large networks that are physically made up of many separate networks. Network layer devices use addressing information to effectively join networks into a large internetwork.

The primary device that operates at this layer is a router, which has more intelligence than a bridge and can calculate an efficient route for a network packet to use to reach its destination. Routers are the keystone devices to Cisco networking. Although you can have a network without a router, it is difficult for a LAN to connect to the outside world, especially the Internet, without a router. In fact, it is downright nearly impossible. You will find all the information you need about routers in Chapters 9, 10, and 11.

Transport me to the gateway

There are no bad gateways, only misunderstood gateways. A gateway can be either hardware or software, or both, but its main purpose is to join two dissimilar systems that have similar functions but cannot otherwise communicate. For example, a PC workstation and a mainframe cannot communicate without a gateway. Although a gateway operates at the Transport layer, it can also operate at any of the top four layers of the OSI model. (See "Betting on the lucky 7" earlier in this chapter for the list of layers.) Table 2-1 summarizes the layers of the OSI model and the hardware that operates on each.

Table 2-1	The Hardware Operating at Each OSI Model Layer
OSI Layer	*Device(s)*
Physical	NIC, cable and transmission media, repeater, hub
Data Link	Bridge, switch, NIC, brouter
Network	Router, brouter
Transport	Gateway
Upper Layers	Gateway

And Now for the Soft Stuff

In addition to hardware, communications activities are provided by software and protocols defined in the OSI model. Just as different types of hardware operate on each of several OSI layers, standards and protocols are also defined on just about every layer of the OSI model. From the Data Link layer (Layer 2) up to the Application layer (Layer 7), each layer defines one or more addressing, connecting, formatting, or converting standard or procedure (see "Betting on the Lucky 7," earlier in the chapter for a description of each OSI layer).

There is one exception to this statement — the Physical layer. The Physical layer defines the physical parts of the network and how they connect and can be laid out, but it doesn't include any software or protocols (see "First, the Hard Stuff," earlier in this chapter).

Although we are discussing the software and protocols of the OSI model in this section, remember that we are doing so on a conceptual level. We can't tell you enough that the OSI model is only a guideline and not a piece of software. Throughout this chapter and the rest of the book, we describe items as being on or at a certain OSI layer. This means only that an item is defined by the standards that exist for that layer. However, eventually you too will begin to picture in your mind the OSI model as a conceptual working model, real or not.

Listing the Functions of Layer 2

Layer 2 (the Data Link layer) is the shipping and receiving dock of the OSI model. It is where data is packaged for transmission on the Physical layer, as well as where data from the Physical layer is unpackaged to be passed to the Network layer (Layer 3) and above. To a certain extent, all OSI layers wrap and unwrap data before sending and after receiving it from the layers above and below it. However, the Data Link layer is the point-of-entry where the data transported over the physical network media enters and leaves your network.

However, a bit more is involved than may appear. In completing these tasks, the Data Link layer performs a number of separate activities, including

- Physical addressing
- Defining the data handling technologies for the various network topologies
- Error checking
- Access to the physical medium (technically called "arbitration")
- Flow control

Stacking up the IEEE 802 standards

Immediately after someone invented networking — by connecting two computers together to share files and pass secret messages — it was immediately apparent that this was a good thing. As local area networks (LANs) began to spread, it became obvious that in order for networks to grow large or to communicate with each other, some rules had to be developed.

Never shy about making rules, those fun-loving, madcap guys at the of Electrical and Electronics Engineers (IEEE) began a project to define Data Link layer standards in February 1980. This date is significant because, for want of a better name, IEEE named the project the 802 Project (as in 80 for 1980 and 2 for February). The 802 Project is actually the name of the committee assigned to develop the networking standards. Each of its subcommittees, assigned to develop standards for a specific networking area, has a subcommittee number, such as 802.1, 802.3, 802.10, and so forth.

Probably the most important of the 802 Project's subcommittees, in terms of Cisco networking, is IEEE 802.3. This is the standard that defines Ethernet, by far the networking standard of choice. The 802.3 standard defines the bus topology, network media (10BaseX), and functions of an Ethernet network. It also defines the functions of the MAC (Media Access Control) sublayer, and of particular interest to the Ethernet world, the CSMA/CD access method.

Each of these activities of the Data Link layer is discussed later in this chapter. First, we need to review some underlying concepts to help you understand the separate activities of the Data Link layer. See Chapter 1 for more information on network topologies.

Probably the most important activities defined on the Data Link layer, as far as your network is concerned, are higher-level message formats and physical-level formats. And the most important parts of these are the IEEE (Institute of Electrical and Electronics Engineers) 802 specification and Media Access Control (MAC) addresses.

Connecting on the LLC sublayer

The Data Link layer is divided into two sublayers by the 802 standards:

- ✔ **Logical Link Control (LLC):** The LLC sublayer is defined in 802.1 and 802.2.

- ✔ **Media Access Control (MAC) sublayers:** The MAC sublayer is defined in the 802.1, 802.3, 802.5, and 802.12.

Don't worry, you don't need to know these numbers. We list them only to demonstrate the complexity of the 802 standards.

The Logical Link Control sublayer creates connections between networked devices. If you want to send data from your workstation client to a server on the same network segment, it is the LLC that creates and manages the connection required to transmit your data.

LLC functions include

- ✔ Managing frames to upper and lower layers
- ✔ Error control
- ✔ Flow control

The LLC works with the Transport layer to provide connectionless and connection-oriented services. A brief description of these two data transfer methods will help you distinguish between them:

- ✔ **Connectionless services:** Messages are not acknowledged by the receiving device, which speeds up the processing. Although it sounds unreliable, this type of transfer is commonly used at this level because the upper OSI layers implement their own error checking and control.

- ✔ **Connection-oriented services:** Because each message is acknowledged, this service is much slower than connectionless services, but it is much more reliable.

Going with the flow control

Flow control is used to meter the flow of data between network devices that may not be running at the same speeds. For situations in which one communicating device is sending information at either a faster or a slower rate than the other device, some form of control is necessary to meter the flow of data between the devices to avoid a loss of data. Flow control prevents the slower device from being swamped and, more importantly, prevents data from being lost or garbled. It works by pausing the faster device to allow the slower device to catch up.

Two types of flow control are implemented in data communications:

- ✔ **Software flow control,** common to networking, involves a process called XON/XOFF, which roughly stands for transmission on/transmission off. In this process, the sending device continues to send data until the receiving device signals, by sending a control character, that it needs to stop the transmission of data until it can catch up. When the receiving device is ready to go, it sends another control signal to begin the data flow again.

✔ **Hardware flow control,** also called RTS/CTS (Ready To Send/Clear To Send), uses two wires in a cable, one for RTS and one for CTS. The sending device uses the RTS signal to indicate when it is ready to send. The receiving device uses the CTS to indicate that the receiving device is ready to receive. When either is turned off, the flow is interrupted.

Detecting errors in the flow

Error detection is the process of determining if any errors may have occurred during a transmission of bits. A calculated value called the CRC (Cyclical Redundancy Check) is added to the message frame before it is sent to the Physical layer. The receiving computer recalculates the CRC and compares it to the one sent with the data. If the two values are equal, it is assumed that the data arrived without errors. Otherwise, the message frame may need to be retransmitted under control of an upper layer. Although the Data Link layer implements error detection, it does not include functions to perform error recovery. This is left for the upper layers to deal with, primarily on the Transport layer.

Communicating on the MAC sublayer

The Media Access Control sublayer provides a range of network services, including controlling which network device has access to the network and providing for physical addressing. The MAC sublayer carries the physical device address of each device on the network. This address is more commonly called a device's MAC (or Layer 2) address.

The MAC address is a 48-bit address that is encoded on each network device by its manufacturer. This works on the same principle that each house or apartment on your street has a unique street address or apartment number assigned to it. The MAC address is used by the Physical layer to move data between nodes of the network. Just like you need to know a friend's address to find his or her house, computers must know each other's address to communicate.

A MAC address is made up of two parts: the manufacturer's ID number and a unique serialized number assigned to the device by the manufacturer. The 48-bits (6 bytes) of the MAC address are divided evenly between these two numbers. The first three bytes of the MAC address contain a hexadecimal manufacturer code that has been assigned by the IEEE. For example, Cisco's IEEE MAC ID is 00 00 0C (each byte holds two half-byte hexadecimal values) and Intel's is 00 55 00. The remaining three-bytes of the MAC address contain a unique hexadecimal serial number that is assigned by the manufacturer to each individual device.

In a workstation, the MAC address is usually burned into the NIC. On a router, each port has its own MAC physical address. The idea is that no two devices should ever have the same MAC address. However, we have heard of instances in which this has occurred in a network with very unpleasant circumstances resulting.

How can we resolve this?

Hardware (MAC) addresses are used to get data from one local device to another. However, not all network operating systems (NOS) use the physical address to reference network nodes. This sets up the conflict between the network (logical) address and the MAC (physical) addresses.

Network operating systems assign a logical network name to each networked device, such as ACCTG_SERVER, NT1, or FRED, to make it easy for its human administrators and users to reference its resources. On the other hand, Layer 1 activities use physical addresses to reference devices on the network. When you request services from the file server FRED, the Data Link layer translates your node name (the name assigned to your computer, most likely your login name) and that of FRED into the MAC addresses of each computer. *Resolving* (the techie term for translating the addresses) these addresses involves a process called, ta da, *address resolution*. Address resolution associates a logical network address with its physical MAC address, and vice versa.

Resolving the issue with ARP

A special protocol, called ARP (Address Resolution Protocol), is used for this service. ARP maintains a small database, called the ARP cache, that cross-references a network's physical and logical addresses. The ARP cache provides each computer with a local network address book. When a device wants to communicate with another local device, it checks its ARP cache to determine if it has that device's MAC address. If it doesn't, it sends out an ARP broadcast request, as illustrated in Figure 2-4, to all devices on the local network. Each device examines the message; if the request is intended for that device, it responds with its MAC address. The sending device stores the address in its ARP cache.

In the example shown in Figure 2-4, USER1 wants to communicate with FRED, a file server. However, USER1 doesn't have a MAC address in its ARP cache for FRED, so it sends out a broadcast message that asks FRED to respond with its MAC address, which FRED does.

When a workstation or server needs to communicate with a device remote to the local network, essentially the same process takes place, with the exception that a router through which the remote device is accessed will likely respond back with its MAC address and not that of the device itself.

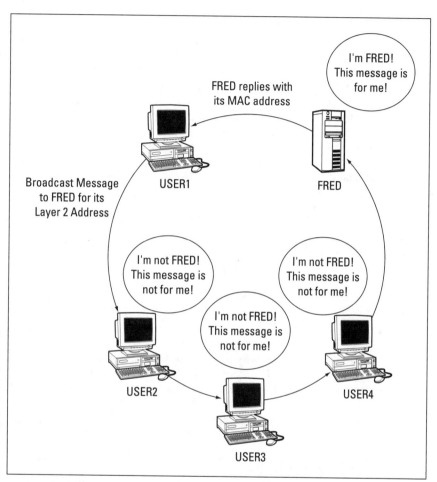

Figure 2-4:
To resolve an unknown address on the network, a broadcast request is sent.

Controlling access to the network

The primary tool defined in IEEE 802.3 for use on the Data Link layer is the CSMA/CD (Carrier Sense Multiple Access/Collision Detection) access method. CSMA/CD is the method used in Ethernet networks for controlling access to the physical media by network nodes. As you may infer from its name, CSMA/CD (quick, say it ten times fast) tries to keep network devices from interfering with each other's communications by detecting access attempts by multiple devices. When sneaky devices avoid detection, and they do, CSMA/CD detects and deals with the data collisions that will undoubtedly occur.

Avoiding collisions

To avoid collisions when two or more workstations are transmitting to the network at one time, CSMA/CD devices "listen" or sense signals on the network backbone before sending a message over the network. If the network is quiet, meaning that it is not in use, the device can send a message. Otherwise, it should wait until the network is not in use. However, if another device sends a message between the time that the first device has decided the network is available and the time it actually transmits its message, the two messages may collide on the network. When this happens, the device that detected the collision sends out an alert to all network devices that a collision has occurred. All devices quit transmitting for a random amount of time to clear the line.

The CSMA/CD process can be described as follows:

1. Listen to see if the wire is being used.

2. If the wire is busy, wait.

3. If the wire is quiet, send.

4. If a collision occurs while sending, stop. Wait a specific amount of time, and send again.

When a collision is detected by a sending device, it sends out a jamming signal that is of sufficient enough duration for all nodes to recognize it and stop broadcasting. Then each device waits a random amount of time to begin the CSMA/CD process again. This random amount of time is determined through a back-off algorithm that calculates the amount of time the device should wait before resuming its attempts to transmit.

Working on a busy intersection

A collision domain is a network segment in which all devices share the same bandwidth. The more devices you have on a segment, the more likely it is that collisions will occur. Too many devices on a segment means that network performance is considerably less than optimal. Increasing bandwidth is one way to deal with the problem, but a better way to deal with this problem is to use the available bandwidth more efficiently.

Segmenting a network for fun and profit

Dividing a network into smaller parts, known as *segments,* decreases the congestion and chances for message collision on each new segment. Yes, each new segment forms a new collision domain, but if the network is segmented properly, the addition of new segments should not cause problems. Devices on the same segment share the same bandwidth. Data passed outside of a segment may enter another segment, or the backbone, which itself is another collision domain on a larger scale. Dividing up a local area network into smaller collision domains, segments, is called *segmentation*.

The benefits of segmenting a LAN are

✔ Increasing bandwidth per user

✔ Keeping local traffic local

✔ Reducing broadcasts

✔ Decreasing collisions

Following the Protocol Rules

A protocol is a set of rules and requirements that two communicating devices must follow in order to conduct an effective communications session. Hundreds of protocols are used in today's networked environment, some general and some specific to a particular operating system, hardware type, or manufacturer.

In general, networking protocols follow the OSI model and its layers. Network servers have suites of protocols, also called protocol stacks, that perform the actions and activities of each layer as a packet passes down or up the OSI model.

Ain't it suite?

A protocol suite is an interrelated group of protocols that have been grouped to help carry out a single activity. For example, the TCP/IP protocol suite is made up of a number of protocols that allow you to interact with the Internet. Most protocol suites, and especially the TCP/IP suite, have different protocols for each layer for the OSI model.

Three general types of protocols exist: Network protocols, Transport protocols, and Application protocols. Figure 2-5 illustrates the general relationship of the three protocol types to the OSI model's layers. Most network administrators spend most of their time working with Transport and Network protocols.

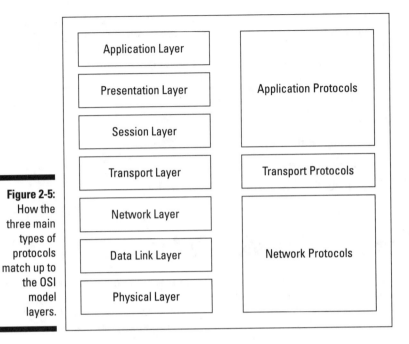

Network protocols

Network protocols provide for packet addressing and routing information, error checking and correction, and enforcing the rules for communicating within a specific network environment. Network protocols provide what are called link services to other protocols operating at other layers. Common Network protocols are

- **DLC (Data Link Control):** DLC is used for network-connected mainframes and Hewlett Packard printers.
- **IP (Internet Protocol):** This is the IP of the famous TCP/IP duo. IP provides addressing and routing information.
- **IPX (Internetwork Package Exchange) and NWLink (NetWare Link):** Novell NetWare's protocol and Microsoft's IPX clone are used for packet routing and forwarding.
- **NetBEUI (NetBIOS Extended User Interface):** This provides transport services for NetBIOS.

Transport protocols

Transport protocols actually do more than just move things around as the name may imply. They do provide reliable end-to-end transport and delivery of data packets, but they also perform error detection in the delivery system. Common Transport protocols are

- ✔ **NetBIOS/NetBEUI (Network Basic Input/Output System)/(NetBIOS Extended User Interface):** While NetBIOS manages communications between computers, NetBEUI provides the data transport services.

- ✔ **SPX (Sequenced Packet Exchange):** SPX is the TCP to IPX's IP. Like TCP, it is used to guarantee data delivery.

- ✔ **TCP (Transmission Control Protocol):** This is the other half of the TCP/IP duo. TCP is commonly misnamed Transport Control Protocol, which is understandable. TCP/IP is responsible for guaranteeing the transport and delivery of packets across networks.

Application protocols

Application protocols provide application-to-application services at the upper layers of the OSI model. Some common Application protocols are

- ✔ **SMTP (Simple Mail Transfer Protocol):** This member of the TCP/IP gang is responsible for transferring electronic mail.

- ✔ **FTP (File Transfer Protocol):** Another protocol wearing the TCP/IP colors, FTP is used to transport files from one computer to another.

- ✔ **SNMP (Simple Network Management Protocol):** This is YATP (yet another TCP/IP protocol) that is used to monitor network devices.

- ✔ **NCP (NetWare Core Protocol):** This is not a TCP/IP protocol! This protocol cluster contains the NetWare clients and redirectors.

How TCP/IP stacks up

The most commonly used protocol suite is TCP/IP, also known as the Internet Protocol Suite (not to be confused with IP, the Internet Protocol). Well, that's why it is commonly called just TCP/IP to represent all the protocols in the suite. Although TCP/IP has been around about ten years longer than the OSI model, it matches up nicely with the layers of the OSI model. Funny how that works out, huh?

Table 2-2 contains an OSI layer by layer breakdown of the TCP/IP suite.

Table 2-2	TCP/IP and the OSI model
OSI model layer	*TCP/IP protocol(s)*
Physical	Physical hardware device connectivity
Data Link	NIC driver, ODI/NDIS
Network	IP, ICMP, ARP, OSPF, RIP
Transport	TCP, DNS, UDP
Upper layers	Telnet, FTP, SMTP

The TCP/IP suite protocols included in Table 2-2 are explained here:

- **ODI/NDIS (Open Data-Link Interface/Network Driver-Interface Specification):** This Data Link layer interface enables NIC drivers to connect to dissimilar networks and have them appear as one.

- **IP (Internet Protocol):** This Network layer protocol provides source and destination addressing and routing.

- **ICMP (Internet Control Message Protocol):** This Network layer protocol carries control messages, such as error or confirmation messages.

- **ARP (Address Resolution Protocol):** This Network layer protocol converts IP addresses to MAC physical addresses.

- **OSPF (Open Shortest Path First):** This protocol is used by TCP/IP routers to determine the best path through a network.

- **RIP (Routing Information Protocol):** This protocol helps TCP/IP routers to use the most efficient routes to nodes on the network.

- **TCP (Transmission Control Protocol):** This primary TCP/IP transport protocol accepts messages from the upper OSI layers and provides reliable delivery to its TCP peer on a remote network.

- **DNS (Domain Name System):** This Transport layer Internet name-to-address resolution service allows users to use human-friendly names.

- **UDP (User Datagram Protocol):** This is another Transport layer protocol can be used in place of TCP to transport simple single-packet messages.

- **Telnet:** This is the protocol used to remotely log into a server, workstation, or router.

- **FTP (File Transfer Protocol):** This is the TCP/IP protocol used to transfer files from a server to a host without analyzing its contents.

- **SMTP (Simple Mail Transport Protocol):** This is the TCP/IP protocol used to move electronic mail from its origination point to the server hosting its destination address.

Chapter 3

Putting the Network Together

In This Chapter

▶ Understanding peer- and server-based networks

▶ Describing internetworking components and terms

▶ Configuring a network interface card (NIC)

*I*f you are new to networking, not to mention Cisco networking, you should go over some of the fundamental hardware, software, and networking concepts before tackling the really technical and complicated router and other Cisco networking stuff in later chapters. If you don't know the basics, understanding the more advanced network concepts and technologies might just be a tad more difficult. The basics include general network concepts, topologies, network structures, networking hardware and software, and a variety of associated concepts and terminology. On a foundation of network basics, you can build a demonstrable understanding of networking technology and practices.

To succeed as a Cisco network administrator, you must have a certain amount of fundamental knowledge in such networking areas as configuring, troubleshooting, fixing, installing, designing, and upgrading networks. For example, it may be difficult, if not impossible, for you to brilliantly deduce the best approach to improving performance on an Ethernet network if you don't know much about Ethernet standards, media, and so forth.

If for no other reason than to be sure that you have an understanding of the fundamental concepts and terminology included in this chapter, you should read through this chapter, because heck, it can't hurt, it can only help, and — you just never know — you could learn something!

Sharing and Sharing Alike

We're going to start you off with the most basic of network basics: *A network is two or more computers connected by a transmission media for the purpose of sharing resources.* That's it! That's what it all boils down to — sharing resources. It doesn't matter whether the network has 2, 20, or 2,000,000 nodes worldwide; it all comes down to sharing resources.

You absolutely must understand this concept. One computer cannot be a network by itself because it can't share. A network is two or more computers connected by some form of communications media so that they can share data, software, or hardware resources. Think about it. Why else would you connect two computers except that you want or need something the other has? Or maybe you have something that another user wants or needs.

Figure 3-1 illustrates a network of the kind we're describing. Adam's computer is connected to Eve's computer so that Adam can use Eve's nifty new laser printer. In this simple network configuration, Adam and Eve are able to share data on each other's hard disks as well. Regardless of its size, Adam's computer and Eve's computer together form a network.

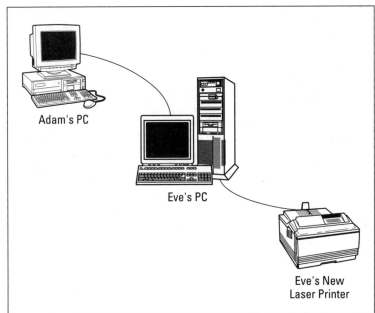

Adam's PC

Eve's PC

Figure 3-1:
A simple
network.

Eve's New
Laser Printer

Sharing resources (yes, data is a resource) is what networks are all about. Networks have advanced to the point where most network users take their network for granted — which is the point when you really consider it. Users only want access to the resources needed to carry out a task on the computer. Whether what they need is software, data, or access to a particular piece of hardware, such as Eve's printer, the user wants the network to make all the resources available on the network seem as if they are directly available on his or her own computer.

Understanding Network Politics

So what happens if you want to connect more than two computers together in a network? Certainly, the more computers you include in your network, the more complicated its administration becomes. But, yes, you can connect three, thirteen, thirty, three hundred, or three thousand computers together to form a network. Essentially, two types of networks exist — and no, Cisco networks and all other kinds are not the two types:

✔ **Peer-to-peer networks** — a.k.a. peer-based networks. As illustrated in Figure 3-1, Adam and Eve have created a peer-to-peer network where neither is the master nor the slave. Participation in a peer-to-peer network is strictly a voluntary, you-trust-me-and-I'll-trust-you affair. If Eve doesn't want to share her resources, no network exists. Each peer (or user) is in charge of his or her own workstation, playing gatekeeper to the other users on the network. Usually a peer-based network is not feasible beyond 10 computers, because of the amount of administration each peer owner is forced to do just to share his or her resources, and at that level, the economies of scale are worth the cost of a server-based network.

✔ **Server-based networks** — also called client/server. These networks have a centralized server or host computer that services the resource requests from the computer workstations attached to the network. The centralized host is called the *server* and the attached workstations are called *clients*. Server-based networks are generally centrally-administered, which means that one or more network administrators handle all of the resource sharing and access rights for the entire network, freeing the users of this task. Figure 3-2 shows the construction of a simple server-based network. Server-based networks can be simple, small networks or very large, complicated networks that take on a personality of their own. If you are creating a Cisco network, it is most definitely a server-based network. Table 3-1 lists a few of the factors that characterize peer-based and server-based networks. Server-based networks have a central administrator, which, depending on the size of the network, may actually be a group of administrators. Nevertheless, the central administrator is responsible for the function, security, and integrity of the entire network, including the workstations.

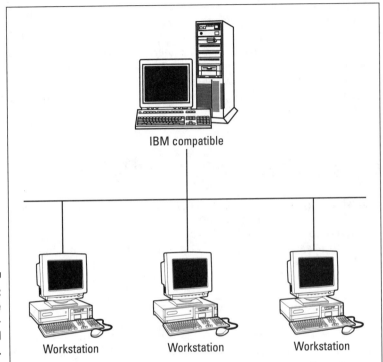

Figure 3-2:
A simple
server-
based
network.

IBM compatible

Workstation   Workstation   Workstation

Table 3-1	Peer-to-Peer versus Client/Server Networks	
Factor	*Peer-to-peer*	*Server-based*
Number of workstations	2-10	Limited only by the network hardware and software in use
Relative cost	Inexpensive	Dependent on network size; can be aggregately very expensive
Security	User managed	Centrally administered
Administration	User managed	Centrally administered
Data backups	Each user responsible for backing up his or her own data	Backups centrally created

Hello, I'll be your server

Many different servers can be on a network, each performing distinctive types of tasks for the network and its workstations. You may think of a server as being a piece of hardware, but typically a server is the software that performs, controls, or coordinates a service or a resource. So, one computer (server) can actually be seen as many different (software) servers to network clients. Table 3-2 lists the most common types of servers implemented on a network.

Table 3-2	Common Server Types
Server Type	*Function or Activity*
File server	A centralized computer that stores network users' data files
Print server	A centralized computer that manages the printers connected to the network and the printing of user documents on the network printers
Communications server	A centralized computer that handles many common communications functions for the network, such as e-mail, fax, or Internet services
Application server	A centralized computer that shares network-enabled versions of common application software, eliminating the need for the software to be installed on each workstation
Database server	A centralized computer that manages a common database for the network handling all data storage, database management, and requests for data

Maxing out on network workstations

A peer-to-peer network is usually effective with no more than 10 workstations. (Of course, you remember that any network must have at least 2 workstations.) Beyond 10 nodes, the administrative tasks required of each user become too much of a burden. Each user is responsible for sharing his or her resources with each of the other users on the network. This task, as well as maintaining any form of security for his computer and resources, can become a real bother and consume much of the user's time. This eventually leads everyone to mutiny and to appoint a central administrator to fuss with it all.

On the other hand, the number of workstations that a server-based network supports varies. For the sake of comparison though, the number of nodes supported by a server-based network is virtually unlimited. The number of nodes on the network is actually controlled by a number of factors, each imposing its own limit. These factors, all of which are discussed in this chapter, include the type of cable in use, the network operating system, and how much money you're willing to spend on connectivity devices.

Building up peer-to-peer relationships

Any workstation in a peer-to-peer network is a peer. Workstations are peers because they are equal and operate at the same level. That's true democracy at work — nobody is the lord, and nobody is the peasant. They are all lords or peasants depending on your viewpoint and cynicism.

Without making this too hard, a peer can also be a server or a client. When a peer workstation requests access to a file on another workstation, the requesting station becomes a client and the servicing workstation becomes the server.

Peer-to-peer networks are constructed in two general ways. The simplest way is to directly connect two computers to each other with a cable attached to their parallel or serial ports. Connecting more than two computers into a network this way is difficult, but for just two workstations that wish to share resources back and forth, this type of peer-to-peer network works very well.

The other, and most commonly used, peer-to-peer network is created by installing a NIC (network interface card) in each computer and connecting each of the computers to a hub. This type of peer-to-peer network can easily connect 2 to 10 workstations. The hub acts as a peer-level interconnection point for the network. The peer-to-peer workstations and any peripheral devices on the network talk with each other through the hub. A printer or another peripheral device can be connected to a specific workstation or connected into the network and be shared by all workstations by connecting into the hub. If the hub is a Cisco hub, then even a peer-to-peer network can be a Cisco network. It doesn't take a full-blown client/server network to be a Cisco network. Any network that uses Cisco equipment, even as little as a Cisco hub, is a Cisco network.

The effectiveness of a peer-to-peer network begins to fade around 10 workstations. In fact, you can find many sources that recommend that a peer-to-peer network be limited to 8 to 10 workstations. Above that number, the administrative tasks that each user must perform to share resources with the network peer becomes such a burden that eventually everyone gives up and elects a central administrator to fuss with it all. This isn't to say that all peer-to-peer networks eventually become server-based networks, but it does happen quite frequently.

You can never be too thin, be too rich, or have too many clients

A server is actually any computer on a network that tends to requests for services from other network nodes. A server performs tasks that service the resource needs of requesting workstations (clients) on the network. A server can perform a variety of functions on behalf of a network and its workstations. A server can be a printer server, a file server, an application server, a fax server, a World Wide Web server, and several other specialized functions. See "Hello, I'll be your server" earlier in the chapter for a little deeper coverage of the different servers.

Workstations that make requests for services on a server are clients of that server. Clients do not share their own resources with other clients on the network. Clients only talk with servers. In some ways, this relationship can be likened to professionals, such as doctors and lawyers, and their clients. However, a more accurate example is when a client needs a certain group of data from a centralized network database. The client sends a properly formatted request and the server responds with the data requested.

If many servers are on a network, they may conceivably be clients to one another. Peer-to-peer workstations can be clients or servers, or both, depending on whether they are asking resources from or providing resources to the other peer workstations on the network.

The number of workstations that can be supported by a server-based network varies, but theoretically, the number is unlimited. The number of clients on a network is actually controlled by a variety of factors. These factors, each of which can impose a limit on the number of workstations on a network, include

- The type of cable used
- The network operating system
- The amount of traffic on the network
- The connectivity devices (routers, bridges, hubs, and so on) in use

Client/server network performance can become an issue as a network grows in number of clients, which can require a larger investment in connectivity devices, specialized software, and network administrators. There is no practical limit on a network, but as we discuss in this chapter and in Chapter 4, some physical and logical limitations can control the design and layout of a network.

Gilster's Law of Network Cost Estimation

Another limiting factor on the size of a network is its cost. Gilster's Law of Network Cost Estimation is: You never can tell, and it all depends. A long list of elements contributes to the overall cost of a network, including, but not limited to, the cabling, equipment, software, and people used to build the network.

A peer-to-peer network is a relatively low-cost affair. At minimum, all you need is a parallel or serial cable and Windows to set up a file- and print-sharing peer-based network between two computers. If you decide to connect three or more computers, it is best to install a NIC in each computer and run cabling to a hub, all of which adds cost. In a peer-to-peer arrangement, you really can't get much fancier than this, so the costs are still relatively minor.

On the other hand, a server-based network really invokes Gilster's Law. The cost can range from that of a peer-to-peer network to thousands, even millions of dollars, depending on the size and scope of the network involved. In the client/server world, every device that is connected to the network, be it a computer, printer, or any other device, is called a *node* and requires some form of a network adapter, usually a NIC, and a length of network-capable cabling. As the network grows, additional equipment is required to balance the network bandwidth and control network traffic.

Size, in terms of the number of nodes on a network, is not the only thing that drives the cost of a network up. Even the smallest networks can have high bandwidth and security demands, which can require specialized, expensive equipment.

Dealing with Security Issues

Aha! Security is where the difference between the two basic network types truly lies. In a peer-based network, security — that is, who can gain access to a computer to use its resources and when they can do it — is controlled by the owner/operator of each node. Security is granted to individual users on the peer network one at a time and in most cases, one folder or file at a time. Permission to share a folder is granted by the owner to each user in the "Network Neighborhood." This type of security is called *share-level security.*

The full responsibility for security on a client/server network, which is no small job we might add, falls directly on the network administrator. This poor soul, excuse us, this highly trained and skilled professional, has the overall responsibility of managing the permissions and rights of all network users. These permissions and rights include access to network resources, such as software, data, and hardware devices. Needless to say, this responsibility is constantly changing. As the network grows, security administration of the network must keep pace. Sometimes, it seems like shoveling sand in a windstorm.

When access is granted by a central administrator who sets the permissions and rights of network users and groups of users to data, software, and hardware resources, the network is using a type of security called *user-level security.*

Who's the peer-to-peer network's gatekeeper?

In a peer-to-peer network, each peer, which is to say each user, is responsible for his or her own workstation, playing gatekeeper to the other users on the network. As described earlier, each workstation user must take responsibility for which other network users can access the data, programs, and devices of her or his computer.

On a Windows 95 or 98 system, the process used to set share-level permissions for file sharing and print sharing is detailed in the following steps:

1. **Click the Control Panel icon on the Windows Desktop or choose Start➪Settings➪Control Panel.**

2. **Double-click the Network icon.**

    The Network window, as shown in Figure 3-3, appears.

3. **Click Add to display the Select Network Component Type window, shown in Figure 3-4.**

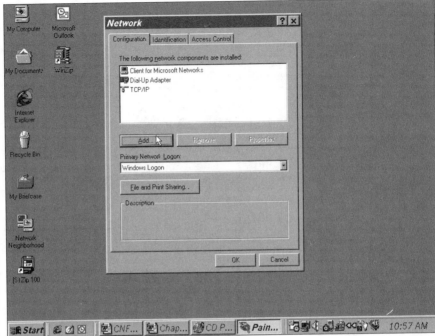

Figure 3-3:
The
Windows
Network
dialog box.

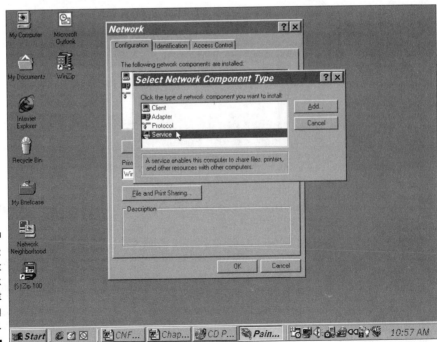

Figure 3-4:
The Select
Network
Component
Type dialog
box.

4. **Select the Service item in the Select the Type of Network Component You Want to Install box and click the Add button.**

   The Select Network Service window, shown in Figure 3-5, appears.

5. **Highlight the service that you want to start, typically File and Print Sharing for Microsoft Networks, and click OK.**

   This action opens the File and Print Sharing service for Microsoft networks and adds it to the system. Now you can share files and printers on your workstation or peer workstations on the network. Sharing occurs at the individual file or device level through the Properties settings of each item.

Another security-related issue on networks is the *integrity* of the data on the network. The data's integrity is the extent to which network users can rely on the data. Users expect the network data resources to be accurate, uncorrupted, timely, and secure. If the data resources on a network are never backed up and one day the server crashes, it is very likely that all of the data on the server will be lost without a chance of recovery. In this case, the integrity of the data is very low. Even where the data is backed up regularly, if the backup media (such as tape cartridges) are not cared for, they could become corrupted and if needed, could not be used to recover the missing data.

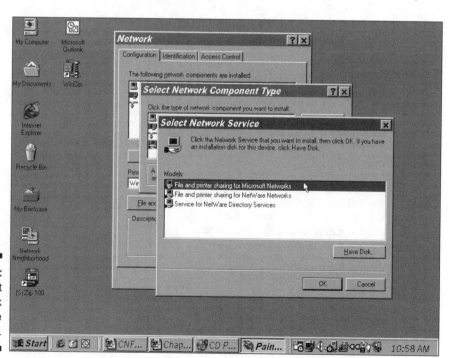

Figure 3-5:
The Select
Network
Service
dialog box.

The most common way to protect the integrity of the data on a network is to copy the data to some form of removable backup media, typically magnetic tape. On a peer-to-peer network, the responsibility for data backups falls straight to each workstation owner. This is another factor that drives peer-based networks to server-based networks eventually.

Providing security on server-based networks

Server-based networks have a central administrator, which, depending on the size of the network, could actually be a group of administrators. Nevertheless, the network's central administrator is responsible for both the security and data integrity of the entire network. This responsibility extends in some cases to include the workstations as well.

Network classifications you really don't care about

You may encounter some other network classifications in the networking world. Generally, these network classifications are used to specifically define particular types of local area and wide area networks to a particular application.

✔ **Campus area network (CAN)** — This type of network connects network nodes located in different physical locations of a geographically small area using only local communications means, such as directly-connected network cabling or a point-to-point wireless system. The CAN is so named because it is used to interconnect buildings on a corporate or collegiate campus into a network.

✔ **Global area network (GAN)** — This type of network connects network nodes located in multiple countries or on multiple continents. Obviously, this requires remote communications connectivity.

✔ **Metropolitan area network (MAN)** — This class of network connects network nodes that are located within the same metropolitan area (defined as being a 50- to 75-mile wide area). MANs may or may not require remote communications connectivity, but likely they do.

✔ **Value-added network (VAN)** — This is a commercial network, one on which the provider adds services or features to an existing network, such as tag switching on an ATM network, and then resells the combined services for a single price. Many ASPs (Application Service Providers) that are also bandwidth providers create VANs for their subscribers.

These classifications of networks are used to specifically define particular types of local area and wide area networks.

The scope of the responsibility of the network administrator depends on the nature of the network and the security requirements of that network. Networks operating in very secure settings may need the central administrator to administer, manage, and audit the security settings and safeguards on all parts of the network, including the workstations. In a general office setting, where security is perhaps not an issue, the central administrator may be concerned only with password access to the network itself, leaving the tasks of workstation security to the users.

The tasks performed by the network administrator to provide security and data integrity to a network involve a number of activities that collectively form the security policies of the network. These include:

- **User and group policies:** Although the maintenance of user and group accounts may seem to be a general administration activity, the ultimate security level is exclusion. Most of the malicious damage done to networks occurs from within. So, who is granted access to the network and to what groups they are assigned has a lot to do with the network's overall security.

- **Password policies:** Whether or not passwords are used and how often they are changed is another important element of a network's security program.

- **User policies:** Are workstations shared by more than one user? Are users allowed to grant share permissions to other users for resources on their workstations? Are users granted roaming accounts or stationary accounts? The answers to these and other related questions form the policies regarding users and their privileges.

- **Backup policies:** The network administrator is generally responsible for how frequently network data, possibly including workstation data, is backed up and how it is safeguarded. Without the protection of a defined and executed data integrity policy and procedure, the data of the network is not safe.

Is It a LAN or a WAN, Man?

In general, nearly all networks fit into one of two network classifications: local area network (LAN) and wide area network (WAN). You probably will run into other network classifications, such as MAN (metropolitan area network) and VAN (value-added network), especially in Cisco documentation, as well as here and there in trade and technical magazines and publications, but they are all just variations of the basic two network classifications:

- **A local area network (LAN)** connects workstations (also called nodes) in a relatively small geographical area, usually a single office, department, or building for the purpose of data and resource sharing.

✔ **A wide area network (WAN)** connects nodes and interconnects LANs located over geographically large areas, such as states, countries, and even globally, using dedicated long-distance, high-speed lines. The Internet is the *ultimate* WAN.

Hardware, Software, and Other Doo-Dads

Any network is a combination of hardware, software, models, standards, and protocols. Some of this stuff you can touch and feel, such as computers, hubs, routers, cables, and the like, and some of it you can't, like software and protocols. Networking is both the art and the science of putting these hard and soft components together so that they support the resource-sharing and information-retrieval needs of the organization.

Included in network hardware are the servers, personal computers, and network connectivity equipment used to create a network's physical infrastructure. The softer side of networks includes the network operating system, client and server software, application software, and the standards and protocols used to control the format, transfer, and reliability of the data exchanged over the network.

The hard parts of networking

The three most basic hardware elements of any network are servers, workstations and nodes, and cabling:

✔ **Cabling** is the physical medium over which information is transmitted between nodes in a network. The five main types of cable used in networking are coaxial, shielded twisted-pair (also referred to as just twisted-pair), unshielded twisted-pair, IBM, and fiber-optic.

✔ **Nodes** are any addressable network device, such as a workstation, peripheral, or other addressable network device. The term *node* is used interchangeably with *workstation*.

✔ **Servers** are network computers from which workstations (clients) access and share files, printing, communications, and other services. Servers can be dedicated to a single service. Examples are: file servers, print servers, application servers, Web servers, and others (see "Hello, I'll be your server" earlier in this chapter).

> ✔ **Workstations** are personal computers connected to a network that are used to perform tasks using services by a network server. A workstation is also referred to as a *client*.

Because we discuss servers earlier in the chapter, we skip the details here, but read on for some information on cabling, networking, and internetworking devices.

Stringing it all together

More than 30 different applications of cable are used in all forms of networking. Here are some of the common applications for network cable (for more information on cable media types, see Chapter 4):

✔ **Adapter cable** — connects a Token Ring network interface card (NIC) to a Token Ring hub or multistation access unit (MAU).

✔ **Backbone cable** — (most commonly called "the backbone") is used to form the main trunk of a network to which individual workstations and peripherals can be directly attached.

✔ **Category *n* cable** — (where *n* represents a category number) is defined in a set of cabling standards developed by the Electronics Industry Association (EIA) and the Telecommunications Industry Association (TIA). You should know the categories:

   • **Category 3** is unshielded twisted-pair cable used for speeds up to 10 million bits per second (Mbps). 10BaseT networks require at least Category 3 cable.

   • **Category 4** is the lowest grade of UTP cabling acceptable for 16 Mbps Token Ring networks.

   • **Category 5** is UTP cable used for network speeds up to 100 Mbps.

✔ **Coaxial cable** — has a central solid wire surrounded by insulation. A braided-wire conductor sheath surrounds the insulation, which is then covered with a plastic jacket. Coax, as it is commonly called, supports high bandwidth with little interference.

✔ **Drop cable** — is a four-pair attachment unit interface (AUI) cable that connects a NIC to an Ethernet network backbone using a clamping connector.

✔ **Fiber-optic cable** — is made of glass or plastic fiber strands surrounded by a protecting jacket that facilitates high-bandwidth transmission by modulating a focused light source. It is commonly used to connect Fiber Distributed Data Interface (FDDI) networks and LAN backbones.

✔ **IBM cable** — is a cable standard developed by IBM that defines cables as Type 1 through Type 9, also designated as I-1 through I-9. IBM cabling is used for Token Ring and general-purpose wiring. You should know these types:

- **IBM Type 3 cable** is UTP with two, three, or four pairs of solid wire.

- **IBM Type 5 cable** is fiber-optic cable.

- **IBM Type 9 cable** is STP with two pairs of solid or stranded wire that are covered with a plenum (see upcoming definition) jacket.

✔ **Patch cable** — is common to Token Ring networks where it is used to connect two MAUs to each other, but it is also used to connect Ethernet hubs together as well.

✔ **Plenum cable** — is used for connections through conduits. This cable has a jacket made from a fireproof plastic that doesn't give off toxic fumes at high temperatures.

✔ **Ribbon cable** — is used to connect internal disk and tape drives. It is constructed with wires placed side by side in an insulating material. One edge of the cable is usually colored red or blue to mark wire number one.

✔ **Riser cable** — is the most commonly fiber-optic cabling and is used to run a connection vertically, for example between floors of a building.

✔ **Thick coaxial cable** — is a coaxial cable with a diameter of 1 centimeter (a little less than ½ inch) that is used with Ethernet networks. It is also called thickwire, Thicknet, and yellow wire.

✔ **Thin coaxial cable** — is a coaxial cable with a diameter of 5 millimeters (about ⅕ of an inch) that is used with Ethernet and ARCNet networks. It is also called thinwire and Thinnet.

✔ **Twisted-pair (TP) cable** — is a cable with two or more pairs of insulated wires twisted together at a rate of six twists per inch. In each pair of wires, one wire carries the signal and the other is grounded. The two common types of TP cable are shielded twisted-pair and unshielded twisted-pair:

- **Shielded twisted-pair cable** is a TP cable constructed with a foil shield and copper braid around the pairs of twisted copper wires to protect against electromagnetic interference (EMI) and radio-frequency interference (RFI). This type of cable is commonly used with Token Ring networks.

- **Unshielded twisted-pair cable** is a cable with no outer foil shield to protect against EMI or RFI. A cable with a high number of twists has lower crosstalk (interference picked up by another wire).

Routers, bridges, and hubs! Oh my!

Another grouping of networking hardware is the devices that connect the network together and allow and process networking signals to move over the cabling of the network or internetwork. This hardware includes a wide range of equipment, from a network interface card (NIC) to repeaters, hubs, routers, and bridges.

Networks are interconnected by cabling and networking devices. These devices improve a network's performance and remove its media or hardware limitations. In the following sections, we define many of the common networking devices.

Can you repeat that?

A repeater is by far the simplest of the network connectivity devices, both in function and application. It is merely an electronic echo machine that retransmits whatever it hears, literally in one ear and out the other. It has no other intelligence. In fact, it has no intelligence at all.

A repeater is used to extend the maximum distance of a network's cabling as a way around attenuation. *Attenuation* is the natural tendency for a signal to weaken as it travels over a cable. The longer the cable, the weaker the signal becomes. By regenerating the signal every so often, the rejuvenated signal is able to reach its destination.

Each type of cable has a different maximum distance limit. Table 3-3 lists the distance limits for the cable likely to be found in a Cisco Ethernet network. As a network administrator, you really should know your cable limitations. By the way, it's likely that you need to know only UTP.

Table 3-3	Attenuation Distances for Common Cable Types
Cable type	*Attenuation Distance*
Thin coax	185 meters (a little over 600 feet)
Thick coax	500 meters (about 1,650 feet)
UTP	100 meters (a little over a football field)
Fiber-optic	2,000 meters (pretty far — about a mile and a quarter)

All segments of cable between the server (or repeater, or active hub, or whatever) and a workstation contribute to the maximum distance of the particular cable type. For example, suppose that a workstation on an Ethernet UTP network has 85 meters of cable from the server to a patch panel, a 5-meter cable to its hub, and a 15-meter cable to its NIC. This is a total of 105 meters of cable, which exceeds the 100-meter attenuation distance for UTP and could be a reason why the workstation begins performing badly.

Patching it all together

It is far easier to connect long cable runs into a distribution facility, such as a wiring closet or demarcation point (the "demarc") with a patch panel. The patch panel provides a connection point for workstation cables and the hub or switch used to connect them to the network.

Patch cables are short cables that are used to connect patch panel ports to a hub, switch, or router port. The benefit of this arrangement is that, when needed, the workstation can be moved easily to another port or perhaps even another hub, for reconfiguring the network or just for troubleshooting, by simply moving the patch cable to a new port.

Meet me at the hub

A hub is a network device that is used to connect workstations to the network. A hub receives a signal and passes it on to all of its other ports. For example, if a four-port hub receives a signal on port 4, it immediately passes the signal on to ports 1, 2, and 3. Hubs, which are common devices on Ethernet networks, are commonly configured with 4, 8, 16, or 24 ports.

Four types of hubs are commonly used:

- **Active hub:** This type of hub acts like a repeater to amplify the signal being passed on, as well as acting like a traffic cop to avoid signal collisions. An active hub is a powered device with a power cord.

- **Passive hub:** This type of hub does not amplify transmission signals; it merely passes them along. A passive hub does not need power and, therefore, does not have a power cord.

- **Hybrid hub:** This is a hub that can mix media types (thinwire, thickwire, and UTP) and serve as an interconnect for other hubs.

- **Smart (intelligent) hub:** This is an active hub with a bigger brain. Smart hubs include some administrative interface, often including SMTP (Simple Network Management Protocol) support or the ability to segment the ports into different logical networks.

Bridging the gap

A bridge is used to connect two different LANs or two similar network segments to make them appear to be one network. A bridge might be used to connect a Novell network with a Windows 2000 network. The bridge builds a routing table of MAC addresses (also called a bridging table) that is used to determine the correct network destination for a message. The overall effect of a bridge on a network is reduced message bottlenecks.

Rooting (or is it routing?) for the home team

You'll hear the word *router* pronounced differently depending on where you are. If you are in England, you'll hear the word pronounced as "rooter," but we Yankees pronounce it as "rowter" which rhymes with pouter and doubter. Regardless of how you pronounce it, a router directs, or routes, packets across networks. A router works with the Internet Protocol (IP) address of a message to determine the path that a message should take to arrive at its destination.

Routers also control broadcast storms on a network. Many messages on a network are broadcast to the whole network rather than to a single workstation. When too many messages are being broadcast over the network, the result is a *broadcast storm.* By routing messages only to certain network segments, a router helps prevent such storms.

Gateways

A gateway, which is usually a combination of hardware and software, is used to connect two networks with different protocols so that they can communicate with one another. Gateways are used in a number of situations involving the conversion of the characteristics on one environment to another, including architecture, protocols, and language. Three different types of gateways exist:

- **Address gateways** connect networks with different directory structures and file management techniques.

- **Protocol gateways** (the most common type) connect networks that use different protocols.

- **Format gateway** connects networks using different data format schemes (for example, one using the American Standard Code for Information Interchange, or ASCII, and another using Extended Binary-Coded Decimal Interchange Code, or EBCDIC).

A gateway is usually a dedicated server on a network because it usually requires large amounts of system resources.

Connecting to the network with a NIC

The most basic of networking devices is the network interface card (NIC), also called a network adapter. This piece of hardware is installed in every networked computer to both physically attach it to the network and to logically connect it to the network system. The primary purpose of the NIC is to transmit data to and receive data from other NICs.

Some of the major characteristics of a NIC are detailed here:

- ✔ **MAC (Media Access Control) address:** Each NIC is physically encoded with a unique identifying address that is used to locate it on the network.

- ✔ **System resources:** A NIC is configured to the computer with an IRQ, an I/O address, and a DMA channel. A NIC commonly uses IRQ3, IRQ5, or IRQ10, and an I/O address of 300h.

- ✔ **Transceiver type:** Some NICs are capable of attaching to more than one media type, such as UTP and coaxial.

- ✔ **Data bus compatibility:** A NIC is designed with compatibility to particular data bus architecture.

Configuring a NIC

Network interface cards are configured either manually with hardware or automatically with software. Many NICs have either DIP (dual inline packaging) switch blocks or jumper blocks that are used to set system resource assignments and transceiver types. Even NICs that have setup software occasionally require a hardware adjustment through a DIP switch or jumper.

One of the key settings on a NIC indicates whether the NIC uses full- or half-duplexing to send its signals. *Full-duplex* NICs can send and receive signals at the same time. *Half-duplex* NICs can either send *or* receive signals, but cannot do both at the same time.

NIC to the network, over

Some NICs have their transceiver (the device that transmits and receives data from the network) on the adapter card itself. Others, especially those supporting thick coaxial media, connect to external transceivers.

NICs that require an external transceiver use an AUI (adapter unit interface) connector, also called a DIX (Digital-Intel-Xerox) connector, on a transceiver cable that connects to a tapping (or vampire) connector that pierces the network cable.

Connecting the NIC

The type of cable used for a network dictates the type of NIC required, as well as the connectors used to connect it to the cable. The most common connector used for each cable type is listed in Table 3-4.

Table 3-4	NIC/Media Connector Types
Media	*Connectors Used*
Thinnet	BNC "T" connectors
Thicknet	AUI connectors
UTP	RJ-45
Fiber-optic	ST connectors

Making the bus connection

In order to connect the computer to the network, a network adapter (NIC) must make two different connections to work properly: to the network media and into a data bus expansion slot in a computer. The expansion slots commonly used for NICs are listed here:

- **ISA (Industry Standard Architecture):** This 16-bit architecture is still one of the most common bus structures used, especially on general-purpose workstations.

- **EISA (Extended Industry Standard Architecture):** This 32-bit architecture is backward compatible to ISA cards.

- **PCI (Peripheral Component Interface):** This 32-bit architecture is also called local bus. This is the data bus of choice in most high-end computers.

- **PCMCIA (Personal Computer Memory Card Industry Association):** Also called the PC Card bus, this NIC is used on notebook and other portable computers.

Operating Systems of the Network Kind

A network operating system (NOS — pronounced "N. O. S.") is a core element of any network. It is the software that manages, permits, and facilitates the sharing of network resources by the network users. These NOSs are commonly used:

- Microsoft Windows NT Server
- Novell NetWare
- UNIX and Linux

Some desktop clients, such as Windows 9*x* and Windows 3.*x*, also provide peer-to-peer networking support through their file-sharing and print-sharing services, but these cannot really be called network operating systems.

The success of your network is equally tied to how well you are able to configure, install, and administer the NOS. Even a good physical network (with good cabling, routers, and switches) cannot overcome a poorly set up logical network (the NOS and the workstation clients). The reverse is also true; a well-configured software system cannot perform well over a badly implemented physical network. But that's the topic of many other books. Depending on the network operating system that your network is or will be using, you may want to check out some of our favorite network books and authors:

  ✔ *Networking For Dummies,* by Doug Lowe

  ✔ *Windows NT Networking For Dummies,* by Ed (Mr. Networking) Tittel, Mary Madden, and Earl Follis

  ✔ *Windows NT Server 4 For Dummies,* by Ed (Networking Is My Life) Tittel

  ✔ *Windows 2000 Administration For Dummies,* by Michael Bellomo

  ✔ *Windows 2000 Server For Dummies,* by Ed (Mr. Know-It-All) Tittel, Mary T. Madden, and James Michael Stewart

  ✔ *Networking with NetWare For Dummies,* by Ed (Novell Man) Tittel, James E. Gaskin, and Earl Follis

  ✔ *Novell's Encyclopedia of Networking,* by Kevin (I'm Not Ed Tittel) Shafer

In spite of this shameless plug for Dummies books, these books in our list are an entertaining and informative way to brush up on your networking knowledge.

Chapter 4

Network Media: A Primer

● ●

● ●

*1*n spite of the fact that our world is fast becoming mostly a wireless one, most networks continue to be on cable and wired infrastructures. The security and reliability of a good, solid piece of copper over which to send your data almost can't be beat. Trust us on this. We wouldn't say it if it weren't true — we all work for a wireless communications company.

The wireless technologies available for local area networks are maturing. But then, so are fiber optic and copper wire technologies, too. We suggest that until such time as wireless becomes cost and functionally competitive with physical media, the hard stuff will remain king.

Perhaps more important than the network's operating system or topology, the physical medium sets the data transmission speed, the network's overall distance, the number and type of connectivity devices required, and the number of devices the network can support. For this reason, any network administrator worth his or her weight in RJ-45 connectors must be familiar with network media. You don't need to be an expert, but you should know the construction and best use of the most common cable and media types, and be able to identify them by sight. No sweat, you say! Well, you also should know their characteristics, limitations, advantages and disadvantages, and the conditions under which each type of cable is an appropriate choice for a network. Piece of cake!

The Fascinating World of Cables

Two materials are primarily used to produce the cables used for local area networks: copper and glass. Yes, the same stuff used to make pennies and windows. Both are relatively inexpensive and abundant, but more importantly, they are both excellent conductors. Copper is an excellent conductor of electricity and glass is an excellent conduit for light. This works out very well, because electricity and light are why you need cable media in the first place.

For one computer to communicate with another computer, a medium must be available over which the electrical impulses that represent commands and data can be transmitted. In a networked environment, whether it be peer-based or server-based (see Chapter 3), the computers and peripherals must be interconnected by some form of a transmission medium so that data can be exchanged and resources can be shared. Cable media has laid (pun intended) the foundation on which networks grew — literally.

The big three of cabling

Four network media types are available today: coaxial cable, twisted-pair cable, fiber-optic cable, and wireless networking (see "A Word about Wireless Networks" later in this chapter). Tracing back in history, other media types have been used for networking, such as smoke, mirror flashes, drums, sneakers, and others, but these have largely proven ineffective for modern networks. For purposes of our discussions here, we will focus on only the three physical media types:

- **Coaxial (coax) cable:** This cable type is a little like the cable used to connect your television set to the cable outlet. Coax cable for networks comes in two varieties: thick coaxial cable and thin coaxial cable. Both are explained later in the chapter.

- **Twisted-pair (no, not the upstairs neighbors):** Twisted-pair cable comes in two flavors, unshielded twisted-pair (UTP) and shielded twisted-pair (STP) cables. UTP is very similar to the wiring used to connect your telephone. These are also explained later in the chapter.

- **Fiber-optic:** Glass fibers carry modulated pulses of light to represent digital data signals. Several different types of fiber-optic cables exist, but they are generally referred to as a group called fiber-optic cable.

The technical stuff about cables

All network cabling has a set of general characteristics to guide you in selecting the right cable for a given situation. These cable media characteristics are
important:

- ✔ **Bandwidth (speed):** Bandwidth is the amount of data that a cable can
  carry in a certain period of time. It is often expressed as the number of
  bits (either Kilobits or Megabits) that can be transmitted in a second.
  For example, UTP cable is nominally rated at 10 Mbps, or 10 million bits
  per second.

- ✔ **Cost:** Cost is always a major consideration when choosing a cable type.
  Look at this relative cost comparison for the major cable media:

  - **Twisted-pair cable** is the least expensive, but it has limitations
    that require other hardware to be installed.

  - **Coaxial cable** is a little more expensive than TP, but it doesn't
    require additional equipment and it's inexpensive to maintain.

  - **Fiber-optic cabling** is the most expensive, requires skilled installa-
    tion labor, and is expensive to install and maintain.

- ✔ **Maximum segment length:** Every cable is subject to a condition called
  attenuation, which means the signal weakens and can no longer be recognized. Every type of cable has a different distance at which attenuation occurs. This distance (measured in meters) is a cable medium's
  maximum segment length, or the distance at which signals on the cable
  must be regenerated.

- ✔ **Maximum number of nodes per segment:** Each time a device is added
  to a network, the effect is like putting hole in the cable. Like leaks from
  pinholes in a balloon, too many devices attached to a network cable
  reduce the distance at which attenuation begins. So each type of cable
  must limit the number of nodes that can be attached to a cable segment.

- ✔ **Interference resistance:** Different cable media have varying vulnerability to electromagnetic interference (EMI) or radio frequency interference
  (RFI) caused by electric motors, florescent light fixtures, your magnet
  collection, the radio station on the next floor, and so on. As the construction of the cable and its cladding (coverings) varies, so does its
  resistance to EMI and RFI signals.

Table 4-1 shows the standard characteristics of the most commonly used network cable types.

Table 4-1		Cable Types and Their Characteristics		
Cable Type	Bandwidth	Max. Segment Length	Max. Nodes per Segment	Interference Resistance
Thin coaxial	10 Mbps	185 meters	30	Good
Thick coaxial	10 Mbps	500 meters	100	Better
UTP	10–100 Mbps	100 meters	1024	Poor
STP	16–1000 Mbps	100 meters	1024	Fair to Good
Fiber-optic	100–10000 Mbps	2000 meters	No limit	Best

Coaxial Cables through Thick and Thin

Although recently deposed as the ruling network cable type, coaxial cable is still a popular choice for networks. It is inexpensive, easy to work with, reliable, and moderately resistant to interference, which makes it a good choice in many situations, such as in environments with a lot of electrical equipment or in instances where longer segment runs are needed.

Coaxial cable is constructed with a single solid copper wire core, which is surrounded by an insulator made of plastic or Teflon material. A braided metal shielding layer (and in some cables, another metal foil layer) covers the insulator and a plastic sheath wrapper covers the cable. The metal shielding layers act to increase the cable's resistance to EMI and RFI signals. Figure 4-1 illustrates the construction of a coaxial cable.

The Institute of Electrical and Electronics Engineers (IEEE) 802 Project defines coaxial cable as either thick or thin. Coaxial cable is used primarily in Ethernet networking environments, where it is also referred to as Thicknet and Thinnet. Other aliases coaxial cable goes by are the generic "coax," 10Base5, thickwire, and yellow wire (all nicknames for thick coaxial cable), and 10Base2, thinwire, and cheapnet (aliases for thin coaxial cable).

What's this 10Base stuff?

In the Ethernet world, the designation of cable is also descriptive of its characteristics. Thick coax cable is designated as 10Base5; thin coaxial cable is designated as 10Base2; and UTP is generally designated as 10BaseT.

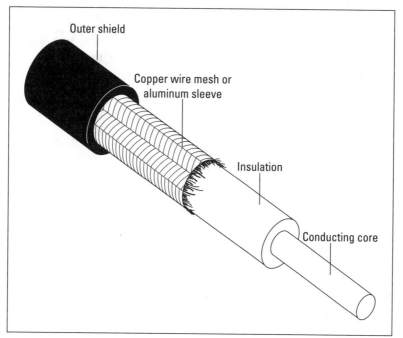

Outer shield

Copper wire mesh or
aluminum sleeve

Insulation

Conducting core

Figure 4-1:
The layers
of a coaxial
cable.

The 10Base part indicates that these cables carry 10 Mbps bandwidths and use baseband, as opposed to broadband, signals. (See Chapter 1 for an explanation of baseband and broadband.) For a coax cable, the 5 and the 2 mean 500 meters and 200 meters, respectively. These distances are the approximate maximum segment length of the cable. Actually, the maximum segment length of thin coax is 185 meters, but 200 works better in this case and besides it's easier to remember than 10Base1.85. The T in 10BaseT refers to "twisted-pair" cable. See "The Ethernet Cable Standards," later in this chapter, for more information.

The coaxial couple has one additional designation: Thick coax is also designated as RG-11 or RG-8 and thin coax as RG-58 (the coax used for television service is RG-59, by the way). The RG stands for Radio/Government and is the rating of the cable based upon the type and thickness of its core wire.

Does this cable make me look fat?

Thick coax is the more rigid of the coaxial twins (fraternal, no doubt). It is about 1 centimeter (about .4") in diameter and is commonly covered in a bright yellow Teflon covering, the origin of its "yellow wire" nickname. Its thicker hide makes it more resistance to interference and attenuation, resulting in a longer segment length and the ability to support a greater number of nodes on a segment compared to its thinner sibling.

Connecting thick coaxial cable to workstations is a fairly complicated, simple process. What we mean is that it really is simple, but it is complicated to explain. An external transceiver attached to a piercing connector (appropriately called a "vampire" tap) is clamped onto the thickwire making a connection that pierces to the central core wire. Then a transceiver cable (called a drop cable) is used to connect to a computer's network adapter with an AUI (attached unit interface) connector. Figure 4-2 illustrates how simple this really is, despite our convoluted description. Table 4-2 lists the characteristics of thick coaxial cable.

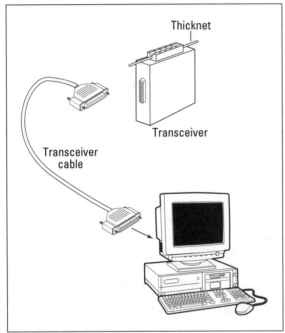

Figure 4-2: A thick coax connection.

Table 4-2	Thick Coaxial Cable Characteristics
Characteristic	*Value*
Maximum segment length	500 meters (about 1,640 feet)
Bandwidth (speed)	10 Mbps
Number of nodes per segment	100
Connector type	AUI (attached unit interface)
Resistance to Interference	Good

The thinner side of things

In contrast to its thicker relative, thin coaxial cable is lightweight and flexible. It is about .2" in diameter and is easily installed. After UTP, this is the second most popular type of network cabling. Thinnet, its more popular nickname, is used to "daisy chain" computers together using BNC-T connectors, a sample of which is shown in Figure 4-3. As is illustrated in Figure 4-4, thin coax cable runs between each network node, connecting one workstation to the next. The characteristics of thin coaxial cable are summarized in Table 4-3.

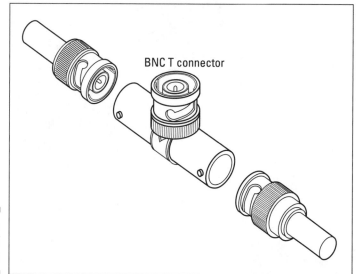

Figure 4-3:
A BNC-T
connector.

Table 4-3	Thin Coaxial Cable Characteristics
Characteristic	*Value*
Maximum segment length	185 meters (a little over 600 feet)
Bandwidth (speed)	10 Mbps
Number of nodes per segment	30
Connector type	BNC
Resistance to Interference	Good

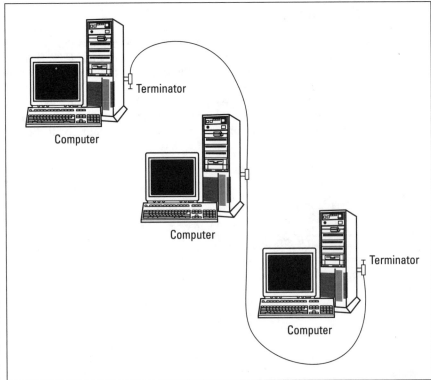

Figure 4-4:
An Ethernet
using
Thinnet
cable.

The Twisted Pair

Although it sounds like the bad title of an even worse movie, the most popular cabling in use for local area networks is twisted-pair copper wire. This media type has all of the attributes to be truly popular: It is the lightest, most flexible, least expensive, and easiest to install of any of the popular network media. The bad news is that it is also vulnerable to interference and has attenuation problems as well. *Interference* is the electrical noise that copper cabling picks up from other wires or electrical devices near it (a good example is what happens to the TV sometimes when the vacuum is running). A signal running through a copper wire begins to lose its strength after a certain distance. This is caused by the resistance in the wire (friction, bouncing molecules, and so on). This condition is called *attenuation*. But, given the right network design and implementation, problems like interference and attenuation are easily overcome.

Two types of twisted-pair wire are used in networks: unshielded (UTP) and shielded (STP), shown in Figure 4-5. Of the two, UTP is the most commonly

used and is very popular on Ethernets. STP wire is common on token ring
networks and in environments where its shielding is required to protect the
cable from electrical noise and other interference.

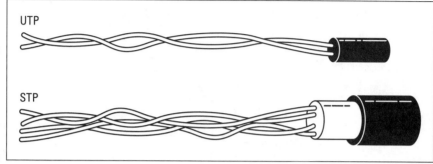

Figure 4-5:
Unshielded
and
shielded
twisted-pair
cables.

Unshielded is not unheralded

Unshielded twisted-pair wire is just about what its name implies — two
unshielded wires twisted together. UTP, commonly referred to as 10BaseT, is
the most commonly used type of cabling used in networks. For all of the reasons discussed in the previous section, it provides the most installation flexibility and ease of maintenance of the big three cabling media types. UTP uses
an RJ-45 connector (as shown in Figure 4-6), which looks very much like the
little clip connector on your telephone, only a little bigger. (RJ stands for
Registered Jack.) Table 4-4 summarizes the characteristics of UTP cable.

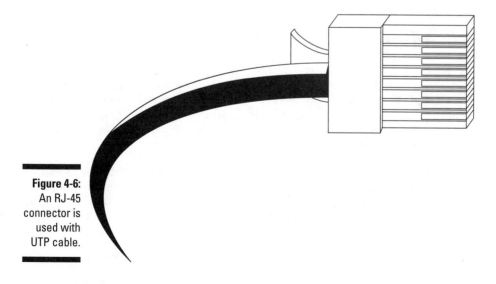

Figure 4-6:
An RJ-45
connector is
used with
UTP cable.

Table 4-4	Unshielded Twisted-Pair Cable Characteristics
Characteristic	*Value*
Maximum segment length	100 meters (not much over 320 feet)
Bandwidth (speed)	10-100 Mbps
Number of nodes per segment	1,024
Connector type	RJ-45
Resistance to Interference	Poor

IEEE 802 groups UTP cable into five categories, or "cats" as the real techies call them (as in Cat 3 or Cat 5):

✔ **Category 1 and 2** — not used in networking. (This isn't here and you didn't see it, but if we left them out, you'd be wondering where they were.)

✔ **Category 3** — a four-pair cable supporting bandwidths up to 10 Mbps and the minimum standard for 10BaseT networks.

✔ **Category 4** — a four-pair cable commonly used in 16 Mbps token ring networks.

✔ **Category 5** — a four-pair cable with bandwidths up to 100 Mbps, used for 100BaseTX and ATM (asynchronous transfer mode) networking.

✔ **Category 6** — a four-pair cable that supports bandwidths up to 1 Gbps (gigabits per second) capable of supporting Gigabit Ethernets.

Leading a shielded life

The other half of the twisted-pair twins is shielded twisted-pair (STP). The best way to tell UTP from STP is that STP is the one with each of its wire pairs wrapped in a grounded copper or foil wrapper. This interference protection helps shield the internal copper wires from interference and helps STP support higher transmission speeds over longer distances, but it also makes STP more expensive than UTP.

STP is most commonly used in token ring networks. In fact, IBM has its own standards for twisted-pair cable for ring networks. The IBM cable standard includes nine categories that range from a two-pair shielded cable (Type 1) to a UTP cable (Type 3), a fiber-optic cable (Type 5), and a fire-safe cable (Type 9).

You Need Your Fiber

Data is carried over fiber-optic cables in the form of modulated pulses of light. To demonstrate how the data is represented as modulated light pulses, you need a dark room, a friend, and a flashlight. Stand in a dark room facing your friend. Now switch the flashlight on and off at the rate of a million times in a second. Although the fiber-optic cable actually uses a faster rate, this rate is adequate to demonstrate the technology in use. The friend? We all need a friend.

The core of fiber-optic cable consists of two or more extremely thin strands of glass. An opaque glass cladding covers each strand, helping to keep the light traveling through the strand and in the strand. The glass strands are capable of carrying signals in both directions, but as you may have guess, only one direction at a time. The glass core (cladding and strands) is then covered by a plastic outer jacket. Figure 4-7 shows the construction of a fiber-optic cable.

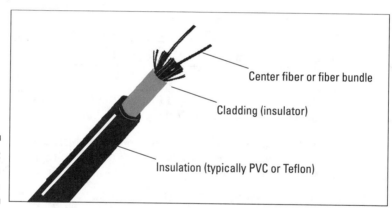

Center fiber or fiber bundle

Cladding (insulator)

Figure 4-7:
Fiber-optic
cable.

Insulation (typically PVC or Teflon)

Because it uses light and not electrical signals, fiber-optic cable is not susceptible to electromagnetic or radio frequency interference. This (and also the very high purity of the glass) gives it incredibly long attenuation and maximum segment lengths. Fiber-optic cable is commonly used for network backbones. Table 4-5 lists the most important characteristics of fiber-optic cable.

Table 4-5	Fiber-Optic Cable Characteristics
Characteristic	*Value*
Maximum segment length	2 kilometers (a little over a mile)
Bandwidth (speed)	100 Mbps to 2 Gbps
Resistance to Interference	Excellent

The Ethernet Cable Standards

Ethernet cable is referred to by a descriptive name, for example 10BaseT, that includes its bandwidth/speed, transmission mode, and a number or letter representing its segment length (coaxial cable) or cable type. Table 4-6 breaks down the meaning of the most common Ethernet cable designations. The "10Base" part of each standard indicates it supports a 10 Mbps transmission speed and uses a baseband transmission mode (see Chapter 1 for a brief explanation of baseband versus broadband transmissions).

Table 4-6	Basic Ethernet Cable Standards	
Cable	*Maximum Distance*	*Cable Material*
10Base2	185 meters (the 2 is for approximately 200)	Thinnet coaxial
10Base5	500 meters	Thicknet coaxial
10BaseF	2000 meters	Fiber-optic
10BaseT	100 meters	UTP

In addition to the standards listed in Table 4-6, the 10BaseF and 10BaseT standards have a few variations, these being the most commonly used standards:

- **100BaseT** — a four-wire 100 Mbps technology usually installed on Cat 5 wiring. This and 100BaseX are the generic terms for four-wire Fast Ethernet

- **100BaseTX** — a two-pair wire version of 100BaseT

- **100BaseT4** — another name for four-wire 100BaseT

- **100BaseFX** — Fast Ethernet using two-strand fiber-optic cable

- **100BaseVG** — a new 100 Mbps standard over Category 3 cable

- **100BaseVG-AnyLAN** — Hewlett Packard's proprietary version of 100BaseVG

A Word about Wireless Networks

Wireless LANs provide all of the same benefits of a wired LAN, plus a few extras. On a wireless LAN, users (especially roaming users) can access shared information without looking for a place to plug in, and the network administrator can set up or augment networks without the need to install or move wires, connectors, or furniture.

The primary thing you should know about wireless networking is that it uses radio frequency broadcasting to send data over the network. Beyond that, a wireless network functions essentially the same as a wired network. The data packets are formatted the same, and the layers of the OSI model and the standard protocols are still in use.

According to the folks who produce wireless LAN systems, a wireless LAN offers a number of productivity, convenience, and cost advantages over a traditional wired network, including

- **Mobility:** LAN users can access information from anywhere in the organization without the need to plug in to a network connector.
- **Installation ease:** You don't have to pull cable through the floor, walls, or ceiling to a new network station.
- **Flexibility:** The network can go where the wire can't.
- **Cost:** This is where there is some debate, but the wireless folks say that although the initial investment may be higher for a wireless LAN, the overall installation and operating expenses can be much lower than those of a wired network. The reasoning is that the expenses involved with moving, adding, and changing workstation locations are virtually eliminated.
- **Scalability:** Changing the topology or configuration of a wireless LAN is easily done. A wireless LAN can be configured anywhere from a peer-to-peer network for a small number of users to a full infrastructure network with thousands of users.

The technical stuff about wireless networks

A range of technologies is used with wireless LANs, each with its own set of advantages and limitations. The most common of the wireless network technologies are spread-spectrum, narrowband, and infrared.

Spreading out the spectrum

Most wireless LANs use the spread-spectrum technology (SST), which is a wideband radio frequency (RF) technique. Spread-spectrum was originally developed by the military as a reliable and secure communications system. It trades off bandwidth efficiency for reliability and security, which means that more bandwidth is needed to transmit data than is needed for a narrowband type of network. However, this results in a signal that is easier to detect, provided that the system is properly tuned.

Spread-spectrum technologies come in two varieties:

- **Frequency-hopping spread-spectrum technology (FHSST):** This type of SST changes frequency in a pattern recognized by both transmitter and receiver, which when properly synchronized, results in a single logical channel. To receivers that don't know the pattern, the transmission looks like background noise.

- **Direct-sequence spread-spectrum technology (DSSST):** This wideband form of SST uses a redundant bit pattern, called a chipping code, for each bit that is transmitted. Statistical techniques in the RF equipment, which are able to determine the data, reduce the need for retransmission of damaged data. To a narrowband radio, DSSST signals appear to be low-power wideband noise and are ignored.

The straight and narrowband

Narrowband radios transmit and receive data using a specific radio frequency, keeping the radio frequency as narrow as possible. Crosstalk (where one channel picks up noise from another channel) between communications channels is avoided by coordinating different users on different channel frequencies.

A radio frequency is very much like a private telephone line. When you are talking on your phone, your neighbors cannot listen to your conversation. Using a different frequency for each user on a network accomplishes this same privacy and noninterference. The radio receiver filters out all radio signals except the ones on its designated frequency.

Lighting up infrared technology

Infrared (IR) systems use very high frequencies that are just below visible light in the electromagnetic spectrum to carry data. Unlike RF signals, but like light, IR signals cannot penetrate solid objects and must use a line-of-sight (LoS). Line-of-sight is also called *diffuse,* or reflective, technology. Most inexpensive systems are LoS, offer a very limited range (around 3 feet), and mostly are used for what are called Personal Area Networks (PANs). A PAN is created around a single computer to connect peripheral devices, such as a keyboard, mouse, and printer via IR technology. Higher performance IR systems are used primarily to implement fixed wireless subnetworks. A diffuse IR LAN does not require line-of-sight to the radio units (called cells), but its range is generally limited to an individual room.

How a wireless LAN works

A wireless LAN is implemented as either an extension to or an alternative for a wired LAN within a single building or campus. Using electromagnetic RF or IR waves, a wireless LAN transmits and receives data through the air, eliminating or minimizing the need for wired connections. The electromagnetic waves are called carriers because they deliver data in the form of energy to a remote receiver. Multiple carriers can exist in the same space at the same time without interfering with each other, provided the radio waves are transmitted on different radio frequencies.

As illustrated in Figure 4-8, transmitter/receiver (transceiver) devices, also called access points, connect to a wired network using standard Ethernet cables. The transceiver receives, buffers, and transmits data between the network's nodes and the wired network's infrastructure. Each transceiver supports a group of user workstations usually within a range of one foot to several hundred feet.

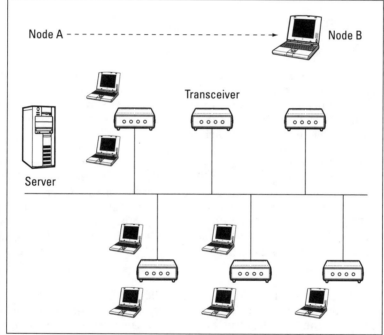

Figure 4-8:
Node A communicating to Node B over a wireless network.

Workstations connect to the network using wireless LAN adapters, in the form of PC cards for notebook computers, specialized NICs for desktop computers, or integrated devices built into handheld computers. These wireless network adapters provide the interface to the network operating system over the airwaves.

Getting Some Backbone (And Segments)

The cable that runs the entire length of a network and is used to interconnect all of the computers, printers, servers, and other devices of the network, is called the *backbone*. Visualize the skeleton of a fish: It is the backbone to which all of the other little-catch-in-your-throat bones attach. A network backbone serves the same purpose of connecting and interconnecting all of a network's resources, only without the smell. The backbone serves as the trunk line for the entire network. Cables commonly used for backbones are 10Base5, 10BaseF, 10BaseT, 100BaseFX, and 100BaseTX (see "The Ethernet Cable Standards" earlier in this chapter). You'll find two main types of backbones:

- ✔ FDDI
- ✔ Ethernet

In the context of a local area network, a *segment* is a group of workstations, servers, or devices that have been isolated on one side of a bridge or router as a part of its logical design or to improve the overall network's performance or security. However, in the context of cabling, a *segment* is a single run of cable terminated at each end.

In the fish skeleton analogy, each of the bones that emanate from the backbone would be segments, just like the cables that attach hubs, workstations, and other nodes to the backbone are cable segments. A very common technology used for network backbones is Fiber Distributed Data Interface (FDDI). FDDI is pronounced "F – D – D – I," but some people insist on pronouncing it "fiddy." Is nothing sacred? FDDI is a 100 Mbps fiber-optic network access method that is excellent for moving traffic around the trunk of a network.

FDDI implements networks as two parallel and interconnected rings. By definition, the two rings run side-by-side around the network in parallel paths, but in reality, they may be strung together or have completely separate paths, coming together only at the points where they are connected. Workstations can be attached to one or both rings of the backbone. The two rings serve as redundant network trunks, and if one breaks or fails, the other takes over, routing around the trouble spot. If both rings are broken, the remaining pieces bond together to form a new ring. Although it sounds like lizard tails or space aliens, FDDI's ability to regenerate the network backbone is what makes it popular.

Ethernet is the technology most commonly used for network backbones. Because network administrators can use the same network technology throughout the network, it is safe to say that most Cisco networks use Ethernet as the overall network implementation.

Part II
Network Operations

GUS, THE OFFICE "FIX-IT MAN" CLEARS A CONGESTED ROUTER

@RICHTENNANT

A little harder please, Gus.

In this part . . .

Many hardware components come together to make a network (see Part I), but even more logical elements give a network its life. Like Part I, this part of the book provides an overview. In this part, though, we review the standards and guidelines that define how a network interacts with its nodes and other networks; and the logical, virtual, and software elements used to transmit or carry data over the network.

Data traveling over a network must be packaged according to generally accepted and implemented standards. It must also be addressed in such a way that there is no doubt of its destination and just where that destination may be.

This part of the book also includes a brief look at the operating system used on network servers. Not that this is an essential part of the Cisco network environment, but it is at least as important to the operation of the overall network.

Chapter 5

Transporting Data: TCP/IP, Datagrams, Packets, and Frames

In This Chapter

▶ Identifying and detailing TCP/IP Transport layer protocol functions

▶ Explaining the functions of ICMP

▶ Defining data encapsulation

*T*his chapter should be subtitled TCFOA (The Chapter Full Of Acronyms). What with UDP, TCP, TCP/IP, FTP, HLEN, IP, SMTP, DNS, SNMP, ICMP, ARP, RARP, and PING, if this chapter has nothing else, it has TLAs (three-letter acronyms) and FLAs (four-letter acronyms) galore. We certainly understand why you may be PTO (Plain Tuckered Out) at the end of this chapter.

A large part of the secret language spoken by Cisco network administrators comes from the TLAs and FLAs of the TCP/IP protocols and services covered in this chapter. Don't be discouraged if you can't remember them all — in spite of what you may hear, nobody can. But, a reward awaits those who learn the secret language of TCP/IP: fame, fortune, clear skin, white teeth, lots of dates, and a better, more fulfilling job. Well, maybe we can't really promise you all that (forget the part about the dates), but being able to read Cisco white papers and articles about WAN networking is its own reward.

How Suite It Is

The Transmission Control Protocol/Internet Protocol (TCP/IP) suite, also known as just the Internet Protocol suite, has quickly become the standard for network communications on both the global (WAN) and local (LAN) levels. A number of factors account for the rapid and widespread growth of TCP/IP:

✔ **Portability:** TCP/IP is platform-independent and is interoperable with virtually every communications system, hardware or software.

✔ **Universal support:** TCP/IP protocols run equally well on every general or network operating system, including UNIX (its native operating system), Windows (9*x*, NT, or 2000), Novell, and so on.

✔ **Adaptability:** The TCP/IP suite contains a protocol that is designed for or can be adapted to just about any communication or networking application.

✔ **Open structure:** Nobody owns TCP/IP. Although many software publishers — including Microsoft, Novell, and others — have their own versions of it, TCP/IP is a public-domain freely distributed set of protocol standards that are available to anyone wishing to use it.

TCP/IP is actually a suite of protocols that interconnect and work together to provide for reliable and efficient data communications across an internetwork. The major protocols of the TCP/IP protocol suite are:

✔ Transmission Control Protocol (TCP)

✔ User Datagram Protocol (UDP)

✔ Domain Name System (DNS)

✔ Internet Protocol (IP)

✔ Address Resolution Protocol (ARP)

✔ File Transfer Protocol (FTP)

✔ Simple Mail Transfer Protocol (SMTP)

✔ Post Office Protocol (POP3)

✔ Interactive Mail Access Protocol (IMAP)

✔ Internet Control Message Protocol (ICMP)

✔ Routing Information Protocol (RIP)

✔ Open Shortest Path First (OSPF)

✔ Hypertext Transfer Protocol (HTTP)

✔ TCP/IP utilities (PING, Telnet, IPCONFIG, ARP, and more)

It's far more important to know the functions of the primary TCP/IP protocols (TCP, IP, UDP, and ICMP) than to memorize the protocols in the suite. You really don't need to know all the protocols in the TCP/IP suite. Knowing how certain protocols behave will be helpful when you configure your Cisco router, but you don't need to waste time memorizing all the protocols. We haven't listed them all here anyway. Look over the preceding list and make mental notes of them.

Stacking up the TCP/IP protocols

The TCP/IP protocol suite can also be arranged into a *protocol stack*. This means that the TCP/IP protocol suite can be broken up into groups of smaller suites that can be stacked or layered on each other to cooperatively complete a task or activity.

The best way to see the makeup of the TCP/IP protocol stack is to view it in contrast to the OSI model (see Chapter 2). The TCP/IP stack contains one or more protocols that function on each OSI layer. Table 5-1 shows how the TCP/IP protocol stack maps to the OSI model. Notice that each layer (or group of layers) has at least two protocols that operate on that layer.

Table 5-1	The TCP/IP Protocol Stack
OSI Layers	*TCP/IP Protocols*
Application, Presentation, Session	Telnet, FTP, SMTP, SNMP, DNS, HTTP
Transport	TCP, UDP
Network	IP, ICMP, ARP, RARP
Data Link, Physical	Ethernet, Token Ring, FDDI*

* These are networking technologies that function at the Data Link and Physical layers. They aren't actually TCP/IP protocols and aren't included as a part of the TCP/IP protocol stack. They're included in Table 5-1 only to show the technologies that function on that level of the model.

The following sections give you a brief overview on the TCP/IP protocols that operate on each layer (or group of layers) of the OSI model.

Applying the application protocols

The TCP/IP application layer (not to be confused with the OSI Application Layer) protocols you will most likely encounter on your Cisco network are listed in Table 5-1 for the top three layers of the OSI model. These OSI layers (Session, Presentation, and Application) are collectively referred to as the Upper Layers of the OSI model. TCP/IP application layer protocols are not actually applications in the sense of Microsoft Word, Lotus 1-2-3, or Duke Nukem. Application layer protocols interface with user-level applications to facilitate the services provided by the other layers of the OSI model and the TCP/IP protocol stack. Application layer protocols commonly used by a Cisco network administrator are FTP, TFTP, SNMP, and Telnet.

Transferring files, trivial or not

The File Transfer Protocol (FTP) is a reliable, connection-oriented tool (see "Connecting ways" later in this chapter) used to copy files from one computer to another over a TCP/IP network, such as the Internet or an intranet. You are likely familiar with this TCP/IP Application layer protocol. It is the workhorse of Web site maintenance and file downloads and uploads. FTP includes functions that allow it to log on to a remote network, navigate its directory structure, list the contents of its directories, and copy files by downloading them to the local computer or uploading them to a remote computer.

Another flavor of FTP is the Trivial File Transfer Protocol (TFTP), which is an *unreliable* (meaning delivery is not guaranteed) file transfer protocol. This TCP/IP protocol is used by Cisco routers to *transfer* (store and retrieve) configuration files from a computer supporting a TFTP server. The *trivial* part of the name refers to the supposition that you would only use this protocol to move files that you don't care much about (trivial data). If you really cared enough to transfer the very best, you would use FTP. However, for small files over a LAN, TFTP works quite well, regardless of how you really feel about the data.

TFTP is actually a very good tool when the data being transferred does not enter or travel on the public network. This tool works very well for transferring configuration and boot files from a local network host to a router or switch. Because of TFTP's lower overhead (it doesn't require packets to be acknowledged), it is much faster and more efficient than FTP for transferring router files (see Chapter 11 for more information on TFTP).

Connecting with Telnet

Telnet is a terminal emulation protocol used on TCP/IP-based networks to remotely log on to a remote device (a computer or router, most likely) to run a program or manipulate data. Telnet was originally developed for ARPAnet (the Department of Defense's early precursor to the Internet) and is now an inherent and highly used part of the TCP/IP communications protocol suite. In the Cisco world, Telnet is used to access and configure routers from remote locations. This is the tool used to connect and log on to virtual terminal interface ports. Remember, you heard it here first.

Running into other protocols

Other Presentation and Application layer protocols that you can count on running into as a network administrator are the Hypertext Transfer Protocol (HTTP), Simple Network Management Protocol (SNMP), Domain Name System (DNS), and Simple Mail Transfer Protocol (SMTP). Of these, the SNMP protocol is the most important to Cisco network administrators.

If your network operating system is or will be Novell NetWare, you should know that IPX/SPX networks, which naturally use the IPX/SPX protocol stack, have two protocols that perform many of the same functions as the TCP/IP Application layer protocols — SAP (Service Advertising Protocol) and NCP (NetWare Core Protocol). However, not all Novell NetWare networks run the IPX/SPX protocol stack. NetWare 5 has made TCP/IP its default protocol suite, instead of IPX/SPX, which is still available. But, legacy networks exist that have not made the switch and still run the IPX/SPX protocol stack. See Chapter 8 for more information on the Novell IPX/SPX protocols.

Moving Packets and Datagrams

The two primary TCP/IP protocols that function on the OSI model's Transport layer are the Transmission Control Protocol (TCP) and the User Datagram Protocol (UDP). These two protocols have a number of things in common, but as we describe in the following sections, they have one major difference, how reliably they transport data over the internetwork.

Controlling the transmission

TCP is a connection-oriented (see "Connecting ways" later in this chapter), reliable, delivery protocol that includes processes to ensure that packets arrive at their destination error-free. TCP provides reliable, point-to-point communications that two devices on a TCP/IP network can use to communicate with each other. To communicate, each device must create a connection to the other by binding a socket to the end of the connection that it controls. The devices read from and write to the application represented by the socket bound to the connection.

Using TCP is similar to sending a registered letter. When you send the letter, you know for sure that it will get to its destination and that you'll be notified that it arrived in good condition. Of course, like registered mail, you pay a higher price to use TCP. Luckily, the higher price doesn't involve money, but rather the amount of bandwidth and time used to complete the transmission, with all that checking and rechecking going on.

This is what's cool about TCP:

- ✔ It's connection-oriented.
- ✔ It offers reliable transfer.
- ✔ It performs error-checking.
- ✔ It has full-duplex transmission.

  ✔ It performs flow control.

  ✔ It even does multiplexing!

Socketing it to me

FTP, Telnet, SMTP, and HTTP are a few of the Application layer protocols that take advantage of the transport services included in TCP. These protocols use TCP to open a socket between two computers. A *socket* directs incoming data traffic to the appropriate application process on a TCP/IP network. A socket is made up of the combination of the IP address of a network node and a port number. We deal with ports a little later in this chapter (see "Getting noticed in all the well-known ports"), but for now, we'll just say that it's a number assigned to a certain type of application, such as FTP, HTTP, Telnet, and so on.

Actually, two types of sockets can be used:

  ✔ **Stream sockets:** This socket works with connection-oriented (see "Connecting ways" later in this chapter) protocols, such as TCP, to transfer data between two computers.

  ✔ **Datagram sockets:** This one works with IP.

Application layer protocols use TCP to open a socket by recording the TCP/IP protocol in use, the destination IP address, and the port number of the application (see "Getting noticed in all the well-known ports" later in the chapter) to be used on the destination device to process the information being transferred.

Connecting ways

Network protocols are either connection-oriented or connectionless. This doesn't mean that some protocols make connections and others don't. What it refers to is the nature of the connection made between two communicating devices while using a specific protocol. This section explains each type:

  ✔ **Connection-oriented protocols** require that a direct connection be established between two devices before data can begin to transfer between the devices. Packets are transferred using a prescribed sequence of actions that includes an acknowledgment to signal when a packet arrives and possibly resending the packet if errors are detected. As a result of this method's reliability and the overhead involved, it is much slower than connectionless protocols. TCP is a connection-oriented protocol.

✔ **Connectionless protocols** are largely based on your faith in the technology. Packets are sent over the network without regard to whether they actually arrive at their destinations. You get no acknowledgments or guarantees, but you can send a *datagram* (as connectionless protocol packets are called) to many different destinations at the same time. Connectionless protocols are fast because no time is used in establishing and tearing down connections. A fair analogy is mailing a first-class letter at the post office. UDP is a connectionless protocol.

Connectionless protocols are also referred to as *best-effort* protocols. This type of delivery system is common to protocols that do not include some form of acknowledgment system to guarantee the delivery of information.

It isn't really important to know whether a protocol is connection-oriented or not, but when setting up a network and looking at the elements included in the network's protocol stack, you will understand more of its inherent behavior if you do know this difference. Here are some of the TCP/IP protocols:

Connection-oriented	Connectionless
FTP	IP
TCP	IPX
SPX	UDP

Making a three-way handshake

Establishing a connection-oriented connection involves setting up sequencing and acknowledgment fields and agreeing upon the port numbers to be used. This is accomplished by a three-step handshake process that works like this:

1. **Handshake one: Host 1 sends a synchronization message to Host 2.**

2. **Handshake two: Host 2 acknowledges Host 1's synchronization message and sends back its own synchronization message.**

3. **Handshake three: Host 1 acknowledges Host 2's synchronization message.**

At this point, the connection is sufficiently synchronized and successfully established, and the applications can begin transferring data. Throughout the communications session, TCP manages the transfer of data packets, ensuring that they reach their destination. If errors occur, TCP supervises the retransmission of the packet.

Checking for errors and closing the window

If TCP ever has a retirement dinner, when they give it the gold socket, they'll say, "You could always rely on good old TCP!" TCP data transfers are reliable. This isn't an opinion; it's a technical characteristic that was designed into TCP. TCP uses two mechanisms to provide its high level of reliability: error-checking and received-segment acknowledgments.

Error checking is accomplished through the use of two numbers stored in the packet header: a checksum and the number of bits in the packet payload. The checksum is calculated through an algorithm, and the bit count is a straight tally. These two values are stored in the packet header and sent along as a part of the packet. The receiving end recalculates, recounts, and checks its numbers against those in the packet header. If they are not equal, a request is sent to the sending station to resend the packet.

The acknowledgment of segment receipts is accomplished through a process called *windowing,* which is a form of flow control. In windowing, a window, which is represented as a number of packets, sets the interval before an acknowledgement must be sent back to the sending station by the receiving stations. The size of the window is the number of packets that are to be sent before an acknowledgement is required to be sent back. Windowing gets its name from the fact that windows can be opened and closed to allow more or less airflow. Of course, you realize that we are speaking of the windows in the walls of your home and not those of the software type.

Windowing works like this:

1. **Host 1 tells Host 2 that it has a certain window size and sends the appropriate number of segments.**

2. **If Host 2 receives all the segments, it sends back an acknowledgment indicating that the next segment should be sent and the size of the window that Host 2 can accept.**

   This tells the sending station that Host 2 is ready for more, and because packets were sent without problems, maybe this time Host 1 should try more if it would like. As the transmission proceeds, the receiving station slowly increases the window size as long as segments are received without errors.

3. **If Host 2 fails to receive a segment, Host 2 resends an acknowledgment for the preceding segment, which means that Host 1 should send that preceding segment again.**

   For example, if errors are detected in segment 3, Host 2 sends an acknowledgement for segment 2, indicating to Host 1 that segment 3 needs to be sent again.

Because Host 1 can't be trusted to send the first experimental number of packets without a failure, Host 2 resets the window to the minimum window size and the trust relationship is rebuilt.

This example uses what is called a *sliding window,* which is so called because the window can be adjusted on the fly to meet the needs of either the sending or receiving device.

Staying connected

After the connection is open, it remains open, providing a virtual circuit. TCP supports *full-duplex transmission,* which means that both the sender and receiver can transfer data simultaneously over the same connection. To accommodate this, the devices at each end of the connection must maintain two windows — one for sending and one for receiving.

TCP allows for *multiplexing,* which is the ability for more than one application to use an open transport connection. This is possible for two reasons:

- ✔ Each TCP segment is self-contained, with its data and addresses encapsulated in the segment packet.
- ✔ Segments are sent on a first-come, first-served basis without regard to what came before or comes after each segment.

Getting noticed in all the well-known ports

A *port* is a logical connection device that allows the system to assign the incoming data to a particular application for processing. Each port is assigned a *port number,* which is a way to identify the specific process to which the message is to be passed.

For example, if you request a file from a remote FTP server, TCP sets the port number to 21 (the standard FTP port number) in order to communicate the nature of the request to the remote server. The remote server sees the request for port number 21 and forwards your request to its FTP program. Both TCP and UDP use port numbers to move information along to the Application layer.

Because someone has to do it, the registering body, IANA (Internet Assigned Numbers Authority), divides port numbers into three groups:

✔ **Well-known ports** are the most commonly used TCP/IP ports. These ports are in the range of 0 through 1023. These ports can be used only by system processes or privileged programs. Well-known ports are TCP ports, but they are usually registered to UDP services as well.

✔ **Registered ports** are in the range of 1024 through 49151. Registered ports are used on most systems by user programs to create and control logical connections between proprietary programs.

✔ **Dynamic (private) ports** are in the range of 49152 through 65535. These ports are unregistered and can be used dynamically for private connections.

You should know this additional information about port numbers:

✔ Port numbers below 256 are assigned to public applications (such as FTP, HTTP, and so on).

✔ Port numbers 256 – 1023 are assigned to companies for saleable applications.

✔ Port numbers above 1023 are dynamically assigned in the host application.

✔ Source and destination port numbers don't have to be the same.

Table 5-2 lists the port numbers and corresponding applications for some of the more common application types. This information is also very useful when doing access lists on a Cisco router (see Chapter 15).

Table 5-2	Well-known Ports
Port Number	*Application*
21	FTP
23	Telnet
25	SMTP
53	DNS
69	TFTP
80	HTTP
110	POP3
161	SNMP

Formatting the TCP segment

On the Transport layer, data packets are referred to as *segments*. Figure 5-1 depicts the format of the TCP segment, and Table 5-3 describes its contents. Compare this to the UDP segment presented in the next section.

Figure 5-1:
The format
of the TCP
segment.

TCP Segment

16 bits	16 bits	32 bits	32 bits	4 bits	4 bits
Source Port	Dest. Port	Seq Number	ACK Number	HLEN	HLEN

	6 bits	16 bits	16 bits	16 bits	0 or 32 bits	?
	Code Bits	Window	Check-sum	Urgent Pointer	Option	Data

Table 5-3	TCP Segment Lengths	
Field	**Size in Bits**	**Purpose**
Source port	16	The number of the calling port
Destination port	16	The number of the called port
Sequence number	32	Ensures correct sequencing of data
Acknowledgment number	32	Sequence number of the next expected TCP octet
HLEN	4	Header length (as number of 32-bit words)
Reserved	6	Set to zero
Code bits	6	Functions that set up and terminate the session
Window	16	Size of window that the sender can accept
Checksum	16	Error-correction feature, sum of header and data fields
Urgent pointer	16	End of the urgent data

(continued)

Table 5-3 *(continued)*

Field	Size in Bits	Purpose
Option	0 or 32 bits per option	0 bits in length if there are no options included or 32 bits for each option included. Maximum TCP segment size is the most common option
Data	—	Data from upper layers

Flying Fast with UDP

User Datagram Protocol (UDP) is the other major Transport layer protocol in the TCP/IP protocol suite. In contrast to TCP and its reliability, UDP is unreliable, which means that it doesn't monitor the transmission of its segments (which, as you probably guessed, are called *datagrams*), and it doesn't require confirmation of datagram delivery. UDP is a best-effort, connectionless protocol best known for its speed.

UDP is fast because it doesn't take the time to check for datagram delivery, acknowledgements, or even error-checking functions like windowing. As shown in Figure 5-2, a UDP header frame, which includes all the fields before the data in the UDP segment, is only 8 bytes long compared to the TCP header frame that can be up to 24 bytes long, if only 1 option is included at the end of the segment. In theory, a TCP header could be up to 60 bytes long if enough options are included. The primary protocols using UDP are SNMP, NFS, TFTP, and DNS.

If you compare the UDP datagram's format and contents, shown in Figure 5-2 and detailed in Table 5-4, you should notice now how much less overhead, in the form of extra fields, a UDP segment contains.

Figure 5-2:
The format
of the UDP
datagram.

UDP Datagram				
16 bits	16 bits	16 bits	16 bits	?
Source Port	Dest. Port	Length	Check-sum	Data

Table 5-4	UDP Datagram Lengths	
Field	*Size in Bits*	*Purpose*
Source port	16	The number of the calling port
Destination port	16	The number of the called port
Length	16	The length of the datagram
Checksum	16	Error-detection feature, sum of header and data
Data	–	Data from upper layers

Transmitting on the Network Layer

A number of TCP/IP protocols operate on the Network layer of the OSI Model, including Internet Protocol (IP), Address Resolution Protocol (ARP), Reverse ARP (RARP), and the Internet Control Message Protocol (ICMP). The OSI Network layer (see Chapter 2) is concerned with routing messages across the internetwork.

Letting you see some IP

While TCP is connection-oriented, IP is connectionless. IP provides for the best-effort delivery of the packets (or datagrams) that it creates from the segments it receives from the Transport layer protocols. IP also provides for *logical addressing* (IP addressing) on the Network layer.

Converting Transport layer segments

The size of IP packets is based on the *maximum transmission unit (MTU)*, which is the largest number of bits that can be transmitted over a certain network protocol. IP selects an appropriate packet size and then proceeds to fragment larger packets. This process, known as *fragmentation*, usually occurs on a router between the source and destination, and results in a fragment that's sized just right to fit into a single frame for shipment over the network. The fragments are then reassembled at the final destination.

IP also provides for logical addressing, which is the hierarchical addressing scheme used on the Network layer. Where Layer 2's hardware addressing only defines a particular network node, logical addressing also defines the node's network and other location information. IP determines the action to take on a packet based on the information in a routing table. On a router, this means that the decision of which port should receive the packet to move it along its way is based on the information contained in its routing table (see Chapter 12 for more information on routers and routing).

Looking inside an IP packet

The IP packet (or datagram) is variable in length, and its format is shown in Figure 5-3 and described in Table 5-5.

Figure 5-3: An IP packet's format.

4 bits	4 bits	8 bits	16 bits	16 bits	3 bits	13 bits	8 bits
Version Number	HLEN	Service Type	Length	ID	Flags	Fragment Offset	TTL

IP Packet

8 bits	16 bits	32 bits	32 bits	Variable	Variable	?
Urgent Pointer	Window	Check-sum	Urgent Pointer	IP Options	Data	Padding

Table 5-5		IP Packet Lengths
Field	*Size in Bits*	*Purpose*
IP version number	4	Identifies the packet as IPv4 or IPv6
HLEN	4	Header length
Type of service	8	How the packet should be processed
Length	16	The total length of the packet including the header and data
ID	16	Used for reassembly of fragmented packets
Flags	3	Used for reassembly of fragmented packets
Flag offset	13	Used for reassembly of fragmented packets
TTL	8	Time-to-live value
Protocol	8	Identifies the Transport layer protocol that passed this packet to IP
Checksum	16	Error-correction feature, sum of header and data

Field	Size in Bits	Purpose
Source IP	32	IP address of sending node
Destination IP	32	IP address of destination node
IP option	Variable	Optional use for testing and debugging
Padding	0 or 8	Used to pad the packet size to allow for the calculation of the checksum
Data	Variable	Data being transmitted

It is okay for the packet to be smaller than the MTU. The checksum of an IP packet is calculated using the number of 16-bit words that make up the packet. If the number of bytes in the packet is an odd number, the padding is used to bring the number of bytes to an even number. The sole purpose of the padding field is to enable the checksum calculation and it is not actually transmitted with the packet.

This is some cool stuff to know about IP and its packets:

- ✔ IP is primarily concerned with routing.
- ✔ IP is a connectionless, unreliable, best-effort delivery service.
- ✔ IP, which operates on the Transport Layer, manages the fragmentation and reassembly of segments being sent by or passed to the upper layers (Session, Presentation, and Application).

Sending notes with ICMP

The Internet Control Message Protocol (ICMP) is another Network layer protocol. It's used primarily for control and messaging services. It carries messages between systems regarding status, passes control codes, and delivers error codes and messages. ICMP is also the underlying protocol to many TCP/IP utilities, such as PING and traceroute.

ICMP has a set of standard messages that it carries. ICMP uses these common messages:

- ✔ **Echo request** — tests connectivity
- ✔ **Echo reply** — replies to echo messages
- ✔ **Buffer full** — indicates that a router's memory is full
- ✔ **Destination unreachable** — indicates that a destination IP is unreachable

✔ **Source quench** — a flow control message

✔ **Redirect** — tells the sender to use a better route for a message

✔ **Time exceeded** — TTL (time-to-live) field time has been exceeded

✔ **Hops** — message failed to reach destination in allotted hops

✔ **Ping** — Packet Internet Groper (technically, the same as echo request and echo reply)

Unraveling the Mysterious World of Encapsulation

As data flows from the top of the OSI model to the bottom, the protocols that operate on each level repackage the message into its own version of a segment, packet, datagram, or frame. Each protocol may add a message header, possibly a message trailer, or divide the original message's data up into smaller chunks to eventually transmit the data over the network or internetwork. As the data passes from one layer (protocol) to the next, its form may change subtly or even radically.

Each protocol (layer) transforms the header, trailer, and message data into a single entity, called a *protocol data unit (PDU)*. This process is called *encapsulation,* and a PDU is the unit passed by one protocol to the next and eventually sent out on the network. Each layer in the TCP/IP protocol stack gives its version of a PDU a different name, as listed in Table 5-6.

Table 5-6	Data Encapsulation Levels
OSI Layer	*Data Encapsulation Level*
Application	Data
Transport	Segments for TCP; datagrams for UDP
Network	Packets (datagrams)
Data Link	Frames
Physical	Bits

Cisco calls the process that moves data up and down the OSI and TCP/IP layers the *Five Steps of Data Encapsulation.* Ooh, sounds so mysterious, like some old monster movie, doesn't it? Actually, all this amounts to is the addition of data headers to a PDU on the way out, and the removal of these headers on the way in, as the PDU passes through the OSI layers. Table 5-6 lists the OSI layer and the name given to the encapsulated data on that layer. Figure 5-4 shows the five data encapsulation levels. This is good to know so that you won't embarrass yourself around network administrators who are really picky about this stuff.

Data	Data		Application Layer
Segment	Transport Header	Data	Transport Layer
Packet	IP Header	Segment	Network Layer
Frame	Data Link Header	Packet · Trailer	Data Link Layer
Bits	11001101010010011110001101001011		Physical Layer

Figure 5-4:
Five steps of data encapsulation.

Chapter 6

Working With Those Weird Numbers

*A*s a Cisco network administrator, you encounter addresses, parameters, table entries, and more uses of binary, hexadecimal, and decimal numbers. Binary numbers are the basis for subnetting and routing; hexadecimal numbers are used for such things as interfaces, operating system interrupt IDs, and port addresses; and decimal numbers are rampant. To a certain extent, your ability to read and understand binary, hexadecimal, and decimal values will determine how successful and efficient your network operates.

Assuming that you are up to speed on decimal numbers, we'd like to focus on binary and hexadecimal numbers in this chapter to give you a solid foundation in these numbering systems.

Feeling Ambivalent about Binary Numbers

Love 'em or hate 'em, binary numbers are integrated into the very fabric of computers and computing. And taking it one step further, binary numbers are an underlying foundation of networking as well. In fact, the binary number system is the basis of the logic, arithmetic, and addressing functions of any computer, router, or other networking device. For no other reason than that, you should be familiar with the binary number system.

In its most complex form, the *binary number system* consists of only two digital values: 1 and 0, which is also its most simple form, by the way. Because a transistor is a semiconductor device that is capable of storing only one of two toggled values, the binary number scheme, with its two digital values, and the electronics of the PC are made for one another.

Assigning power to the places

To understand the basics of binary numbers, you should begin with a brief review of decimal numbers. What, you say you know decimal numbers and don't need a review? Trust us, you need this review.

When doesn't 101 equal 101?

When you encounter the number 101, we'll assume you think of one hundred and one. Sure, anyone would. But, what if you were asked to prove why 101 was equal to one hundred and one? "Just because" doesn't explain how you know that these three numbers represent that value. Chances are that you have become so familiar with the decimal number system that you've forgotten what you learned in primary school about number systems.

The number 101 actually represents 1 unit of 100^2 plus no units of 10^1 plus 1 unit of 1^0, or 100 plus 0 plus 1, or one hundred and one (101).

However, if the number system being expressed were to change from decimal to binary, octal, or hexadecimal, the value represented by the numbers 1, 0, and 1 changes dramatically. Table 6-1 shows the effect of changing the number system on the value represented by the digits 101.

Table 6-1	Values in Different Number Systems	
Number System	*Base*	*Decimal Equivalent of Value Represented by 101*
Binary	2	5
Decimal	10	101
Hexadecimal	16	257
Octal	8	65

What the entries in Table 6-1 show is that although the digits 101 are somewhat universal, the value represented by these digits is quite different under different number systems.

The base of a number system indicates how many characters are used to represent numbers. For example, a number system with a base of 2 means that all numbers in that system are represented by one of two characters. In the binary system, all numbers are represented by 1 and 0. In the decimal system, all numbers are represented by 0, 1, 2, 3, 4, 5, 6, 7, 8, and 9 (that's a total of 10 numbers, by the way). The hexadecimal system, as you might imagine, uses 16 characters, and the octal system uses 8 characters.

Keeping the columnar score

When you write a number in any number system, what you are really writing is how many of each successive columnar value is included in generating the value being represented. Here's an example, using the old trusty 101 again (remember that any number raised to the zero power produces 1).

In decimal, the columnar values represent the powers of ten:

$$10^7 \quad 10^6 \quad 10^5 \quad 10^4 \quad 10^3 \quad 10^2 \quad 10^1 \quad 10^0$$

To represent the value one hundred one, tallies are placed in the appropriate columns to represent that value:

10^7	10^6	10^5	10^4	10^3	10^2	10^1	10^0
0	0	0	0	0	1	0	1

This is proof that the digits 101 equal one hundred one in the decimal system.

Turning numbers on and off to create value

Binary values are the result of combining the number 2 being raised to different exponential powers in the same way as decimal numbers. The difference between decimal and binary is that in decimal, although we avoided using them, you can represent columnar values with the numbers 0 through 9. The number placed in the column represents how many of that column's values are used in the number being represented. However, in binary, although the same function is in use, the numbers that can be used to represent how many of a column value are in use are limited to either a 0 or a 1. It is easier to think of binary columns as having an on-and-off switch. If a 1 is used in a column, that column's value is included; if the column has a 0, then that column is off and no value is represented.

Binary numbers all in a row

The majority of what you need to know about binary numbers for use in networking is the value for each of the 8-bits in a byte. Each of the 8 bits represents a different power of two, in exactly the same pattern used for decimal numbers.

The decimal values for each position of the 8 bits of a byte are:

2^7	2^6	2^5	2^4	2^3	2^2	2^1	2^0
128	64	32	16	8	4	2	1

Using these values, you can determine that the binary number 10101101 represents 128 + 32 + 8 + 4 + 1 or 173 in decimal values. Those positions with a one are included; those positions with a zero are not. It's really just that simple.

As a network administrator, you unfortunately need to know enough about the binary number system to express decimal numbers as binary numbers and which binary positions are used to yield a specific decimal value. You don't need to know binary arithmetic, you know, addition, multiplication, and so on. That should be a relief.

Working with binary numbers is a required skill in developing and applying subnet masks to IP addressing (see Chapter 7). And the key component of this application is the 8-bit byte, four of which make up an IP address. The commonly used IP address (IP version 4 addressing) consists of four 8-bit binary octets that are typically, and thankfully, expressed as decimal numbers. See Chapter 7 for the details on why this is important to know.

Proving the value of another 101

The key to binary numbers is to remember that each bit in the 8-bit byte represents a power of 2, starting with 0 on the right end up through 7 at the left end. For example, the binary number 00000101 contains the following values:

$1 \times 2^0 = 1$ (any number to the zero power is 1)

$0 \times 2^1 = 0$ (any number to the one power is the number)

$1 \times 2^2 = 4$ (two times two)

$0 \times 2^3 = 0$ (two times two times two)

$0 \times 2^4 = 0$ (two times two times two times two)

$0 \times 2^5 = 0$ (two times two times two times two . . .)

$0 \times 2^6 = 0$

$0 \times 2^7 = 0$

Totaling 5

So 00000101 in binary is the same as 5 in decimal. The largest value that can be stored in 8 bits is 255. This is the decimal value of the binary number 11111111 which is the same as saying $128 + 64 + 32 + 16 + 8 + 4 + 2 + 1 = 255$.

Practice makes perfect conversions

As we said earlier in this section, you should know how to convert decimal values to binary and especially binary values into decimal. Use these steps to convert a decimal number into a binary number:

1. **Determine the largest power of two that can be subtracted from the number.**

   For the number 248, the largest binary value that can be represented in 8 bits is 128, or 2^7. The easiest way to determine this is to find the highest value that is less than the number you are converting. Because you know for sure that 128 is less than 248, you can place a 1 in the left-most position of the 8-bit set. So far, your binary number is 10000000.

2. **Subtract the bit value from the original number.**

   The difference of $248 - 128$ is 120. Repeating the process used in Step 1, the next highest value that can be subtracted from the number is 64, or 2^6. Your binary number is now 11000000.

3. **Until the remaining value of the original decimal value reaches zero, repeat Step 1.**

   The final binary number for 248 is 11111000.

Now try these steps for any number between 11 (no reason to make it too easy) and 255.

You can also convert a decimal number to binary in a less complicated way. You simply divide the number by 2 and save the remainder (it will be either 1 or 0). Continue dividing the quotient (the answer in a division problem) by two and saving the remainder until all you have is remainder. For example, in our original problem of converting the decimal 248, you would:

1. **Divide 248 by 2 to get 124, with a remainder of 0.**

2. **Next divide 124 by 2 to get 62, with a remainder of 0.**

3. **Divide 62 by 2 to get 31, with a remainder of 0.**

4. **Divide 31 by 2 to get 15, with a remainder of 1.**

5. **Divide 15 by 2 to get 7, with a remainder of 1.**

6. **Divide 7 by 2 to get 3, with a remainder of 1.**

7. **Divide 3 by 2 to get 1, with a remainder of 1.**

8. **Divide 1 by 2 to get 0, with a remainder of 1.**

Now write down the remainders, last to first, 11111000, and you have the binary number for the decimal 248. Try this one yourself on another number.

Of course, an even simpler way is to use a scientific calculator or the Windows Calculator (in Scientific view) to convert these numbers, but you won't always have one with you, so being able to convert decimal numbers to binary is a good skill for a network administrator to have.

Hexing the Numbers

The word *hexadecimal* means six and ten, and that's just what this number system is about. Where binary includes only 0 and 1, hex, as it's known to its friends, includes the decimal numerals 0 to 9 (the ten) and replaces the decimal values of 10 to 15 with the symbols A, B, C, D, E, and F (the six).

In networking, the principal use of hexadecimal numbers is to provide a shorthand way of recording and displaying long binary numbers. Hexadecimal is commonly used to display the long binary addresses of memory, ports, and interfaces, which would be too prone to error, not to mention tedious to work with, if their addresses or information were entered or displayed in binary. Computer technicians use hex numbers to identify IRQs, LPT, or COM ports. For example, the hex number 2F8 is the default address of IRQ3 and COM2.

In most cases, you rarely need to know the decimal equivalent of a hexadecimal number. However, the ability to convert hexadecimal numbers is a good basic skill for anyone working with personal computers and networking hardware, because you often need to convert a range of hex addresses to decimal to determine the size of a block of memory or storage, or an address range. One more bit of good news is that you never, repeat never, should need to convert a decimal number to a hexadecimal number, although you should probably know how, just in case.

Hexing decimal numbers

The number base (technically, the radix) for decimal is 10, for binary it's 2, and for hexadecimal it's 16. While you roll that around in your head for a while (not too long — it causes headaches), remember that you have nothing to fear. What we have is just another way to represent exponential powers of a base in columns.

Hexadecimal numbers are expressed as powers of 16, in exactly the same way that we've shown earlier in this chapter for decimal and binary:

16^5	16^4	16^3	16^2	16^1	16^0
1,048,576	65,536	4,096	256	16	1

As you can see from the preceding, hexadecimal numbers can represent very large numbers with only a few characters. Although you will rarely need to think of it, the hexadecimal number 101 is equivalent to decimal 257. This is 256 + 0 + 1 = 257.

Bear in mind that, like decimal with its 10 numeric values that can be used in each column of the number, hexadecimal has 16 values that are used to represent how many of a power of 16 are included in the number being represented. For example, the hexadecimal number 3A7F9 has the decimal equivalent of 239,609.

Converting hexadecimal numbers

To convert any non-decimal number system into decimal is a matter of knowing two things: the base value of the number system and the numeric value of each position. In binary numbers, each position represents a different power of two; the same holds true in any number system, including hexadecimal. The difference with hexadecimal is that each position represents a different power of 16.

The base value of a number is the value represented by the expression "10." The base of decimal is 10, the base of binary is 2, and the base of hexadecimal is 16. Therefore, 10 in decimal is 10; 10 in binary is 2; 10 in octal (base 8) is 8; and 10 in hexadecimal is 16.

Use the following steps to find the decimal equivalent for the hex number A012F:

1. **Figure the value of the first character.**

   Because each position represents a power of 16, the A in A012F represents the positional value of 16^4. The A has the decimal equivalent of 10. So this position is worth 10 x 16^4, or 655,360.

2. **Repeat Step 1 until you have figured the values for the rest of the characters.**

   The next position of value is a 1 in the position of 16^2, which is worth 256.

   The next position has a value of 2×16^1, or 32.

   The last position has the value of F (15) $\times$ 16^0, or 15. Any number to the zero power is worth 1, so this is the same as 15 x 1.

3. **Add up the values for the final value.**

   Add 655,360 + 256 + 32 + 15, and you get the sum of 655,663, which is the decimal equivalent of A012F hexadecimal.

Just a nybble more on hexadecimal

If you understand how hexadecimal works and how it is used to represent decimal numbers (see the preceding two sections), you are ready to deal with how hexadecimal is used to display binary numbers.

Each 8-bit byte can be divided into two 4-bit halves, each of which is called a *nybble*. Seriously, that is what it's called. A nybble is perfect for holding one hexadecimal number, because four binary bits are capable of storing the decimal values 0 to 15.

If you were to convert the binary number 11111111 (decimal 255) to hexadecimal, the resulting hex number is FF. Converting the decimal address 2587469 to binary yields 1001110111101101001101, but this same value in hexadecimal is 277B4D. Hexadecimal takes the bytes holding the binary number, splits them into nybbles, and then converts each nybble to a hex number.

Table 6-2 shows how this works for the numbers in the preceding paragraph.

Table 6-2	Converting Binary to Hexadecimal
Nybble Contents	*Hexadecimal Number*
0010	2
0111	7
0111	7
1011	B
0100	4
1101	D

Using the tool available

Probably the best, because it is the most readily available, tool you have for converting decimal, binary, or hexadecimal numbers is the Windows Calculator. This handy tool is found on the Windows Start➪Programs➪Accessories menus of just about any Windows version, including 98, NT, and 2000.

Using a calculator is by far the easiest way to convert number systems, but knowing how to convert them can come in handy, especially when working with debugging and troubleshooting tools, configuring a router, or subnetting a network.

As Table 6-2 shows, long binary numbers are easily represented as hexadecimal numbers for entry and display. If you ever really want to know the value of an address (and there may or may not come a time that you do), simply convert it to binary and then to decimal.

Hexadecimal numbers are usually written with a small *h* following them. For example, the number used in the preceding steps is commonly written as A012Fh. You will also see hexadecimal numbers represented as 0xA012F, where the *0x* is another way to designate a hexadecimal number. However, as you will see in later chapters, some Cisco router commands expect hexadecimal parameters without any designation characters.

Chapter 7

The Curse of the Subnet Mask and Other Boolean Tales

*N*etworking is like delivering pizza — without the right address, it doesn't matter how good the pizza is or how fast the delivery service. Your product is wasted if it can't reach its destination. On the network, a message, like the pizza, must have a valid address if it ever hopes to reach its destination. Knowledge and understanding of network addressing schemes, especially the IPv4 (IP addressing, version 4), are essential to your success as a network administrator. This is true, whether or not your network connects to the Internet. In this chapter, we look at all aspects of networking address. Well, at least, as it relates to Cisco networking, that is.

How May We Address You?

Just like the post office and the pizza dude expect you to have an address that uniquely finds you and your home, each node on a network must also be uniquely identified. If you wish to log onto a network, use a network's resources, download information from a Web site, or receive e-mail, the workstation you are working on must be able to be found on the network. Without some unique identification for your node, the network won't know where to send any information, e-mail, or files intended for you.

As a person, you also have many ways to be identified, including your social security number, your phone number, your Wal-Mart frequent shopper card number, and others. On a network, a computer also has several ways to be identified. It can be addressed by its MAC address, an IP address, perhaps an IPX address, and perhaps even a URL.

Two forms of addressing can be used to locate a node on a network:

 ✓ **Network address:** A network address relates to all other addresses on the network in the sense that the address is assigned as a part of a logical grouping, such as with an IP address, and uniquely identifies both the network node and the network on which it is found.

 ✓ **Physical address:** A physical address bears no relationship to any other physical address on the network, as it is randomly assigned by a manufacturer of network adapters and therefore identifies only the network interface of a single workstation or node.

Dissecting the network address

A network address has two parts: a host ID, which identifies an individual node or workstation, and a network ID, which designates the network or network segment, on which the host ID can be found. Various network addressing schemes are in use, but the IPv4 addressing scheme is the one most commonly used on Cisco networks.

Look at this example of an IPv4 network address:

    204.106.100.131

In this example, 204.106.100 represents the network ID of this Class C address and the .131 portion is the host ID.

Getting physical with MAC addressing

The most common physical addressing scheme used on Cisco networks, and all other networks as well, is the media access control (MAC) address. The MAC address is a Data Link layer (Layer 2 of the OSI Model) address and is generally the address of a network interface card (NIC). The MAC address is also referred to as the Ethernet address, physical address, or the burned-in (as opposed to burned-out) address. See Chapter 2 for information on the OSI Model, its layers, and the Ethernet standards.

MAC addresses are flat addresses, which means they identify only the node to which they are attached and have no relation to the rest of the network. In a network address, the hosts on a single network segment all have the same network ID, but MAC addresses are issued individually to network adapters and other networking devices when they are manufactured. In case you didn't know it, the equipment on your network doesn't all have to be from the same manufacturer, no matter what the kid at the computer store told you. Therefore, the chance of having even two MAC addresses in sequence on one network is extremely slim. Think of a MAC address like the number on your credit card — that number is assigned to you and can be used to identify you, but it doesn't tell much about you other than your name.

A MAC address is a 48-bit (6-byte) number that is commonly represented as six two-digit hexadecimal numbers separated by dashes. Figure 7-1 shows the display generated by the Windows utility WINIPCFG that includes the Adapter Address box, which contains the MAC address of a computer's network interface card.

In the MAC address shown in Figure 7-1, the first three bytes (24 bits) contain a code assigned to the manufacturer of the card by the IEEE (in this case 44-45-53), and the last three bytes (24 bits) contain a unique serialized number assigned to this particular network interface card by the manufacturer when it was manufactured (54-00-00).

Just so you know, the MAC address manufacturer code assigned to Cisco Systems is 00 00 0C.

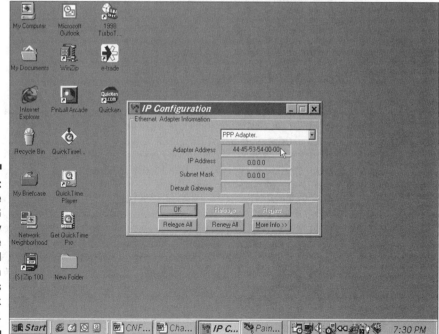

Figure 7-1:
The
WINIPCFG
display
includes the
physical
address of a
computer's
network
adapter.

MAC address manufacturer codes for the terminally bored

The first three bytes of a MAC address contain a hexadecimal manufacturer code. The following are examples of IEEE assigned MAC address manufacturer codes and the manufacturers they identify:

00 00 3D	AT&T
00 00 1D	Cabletron
10 00 D8	Data General
08 00 5A	IBM
00 55 00	Intel
40 00 65	Network General

00 00 1B	Novell/Eagle
00 00 03	Standard Microsystems
00 00 11	Tektronix
40 00 14	TI (Texas Instruments)
00 DD 00	Ungermann-Bass
00 00 2A	TRW
40 00 AA	Xerox
00 01 E3	Xircom

Networking devices, such as routers, often use a couple of protocols — ARP and RARP — to learn about addresses on their network. ARP (Address Resolution Protocol) is used to find a MAC address from a known IP address. RARP (Reverse Address Resolution Protocol) is used translate a MAC address into an associated IP address.

Working with MAC addresses

What you should know at this point is that a MAC address is the unique identifier of the adapter, usually a NIC, used to connect a device to the network. This is all well and good as long as the only addresses ever used on a network are MAC addresses. What happens when somebody from outside your network wants to address one of your network's nodes with something other than the MAC address, such as an IP address? What then?

If your network is using a network protocol that allows for addressing other than the MAC address, it will have a mechanism for translating these other addresses to the MAC address of each node. For example, if your network is using TCP/IP, (a wise choice we might add) then each of your network nodes also have an IP address. This is great for communicating over a WAN, but on the LAN, it is the MAC address that is king.

TCP/IP includes two protocols that are used to resolve (which is the really cool network way of saying "translate") the MAC and IP addresses of a node, ARP and RARP:

- **ARP (Address Resolution Protocol):** Sends out a broadcast message to learn the MAC address of a specific IP address. The node with the broadcasted IP address responds with its MAC address, completing the set. There are no discounts for older networks on this protocol.
- **Reverse ARP (RARP):** Broadcasts messages to learn the IP address corresponding to a specific MAC address. This requires the presence of a RARP (pronounced "rarp," what else?) server on the network.

The associated pairs of addresses, the MAC and IP addresses, for a network node are stored in memory in a table referred to as the *ARP cache.*

What a Novell idea!

Some network addresses incorporate a MAC address. A primary example of this is Novell's IPX protocols. IPX addresses are not classified into address classes, as are IP addresses. The IPX address is ten bytes (80 bits) long. Of these ten bytes, four bytes (32 bits) represent the network ID, and six bytes (48 bits) are used for the hexadecimal node ID, which is normally the MAC address of the node. The ten-byte length of the network ID is often misleading because any leading zeroes, something quite common, are not usually shown in the number.

For example, look at the following IPX address:

4b2c.0000.06d2.ef67

In this example, the network ID is 4b2c (actually it is 00004b2c, but the leading 0s are suppressed), and the node ID is 0000.06d2.ef67 (notice that leading 0s are shown in the node ID).

The Wondrous World of IP Addressing

The most commonly used addressing scheme on Cisco networks is the IP (Internet Protocol) addressing scheme. In fact, the IP addressing scheme is the scheme of choice on the Internet as well. As a network administrator of a Cisco network, IP addressing will become second nature, as well as a second language, for you.

Keep these IP address basics in mind:

- ✔ IP addresses are assigned by the American Registry for Internet Numbers (ARIN), the agency responsible for assigning and tracking the network IDs used on the Internet.

- ✔ IP addresses are made up of four 8-bit binary numbers connected by periods (dots). The IP address for `www.dummies.com` is 206.175.162.18.

- ✔ IP addresses are 32 bits in length, with each of the four numbers using 8 bits.

- ✔ Each of the 8-bit numbers is called an *octet*.

- ✔ What each separate octet means depends on the class of the IP address.

- ✔ The octets in an IP address, depending on the address class, are a part of either the network identity or the host (node) identity.

- ✔ IP addresses are divided into five address classes: Classes A, B, C, D, and E.

The four octets are usually written as what is called *dotted-decimal notation*. The four octet number format is also commonly known as IP version 4. The four does not have anything to do with the four octets. In fact, the rapid expansion of the Internet is causing a shortage of IPv4 addresses, and on the horizon is the 128-bit IP version 6. An IPv6 address has 16 octets.

Bringing on the binary

The binary system is a numbering system that uses only two values (0 and 1) to represent numbers. Computers, unlike most humans, flourish in binary. In order for a computer to process an address, it must be expressed in terms that the computer can understand. This is the reason for the binary values. Fortunately for us humans, binary numbers can be expressed as decimal numbers by converting the binary value into a decimal value — a talent that you will acquire as a network administrator.

We aren't going into too much detail here on the binary number system. If you aren't too familiar with binary numbers, you really should review Chapter 6 before you continue with this chapter. IP addressing and subnet masks require that you have at least a basic understanding of the binary number system and how it represents values.

You must absolutely know two fundamental and essential principles of binary to work with network addresses: the largest decimal number that can be expressed in an 8-bit binary number is 255 and the lowest value that can be expressed in 8-bits is 00000000. So, if an 8-bit binary number is all 1s (11111111), it represents 255 and if it is all 0s, it is 0. Actually, you do need to understand why. If you don't, check out Chapter 6.

As discussed earlier in this chapter, an IP address consists of four 8-bit binary numbers, called *octets*. In binary, an IP address may look something like this, at least to routers and computers:

11111111.11111111.11111111.11111111

But, because binary values are difficult for humans to deal with, IP addresses are typically displayed (at least among the humans) as decimal numbers, for example

255.255.255.255

This may seem pretty straightforward, but as we discuss later, it is the binary value in the octet, and not the decimal value it represents, that is important.

Separating the IP Classes

Before reading this section, you may want to review the IP addressing rules in "The Wondrous World of IP Addressing," earlier in the chapter to refresh your understanding of how an IP address is constructed.

IP addressing is divided into five address classes that are designated as A through E. As you read about the different IP address classes, bear in mind that the inventors of this class system thought the Internet would remain a fairly small and exclusive club. The original meaning has eroded a bit, but by and large the address classes represent a hierarchy of IP address assignments in which Class A addresses are intended to be assigned to larger, complex networks, Class B addresses to less complex and somewhat smaller networks, and Class C addresses to local networks and ISPs (Internet service providers).

Class A IP addresses

Class A IP addresses are awarded to large networks. Class A addresses use only the first octet (8 bits) for the network ID. The other three octets contain the host address. These addresses range from 1.*hhh.hhh.hhh* to 127.*hhh.hhh.hhh,* where all of the *hhh*s identify a host computer's address, and the numbers indicate the address ranges assigned to this address class. Fifty percent of all IP addresses are Class A addresses.

There are 128 network (0 to 127) values available, but the network addresses with all 0s or 1s and the network addresses in the 127 group are reserved as special network addresses (see "Using Special Network Addresses," later in this chapter). So, the net effect (no pun intended) is that the available group of Class A networks is essentially 1 through 126.

Each Class A network can address 16,777,214 network nodes. To compute the number of hosts or nodes that can be addressed on a Class A (or Class B or C, for that matter), use this formula:

$$(2^n - 2) = \text{\# of available hosts}$$

In this formula, n represents the number of bits in the host ID portion of the address.

In a Class A address, 8 bits are used for the network ID and 24 bits are used for the host ID.

The number of bits in the network ID plus the number of bits in the host ID will always equal 32. Another way to think of this is that the number of bits in the host ID is 32 minus the number of bits in the network ID, which you know from the address class. How do you know the address class? By the number in the first octet.

So, for the Class A address, the number of host ID bits is 24. Two to the 24th power is 16,777,216 (Gilster's lucky number), and this number minus two is 16,777,214. So the number of hosts that can be addressed on a Class A network is 16,777,214. Why subtract two addresses? Two are subtracted because IDs (addresses) with all 1s and all 0s have special purposes (see "Using Special Network Addresses," later in this chapter).

To compute the number of networks available, a completely different formula is used:

$$(2^n - 2) = \text{\# of available networks}$$

Notice how completely different this formula is compared to the one used for computing the number of hosts on a network. The difference is that now the "n" represents the number of bits used to represent the network ID. We must tell you the trick to this, however. In a Class A address, the first bit of the first octet is used to indicate that the address is a Class A address. This leaves only seven bits for the network ID. So, two to the seventh power minus two is 126, and a Class A network has 126 networks, each of which can have 16,777,214 hosts.

Class B IP addresses

Class B addresses are assigned to medium-sized networks. Twenty-five percent of all available IP addresses are in this class. Class B addresses use 14 bits to identify the network (2 bits are reserved to indicate that the address is a Class B address), which limits the number of Class B networks to 16,382 ($2^{14} - 2$). Class B networks are in the range of 128.0.*hhh.hhh* (*hhh* represents the host address) to 191.255.*hhh.hhh*. This means that each Class B network can address more than 65,534 hosts.

!gnore the percentages

Yes, we know that the percentages in the IP address classes do not add up to 100 percent. Don't worry about why. In fact, don't worry about these percentages at all. We included them to give you a sense of scale. But, now that you've asked, the remaining addresses are special IP addresses or unassigned addresses.

Characteristics of the IP Address Classes

Class	Bits in Network ID	Number of Networks	Bits in Host ID	Number of Hosts/Network	Address Range
A	8	126	24	16,777,214	1.0.0.0 to 126.255.255.255
B	16	16,384	16	65,536	128.0.0.0 to 191.255.255.255
C	24	2,097,152	8	254	192.0.0.0 to 223.255.255.255
D	0	0	32	268,400,000	224.0.0.0.0 to 239.255.255.255
E	Class E addresses are reserved for future use				

Class C IP addresses

Class C networks are assigned to relatively small networks. Class C addresses account for 12.5 percent of all available IP addresses. Class C addresses use 21 bits to identify the network (three bits are used to indicate that the address is a Class C address), which allows for more than 2 million networks to be identified in the range of 192.0.0.hhh to 223.255.255.hhh ($2^{21} - 2 = 2,097,152$). This leaves 8 bits to identify the host computers and, as is the case with all IP addressing, the host addresses with all 0s or 1s are special function addresses (see "Using Special Network Addresses," later in this chapter). Each Class C network can address a maximum of 254 host addresses ($2^8 - 2 = 254$). If you understand your binary, you're probably wondering why — if there are 8 bits available to identify the hosts — there are only 254 hosts possible. The hosts with all 1s and all 0s are reserved for special address functions.

Class D and Class E IP addresses

Class D is set aside especially for *IP multicasting* and does not have network and host ID parts. IP multicasting sends datagrams to a group of hosts, which may be located on many separate networks. Class D addresses are in the range of 224.*hhh.hhh.hhh* to 239.*hhh.hhh.hhh.* Address 224.0.0.0 is reserved and cannot be used, and address 224.0.0.1 is reserved for addressing all hosts participating in an IP multicast.

Class E addresses are reserved for future use. This means that a little over three percent of all IP addresses are in the range from 240.0.0.0 to 254.255.255.255. Before you ask about 255.255.255.255, think about it for a minute.

Using Special Network Addresses

Network addresses that contain all binary 0s and 1s and network addresses beginning with 127 are special network addresses. Table 7-1 lists the special network addresses.

Additional ranges of numbers are set aside for use by network managers for intranets and internal networks that do not connect to the Internet. These addresses are in three ranges:

> 10.0.0.0 through 10.255.255.255
>
> 172.16.0.0 through 172.31.255.255
>
> 192.168.0.0 through 192.168.255.255

Table 7-1	Special Network Addresses		
Network Part	*Host Part*	*Example*	*Description*
All 0s	All 0s	0.0.0.0	This host
All 0s	A host ID	0.0.0.34	A host on this network
All 1s	All 1s	255.255.255.255	Broadcast to local network
A network ID	All 1s	197.21.12.255	Broadcast to the network
127	All 1s or 0s	127.0.0.1	Loopback testing

Subnetting a Network

Okay, we put it off as long as we could, but we can't avoid it any longer, we have to use the "S" word — subnetting. We're sorry to be so blunt and just blurt it out like that, but we've found that the best way is to just jump on in and either sink or swim.

Subnetting is the process of logically dividing the network IP address into a group of segments, called subnetworks. The subnet mask is the 32-bit binary number used by the router to *extract,* or *mask out,* the subnet address.

Subnetting a network can solve many networking problems, including reducing traffic, increasing throughput, improving performance, curing dandruff, getting dates, and others. But, the best reason for subnetting is simplified management of the network. Oh, and by the way, we were just kidding about the dandruff. The two main reasons to subnet are

- **An unlimited number of IP addresses are available.** We have to do more with what we have until the next version of IP is completely rolled out. (See "Expanding the IP Horizon" later in this chapter.)

- **A router needs a way to identify the network portion of an IP address.** All classes of addresses (A, B, and C) have a definite number of bits that are required for their network address, as shown in Table 7-2.

Table 7-2	IP Address Class Breakdowns	
Class	*Network Bits*	*Host Bits*
A	8	24
B	16	16
C	24	8

You should be able to easily spot the pattern in Table 7-2. Take your time; we'll wait for you. That's right! As the Class level decreases, from A to C, more bits are used for the network ID and fewer are used for the host ID.

The other part of subnetting is the subnet mask. Table 7-3 lists the default subnet masks used as the basis for developing your own subnet mask. Don't worry about the default masks right now, but remember where you saw them for later reference.

Table 7-3	Default Subnet Masks
IP Address Class	**Subnet Mask**
Class A	255.0.0.0
Class B	255.255.0.0
Class C	255.255.255.0

For many people, subnet masks and subnetting are the most difficult parts of the network administrator's job to master. But, the need to memorize the details of subnetting is lessened every day. As the tools get more sophisticated, the network administrator can rely on them more and on his or her memory less. One such tool is a subnet calculator that you can use to help plan out your network, but even with this tool, you should try to gain as much ability as you can in doing those subnetting calculations.

May we borrow a couple of bits until Tuesday?

What is involved with subnetting is borrowing bits from the host ID portion of the IP address to allow for more networks (actually subnetworks). Remember that the number of networks in an IP address class is determined by the number of bits used to identify the network ID. By adding more bits to the network ID, you can naturally identify more networks. Of course, this ability comes with a price. There are still only 32 bits in the IP address, so if you use more for the network ID, then fewer are available for the host ID portion. This is okay, because the goal is to have more addressable networks with fewer hosts on each subnetwork.

The trick is to borrow just enough bits from the host ID so that you can address the subnets you need and still be able to address all the host IDs you need as well. The 32-bit IP address is a fixed-length entity; you don't have more bits to use. Also remember that you, as the network administrator, control only the host ID portion of the address, so you can borrow bits only from that part of the address.

Most subnetting in real life, as opposed to the fantasy world of this book, typically involves only Class B and C addresses, because that's what is really available to smaller local area networks. If you will be working with a Class A network involving millions of nodes, just remember that the applications are the same, but the scale is much grander. But, chances are good that you will work with Class C addressing on an internal private network address scheme, just like we do.

The best way to learn subnetting is to do it. Our explanations cannot possibly be so good that anyone can safely begin subnetting a network without some practice. Yes, subnet calculators are available. But, you really can't do better than some paper-and-pencil practice to help you lock in the concepts and fundamentals of subnetting and subnet masks away.

Subnetting a Class A network

The Class A IP address includes only 8 bits for the network ID, leaving 24 bits for the host. If you wish to subnet a Class A network, you need to borrow a sufficient number of bits from the host ID portion of the mask to allow the number of subnets you plan to create, now and in the future.

For example, if you wish to create two subnets with over 4 million hosts per subnet, you can borrow 2 bits from the second octet and use 10 masked (positions in the mask with a 1 value) bits for the subnet mask (11111111 11000000) or 255.192 in decimal. This results in a new subnet mask of 255.192.0.0

Keep in mind that the 8-bit octets have binary place values, as shown in Table 7-4. When you borrow bits from the host ID portion of the standard mask, you don't change the value of the bits; you only change how they are used and the decimal value that results from adding them.

Table 7-4	IP Address Octet Binary Values	
Bit Number	*Power of 2*	*Decimal Value*
8	2^7	128
7	2^6	64
6	2^5	32
5	2^4	16
4	2^3	8
3	2^2	4
2	2^1	2
1	2^0	1

For a Class A network that needs a maximum of 254 subnets with 65,534 hosts on each subnet, you must borrow 8 bits from the host ID, creating a subnet mask with 16 masked bits, 255.255.0.0.

Table 7-5 includes a sampling of subnet mask options available for Class A addresses.

Table 7-5	Class A Subnet Masks		
Subnet Mask	*Number of One Bits in Mask*	*Number of Subnets*	*Number of Hosts per Subnet*
255.0.0.0	8	0	16,777,214
255.192.0.0	10	2	4,194,302
255.240.0.0	12	14	1,048,574
255.255.0.0	16	254	65,534
255.255.128.0	17	510	32,766
255.255.240.0	20	4,094	4,094
255.255.255.128	25	131,070	126
255.255.255.240	28	1,048,574	14
255.255.255.252	30	4,192,302	2

The third entry in Table 7-5 lists a subnet mask of 255.240.0.0 that uses 12 bits to indicate the network ID. You know that 8 bits of the network ID are used for the Class A network ID, so 4 bits are used for the subnet portion of the address. Applying the number of networks formula ($2^4 - 2 = 14$), you know that you can address 14 subnets. The number of hosts formula ($2^{20} - 2 = 1,048,574$) indicates that over a million hosts are available on each subnet.

How would you know that 12 bits were used in the network portion of the mask if Table 7-5 wasn't available? Well, if you convert the subnet mask to its binary equivalent, you get this:

11111111.11110000.00000000.00000000

You know that 11111111 is the binary equivalent for the decimal value 255, which is the first value in the mask. The next portion indicates that the binary values (refer to Table 7-4) of positions 8 (2^7), 7 (2^6), 6 (2^5), and 5 (2^4) are to be added. These are 128 + 64 + 32 + 16, which equals 240, the value in the second position.

The number of 1s in a subnet mask cannot be more than 30 bits in length (the subnet mask is always 32 bits long). Also remember that the addresses with all 1s and all 0s cannot be used because they have special meanings (see "Using Special Network Addresses" earlier in this chapter).

You should see a pattern (a bit pattern actually) in Table 7-5. As more bits are taken from the host ID and used in the subnet mask to identify subnets, more subnets are possible but with fewer hosts per subnet.

Subnetting a Class B network

For a Class B network, 14 bits are available to be borrowed from the host ID (8 from the third octet and 6 from the fourth octet). The subnet masks available for a Class B network are listed in Table 7-6.

Table 7-6		Class B Subnet Mask Values	
Bits Used		*Binary Value*	*Decimal Value Subnet Mask*
14	11111111 11111100	255.252	255.255.255.252
13	11111111 11111000	255.248	255.255.255.248
12	11111111 11110000	255.240	255.255.255.240
11	11111111 11100000	255.224	255.255.255.224
10	11111111 11000000	255.192	255.255.255.192
9	11111111 10000000	255.128	255.255.255.128
8	11111111 00000000	255.0	255.255.255.0
7	11111110 00000000	254.0	255.255.254.0
6	11111100 00000000	252.0	255.255.252.0
5	11111000 00000000	248.0	255.255.248.0
4	11110000 00000000	240.0	255.255.240.0
3	11100000 00000000	224.0	255.255.224.0
2	11000000 00000000	192.0	255.255.192.0

For a Class B network with an IP address of 172.16.31.0 and a subnet mask of 255.255.255.252, how many subnets and hosts are available per subnet?

Do this one the hard way:

The decimal value in the fourth octet is 252, which has the binary equivalent of 11111100; we used the handy Windows calculator to convert this number (see Figure 7-2). You could do it the really hard way, but why?

The binary equivalent of 252 (11111100) tells you that 6 bits have been borrowed from the last octet. Don't forget that we are working on a Class B subnet and we must account for the value 255 in the third octet as well. If you haven't already done so, commit to memory that the value 255 means that all 8 bits are in use. So, if you add up all the bits used to create the subnet mask in the third and fourth octets and insert them into the formulas, you'd get:

Number of Subnets = $2^{14} - 2$

Number of Subnets = $16,384 - 2$

Number of Subnets = $16,382$

Again, 6 bits were used for subnetting, so only 2 bits remain for identifying host IDs.

Number of Hosts = $2^2 - 2$

Number of Hosts = $4 - 2$

Number of Hosts = 2

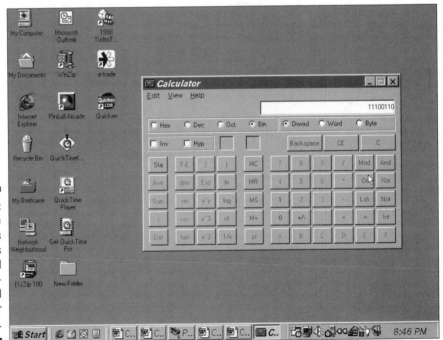

Figure 7-2:
The Windows Calculator is a handy tool for converting decimal to binary or vice versa.

This tells us that a Class B network with the address 172.16.31.0 and a subnet mask of 255.255.255.252 can address 16,382 subnets of two hosts each. Table 7-7 lists the rest of the Class B possibilities.

Table 7-7	Class B Subnetting		
Subnet Mask	*Subnet Bits*	*Subnets*	*Hosts*
255.255.255.252	14	16,382	2
255.255.255.248	13	8,190	6
255.255.255.240	12	4,094	14
255.255.255.224	11	2,046	30
255.255.255.192	10	1,022	62
255.255.255.128	9	510	126
255.255.255.0	8	254	254
255.255.254.0	7	126	510
255.255.252.0	6	62	1,022
255.255.248.0	5	30	2,046
255.255.240.0	4	14	4,094
255.255.224.0	3	6	8,190
255.255.192.0	2	2	16,382
255.255.128.0	1		Not a legal subnet
255.255.0.0	0	1	65,534

Subnetting a Class C network

On the standard Class C address, 24 bits are used to identify the network ID, and 8 bits are used to identify the host ID. To create a subnet, bits are borrowed from the host ID for the network ID. You can borrow up to 6 bits of the fourth octet to create your subnet. The more bits you borrow, the more subnetworks you can create, but at the expense of fewer hosts per subnetwork. You must leave at least 2 bits for the host (no, not a tip; you leave the last two numbers on the right) in the octet; bits are borrowed from left to right. Table 7-8 lists the resulting subnet values created from borrowing bits from the host ID.

Table 7-8	Class C Subnet Mask Values	
Bits Used	*Binary Value*	*Decimal Value Subnet Mask*
6 11111100	252	255.255.255.252
5 11111000	248	255.255.255.248
4 11110000	240	255.255.255.240
3 11100000	224	255.255.255.224
2 11000000	192	255.255.255.192

Table 7-9 summarizes Class C network subnetting. This table can come in handy when you are working on networks and your computer and subnet calculator aren't available.

Table 7-9	Class C Subnetting		
Subnet Mask	*Subnet Bits*	*Subnets*	*Hosts*
255.255.255.252	6	62	2
255.255.255.248	5	30	6
255.255.255.240	4	14	14
255.255.255.224	3	6	30
255.255.255.192	2	2	62
255.255.255.128	1		Not a legal subnet value (Trust us!)
255.255.255.0	0	1	254

Examining your subnet options

After you understand where subnet numbers come from (you do, don't you?), then you need to determine how many subnets and hosts per subnet are created for the various available subnets.

Two simple formulas calculate these numbers for us:

Number of hosts per subnet = $(2^{\text{number of bits used for host}}) - 2$

Number of subnets = $(2^{\text{number of bits used for subnets}}) - 2$

These formulas look somewhat familiar to others we talked about earlier in the chapter (see "Separating the IP Classes"), but if you look closely they are completely different from those, as well as from each other. These two formulas are used independently to determine the number of hosts available on a subnet and the number of subnets available given the number of bits used in the subnet addressing. Which formula you use depends on what you are using the bits for, the host or the subnet.

Work through this example with us.

A Class C address 192.168.1.1 has a subnet mask of 255.255.255.252. To create this subnet mask, 6 bits have been borrowed (see Table 7-8). So the calculation is this:

Number of subnets = $2^6 - 2$

Number of subnets = $64 - 2$

Number of subnets = 62

If 6 bits were borrowed for subnetting, then 2 bits are available for host IDs. The calculation to determine the number of hosts available on each subnet is as follows:

Number of hosts = $2^2 - 2$

Number of hosts = $4 - 2$

Number of hosts = 2

Applying Your New Knowledge

In this section, we provide you with a bit of practice on developing network subnetting. If you are a genius at subnetting, this may be child's play for you, but if you are learning about subnets, masks, and IP addressing for the first time, the problems in this section should draw on your knowledge of:

✔ **Binary numbers:** see Chapter 6 for a review

✔ **IP address classes:** see "Separating the IP Classes," earlier in the chapter

✔ **Subnetting a network and developing a subnet mask:** see "Subnetting a Network," earlier in the chapter

Using what you know, can you determine the subnet address of the Class C address 192.168.1.1 that has a mask of 255.255.255.192? To really show off, go ahead and do it longhand.

In binary, the host address in question is this:

11000000(192)   10101000(168)   00000001(1)   00000001(1)

The subnet mask is this:

11111111(255)   11111111(255)   11111111(255)   11000000(192)

If we "and" these two together using Boolean algebra, the process is as follows. (see "Taking the *boo* out of Boolean algebra," later in the chapter, for information on Boolean algebra and "anding"):

11000000 10101000 00000001 00000001 (Host address)

11111111 11111111 11111111 11000000 (Subnet mask)

11000000 10101000 00000001 00000000 (Network address)

The resulting network address is 192.168.1.0. This is exactly the process used by the router to determine to which of its interfaces an IP address should be forwarded. By stripping away the host portion of the IP address, the network (interface) address is exposed. That, in a nutshell, is how and why subnetting and subnet masks help you to logically subdivide the network into smaller administrative groupings.

Developing valid subnets, hosts, and broadcasts

What are the valid subnets, hosts, and broadcast addresses for the network 192.168.1.0 using a subnet mask of 255.255.255.192?

Piece of cake! You know that the address is a Class C address (Class C addresses are between 192 and 223 — see "Class C IP addresses" earlier in the chapter) and with a Class C subnet mask value of 192, two subnets are available with 62 available hosts per network (refer to Table 7-5).

Now for a new piece of information: To calculate the number of valid subnets on a network, subtract the subnet mask (192, in this case) from 256. The equation is: 256 – 192 = 64. Now, beginning at zero, count the number of times you can increment by this number (64, in this case) to reach the mask value, not counting the last increment. In this example, you can increment from 0 to 192 twice:

192.168.1.64

192.168.1.128

These IP addresses are valid subnet addresses, which are also known as the *wire addresses* of the subnets.

The *broadcast address* of a subnet is the highest number available in the subnet (for example, 192.168.1.127), which should be one less than the next subnetwork address. Outside of subnetting, the broadcast address of a network is one in which the host address is all binary 1s, or a value of 255. However, in subnetting, this is not the case. In this particular example, the broadcast addresses are:

192.168.1.127

192.168.1.191

On each subnetwork, the available range of hosts is all of the IP addresses between the subnet address and the subnet's broadcast address:

192.168.1.65 through 192.168.1.126

192.168.1.129 through 192.168.1.190

Avoiding the subnet mask trap

Try this one to really show-off: What are the subnetwork and broadcast addresses of the address 172.16.1.128 that uses a subnet mask of 255.255.255.0? Don't be misled by the subnet mask in this problem. The default mask (see Table 7-3 in "Subnetting a Network" earlier in the chapter) for a Class C address is 255.255.255.0, but you were too sharp to fall into that trap. You knew from the host address that this is a Class B address. This also tells you that only 8 bits of the possible 14 are used in the subnet mask. This allows you to calculate that 254 subnets are available ($2^8 - 2 = 254$ subnets). Because only 8 bits are borrowed for the subnet mask, 8 bits must be left for the host ID. As you know, this means that 254 hosts are available per subnet and that the entire fourth octet is used for each subnet (254 hosts plus 1 broadcast address equals 255 addresses).

To determine the valid subnetworks, you calculate 256 – 255 = 1, and you find that the valid subnetwork numbers are 172.16.1.0, 172.16.2.0, ... 172.16.254.0. So the subnetwork address is 172.16.1.0, and the broadcast address is 172.16.1.255.

Planning a subnet: An exercise

Resolve the addressing problem in this scenario:

Your company has been assigned a Class C address with a network number of 192.168.250.0. Your boss wants you to plan for network expansion but doesn't want to have more than 20 people on any LAN. Come up with a networking scheme.

In this scenario, the driving factor is the number of hosts per subnet. You know that in subnetting a Class C network, you can have a maximum of 62 hosts with two subnets or a minimum of two hosts with 62 subnets depending on the subnet mask you choose.

To allow for 20 hosts per subnetwork requires a subnet mask of 255.255.255.224. (Remember that to discover the number of host addresses, you take 2 to the power of the number of bits used for the host portion and then subtract 2 from this number) $2^5 - 2 = 30$.

Using this data, you realize that you have six subnets available. To figure out the subnet numbers, you subtract $256 - 224 = 32$. This would leave you with the values listed in Table 7-10.

Table 7-10	Subnets Available for 192.168.250.0	
Subnet Address	*Hosts*	*Broadcast Address*
192.168.250.32	.33 – .62	.63
192.168.250.64	.65 – .94	.95
192.168.250.96	.97 – .126	.127
192.168.250.128	.128 – .158	.159
192.168.250.160	.161 – .190	.191
192.168.250.192	.193 – .222	.223

Who Was That Subnet Masked Man?

In order for a router to know whether a particular host is located on the network attached to it, it must be able to extract the network ID from a destination address. To do this, a filtering mechanism is applied to the IP address to highlight the address portion needed. This filtering mechanism is the *subnet mask,* which is actually short for subnetwork address mask.

The purpose of a subnet mask is to determine whether an IP address exists on the local network or on a remote network, in which case the data must be routed to the next router. The subnet mask extracts the network ID from a message's destination address, which is then compared to the local network ID. If they match, the host ID is on the local network. Otherwise, the message must be routed beyond the local network.

Taking the *boo* out of Boolean algebra

The process used to apply the subnet mask uses what is called *Boolean* (boo-lee-uhn) *algebra* to filter out all non-matching bits and identify the network ID. Not to worry; we're not making you do algebra, at least not the kind you remember from high school. Boolean algebra applies binary logic to yield binary results. See, nothing to worry about.

Working with subnet masks, you need only four basic principles of Boolean algebra:

- 1 and 1 = 1
- 1 and 0 = 0
- 0 and 1 = 0
- 0 and 0 = 0

Translation: The only way to end up with a 1 is to combine two 1s; everything else yields a 0. This is the fundamental operation in Boolean algebra. Boolean algebra is a crusader — it is always searching for truth. True and True equals True; a False in any pair results in a False.

When the subnet mask is applied to an IP address, a process called *anding* is used to align each of the 32 bits right to left and left to right. Then each pair of bits (one from the IP address and one from the subnet mask) is anded. Any pair that contains two 1s, results in a 1; all others result in a 0.

Table 7-11 illustrates how the Boolean algebra anding process works:

Table 7-11	Boolean Algebra Anding	
Element	*Dotted Decimal*	*Binary Equivalent*
Class A address	123.123.123.001	01111011 01111011 01111011 00000001
Default subnet mask	255.000.000.000	11111111 00000000 00000000 00000000
Network ID	123.000.000.000	01111011 00000000 00000000 00000000

Study the Binary Equivalent column of Table 7-11. The result in the Network ID row has only 1s where 1s were present in both the network address and subnet mask rows.

Similarly, a default Class B subnet mask strips out the 16 bits of the network ID, and a default Class C subnet mask strips out the 24 bits of the network ID. The example in Table 7-11 is fairly easy and straightforward. If you agree, then you have the fundamentals sorted out and will be ready when we start borrowing bits from the host ID to create subnetworks.

Using the magic of the mask to find subnets

IPv4 addresses are a scarce commodity. We want to emphasize this so that you get the idea that when you design a network, you must do so with IP address conservation in mind. Subnetting provides a way to segment a single network IP address into many segments, which creates more networks with fewer hosts each.

A network has its own unique address. In a network address, the host ID portion is all binary 0s. For example, a Class B network address (16 bits in the network ID) like 172.20.0.0 creates a network with 65,536 individual hosts. Imagine that many workstations are trying to contend for access to the wire! Subnetting allows you to divide this network into a series of subnets with fewer nodes on each subnetwork. Not only does this improve the available bandwidth, but it also cuts down on the amount of broadcast traffic generated. You see, subnetting can be your friend!

In our example network of 172.20.0.0, the network administrator could subnet the network into five smaller networks: 172.20.1.0, 172.20.2.0, 172.20.3.0, 172.20.4.0 and 172.20.5.0. To the outside world, the network is still 172.20.0.0, but internally, routers are able to break the address down into the five smaller subnetworks.

Just in case you are wondering, subnet masks apply only to Class A, B, and C IP addresses.

The subnet mask is the strainer applied to a message's destination IP address to determine whether the destination network is the local network. It works like this:

1. **On the Dummies Class C network, if a destination IP address is 206.175.162.18, its binary equivalent is 11001110 10101111 10100010 00010010.**

    Trust us on this.

2. **The default Class C subnet mask is 255.255.255.0, and its binary equivalent is 11111111 11111111 11111111 00000000.**

   Really, that's it!

3. **These two binary numbers (the IP address and the subnet mask) are combined using Boolean algebra, which yields the network ID of the destination:**

206.175.162.18	11001110 10101111 10100010 00010010
+	
255.255.255.0	11111111 11111111 11111111 00000000
=	
206.175.162.0	11001110 10101111 10100010 00000000

4. **The resulting ID (206.175.162.0) is the IP address of the network, which means that the message is addressed to a node on the local network.**

Subnet masks for Class B and Class C networks

The pattern shown in Table 7-11 for Class A subnets continues with Class B and Class C IP addresses and subnet masks. The only differences are that you have fewer options (because of the fewer bits available) and that you are much more likely to work with these networks in real life. Table 7-12 lists a few of the subnet masks available for Class B networks, and Table 7-13 lists all of the subnet masks available for Class C networks.

Table 7-12	Class B Subnet Masks		
Subnet Mask	**Number of One Bits in Mask**	**Number of Subnets**	**Number of Hosts per Subnet**
255.255.0.0	16	0	65,534
255.255.192.0	18	2	16,382
255.255.240.0	20	14	4,094
255.255.255.0	24	254	254
255.255.255.240	28	4,094	14
255.255.255.252	30	16,382	2

Table 7-13	Class C Subnet Masks		
Subnet Mask	*Number of One Bits in Mask*	*Number of Subnets*	*Number of Hosts per Subnet*
255.255.255.0	24	0	254
255.255.255.192	26	2	62
255.255.255.224	27	6	30
255.255.255.240	28	14	14
255.255.255.248	29	30	6
255.255.255.252	30	62	2

Donning the Subnet Mask

When you begin planning a network, one of the first things you do is figure out the number of network IDs and hosts your network will require. To accomplish this, you must account for every WAN connection (connections to outside routers) and every subnet within the network.

Network IDs are assigned by ARIN (American Registry for Internet Numbers), but the local network administrator assigns the host IDs. The host ID identifies an addressable device on the local network. This can be almost any addressable device on the network, including computers, routers, bridges, switches, and so forth. You don't have to follow any set-in-concrete rules governing the assignment of host IDs, but some general guidelines are around.

A number for everything, and everything is numbered

A commonly accepted practice is to assign host IDs in groups based on the type of host and to give routers the lowest range of numbers in the host range. For example, if you were to use this scheme to assign host IDs on a network or network segment, your host IDs would be grouped as follows:

a.b.c.1 through a.b.c.255 — Routers

a.b.200.1 through a.b.200.254 — NT servers

a.b.240.1 through a.b.240.254 — UNIX hosts

Configuring the router for IP

After your network is completely worked out, that is, after the network has its subnets and subnet masks, this IP addressing scheme should be configured onto the appropriate interfaces on your local router. Each router interface, like each host computer, must have its own IP address if it is to communicate on an IP network. Each of the interface ports should also be configured with the subnet information for the subnet to which it is attached. Routers can be attached to multiple subnets, by each subnet attached to a different router interface. See Chapter 14 for more information on routers and their interfaces.

The **ip address** command is used to configure a router interface to its own IP address, subnet, and mask. A router with four interfaces will have four distinct IP addresses, because each address is on a different network or subnetwork. The **ip address** command is entered from the **config-if** (configure-interface) mode of the Cisco IOS because the command's action affects only a specific interface. In this command, both the IP address and the subnet mask are assigned.

The subnet mask can be entered in dotted decimal notation. However, it can be displayed in dotted decimal notation or in the bit-count format by using the **term ip netmask-format** command. Bit-count format refers to an 8-bit mask (255.0.0.0), 16-bit mask (255.255.0.0), or 24-bit mask (255.255.255.0). An example of what this might look like on a Cisco router is shown in Figure 7-3.

Figure 7-3:
The Cisco
IOS
commands
used to
configure
a router
interface's IP
assignment.

```
CISCO_Networking#config t
Enter configuration commands, one per line. End with CNTL/Z.
CISCO_Networking(config)#int e0
CISCO_Networking(config-if)#ip address 192.168.1.6 255.255.255.0

CISCO_Networking#term ip netmask-format decimal
CISCO_Networking#show int e0
Ethernet0 is up, line protocol is up
    Some display deleted for clarity
    Internet address is 192.168.1.6 255.255.255.0

CISCO_Networking#term ip netmask-format bit-count
CISCO_Networking#show int e0
Ethernet0 is up, line protocol is up
    Some display deleted for clarity
    Internet address is 192.168.1.6/24
```

Routing IP Addresses

When you build a network, you need to figure out how many network IDs your network requires. To do so, you must account for every WAN connection and subnet on the network. Every node and router interface requires a host address, or ID. There's no hard and fast rule on how you should dole out your allotted IP addresses. Commonly, though, the lowest numbers (1 through 10) are assigned to routers and servers, but how you assign addresses is strictly up to you and your network policies and guidelines.

Configuring an IP address

The proper way to configure an IP address on the router is through the **ip address** command, which assigns each router interface its unique IP address. A router with four interfaces needs four distinct IP addresses because, technically, each interface (and address) is on a different network. The **ip address** command is entered from the config-if mode because the action affects only that interface. Both the IP address and the subnet mask are defined in the command. Here is a sample **ip address** command session:

```
Cisco_Networking#config t
Enter configuration commands, one per line. End with CNTL/Z.
Cisco_Networking(config)#int e0
Cisco_Networking(config-if)#ip address 192.168.1.6
        255.255.255.0
Cisco_Networking#term ip netmask-format decimal
Cisco_Networking#show int e0
Ethernet0 is up, line protocol is up
Some display deleted for clarity
Internet address is 192.168.1.6 255.255.255.0

Cisco_Networking#term ip netmask-format bit-count
Cisco_Networking#show int e0
Ethernet0 is up, line protocol is up
Some display deleted for clarity
Internet address is 192.168.1.6/24
```

The subnet mask is entered in dotted decimal notation as shown in the fourth line of this example. However, it may be displayed in either the dotted decimal notation by using the decimal option on the **term ip netmask-format** command. It can also be displayed in the bit-count format by entering the bit-count option of that same command. Bit-count format refers to a standard that is commonly used with a notation type called Classless Interdomain Routing (CIDR). CIDR expresses the subnet network address in the form "/n," where "n" represents the number of bits used to designate the network address. For example, an IP address that uses 8-bits (Class A) to designate its network address (255.0.0.0) is expressed as /8 CIDR block, a 16-bit address (255.255.0.0) is expressed as /16, and a 24-bit address (255.255.255.0) is represented /24, and so forth up to a /30. Classless or bit-count format is not limited to class A, B, and C addresses. In fact, a network address can use any number up to 30 bits on a subnetted network, which would be expressed in bit-count format as /30.

Verifying an IP address

IP addresses can be verified using PING, Trace, and Telnet. These are very handy commands to know. PING is used to verify IP address connections to the Network layer. Trace (or traceroute) is used to verify the route to be used between two IP addresses. Telnet is used to verify network IP address connections to the Application layer.

Verifying with Telnet

The reason you need to verify IP addresses is to ensure that the various parts of a network can properly communicate with the other parts. For example, if you can Telnet (terminal emulation protocol) into a router from a remote location on the same network, you can verify that the interface and route are up and available. Because Telnet operates on the OSI Model's Application layer, when it's functioning, it's safe to assume that all lower layers are also functioning.

Here's a sample Telnet session used to verify the connection and route at IP address 205.7.5.1.

```
Cisco_Networking#telnet 205.7.5.1
Trying 205.7.5.1 ... Open
Greetings from a Generic Cisco Lab
User Access Verification
```

Verifying with PING

The PING (Packet Internet Groper) command verifies OSI Layer 3 (Network layer) connectivity. PING sends out ICMP (Internet Control Message Protocol) messages to verify both the logical addresses and the physical connection. The PING command issued from a Cisco router responds with a number of single character responses, which are listed in Table 7-14.

Table 7-14	Cisco PING Response Codes
Response	*Meaning*
! (exclamation mark)	Success
. (period)	Timed out waiting for reply
U	Destination unreachable
I (vertical bar)	Ping process interrupted
? (question mark)	Unknown packet type
C	Congestion-experienced
& (ampersand)	Time to live exceeded

Here are two sample PING sessions on a Cisco router, one successful, the other not so successful:

```
Cisco_Networking#ping 205.7.5.1
Type escape sequence to abort.
Sending 5,100-byte ICMP Echoes to 205.7.5.1, timeout is 2
        seconds:
!!!!!
Success rate is 100 percent (5/5), round-trip min/avg/max =
        104/110/128 ms

Cisco_Networking#ping 205.7.5.5
Type escape sequence to abort.
Sending 5, 100-byte ICMP Echoes to 205.7.5.5, timeout is 2
        seconds:
.....
Success rate is 0 percent (0/5)
```

For some very good coverage on the PING command in general, visit www.freesoft.org/CIE/Topics/53.htm. We should caution you that the PING command used on a Cisco router is proprietary to Cisco and may not perform exactly like the general TCP/IP PING command. For information specific to the Cisco PING, visit www.cisco.com.

Verifying with traceroute

The **traceroute** or **trace** command is used to show the complete route from a source to a destination. Trace sends out probe packets one at a time to each router or switch in the path between the source and the destination IP address entered. Traceroute displays the round-trip time for each packet sent to each upstream router. Traceroute has really only two results, time exceeded or destination unreachable. Trace is used to determine where a breakdown in a route may be occurring.

Here's an example of how trace is used: A network has four routers (A, B, C, and D). A trace command is issued on router A to trace the route from itself to router D. A timing response comes back from router B, but the next message indicates that router C is unreachable. You can be fairly certain that the problem lies somewhere on the route between router B and router C. The problem could be with B or C themselves or on the network media connecting them.

Like PING, trace also has its own set of response codes, listed in Table 7-15.

Table 7-15	Trace Command Response Codes
Response	*Meaning*
*	timed out
!H	router received packet but did not forward it (usually, but not necessarily, due to an access list)

Response	Meaning
N	network unreachable
P	protocol unreachable
U	port unreachable

Here are the results of a sample traceroute session in which all stations were reachable:

```
Cisco_Networking#traceroute 192.5.5.1
Type escape sequence to abort.
Tracing the route to LAB-A (192.5.5.1)
1 LAB-D (210.93.105.1) 4 msec 4 msec 4 msec
2 LAB-C (204.204.7.1) 20 msec 32 msec 28 msec
3 LAB-B (199.6.13.1) 44 msec 48 msec 44 msec
4 LAB-A (201.100.11.1) 64 msec * 60 msec
```

Expanding the IP Horizon

A newer version of the Internet Protocol (IP version 6 or IPv6) that radically adapts the addressing structure of IPv4 is now available for use. We doubt that anything can be done to prevent IPv6 from taking over the Internet addressing realm someday. In a way, IPv6 is good news; we are running out of IPv4 addresses, and IPv6 certainly solves that problem. But the real problem, as is common when exchanging one system for another, is that in order to change to IPv6, your network operating system, routers, switches, and workstations must all support its use. If they do, great! You have an ample supply of IPv6 addresses available for your network. If your equipment is not compatible, and you do not want to throw out your existing network and replace it with nifty new IPv6-compatible gear, then you'll need to continue finding ways, such as subnetting, to extend IPv4's limitations.

Just in case you're curious, IPv5 (which was also called Internet Stream Protocol or ST2) added ATM (Asynchronous Transfer Mode) support to the Internet Protocol without affecting its addressing structure.

IPv6 uses a 128-bit address structure. This is four times bigger than the current 32-bit IPv4 address structure and should supply ample addressing, for now, for all networks and hosts. Other advantages of IPv6 over IPv4 include security, enhanced support for real-time traffic, and automatic IP configuration from plug-and-play devices. Real-time traffic includes video-conferencing and voice over IP (VoIP). IPv6 includes a flow label that identifies the end-to-end flow that a packet is using to routers, allowing packets to move from source to destination much faster. Plug-and-play is supported in IPv6, allowing automatic IP address configuration.

The 128-bit address of IPv6 is a hexadecimal format that is broken into eight 16-bit sections delineated by colons. Look at these examples of an IPv6 address:

A733:0000:FEDC:EB62:4532:0000:FA39:4321

or

A733:0:FEDC:EB62:4532:0:FA39:4321

or

A733::FEDC:EB62:4532::FA39:4321

The first example shows the full representation of an IPv6 address, but the second and third examples are alternate representations that reduce and then eliminate the zero octets.

Because an IPv6 implementation worldwide cannot happen overnight, both 32-bit IPv4 addresses and 128-bit IPv6 addresses must be routed at the same time. In order to do this, IPv6 will need to be implemented on one autonomous system at a time with an address translation process in place to convert the 128-bit addresses to 32-bit addresses when sending from IPv6 to IPv4.

Chapter 8

Operating the Network

● ●

In This Chapter

▶ Differentiating the major network operating systems (NOSs)

▶ Identifying popular client operating systems

▶ Describing NOS directory services

▶ Associating IPX, IP, and NetBEUI with their functions

● ●

A softer side to networking on a local-area network (LAN) contrasts to the hardware side (which is not necessarily the harder side of the network). This softer side is actually the software side — the network operating system (NOS). Please don't mistake softer to mean easier. That isn't what we mean at all.

In this chapter, we detail the kinds of things that you should know about operating systems. We have included information on what we think are the major network operating systems (Novell NetWare, Windows NT Server, and the UNIX/Linux operating systems) and their directory services, clients, and protocols. For the sake of space (we could write an entire book on each of these systems!), we have tried to weave the generic among the specific of each NOS.

What You Need to Know about an NOS

You should know that Novell NetWare, Windows NT Server, and UNIX/Linux are the three most popular NOSs. In addition to that, you should remember these two important things about network operating systems:

✔ What clients are used to connect each NOS to a Windows-based workstation

✔ What directory services and file systems each NOS uses

Imposter NOSs!

If the three services listed in "Network operating systems 101" represent the true definition of a NOS, then Novell NetWare is the only one that is truly and solely an NOS. The others (Windows NT, Mac/OS, UNIX, and Linux) are actually multi-purpose operating systems, but for what we are trying to explain here, they are just network operating systems.

Okay, lumping UNIX and Linux together may be controversial, but for what we are discussing here, they are essentially the same. Remember that this book is about Cisco networking. For more detailed information on these two network operating systems, check out some of my favorite books and authors:

- *UNIX For Dummies,* 4th edition, by John R. Levine and Margaret Levine Young
- *Linux For Dummies,* 2nd edition, by Jon "Mad Dog" Hall
- *Linux Administration For Dummies,* by Michael Bellomo

Network operating systems 101

A network operating system (NOS) is a specialized piece of system software that runs on a network server to provide the following services:

- Connects computers and peripheral devices into a local-area network (LAN) and services their requests for resources
- Manages who can access data and shared network resources (such as printers, CD-ROMs, disk drives, software, and so on)
- Monitors the performance and activities of the network.

NOS core services

Most network operating systems perform or provide for a group of core services that network users depend on to help them share networked resources. Core services are those services provided only by the NOS as server-based functions to the network clients. The following are included within the NOS core services:

✔ **File services** provide shared access to directories and files and provide fault tolerance services on network storage devices.

✔ **Print services** provide a common utility for local and remote printing on shared network printers, and manage print queues, devices, forms, and user access.

✔ **Directory services** provide users with transparent access to network resources and services. By transparent, we mean that users do not need to know where the data or resources are physically located. Directory services create the illusion that all resources are local. Novell NetWare includes NetWare Directory Services (NDS), and Windows NT uses its Explorer.

✔ **Security services** provide network security and data protection for local and remote access, including user-level (password-based), share-level (permissions-based), and data encryption services.

✔ **Messaging services** provide message (e-mail) store and forward services and support for mail-enabled applications. Messaging services, along with security services, are fast becoming primary NOS services as internetwork computing continues to evolve.

✔ **Routing services** provide multi-protocol services for transferring packets between routers, including options for common LAN protocols (IP, IPX, and AppleTalk).

✔ **Network administration services** provide SNMP (Simple Network Management Protocol) and resource and directory structure management tools.

Listing their attributes

One of the attributes of a NOS is that it provides security services for data stored on the network. Virtually all NOS and general operating systems have a mechanism for granting or restricting access to individual users or groups of users.

In this book, we discuss two-levels to protecting data: limiting what can be done to files and directories, and limiting who has access to them.

Table 8-1 shows the differences between file properties used in NetWare and those used in Windows NT.

Table 8-1	File Properties Used in NetWare and Windows NT		
NetWare Attribute	*Windows NT Permission*	*Meaning*	*Purpose*
A	A	Archive	Directory or file is new or has been changed and needs to be backed up.
C	-	Copy inhibit	Blocks a file from being copied. Handled through Windows NTFS permissions.
H	H	Hidden	A file that cannot be viewed with directory list commands.
P	-	Purge	Permanently removes deleted file and directories. Handled by Windows NT Recycle Bin.
RO	R	Read-only	Restricts access to read-only and prevents changes to the file.
RW	-	Read-write	Directory or file can be viewed, changed, or deleted. No direct Windows NT equivalent (absence of read-only attribute allows same action).
SH	-	Shareable	More than one user can access the file at a time. Handled in Windows NT by creating a network share.
SY	S	System	Operating system files.

The list of file properties used in the UNIX and Linux systems is much shorter, as shown in Table 8-2, but essentially the file properties provide the same types and levels of control. Without going into the gory details, UNIX/Linux systems restrict access to folders and files by specific users and groups of users. When access is granted to a file or folder (called a directory in this world), the file may be read, written to (in effect, this is permission to change a file), or executed. In one way or another, the permissions listed in Table 8-1 are accomplished in this scheme as well.

Table 8-2	UNIX/Linux File Permissions
File Permission	*Meaning*
r	Read-only
w	Read/Write (Change)
x	Execute

Networking with NetWare

Novell NetWare has undergone a number of name changes in its time. It has been called at one time or another Novell ZenWorks, NetWare 3.x, NetWare 4.x, NetWare IntraNetWare, and most recently NetWare 5. But you just need to remember its original, more commonly used name — Novell NetWare.

A popular LAN operating system developed by Novell Corporation, NetWare supports a variety of different types of LANs, including Ethernet, and Token Ring networks. Like most operating system software, Novell has gone through changes, enhancements, and fixes, but it has remained mostly constant in its structure and function. If you are working with a NetWare NOS as a part of your Cisco network, you really must know these three things:

- ✔ The IPX, also known as IPX/SPX, protocol
- ✔ NetWare's physical and logical file system organization
- ✔ NetWare Directory Services (NDS)

History 010: The "unhistory" of networks

We have not included in this book lengthy histories of NetWare, Windows NT, and UNIX. This is not information you need on the job, and we don't want to confuse you with it. However, if you are a true networking professional, you subconsciously seek out all the interesting trivial details of things, if for no other reason that to have a diversion from the things on which you seek details.

You can find all the background material that you need on these and other network operating systems on the Web. We recommend that you visit the following sites for good background information:

- ✔ NetWare:
  www.netware.novell.com/
  discover
- ✔ Windows NT:
  www.microsoft.com/ntserver
- ✔ UNIX:
  www.yahoo.com/computers/
  operating_systems/unix/

In case we haven't mentioned it, NetWare is installed on top of the 16-bit DOS environment, which it quickly and completely replaces with a snazzy 32-bit multitasking multi-user NOS. NetWare replaces the DOS file handling system with its own file system, known as *NetWare file system* (NFS). A file system is the way that an OS handles and stores files, or in this case, how NetWare stores and handles files on the network.

Making it up in volumes

NetWare divides the physical disk media into logical groupings called volumes. A *volume* is the highest level in the NetWare file system. It represents a fixed amount of hard disk space. A volume may be created on any hard disk that has a NetWare partition, and a NetWare server can support up to 64 volumes on a network.

The NetWare file system has two kinds of volumes:

- ✔ **Physical:** Consists of up to 32 volume segments that can be stored across one or more hard disks. To further complicate this, a disk drive can hold up to 8 volume segments from one or more physical volumes.

- ✔ **Logical:** Divided into directories and used to locate files. The NetWare installation creates the first volume, which is named SYS. A volume must be "mounted" to be visible to the system.

The volume name is used in directory paths followed by a colon. This format is much like the DOS device designator (for example, A:). The path to the PUBLIC directory on the SYS volume looks like this:

```
SYS:PUBLIC
```

Queuing up to print

Network print services are a part of the transparent world created for network users. Figure 8-1 is a simplistic illustration of the difference between what the user believes and network reality.

NetWare controls printing through a mechanism called a printer queue, which is accessed and controlled by the administrator through the PCONSOLE utility. The queue accepts and holds requests for print services until the printer in question becomes available. Incoming print jobs are held by one or more print servers on the network until they can be serviced.

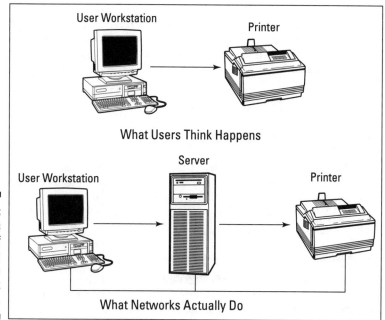

User Workstation

Printer

What Users Think Happens

Server

User Workstation

Printer

What Networks Actually Do

It's in the directory

In general, an NOS (pronounced enn-oh-ess) directory service is used to identify the resources on a network, such as e-mail addresses, computers, and
printers, and to make them accessible to users and server- and client-based
applications. Ideally, the directory service shields the user from the network's physical topology and protocols, creating a transparent working environment. The Windows Explorer in Windows 95/98 is an example of a simple
directory service.

Network directory services come generally under the ITU (International
Telecommunications Union) X.500 standard. However, because this standard
is so large and complex, virtually none of the network directory services in
use comply with it totally.

Most of NetWare's core services come from its NetWare Directory Services
(NDS). NDS serves as an agent for the user in requesting and accessing network resources. When the user logs in, NDS captures information about the
user to facilitate any requests the user makes then or later for system
resources. This allows the user to concentrate on what he or she wants to do
and largely be unconcerned with how it happens.

From a network administrator's point-of-view, NDS helps manage users and applications and what they can access. Through NDS, the administrator creates and controls a database of users and resources, including resources in remote locations. Although NDS is an integrated part of a NetWare installation, it can also be installed on a Windows NT network and on several flavors of UNIX as well.

Keeping it secure

Any NOS worthy of being called that must provide some means for keeping out the mean-and-nasties while allowing the good-and-deserving to access the resources they need. NetWare is no different. It uses a two-level model of SUPERVISOR and non-SUPERVISOR (what you might call users, peons, pests, nags, and so on) accounts.

The all-knowing, all-powerful SUPERVISOR

Supervisor-level accounts (SUPERVISOR and ADMIN) are the omnipotent, anointed rulers of the NetWare network. Supervisor accounts have the power to add and remove users from the network and to set which network resources each user can and cannot access.

Supervisor accounts also have the ability to run administrative software utilities for a wide range of security, fault tolerance, and user management functions.

The lowly, needy groups and users

On a NetWare system, a user is represented by a login account. Each login account can be assigned its own set of resource access rights. Groups are used to collectively administer users that use the same software and access the same directories and files. On all NetWare systems, all users automatically belong to the group EVERYONE. However, to restrict access to accounting files, a group named BEANCNTR may be created to include only the accounting office users. All file rights and permissions assigned to BEANCNTR are automatically extended to the users in this group.

In addition to file attributes (see "Listing their attributes," earlier in this chapter), group and user accounts can be assigned specific rights to specific volumes, directories, and files. This is the mechanism by which you can keep all other users out of the accounting files, except those in the BEANCNTR group.

User security rights work with file attributes to determine who has access to a file and what users can do with it. Table 8-3 includes a list of the NetWare user security rights that can be assigned to NetWare files and directories. In NetWare, much of the data resource security is set through user right assignments. This is also known as *user-level security.*

Table 8-3	NetWare Security Rights
Name	*Description*
ACCESS CONTROL	This is like granting supervisor-level rights to a user for a particular directory or file.
CREATE	This allows a user to make sub-directories and create files.
ERASE	Provided the file is not read-only, the user can delete a file or directory.
FILE SCAN	The user can use the DIR command to view the contents of a directory.
MODIFY	The user can change files, including renaming them, and can change file attributes.
READ	The user can open or execute files.
WRITE	The user can write to files that do not have read-only attributes set.

Restricting access to your account

Additional access and login limits can be set for a NetWare network. Using NWADMIN, NWADMN32, NETADMIN, or SYSCON depending on the NetWare version, a variety of other restrictions can be placed on a user account. These include indicating the number of active logins that a user can open, a designated workstation for a user, the time of the day or the days of the week that an account is valid, and setting an account expiration date, a limit on disk space used, and password characteristics.

Leave it with my messaging service

Although most people think of e-mail when they hear the term messaging, it refers to the technology employed by the network to move service requests and data around the network. As far as e-mail goes, NetWare supports the protocols that enable e-mail clients and mail-enabled applications, but its primary messaging functions are carried out through the IPX protocol.

The Internetwork Packet Exchange (IPX) and its companion protocol, Sequenced Packet Exchange (SPX), together commonly referenced as IPX/SPX, provide a combination of function to ensure that a network message — a packet — gets to where it was addressed:

1. IPX sends the packet to its destination.

2. SPX requests verification (in the form of a checksum) from the destination location that it has received a packet.

3. SPX verifies the checksum against the value it calculated before sending the message. If the two match, the packet reached its destination intact. If the two sums do not match, the packet is sent again.

4. IPX routes packets across the network to their destinations and directs replies and returning data to their appropriate locations.

The IPX protocol works well with many different network topologies, which is one reason why Microsoft created its own version of IPX for Windows NT.

IPX is a best-effort protocol. This means that it does not include a message acknowledgement system to guarantee delivery of a message. This is where SPX comes in. SPX enhances IPX by supplying acknowledgement services. See Steps 2 and 3 for the details. SPX also manages larger messages that must be broken into smaller packets, verifying their sequencing as well.

Don't confuse IPX with IP (Internet Protocol). IP is the TCP/IP protocol that provides the mechanism for transferring data across an internetwork, and IPX is the native transport protocol of NetWare.

One drawback to IPX comes with trying to use it over a wide-area network. Because IPX requires each packet to be acknowledged before sending the next packet, sending messages over slower transmission links, such as telephone lines, can be extremely slow, although quite reliable. The remedy for this, the slowness – not the reliability, is the use of *packet burst mode,* which requires an acknowledgement only after a burst (bundle) of packets is received correctly at its destination.

Routing around NetWare

NetWare provides support for multi-protocol routing services through a suite of software tools called the IntraNetWare bundle. These elements are included with the IntraNetWare suite:

✓ **NetWare MultiProtocol Router with WAN Extensions** — provides concurrent routing support for IPX, TCP/IP, AppleTalk, NetBIOS, and SNA/LLC2 (Systems Network Architecture/Logical-Link Control Type 2) protocols and applications. The WAN extensions package provides NetWare with the ability to connect over ISDN (Integrated Systems Digital Network), frame relay, or ATM (Asynchronous Transfer Mode) without an external router.

- ✔ **NetWare IPX/IP Gateway** — allows network clients to connect to the Internet to access resources without running a TCP/IP client. The gateway translates between NetWare's native IPX protocol (used to communicate on the local network) and the IP protocol (used to communicate with remote network hosts).

- ✔ **RIP (IPX)** — is NetWare's version of the standard Routing Information Protocol (RIP), which is used to determine the best route that a message should follow to its destination.

- ✔ **NetWare Web Server** — enables the NetWare server to act as a World Wide Web server, including browser-level access to NDS.

- ✔ **FTP Services for NetWare** — enables the NetWare server to provide file transfer protocol support to local and remote users.

Checking Out Windows NT Server

Like NetWare, Windows NT has several versions still in use around the networking world. The most popular current version is Windows NT Server 4.0 with service packs (error corrections and enhancements) almost in double digits. Some later versions exist (Windows 2000, for example, which is slowly gaining acceptance), but we've chosen to focus on Windows NT 4.0 here because it represents most of the features used within a Cisco network environment.

Although we cover network operating systems in this chapter, this is still a Cisco networking book and that is still our main focus.

If you want to learn more about Windows, this is an excellent source for reference materials that are easy to read and understand: www.dummies.com. Okay, so it's a plug, but it really is a good source for reference (for the rest of us) books.

Yippee, yippee, it's a GUI

Windows NT looks very much like the Windows graphical user interface (GUI) found on nearly all desktop computers these days. However, after its pretty face, the similarities begin to fade. Make no mistake about it, Windows NT Server was designed to compete with Novell NetWare as a network operating system and provides each of the NOS core services (listed earlier in this chapter in "NOS core services").

NetWare has NDS that provides the lion's share of its core services; Windows NT uses a family of specialized services to provide its core functions. Table 8-4 lists the Windows NT service that provides each of the NOS core services.

Table 8-4	Windows NT Core Services
Core Service Area	*Windows NT Service*
File services	NTFS (New Technology File System)
Print services	Windows NT File and Print Services
Directory services	Windows NT Explorer and User Manager
Security services	Security Access Manager and Remote Access Services
Messaging services	Microsoft Exchange, Outlook, Mail, and other add-on products
Routing services	Routing Information Protocol (RIP)
Network administration services	Windows NT Control Panel

Does this system make the network look FAT?

An operating system uses a file system to organize and catalog its data. Virtually every OS and NOS has a file system. Table 8-5 lists the file system used by several of the more popular operating systems.

Table 8-5	Operating Systems and their File System
OS/NOS	*File System*
DOS	FAT (File Allocation Table)
Linux	LFS (Linux File System)
Mac/OS	HFS (Hierarchical File System)
Novell	NFS (Novell File System)
OS/2	HPFS (High Performance File System)
UNIX	NFS (Network File System)
Windows 9x	FAT, FAT32 (FAT 32-bit)
Windows NT/2000	FAT, NTFS (NT File System)

Windows NT gives you a choice of two file systems:

- ✔ **FAT (File Allocation Table):** FAT is the easiest and less expensive way to go, in terms of hardware and labor. The FAT file system allows users to store and read files on server disk drives, but unfortunately, little data protection exists beyond basic user-level security.

- ✔ **NTFS (New Technology File System):** NTFS is a driver that loads at the I/O layer of Windows NT to process input/output requests for its files, directories, and volumes, and provides file- and directory-level security. Because of the limitations of file allocation tables, NTFS is the file system of choice for Windows NT Server servers.

The disk bone's connected to the partition bone...

Under Windows NT, hard disk drives are organized in a fairly simple hierarchy. At the top of the storage tree is the physical storage medium itself. Using FDISK.EXE (yes, the old DOS FDISK), the hard disk is divided into one or more partitions. No matter how many disks are installed on a computer, at least one primary partition (usually designated drive C:) must serve as the boot partition for the system. Any other partitions created on the disks are extended partitions.

Okay, here is the wrinkle in this otherwise simple hierarchy: Each extended partition can also be sub-divided into as many as 23 logical partitions, each of which can be assigned a drive letter. One or more partitions form a volume, which is assigned to a file system, such as NTFS or FAT. And that brings you back full circle.

Share and share alike

Network shares allow users to access data and resources on the network. Although they are part of the file system, network shares create a new level of security called share-level security. Before a user can access data on the network, that user must be assigned the appropriate user-level security and a network share must be created for the directory or file that the user wants to access.

You create a share by giving the file or directory a share name, which is normally the same as its file system name, but it can be different. You could assign the directory BEANCNTR the share name ACCTONLY, if you like. In either case, users would access the shared resource using the following syntax:

```
\\SERVER_NAME\SHARE_NAME
```

or

```
\\THUNDER_BIT\ACCTONLY
```

The first sample shows the general syntax — two backward slashes, followed by the server name, followed by a backward slash, followed by the share name. As illustrated in the second sample, the user can share the directory ACCTONLY on the THUNDER_BIT server.

It's a hard (copy) world

Windows NT Server print services have four components: print servers, print queues, print jobs, and of course, printers. Actually you can have two types of printers:

- **Physical printers:** This type of printer is an actual printer that is connected to the network or to a workstation that is connected to the network. Physical printers can be divided further into server-attached, network-attached, and workstation-attached. These three configurations are also known as server printer, network printer, and remote printer, respectively.

- **Logical printers:** A logical printer can be a piece of software that functions as a printer, such as a fax server or fax software running on a desktop. The concept of a logical printer is also embedded in the object definitions of a Novell network as well to connect users to printers on the network.

The good news is that beyond this naming quagmire, Windows NT printing works very well. It's just a matter of organization and using the right name. Print servers are either computers dedicated to that task or network workstations that have been assigned this additional duty. Print queues form the line of print jobs (stuff to be printed) submitted by the user, each awaiting its turn on the printer. When the user sends something to the printer (refer to Figure 8-1), the print server stores it in the queue for the destination printer until the printer is available.

You can use three printer configurations for printers on a Windows NT Server network:

- **Server-attached (server printer):** This is just what it sounds like — a printer attached directly to the server computer.

- **Network-attached (network printer):** A number of printers can be attached directly to the network as addressable nodes on the network. These printers use special network adapters, such as HP's JetDirect card, to connect to the network.

- **Workstation-attached (remote printer):** This is a printer cabled directly to a network workstation. In order for other network users to access it, the workstation user (owner) must make it available with share-level permissions (see "Securing the Windows NT world," later in this chapter).

Windows NT workstations do not need to have a driver installed locally for a network- or server-attached printer. Windows NT print services use a server-based printer driver to properly prepare the print job for the printer.

Exploring Windows directory services

Those of you who are veteran Windows users, which means that you have used a Windows version with a number less than 90 in it, should be familiar with the Windows NT Explorer. At first glance, it looks exactly like the Explorer found in Windows 98. But beneath its façade, the Windows NT Explorer separates itself from the Explorer pack.

The Windows NT Explorer is the file and directory management tool for Windows NT Server. Using its tools and utilities, you can add or delete directories (called folders) and network shares, or you can alter the structure of the network. This is also where file permissions, auditing, and ownership properties are managed.

File permissions (refer to Table 8-1) control the actions that can be performed on a file or directory. Auditing sets up a tracking procedure that logs access and other activity on a share, file, or directory. Only the owner of a network resource can change its properties. On occasion, the administrator must take ownership of a resource to solve a problem.

Securing the Windows NT world

Security on Windows NT Server operates much like that discussed earlier for Novell NetWare with three levels of security: user-level, share-level, and resource permissions. Users and groups are assigned rights to access shared network resources. Permissions govern the type of actions permitted on a resource. The rights of the user are re-established each time the user logs in.

As discussed earlier, network shares can be created for a directory, file, printer, CD-ROM drive, and so on, to allow users to access network resources. A network share can be restricted to certain groups or accounts, or it can be left open to all network users. This also establishes the share-level security for the shared resource. Only network resources can be shared in this way. Local resources, those attached or inside a local workstation, must be shared in the same way by the workstation user (owner).

The Windows NT administrator can set the share permissions to those listed in Table 8-6. The User Manager for Domains is an especially useful tool available in Windows NT. This tool is invaluable for managing group and user accounts, rights, and permissions on a Windows NT Server network with multiple domains.

Table 8-6	Share Permissions
Permission	**Description**
No Access	This is a kind of backhanded permission. With this permission "granted," a user or group cannot see or access the shared resource.
Read	Read-only access is granted. No changes can be saved to the shared file.
Change	This share permission allows users to make changes to a shared file or directory.
Full Control	Whoa, there! You have just assigned full access and control to a share (including the ability to remove it).

File and directory permissions are a part of share-level security on a network. They control the action that can be taken on a file or directory. Just because a user has access to a file or directory doesn't mean that a user can have his or her way with it. You may want to give read-only permission to some users, while others may have earned your trust.

Messaging in and around Windows with protocols

At its most basic levels, Windows NT/2000 uses two protocols, NetBIOS (Network Basic Input/Output System) and NetBEUI (NetBIOS Extended User Interface) that are really one protocol, to carry network messages around the network. However, NetBEUI is somewhat limited in what it can do, should you want the network to grow or connect to the outside world — for example, to the Internet.

Remember this news flash when setting up routing on your network: NetBEUI is a non-routable protocol. It is not a bad protocol; in fact, it is a connection-oriented protocol that works well on small networks. Non-routable means that it cannot be used to connect with another physical network without passing it through a bridge. Connection-oriented means that it operates with a form of point-to-point connection much like that used to dial another computer over a modem. One benefit of a connection-oriented protocol is that when a packet arrives at its destination, its arrival is confirmed to the sender.

Windows NT/2000 Server also supports virtually every one of the popular networking protocols in use, including IPX, TCP/IP, and AppleTalk. This support is provided through two service bundles:

- **NWLink (NetWare Link):** NWLink is Microsoft's version of NetWare's IPX. It is fully compatible to IPX and is often called Microsoft IPX.

- **Microsoft TCP/IP (Transmission Control Protocol/Internet Protocol):** This implements the hugely popular open protocol suite used primarily for the Internet, but it is gaining some favor as a LAN protocol as well. Windows NT/2000 Server supports and implements TCP/IP protocols and IP address resolution.

Windows Server also supports the DLC and AppleTalk protocols, as well. It is not a bad idea for you to know at least something about these two common protocols. They seem to show up in unusual situations and usually when you least expect them.

- **DLC (Data Link Control)** is a protocol used to connect networks and workstations to mainframe computers or to network-attached printers.

- **AppleTalk** is the Apple Macintosh networking protocol. This protocol is implemented on a Windows Server network as Services for Macintosh. Another Macintosh network protocol that you might run into is TokenTalk, the token ring equivalent of the Ethernet AppleTalk.

Routing around a Windows network

Routers are either dynamic or static. Dynamic routers, such as a TCP/IP or IPX router, are protocol dependent. Windows Server implements dynamic routers for both IPX (RIP IPX) and TCP/IP (RIP) using a choice of frame (packet) standards:

- **IEEE 802.2:** Standard for Logical Link Control formats.
- **IEEE 802.3:** Standard for bus networks.
- **Auto-detect:** Looks at the packet and determines which format it uses.

Cross-Platform Connectivity: Windows Support for NetWare

It is not unusual to have both Windows NT/2000 Server and NetWare servers in the same network, especially if the network is being migrated to one or the other. Both of these NOSs include utilities and service packages to provide for cross-platform connectivity on the network.

Microsoft Windows Server, which is far more accommodating of NetWare than vice versa, includes a variety of cross-platform connectivity services to all Windows clients to access a NetWare server. Included are these services:

- ✔ **Gateway Service for NetWare (GSNW)** — allows a Windows server to act as a bridge for Windows clients to access resources on a NetWare server.

- ✔ **Client Service for NetWare (CSNW)** — allows a client to access and use file and print services from a NetWare server. (This is included in Windows NT Workstation and Windows 2000 Professional.)

- ✔ **File and Print Services for NetWare (FPNW)** — allows a Windows server to be seen as a Novell NetWare 3.x-compatible server by NetWare clients for file and print services.

- ✔ **Directory Service Manager for NetWare (DSMN)** — allows for user and group accounts to be managed on both the Windows and NetWare servers, with the changes of one updated automatically to the other.

Giving UNIX the Once Over

In the UNIX and Linux worlds, most networking configuration occurs when the network interface card is configured on the computer. You don't need to know much about the UNIX (or Linux) operating system itself to connect one to a router. What you do need to know is how this operating system supports networking and especially internetworking.

UNIX and Linux have clients available for virtually every commonly used protocol in use on networks, but the three protocols with native support on these systems are:

- ✔ SLIP
- ✔ PPP
- ✔ TCP/IP

SLIPping into the Internet

Before the advent of the World Wide Web, UNIX computers and servers were connected to the Internet (to each other actually) over serial line connections using modems and telephone lines. UNIX computers then, and now, use the Serial Line Internet Protocol (SLIP) to make this connection. The SLIP protocol allows IP packets (also called *datagrams*) to be sent over the serial connection.

Getting straight to the point

The Point-to-Point Protocol (PPP) is another serial line IP protocol that has many of the features lacking in SLIP. PPP's main advantage over SLIP is that it can transmit a packet from any protocol, placing it in a container called a frame, and not just those from IP. PPP also includes options to negotiate an IP address and the maximum packet size, as well as client authorization. The overall effect of PPP is that it allows the modem to act like a network interface card (NIC).

PPP is made up of a number of separate protocols, including these:

- **High-Level Data Link Control Protocol (HDLC):** HDLC defines the individual PPP frame and provides a 16-bit checksum. Unlike SLIP packet encapsulation, a PPP frame is capable of carrying packets from protocols other than IP, including IPX and AppleTalk. The basic HDLC frame includes a protocol field that identifies the type of packet included in the frame.
- **Link Control Protocol (LCP):** LCP runs on top of HDLC to establish data link options, such as the Maximum Receive Unit (MRU), the maximum frame size that the receiving side of the PPP connection agrees to receive.

UNIX and its TCP/IP alternatives

TCP/IP on UNIX is no different that TCP/IP on any other operating system or NOS. However, UNIX networking services have some options, the most common of which are the User Datagram Protocol (UDP) and the Internet Control Message Protocol (ICMP). In case you haven't noticed, data packets are called *datagrams* in the UNIX world.

- **UDP:** This is designed for applications that don't need messages divided into multiple datagrams and don't care about the sequence in which they are received. UDP is a direct replacement for TCP and works with IP. However, it doesn't split data into multiple datagrams, and it doesn't track what has been sent so it can be resent, if necessary.
- **ICMP:** This is used to transmit error messages and messages intended for TCP/IP itself. For example, if you attempt to connect to an Internet host server, you may get back an ICMP message that states, "Host unreachable."

Presenting the ever-popular NFS and the lovely NIS

NFS, the network file system, provides network services using a mechanism called *remote procedure call* (RPC). NFS allows users to access files on remote hosts in the same way that they would access files on their local system. The remote file access is completely transparent to the user and is compatible with a variety of server and remote host architectures. The true benefit of NFS is that centrally stored files can be "mounted," or linked, to the local workstation when it is logged on, and the file is as good as local to the user without actually being so. Large files or commonly shared files are installed only once and then are shared throughout the network.

The Network Information System (NIS) is a UNIX service, developed by Sun Microsystems. It distributes information, such as that contained in the user accounts, and groups files to be distributed to all servers on a network. NIS makes the network appear to be a single system with the same accounts supported on all servers.

Workstation Welfare: For the Good of the Client

Regardless of the network operating system running on the network servers, each workstation must have its own operating system, preferably one that is compatible with the NOS and its protocols. In some situations, it is necessary for the NOS to adjust to the OS running on its clients.

The Microsoft Windows operating systems as a group are the most popular client operating systems. Windows systems (Windows 3.x, Windows 9x, Windows NT Workstation, and the Windows 2000 Millennium and Professional versions) all include client software to allow the workstation to communicate with a network running the IPX, TCP/IP, or NetBEUI protocol. The latest releases of Windows also include clients and services providing cross-platform support for file, directory, and print services for NetWare and Macintosh AppleTalk networks.

The Linux operating system is gaining popularity as a workstation (and network) operating system, because it too includes clients for TCP/IP, IPX, and NetBEUI networks.

Network-specific client-based protocols are also called redirectors, which basically describes what they do. Messages sent to the network are redirected to the protocol it serves. (In other words, messages are properly formatted and structured specifically for a certain protocol.) A workstation may run multiple clients, depending on the number and type of servers it has access to and the NOS and protocols running on the servers.

Part III
Cisco Networking

The 5th Wave   By Rich Tennant

"I find it so obnoxious when people use their cellular phone in public that I'm making notes about it on my HPC for a future opinion piece."

In this part . . .

Okay, we're finally getting to the good stuff, the first of four parts of the book that relate to Cisco networking and Cisco Systems' routers, switches, and other networking and internetworking devices.

We start by looking at the role a router or switch can play on a local area network (LAN) and then expand into the different Cisco routers and how they are used, how they are configured, and how their protocols are established. All right, this does sound like more fundamentals, but we're getting there. The point of the material in this part of the book is to help you understand how a router works, how it fits into your network, and how it can best serve your needs, which is exactly the point, isn't it?

Chapter 9

Installing Routing and Switching on the LAN

Throughout this book, you find lots of great technical stuff to help you plan, design, and work with your Cisco network. This is fine, but we thought that we should devote at least one chapter to the common sense stuff, such as planning, preparing, and installing your Cisco networking systems. So, to that end, we have included in this chapter a discussion of planning activities, safety considerations, and installation steps that you should use to install your Cisco routers, switches, and hubs.

It may not be the most exhaustive checklist of what you must do before and during the installation of your Cisco equipment, but we do hit the high points of what you should consider. You'll find that the manuals included with just about every piece of Cisco equipment have a very complete installation guide. If this isn't enough, then by all means, visit the Cisco Systems' Web site at www.cisco.com.

Preparing to Install Cisco Equipment

Before you even begin to install your Cisco router, switch, or hub, you need to think about, plan for, and do some specific things. We know that when you see that box with the bridge logo in blue and red, you're just so excited and all you want to do is get it out of the box and into the network. But, for the sake of safety for you and your equipment and to ensure that your equipment is installed so it will operate properly, you should take the time to do a few get-ready steps:

1. **First and foremost, read the safety booklet packed with your equipment.**

   It is titled something like *Regulatory Compliance and Safety Information for Cisco xxxxx*, where "xxxxx" is the name and model number of the switch, router, or hub.

2. **Be absolutely sure that the device you have is exactly the device you ordered, and be sure beyond any doubt whatsoever that it is configured with the power source type that you intended.**

   Many Cisco devices are available in either AC or DC power types.

3. **Always read the installation instructions for your Cisco device completely, before connecting it to its power source.**

   The Cisco installation guide will tell you that Cisco devices are designed for "TN power system," which means that your electrical system has a direct earth ground.

4. **If the device is a table or desktop type, never place anything on its top that weighs more than 10 pounds.**

   The case or chassis of a desktop device is not designed to support excessive weight, and the device could be damaged. This is also good advice for any networking device regardless of its size or case design.

5. **Be sure that you are able to properly lift and install your Cisco gear.**

   For devices that must be installed in a rack mounting, such as the larger switches, routers, and firewalls, use the buddy system and get somebody (or two bodies) to help you.

Snap, crackle, pop

Under the category of "it's only obvious" is the advice to not work on electrical devices, including Cisco equipment, during a lightning storm. If a thunder and lightning storm is raging outside, wait until it passes to work on your equipment. This includes actions as simple as plugging them in or unplugging them from the power source. Not even an anti-static wrist strap will protect you if you are holding the power cord when lightning strikes your building.

Readying the installation site

Like most computers and networking equipment, Cisco systems are designed to operate in a certain environment. Cisco defines this environment fairly tightly, but most of its parameters are only common sense anyway, so setting up the installation site shouldn't be too tough. The information in this section provides you with some guidelines and advice for choosing an installation site and connection your system to the electrical source.

Choosing an installation site

Where would you put a very expensive key component of your LAN or WAN? Would it be in a site that meets the criteria in this list? We think so.

- ✔ Access to the room, desk, cabinet, or rack where the system is installed should be restricted to only those that need access to the area. This is a little overkill for a desktop switch or router, but to protect your rack mounted systems, you probably want to restrict access by using some form of physical security, such as a special lock or maybe even some form of James Bond-like biological identification system.

- ✔ To ensure that the site is safe, install your systems in an area that has ample space for people, tools, and documentation around it. Make sure that the area has adequate space for tools, cabling, and other equipment while you are working and that all tools and spare (leftover?) parts are stowed properly and out of the way.

- ✔ In general, the site should be clear of all possible hazards, including such things as wet floors, ungrounded power cables, and any conductive materials, such as metal filings or other manufacturing debris.

- ✔ The location of your networking equipment should be clean, well ventilated, dry, and dust-free. Like computers, networking equipment pieces have fans and ventilation systems of their own, which can become clogged and stop ventilating.

- ✔ You may also want to air-condition the area to prevent high operating temperatures. Consistently high operating temperatures can damage electronic equipment and cause the equipment to perform erratically. And it's also uncomfortable for you. Cisco recommends that the temperature be maintained at between 32° F (Brrrrr) to 104° F (whew!). For those of you using the Centigrade scale, this is 0° to 40°.

Connecting to the electrical source

Cisco has not quite completed its self-generating power option package for its routers and switches just yet, so you will need to plug your devices into an electrical power source. Follow these tips when plugging in your equipment:

✔ Never, repeat never, cut the ground conductor off the AC plug on the unit. If you have only an electrical outlet with two holes (which means it doesn't have the third grounding hole), move to a location that has the properly outlet, or get your local electrician in to fix the socket.

✔ Make sure that the electrical outlet is connected to an earth ground. If you are unsure of this, call your local electrician to make sure.

✔ Your Cisco equipment does not include any internal circuitry to protect itself from the local power. If any surge suppression, power conditioning, or battery-backup services are needed, you must supply them. Because you are likely to want the network and its components to continue running for some amount of time in the event of a power failure, you should install an uninterruptible power supply (UPS). But, don't overlook surge suppression; power spikes can do as much, if not more, damage as a power failure.

Safeguarding your system from ESD and EMI

ESD (electrostatic discharge) results from static electricity building on you or on your equipment, or both. If safety precautions are not taken, even a small amount of ESD can cause major damage to electronic components in your Cisco systems. Even a small ESD — one that you can't see, hear, or feel — can result in complete or intermittent failures of your systems.

We recommend that you observe the following safeguards when installing or servicing any computing or networking equipment:

✔ Wear an ESD wrist or ankle strap anytime you are handling electrical devices or electronic components. Clip the strap to any unpainted metal surface of the device or to an ESD jack, if one is available. The ESD strap will protect the system from any static buildup on your body, but not that in your clothing, so avoid touching components to your clothes.

✔ After removing an electronic component from a system, lay it on an anti-static surface or place it in a static-shield bag. Never stack electronic cards directly on top of each other.

✔ If you must handle electronic components, such as circuit boards and edge connectors, take care to touch only card edges that do not have connectors and never touch the electronic circuits and components on the faces of the circuit board.

If you need to run the cabling for your system for an extended distance, say from one room to the next, you need to be aware of the potential for EMI (electromagnetic interference), which is generated by just about every type of electrical or electronic equipment at some level. Take care to avoid noisy electrical motors and any existing non-data wiring running near your cabling or power lines.

A strong radio transmitter in the vicinity can, over time, begin to degrade the signal drivers or receivers in your system. Lightning is another system killer. Protect your system from these electrical problems. To safeguard against or to fix these types of problems, we recommend that you consult your electrician or an RFI (radio frequency interference) expert.

Racking it up

Identifying a rack mountable Cisco device from one that isn't rack mountable is easy. Figure 9-1 illustrates the differences in appearance of desktop and rack mountable systems.

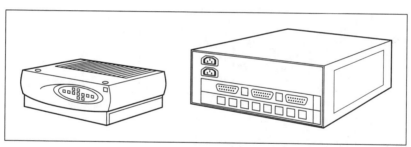

If your router or switch is rack mountable, a rack mount kit is usually included with the system. The rack mount kit allows you to mount the device into an upright 19-inch rack system. Before locking down your system in the rack, be sure that no obstructions, such as power strips or support bars, could get in the way later when you need to access the device.

You can install these types of rack systems in your equipment:

- Two-bar open (Telco) racks
- Four-bar open racks
- Cabinets

Many variations and combinations of these exist. The best rack for your installation is the one that works best for your installation; it all depends on your needs and the amount of room available and the amount of money you want to spend. If aesthetics are important, and remember this is strictly in the eye of the beholder, than you may want a cabinet. Otherwise, an open rack may do the job. Figure 9-2 shows a typical rack mount system.

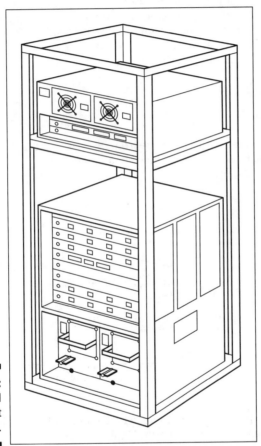

Figure 9-2:
A typical
rack mount
system.

Cisco recommends that you install your system in an open rack if at all possible. An open rack ensures that the system will get proper airflow. If you have to use a cabinet, be sure that it has proper ventilation, such as fans at the top of each bay.

These tips for installing Cisco equipment into a rack system should be helpful.

▶ **Let the air flow.** Your systems require an ample, unobstructed flow of cool air to maintain their normal operation. The systems could overheat and perform badly otherwise.

✔ **Give it space.** You need at least six inches of open space around the ventilation openings on the equipment's case or chassis.

✔ **Blow hot air.** Here's a news flash — heat rises. When laying out a rack, remember that the equipment located at the bottom of the rack puts out heat and that you don't want heavy heat pumpers located at the bottom of a rack. The hot air coming from lower equipment can be drawn into the equipment located higher in the rack and cause it to overheat.

✔ **Start at the bottom.** After installing stabilizers for the rack itself, mount equipment on a rack starting at the bottom. If you place heavy equipment at the top first, the rack may fall over.

✔ **Nail it down (or up).** If you are using a Telco-style rack (the type commonly used by the local telephone company), bolt it to the floor, ceiling, or both, before installing any equipment. Be absolutely sure that the rack is capable of holding the weight that you will be mounting on it.

Connecting to power

Most Cisco systems have AC (alternating current) and DC (direct current) power supplies. *AC* power is the type of electricity supplied by the normal, everyday electrical outlets on the wall of your office or home. *DC* power is commonly used in high-volume and high-end networking situations where a cleaner power source is desired.

If your network is designed around high-availability principles, Cisco provides optional redundant power supplies for most of its higher-end routers and switches. The two principles that we have just introduced to you, high-availability and redundant power supply, are frequently design elements of systems that must not fail.

Keeping it up

The design and operational concepts of high-availability are used to define and build a network infrastructure that does not have a single point of failure. In every place possible, redundant (spare) systems are included to provide for a continuity of services if any component of the system fails. High-availability often focuses on the power source, but truly reliable systems also include redundant servers, routers, disk drives, and more.

Being redundant isn't a bad thing

A redundant power supply is an optional feature of many Cisco routers and switches (and other Cisco devices as well). The redundant power supply automatically kicks in to supply a power source to the device if the primary power supply module fails. The power supply is the component of electrical computing and networking equipment that fails most often because it must suffer the slings and arrows of electrical spikes, brown outs, and noise. Therefore, if you are designing a system that must not fail, a redundant power supply is a good idea. Check with your Cisco reseller to see if one is available for your particular equipment.

Plugging in to AC power

As we mentioned earlier in this chapter, Cisco systems that operate on AC power are designed to connect to electrical systems that have at least one direct earth ground. This means that, somewhere in the system, a metal rod has been sunk into the ground and a grounding circuit has been attached to it. This literally grounds your electrical system.

Other than the obvious (we hope) things you should observe when working with AC power, such as don't stand in water when plugging in or unplugging the power cord, the one recommendation we have is that you allow for access to the AC connections. You should have clear, unobstructed access to both the electrical outlet where the unit is connected and to the back of the device where the power cord attaches to the unit. These power connections are generally the only means available to disconnect the device from the power.

Connecting to DC power

Direct current (DC) power is used in virtually all computing and networking systems. It is especially popular in large-scale high-availability systems that are connected to large battery backup installations. For equipment to be installed in this type of environment, Cisco has a DC power supply that can be used in place of the AC power supply.

If you plan to use DC power for your system installation, we recommend that you consult the manuals that came with your device for installation and safety instructions or visit the Cisco Systems Web site for specific DC power guidelines.

Following the power requirements

Cisco has a long list of power requirements for the location of your systems. If you fail to meet these conditions in your installation, your ability to make a warranty claim due to a power supply failure or the like could be affected. If you are uncertain whether your equipment room meets the electrical requirements prescribed by Cisco, we recommend that you hire a certified electrician to install or inspect your facility. This will avoid some very costly potential problems with your Cisco gear down the road.

At minimum, your installation site should meet one of the following electrical codes:

> ✔ **United States:** Use the National Fire Protection Association (NFPA) 70 and the United States National Electrical Code (NEC).
>
> ✔ **Canada:** Use the Canadian Electrical Code, Part I, CSA C22.1.
>
> ✔ **Other countries:** Use the local and national electrical codes or refer to IEC 364, Part 1 through Part 7.

Installing the System

Each Cisco system comes with complete installation instructions that are available online from the Cisco Systems Web site as well. Follow these instructions to the letter, and you should have little trouble. Each of the instruction sets includes some generic guidelines on working with electricity, preventing ESD damage, and connecting to a LAN or WAN. The instructions for each specific device focus on installing it in a rack system, if appropriate, connecting up its interfaces, configuring the operating system, and dealing with any cabling and wiring issues unique to the system. The following sections review some of the specific or unique installation requirements for routers, switches, and hubs.

Installing a router by the book

Cisco recommends the use of an installation checklist when installing a router in your network, and we agree. Cisco provides a copy of its recommended checklist format in the installation materials and product documentation. This checklist includes the materials, considerations, and steps that you should have and take to ensure a quality installation.

Our version of the installation checklist that would be used with a router is included in Table 9-1.

Table 9-1	Router Installation Checklist	
Task	*Completed By*	*Date*
Review installation site power for ability to support additional load		
Review backup power source for ability to handle additional load		
Test power source for router		
Unpack router and verify contents against packing slip(s)		

continued

Table 9-1 (*continued*)

Task	Completed By	Date
Review "Regulatory Compliance and Safety Information" document		
Review product documentation (printed or CD-ROM)		
Inspect the router for damage and verify installed features and modules		
Power on router prior to installation in rack system		
Test VTY terminal or modem connection		
Install in rack system or at operating location		
Perform startup and initial configuration setup process		
Test initial operations (login, interface configuration, and so on)		
Back up running configuration		

Keeping an installation log

Cisco also recommends that you keep a record of any action performed on the router (or another Cisco device, for that matter), including any background information on the criteria used to choose the particular router model installed. The installation log should be kept near the router so that anyone needing to perform maintenance or upgrade on the router can refer to the device's history, as well as record their actions, including installation or removal of modules, software upgrades, a record of intermittent problems, and so on. The installation log should also include a copy of the installation checklist and a schedule and record of any regularly scheduled maintenance activities.

Connecting a router to the network

After your router is installed in its operating location and has had its initial operating configuration setup and backup (see Chapters 11 and 13 for information on configuring and backing up the router), the next steps involve connecting its interface ports to the network media. You must deal with a series of considerations for each different cable medium used on the network.

In this section, we discuss how a router is connected to the more common media and connector types: Ethernet, serial, and ISDN BRI connections. The examples shown in this chapter are of the Cisco 2600 router, but you'll find that most Cisco routers are very similar to this model.

Identifying the ports

Cisco routers all support three standard types of interface ports: Ethernet, console, and auxiliary. Each of the ports is accessed through an RJ-45 connection on the back of the router. Some router models also allow for the addition of other port/interface types, including fiber-optic, coaxial cable, and serial connections. Figure 9-3 illustrates the port connections on the Cisco 2600 router.

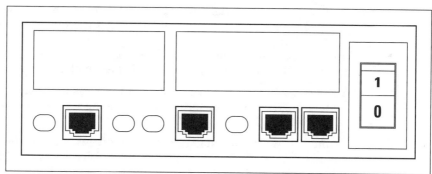

Figure 9-3:
The ports on the Cisco 2611 router.

Cisco routers starting with the 2600 series have one or more slots into which you can add interface cards or network modules. Check with your Cisco reseller for the following information:

- ✔ Type of interface cards available
- ✔ Number of ports supported on each card
- ✔ Connection restrictions, if any, of each interface

Making the Ethernet connection

Ethernet networking is the most common networking technology in use. Its popularity is based on its relative ease of installation and its established standard IEEE (Institute for Electrical and Electronic Engineering) 802.3. Within Ethernet are a number of implementations, all of which are supported by Cisco routers. Table 9-2 lists the most common of the Ethernet formats.

Table 9-2		Ethernet Implementations	
Type	*Speed*	*Cable Media*	*Connector Used*
10BaseT	10Mbps	Copper UTP	RJ-45
10Base2	10Mbps	Thin coaxial	BNC
10Base5	10Mbps	Thick coaxial	BNC/AUI
100BaseT	100Mbps	Cat5 UTP	RJ-45

Connecting to a serial line

If you want to make a serial connection to your Cisco router, normally you have to add a WAN interface card or a serial network module to your router. To properly connect a network device to a serial port on your router, you need to know a little bit about the connection to be made:

- **DCE or DTE:** Is the serial device DTE (data terminal equipment) or DCE (data communications equipment)? Devices that communicate over a synchronous serial interface are DCE and DTE devices. DTE devices do not provide a clock signal, but DCE devices do. The clock signal is used to control the communications between the serial device and the router.

- **Signaling:** What is the signaling standard used by the device? Cisco routers support a wide-range of serial signaling standards: EIA/TIA-232, EIA/TIA-449, V.35, X.21, and EIA-530.

- **Connector:** What type (standard, number of pins, male or female) of connector is used? Cisco serial interface cards and network modules require a Cisco DB-60 connector at the router, but the other end can be whatever connector your serial device needs. You can order a cable to meet your needs from your Cisco reseller.

One thing to be careful of is the distance limitations of serial interfaces. Distance and data speed are directly related to one another in serial communications. The greater the distance, the slower the speed you can use, and *vice versa*. Each Cisco serial interface card and network module lists the recommended distances for each type of signaling standard and connection supported. One rule of thumb is that you can generally exceed the standard distances, but by how much depends on how clean your cabling and environment are from electrical interference. Table 9-3 lists some of the distance and speed trade-offs for different serial signaling standards.

Table 9-3	Serial Communications Speeds and Distances	
Rate (Kbps)	*EIA/TIA-232 Distance (Feet)*	*X.21/V.35 Distance (Feet)*
2.4	200	4,100
4.8	100	2,050
9.6	50	1,025
19.2	25	513
38.4	12	256
56.0	9	102
1544.0 (T1)	Virtually none	50

Making the BRI connection

If you need to connect a BRI ISDN (Basic Rate Interface Integrated Services Digital Network) service to your router, then trust use that you will most likely need to order a network module or an interface card. What you will need to know about the connection is the type of interface your ISDN service uses. Most likely it is either an S/T class interface that requires an external NT1 (Network Terminator 1) terminator or a U class interface with a built-in NT1.

Installing a router in a WAN

It is not uncommon for a router to be installed in a WAN environment. In fact, it is the router that connects a LAN to its WAN. Router installation instructions include some guidelines on installations in a WAN. These types of guidelines are included:

✔ Telephone lines do carry electricity, so to avoid a shocking experience, be careful when working with telephone lines.

✔ Working with telephone lines during a lightning storm is not a good idea. Actually, our message is "don't do it!" Treat telephone lines the same as you would electrical lines in this situation, and stay clear. In fact, don't even use a telephone (except for cordless types) during an electrical storm.

✔ A WAN port carries a hazardous level of voltage even when the power is off. So always detach the cable end that is away from the system first, before working on a port.

Switching Your LAN

If you require a switch in your LAN, the planning and preparation you should do are very much the same as you would for a router. You must consider all the interfaces to be made to the switch, the distance limitations of each interface and signal type, the specific types of cabling and connectors required, and any special interface equipment needed to make the connections, such as modems, network transceivers, or connectors.

Figure 9-4 illustrates how switching is applied to a LAN to connect each floor of a building to the backbone and to act as a distribution point for each floor. You must consider the following in such an environment:

 ✔ The connection to the backbone

 ✔ The different types of connections in use in the distribution field of each switch

Cisco switches use Ethernet connections (10/100BaseT) as their standard, but other types of connections are supported by different Catalyst switches. If your network requires a connection to the switch other than Ethernet, study the Cisco product guides and consult with your Cisco reseller.

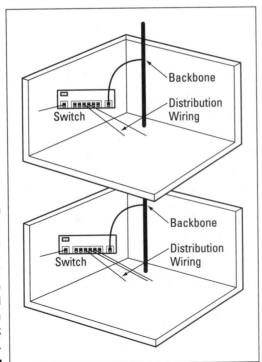

Figure 9-4: Switches used to distribute LAN signals to individual floors off a network backbone.

Hubbing Your Network

If you have designed one or more hubs into your network, different installation considerations are made depending on whether you are using more than one Cisco Micro Hub:

- ✔ **Stacking multiple hubs:** If you are using only one hub, then this is not an issue. If you want to stack two or more Cisco Micro Hubs (but not more than four), you can stack one on top of the other and then connect them together through ports located on their rear panels. Cisco Micro Hubs ship with a stacking clip (which looks something like a stick figure Gumby) and a screw that you can use to anchor them securely together in a stack. If you are using managed hubs (Cisco 1538M hubs), you are limited to two hubs in your stack, and the upper hub must be the primary.

- ✔ **Connecting the stacked hubs:** If you have stacked more than one Cisco Micro Hub, the next step is to connect them together with the connecting cables supplied with the hub. You need to follow one rule for cabling your stacked hubs: The hub on the top of the stack must have its UP connector open and the bottom hub must have its DOWN connector open. This means that the bottom hub is connected to the next higher hub from its UP connector to the DOWN connector of the next higher hub, and so forth all the way to the top. Don't worry, although you shouldn't foul it up, if you connect it up, or down, incorrectly, you won't hurt anything. It may just not work right.

- ✔ **Connecting network devices to the hub:** You can connect network devices, such as servers and computer workstations, and other Ethernet hubs or switches to your hubs. Each device that you connect to a hub must have an Ethernet 10/100BaseT connection. You'll know the connection is okay if the LED (light emitting diode – the little light above the port) is on and blinking.

Filling in Those Ugly Gaps

Some Cisco devices have module slots where additional ports or features can be added to a router or switch. When the installation of the system changes and the ports, interfaces, or function are no longer needed, these modules can be removed. When this happens, always remember to put a faceplate over the empty module slot. Faceplates are the covers used to fill empty module bays when they are empty. By replacing the faceplate, you prevent a number of other problems:

✔ Accidentally touching the components inside the chassis and damaging the system or causing other problems for the device

✔ The potential for damage to the system by EMI and RFI

✔ An open slot on the system disrupting the design and efficiency of the airflow through the chassis intended to cool the system's components

Chapter 10

Working with Routers

. . . .

In This Chapter

▶ Defining router elements

▶ Using a router to segment a LAN

▶ Describing the benefits of LAN segmentation

▶ Differentiating a Cisco router's memory types

▶ Reviewing CDP and basic show commands

▶ Listing Cisco router interface options

▶ Preparing to install a router

. . . .

A router is one thing you definitely must be familiar with to implement a Cisco network. This includes how a router "thinks," how it relates to other devices, and its role in the networking world. The challenge to succeeding as a Cisco network administrator is in the router.

However, some things you really don't need to know about routers. We realize that if you are starting from scratch, IT routers, and especially Cisco routers, can be intimidating. Just so you don't end up wasting valuable time learning the wrong stuff, don't worry about the following things as you become a Cisco network administrator, even if you wish to become certified:

✔ You don't need to be able to field strip and reassemble a router, either blindfolded or not.

✔ You don't need to memorize the processor speeds and specific memory amounts in particular Cisco router models, and normally, determining the proper memory or processor configuration for a router is not a big requirement.

✔ About the only components on the router that you really care about are the interfaces and memory. You don't need to know the general anatomy of a router.

A Layered Approach to Networks

Cisco uses a three-tier hierarchical network model, like that illustrated in Figure 10-1. The Cisco network model consists of three layers: the core layer, the distribution layer, and the access layer.

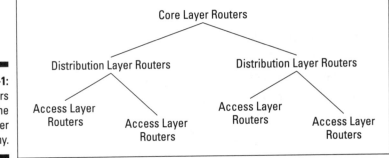

Figure 10-1:
The layers
of the
Cisco router
hierarchy.

- ✔ **Core layer:** Also called the Backbone layer, this layer provides transportation of data between networks. Core layer routers are in the 7000 series or higher.

- ✔ **Distribution layer:** This layer acts as a demarcation between the core and access layers and provides differentiation between dynamic and static routing and other policy-based functions (See Chapter 12 for information on dynamic and static routing). Distribution layer routers are in the 3600 series.

- ✔ **Access layer:** Users are allowed access to a network or internetwork on this layer of the Cisco network model. Access layer routers are in the 2500/2600 series.

Familiarizing yourself with the model series might be a good idea. You can use a core layer router on the distribution or access layers, but it would be a terrific waste of capability and money. You cannot, repeat cannot, effectively do the reverse. An access layer router is not a good choice on the core layer.

Understanding the primary purpose of each layer of the Cisco network model helps you to understand why a certain router, switch, or module is appropriate for a particular application on a network. Applications can be defined to one of the layers of the Cisco network model, which means that each application can be associated with the devices appropriate on that level.

Moving traffic over the core layer

The core layer is where the biggest, fastest, and, not surprisingly, most expensive routers, with the highest model numbers, are found. Core layer routers are used to merge geographically separated networks. The core layer focuses on moving information as fast as possible, most often over dedicated or leased lines. The core layer of any network should be its high-speed switching backbone and, as such, should be designed to switch packets as fast as possible. This means that no packet manipulation, such as access control lists or packet filtering, should be done on the core layer, because these activities would slow down packet switching.

The primary concern on the core layer is reliability. Usually, when the network backbone fails, the network does also. So the core layer of any network must be designed for *high availability,* which is the design philosophy aimed at eliminating points of network failure. Another concern about reliability is avoiding devices and protocols that have slow convergence. Switches and routers that have faster convergence and can provide load balancing over multiple links are best suited for use on the core layer. *Convergence* is the ability of a network's routers and switches to agree to a new topology of the network after a change has been made to the network. Core layer routers and switches should provide both routing and Layer 2 switching and bridging over different Layer 3 protocols (see Chapter 2 for information on the OSI model and its layers). The overall design goal for a network's core layer should be to eliminate single points of failure.

Distributing data around the network

In the Cisco world, the campus backbone exists on the distribution layer. We realize that including the backbone on the distribution layer may contradict the definition that we gave in the preceding section for the core layer. But please understand that we are actually dealing with different backbones here. The core layer backbone is a more universal internetworking backbone than that used within a single LAN or campus area network (CAN).

Routers on the distribution layer of the model are used to connect buildings or departments, such as accounting, production, and distribution — each of which is known in Cisco-speak as a large functional group (LFG). Distribution routers represent the intermediate level of the Cisco model. On this layer, the packets of the network are filtered and forwarded up and down router layers. Most routing policy decisions that decide the best routing for messages on your network are made on the distribution layer. Mid-level network servers, such as department or network segment servers, can also be found on the distribution level.

The distribution layer serves to separate the access and core layers and acts as a gateway to the core. It is on the distribution layer of the Cisco network model that the boundaries of a network are defined and packet manipulation takes place. Several other activities performed on the distribution layer are:

- Aggregation of addresses or links
- Access to LFGs
- Definition of broadcast and multicast domains
- Routing for Virtual LANs (VLANs) (see Chapter 16)
- Router and switch-based security (access lists)

Providing access to the network

The access layer is where the rubber meets the road. The access layer is where host computers access a network and where most network traffic finds its destination. Access layer routers and switches are used to segment LANs, which we talk about in a later section (see "Segmenting a LAN with a Router"). They also provide remote access to a network using WAN services.

We don't have much to say about access layer devices, primarily because the access layer operates essentially on the local area network. Devices on the access layer do not make sophisticated decisions or worry about convergence or interconnectivity. The bulk of their responsibility is to provide functionality and access to the local network.

Segmenting a Network with a Router

Segmenting a LAN with a router may not be the least expensive way to go, but it does have its benefits. You can find less expensive ways to segment a network, such as with a bridge, and you can find faster, simpler ways, such as with a switch, but a router can provide benefits other devices cannot.

This chapter is about routers, so we focus on some facts and characteristics of LANs segmented with a router. In case you're wondering, a WAN, because it is made up of separate networks already segmented behind their routers, cannot be further segmented.

Most networks began life as a fairly simple affair with a small group of client workstations receiving services from a single server. But like weeds, kudzu, and children, networks always seem to grow and in unexpected ways. A network can grow into a bandwidth-starved monster with the network carrying more broadcast messages than anything else. Sound familiar? No? Then you really must be new to networking. Or, you are among those saintly administrators that already know the value of segmenting a network.

Regardless of how you segment a network or what devices you use, some general benefits are almost always generated:

✔ **Keeps local traffic local:** Breaking up a large network into smaller segments with fewer workstations on each segment reduces congestion on the network by reducing the traffic load being carried over the entire network.

✔ **Increases the bandwidth available to each user:** Bandwidth is a shared entity, but segmenting the network allows each segment and its workstations to have full use of the bandwidth available. For example, if 100Mbps network has 100 users, each user has 1Mbps of bandwidth available, on average. However, if this network were segmented into 10 segments with 10 users on each segment, each user would have an average of 10Mbps of bandwidth available, on average.

✔ **Reduces collisions:** On a large network, as the number of workstations grows, so do the interruptions on the network to handle collisions. After segmenting the network, the traffic from a segment tends to stay within its segment, with less traffic being routed outside of the segment to contend for access to the backbone.

✔ **Reduces Ethernet distance limitations:** An Ethernet network (see Chapter 4) has inherent distance limitations. When you segment a network with a router (and only a router — not a bridge and not a switch), you re-establish the beginning point from which the maximum distance for the cabling is determined.

Segmenting a LAN with a Router

For most LANs, a bridge or switch is used to segment the network for reasons discussed in Chapter 16. But several reasons exist to use a router to segment a LAN. One reason may be as simple as this: You have money to burn, or you have always wanted to get your hands on a Cisco router. The real reasons, or at least the ones you should tell your boss, can be summarized as

✔ **Reduced size of broadcast domains:** Routers block broadcasts unless specifically instructed to forward them.

✔ **Smaller networks:** Routers create smaller networks, as opposed to dividing a large network into smaller pieces of itself.

✔ **Flexible addressing:** Routers segment a network by using logical, rather than physical, addresses. For example, a bridge uses the MAC (Media Access Control) or physical address to make its addressing decisions, whereas a router uses the logical or IP address.

✔ **Better administration:** A system administrator has more management tools available when using a router, thanks to the increased memory in a router and its ability to make routing decisions based on a multitude of factors.

Deciding on segmenting your network

You really do need to figure out what it is you are trying to accomplish by breaking a network into smaller segments. With your goals established, determining whether you need to use a router, switch, or bridge is much easier. Needless to say, if all you need is a bridge, paying for a bridge is much better than paying for a router. Routers are expensive devices with a high degree of sophistication. When you need a router, certainly you should use a router, but when something else will work as well as or better than a router, then by all means, use something else.

Consider these things before you segment a LAN with a router:

✔ A router can segment a LAN that includes different media types. For example, a LAN may have both Category 5 and Thinnet (coaxial) cable connecting to fiber-optic cabling.

✔ A router can interconnect LANs that are using different protocols, provided they are all routable.

✔ A router increases latency, the amount of delay introduced by networking devices, by adding the delay caused by the router examining each packet entirely before sending it on.

✔ A router can also provide more than one active link or route to a destination. On a larger LAN, this can provide route diversity and redundancy, which are always good things.

From here, you should do the following things as you set up your router:

✔ Choose the best spot for the router.

✔ Understand your router's memory capabilities.

✔ Determine which port you want to install on your router.

✔ Consider environmental factors.

Picking your router spot

We can't really give you a how-to for segmenting a LAN with a router. Although it is really more complicated than it sounds, you just add a router to the network at some point that makes logical, physical, and routing sense. That's about it. However, doing it right involves some knowledge of the network, its traffic, and its topology. You could just pick a point in the LAN and plug the router in, but most likely, unless you are extremely lucky, you wouldn't see much improvement in the performance of the LAN. Segmenting the LAN with a router really requires that you know where the segmentation would make the most sense for the outcome that you want to obtain.

Routers are generally used to segment fairly large networks, in terms of geography, number of nodes, or volume. What's a good network to segment with a router, you ask? These criteria give you some ideas:

- One spread over several floors or buildings

- One that has a high number of nodes in comparison to the bandwidth available, so that the desired average bandwidth goals are not being realized

- One that must provide each workstation or segment with a high amount of bandwidth regardless of the number of nodes or its size

Remembering the Router's Memory

Just because a Cisco router has four kinds of memory doesn't mean that understanding them is difficult. Cisco routers don't really have any more or fewer types of memory than your personal computer. Thinking of the Cisco router as a special-purpose personal computer may help you to keep the memory types straight. In fact, Cisco claims that it is a software company, not a hardware company. Table 10-1 summarizes just about everything you need to know about the memory in a Cisco router.

Table 10-1	Different Memory Types in a Cisco Router
Memory/Type	*Contents*
RAM/DRAM	Active program and operating system instructions, the running configuration file, routing tables
NVRAM	Startup configuration file
ROM	POST, bootstrap, and startup/power-up utilities, usually limited version of Cisco IOS
Flash	Cisco IOS

To simplify your life, don't worry about how much memory is in each router configuration. You should, however, have a very good general understanding of the different types of memory in the router and how and when each is used.

RAM/DRAM a ding dong

The primary working memory in a Cisco router is called RAM (random-access memory). Like your PC, the router uses RAM for storing its working files and data. The RAM in the router is specifically DRAM, which stands for dynamic random-access memory and is pronounced "dee-ram" (not to be confused with de Bulls, de Bears, or de Rams, for that matter), which is the same memory type found in most personal computers. And like the RAM in your PC, if the power is switched off or the power fails, any files and data stored in RAM/DRAM are lost. That's where the "dynamic" part of the DRAM name comes in. DRAM is volatile RAM, which means that it must have an electrical power source in order to hold data. It's simple: no power = no data.

Just remember that a Cisco router's RAM is volatile DRAM that holds the router's working configuration, data, and files. When the power is turned off, the contents of the RAM simply cease to exist. The contents are lost and cannot be recovered.

In the Cisco router, RAM is used to hold

- A working copy of the Cisco IOS software (see Chapter 11)
- The command executive, also known as EXEC, which interprets the commands you enter from the router console
- Routing tables (see Chapter 12)
- The active configuration file (see Chapter 14)
- The ARP cache (see Chapter 12)
- Packet buffers, which are temporary I/O areas used for processing a packet
- Packet hold queues, which are used to hold incoming and outbound packets awaiting services by the router

Did we mention that anything stored in RAM is lost when the router is powered off? We hope that you are beginning to see that providing a good power source to your routers, such as an uninterruptible power supply (UPS) with a long standby battery life, is essential. If the power fails or if you turn the router off for some reason (although what the reason could possibly be escapes us), the only real catastrophe will be that you might lose any changes you've made to the active configuration file and haven't copied to NVRAM. Everything else — the routing tables, the ARP cache, and so on — will be reconstructed by the Cisco IOS as soon as power is restored and the router completes its power up sequence.

NVRAM for static storage

While DRAM is volatile and must have a power source so that it can hold any data or instructions placed in it, NVRAM — which is nonvolatile RAM — can hold its contents whether its power source is on or off. NVRAM can statically hold its contents without an active power supply.

What Cisco calls NVRAM, your personal computer calls SRAM (pronounced "ess-ram"), or static RAM. It's the same thing — trust us. The most important thing stored in NVRAM on a Cisco router is the startup configuration file that is loaded to RAM during the router's boot sequence.

Any changes made to the working (or running) configuration in RAM should be backed up to NVRAM in order for those changes to become a permanent part of the router's configuration. Any changes made to the running configuration that are not stored in NVRAM will be lost if you ever need to restart the router.

ROM with a vie

Another type of memory, called ROM (read-only memory), is even more reliable than NVRAM. Like NVRAM, ROM is nonvolatile and does not lose its contents when the power goes off. Information or programming stored in ROM is put there when the integrated circuit (IC), on which the ROM is based, is manufactured. This process burns in the ROM IC's contents, which permanently locks in the information or programming instructions on the chip.

The ROM in a router is exactly like the ROM in your personal computer and is used for much the same thing. ROM holds the instructions used to start your system each time you power it up. These instructions are called firmware, as opposed to hardware and software, and are literally burned into the PROM (programmable read-only memory) chip when it is manufactured. A PROM usually is not upgradeable.

On the Cisco router, ROM holds the instructions used to perform the power-on self-test (POST) diagnostics, the bootstrap program (which is the startup program for the router), and the router's operating system (which will always be the Cisco IOS). Cisco routers contain two copies of IOS, a stripped-down version that is stored in ROM and the fully up-to-date version stored in Flash memory (see the next section, "Flashing the EPROM").

Flashing the EPROM

A specific type of PROM can be updated. An EPROM (erasable programmable read-only memory) can be updated. An EPROM is erasable and can be written to and updated using a software-controlled operation called *flashing*. As temporary and volatile as this may sound, it isn't. EPROMs are nonvolatile and retain their contents indefinitely, even without a power source, or at least until the next time they are flashed. And no, the software used to update an EPROM is not called a flasher.

On the Cisco router, the Flash memory is an EPROM IC chip that holds the image and microcode of the router's operating system, the Cisco IOS. Storing the fully up-to-date IOS version in Flash memory enables you to upgrade it without having to remove and replace ROM chips on the router's CPU board, or — worse yet — continually purchase new routers to get the new and improved features.

Discovering CDP

The Cisco Discovery Protocol (CDP) is a proprietary Cisco protocol that allows you to get (discover) information about directly connected Cisco routers, bridges, and switches. CDP, which is included throughout Cisco's product line, uses a Data Link layer protocol called SNAP (Subnetwork Access Protocol) and frames to communicate with routers and other network connectivity devices. Virtually all LAN media and transmission modes support CDP, including Frame Relay and ATM (Asynchronous Transfer Mode), see Chapter 17.

CDP automatically starts when the router is powered on and immediately goes to work by multicasting Data Link layer discovery messages to the network looking for other Cisco devices. Any device wishing to be discovered sends back an SNMP (Simple Network Management Protocol) message containing configuration data on itself. The information in this message allows CDP to display information about the discovered devices, including information about different Network (or higher) layer protocols. CDP caches whatever it discovers in its router's RAM and updates it periodically as the information changes.

So why are we discussing a protocol?

If this chapter covers the most basic components and activities of a Cisco router, why does it include a section on a protocol? CDP is covered here because it is a foundation protocol that performs one of the most basic functions of a router: discovering information about the router's neighbors.

Many of the routing decisions made by the router are based on what the router knows about its neighboring routers. If a neighboring router is up or down or just not responding, this has a direct impact on whether or not that router should be included in the routes available for use. So, we thought it would be a good idea to mention how the router learns about the health and well-being of its neighbors.

CDP does the following things for you and your routers:

- ✔ CDP uses SNAP at the Data Link layer, which makes it protocol independent.

- ✔ CDP detects attached devices regardless of what protocol they're running (for example, TCP/IP, IPX, or AppleTalk).

- ✔ CDP is enabled by default when the router is booted on all interfaces.

- ✔ CDP update requests are multicast by default every 60 seconds using Layer 2 multicast messages.

- ✔ CDP has a default hold-time. The amount of time that a device holds a CDP update before discarding it is 180 seconds.

Working with All the Best Connections

Cisco routers connect to the world through a wide array of interface ports. Your particular interface needs will determine exactly which ports you configure on your router. But regardless of your need, Cisco has either a router or an add-in module to provide the type of interface you need.

The ports installed on your router should reflect the interface needs of your network. In the 17 router families offered by Cisco Systems, you are bound to find a router to fit your needs and requirements. However, sometimes the router you need operationally just doesn't have just the ports you need. This is where the modularity of the Cisco router line can help you. For the Cisco 1600 router series and above, you can add interface modules to the router to configure it to fit your particular needs. If you do customize your router, add only the functions you need in the near future. The interface modules aren't inexpensive and can be added in the future when you actually need them.

Taking command of the console

Every Cisco router comes with one particularly essential interface port. This port, a 25-pin serial port, is called the *console port*. It is through the console port that you install and configure the router initially and perhaps in the future.

To install and configure a Cisco router, you connect the console port into a terminal, such as a computer running terminal emulation software that has an EIA/TIA-232 DTE port using an EIA/TIA-232 DCE console cable that has DB-25 plugs at both ends. What all of that alphabet soup means is that you can use your portable computer's serial port with a null modem cable and software such as Windows' HyperTerminal utility. After you have completed the initial configuration of the router, don't leave your computer connected to the router. You should log off the router and remove the cable. This connection should be used only when it is needed for configuration or administration of the router.

Making the router feel at home

You should consider a number of factors for each interface type in use when preparing to install a router. Chapter 4 provides some detail information on the specific considerations for each type of media in use, but consider these general things:

- ✔ **The type of cabling needed for each port** (fiber, thick or thin coaxial, or twisted-pair cabling) — Ensure that you have the appropriate connectors and cable management materials before starting the installation.

- ✔ **The distance limitations for each signal type** — Cisco has a specification on the distance limits that you should use for each of the different signal types it supports.

- ✔ **The cables you need for each specific interface** — Make sure that you have the right kind of cable with exactly the right connectors for each interface port.

- ✔ **The interface equipment needed to support your media type** — Be sure that you have things such as transceivers, modems, channel service units (CSUs), and data service units (DSUs).

Before you install your router, make sure that you have everything you need on hand. If you are really brave, you might consider building your own cables, but unless you have had extensive experience building cables, you're better off just buying them. If you insist on building your own cables, refer to the cable pin outs in the "Cabling Specifications" appendix of the "Planning for Installation" white paper.

Take our advice: Call your Cisco representative or reseller to order your connecting cables. Yes, you'll pay more, but you'll thank us in the end. You can find the Cisco "Planning for Installation" white paper at this Web site (a PDF document is available on the site):

www.cisco.com/univercd/cc/td/doc/product/core/cis7010/7010_him/
7010prep.htm.

Providing a powerful plethora of ports

A long list of interface modules is available for Cisco routers, should you need to add additional ports to one of the modular routers. This list is representative of the interface modules available from Cisco:

- ✔ AnyLAN (voice grade)
- ✔ ATM (OC-3 rate) single-mode or multimode
- ✔ Channelized DS3 and E3

- DS3 high-speed interface
- E3 medium-speed interface
- ESCON adapter
- Ethernet 10BaseT and 10BaseFL
- Fast Ethernet 100BaseTX and 100BaseFX
- FDDI single-mode and multimode (half-duplex and full-duplex)
- HSSI
- ISDN BRI
- Multichannel PA (DSX1, E1, E3, T3)
- Synchronous serial (V.35, X.21, EIA/TIA-232, E1, EIA/TIA-449, EIA-530)
- Token Ring half-duplex and full-duplex

And a remarkable range of routers

The information in Table 10-2 provides you with an overview of the different Cisco router series. Please understand that Cisco, like all high-technology companies, is constantly updating and upgrading its lines, with products being added or discontinued all the time. What we really mean is that the list in Table 10-2 could very well be obsolete the second this book is printed, but it's our educated guess that the majority of it will be valid for at least a couple of years.

Your best bet for an up-to-date list of Cisco routers is to visit Cisco's router products Web site at www.cisco.com/warp/public/44/jump/routers.shtml.

Table 10-2	Cisco Router Series	
Product Series	*Description*	*Applications*
Cisco 12000	Gigabit switch routers	Accepts data from PSTN, ATM, Frame Relay, DSL, and PBX for high-speed transmission over the IP backbone
Cisco 10000	Edge services routers	High-density T1-aggregation IP edge routers
Cisco 7500	Data, voice, and video routers	Supports multiprotocol, multimedia routing, and bridging with a wide variety of protocols and LAN and WAN options

(continued)

Table 10-2 *(continued)*

Product Series	Description	Applications
Cisco 7200	High-performance multifunction routers	Chassis-based, modular central site router that provides high-performance and avilability with serviceability and manageability features
Cisco 7100	VPN routers	Integrated VPN solution that combines high-speed routing with VPN services
Cisco 4000	Modular, high-density routers	Modular access routers with a broad set of connectivity features and internetworking software set; a good choice where protecting a legacy system investment is important
Cisco 3600	Modular, high-density access routers	Multi-service access routers for medium-size and large size offices and smaller ISPs
Cisco 2600	Modular access routers	Cost-effective, modular access router for branch offices that supports voice, data, and dial-up access
Cisco 2500	Fixed and modular access routers	Flexible branch office choice that features intergrated hubs and access servers for either Ethernet or Token Ring
Cisco 1700	Modular access router	For secure Internet, intranet, and extranet access with optional VPN and firewall service designed for small branch offices or small and medium businesses
Cisco 1600	Modular desktop access routers	Small footprint routers that are excellent choices for small business or branch offices to connect an Ethernet LAN to the Internet or a corporate WAN
Cisco 1400	xDSL routers	Secure router that features both Ethernet and ATM interfaces that include VPN and firewall support

Product Series	Description	Applications
Cisco 1000	Fixed-configuration desktop access routers	For connecting small offices to ISDN or serial WAN connections
Cisco 900	Cable access routers	Provides telecommuters and small offices with high-speed secure connection and access
Cisco 800	ISDN, serial, and IDSL routers	Inexpensive router series that connects up to 20 users to the Internet or intranet over ISDN, IDSL, or a serial connection; small office router for offices of up to 20 users and corporate telecommuters
Cisco 700	ISDN access routers	A series of affordable, fast routers that connect small office and home office workers to the Internet

Protecting the Router from the Environment

You should consider a number of environmental factors before slapping that router into place. Cisco routers have built-in environmental monitoring. They won't give you an air quality report or test your local drinking water, but they will protect the router from potential damage from electrical spikes and high-temperature operating conditions.

Some of the recommended environmental considerations are obvious, or at least they should be, and others more subtle. To protect the investment you've made in a Cisco router, you should definitely include these things in your site preparations:

✔ **Temperature:** Maintain an ambient temperature of 32°F through 104°F (0°C through 40°C) and keep the area as dust-free as possible. A good rule of thumb is if you can stand the temperature, so can the router. If you turn either blue or red, something is wrong!

✔ **Power:** The router needs voltages between 100 and 240 VAC and 50 through 60 Hertz. Some routers also have options for DC power. Be sure to read the product specifications carefully for the power requirements of your specific router.

✔ **Wiring:** When setting up the router site, consider distance limitations, EMI, and connector compatibilities.

✔ **Equipment rack:** Your Cisco router comes with rack-mounting hardware compatible with most 19-inch rack systems and Telco-style racks. When mounting the router, be sure that you have free access to both the interface processor and the chassis cover panel. You can also set the router on a rack shelf as long as the router can be secured to the shelf. This may be a no-brainer, but don't set the router directly on the floor or in any other area that may collect dust.

✔ **Airflow:** You must maintain two inches or more clearance between the sides of the chassis and the enclosure walls to allow air to properly flow through cooling ports on the router.

✔ **Cooling:** Just because a room has air conditioning doesn't mean that it can stay properly cooled after you have installed a router and any associated networking equipment. Electrical equipment puts out heat and you may need to add additional cooling capacity to keep the room at acceptable operating temperatures.

✔ **ESD (electrostatic discharge):** When working on, in, or near the router, follow standard ESD-avoidance procedures to protect the router and its modules from damage. A good reference site for ESD information is Indiana University's Knowledge Base at kb.indiana.edu/data/aeoh.html.

After your Cisco router is installed and configured, you can use the **show environment** command to monitor the internal system environmental conditions. The router's environmental monitor continuously checks the interior chassis' environment, looking for marginal or alarm-level conditions such as high temperatures and maximum and minimum voltages. Any out-of-range conditions are recorded and reported.

If your router ever displays warning messages like this

```
WARNING: Fan has reached CRITICAL level
```

or this

```
%ENVM-2-FAN: Fan array has failed, shutdown in 2 minutes
```

be sure that you take immediate action to identify and isolate the problem and then correct it. Of course, you will only see these messages if you maintain a console on the router. Otherwise, you should check the router's log file frequently.

Chapter 11

Setting Up and Saving the Router

· ·

In This Chapter

▶ Using the setup command

▶ Identifying IOS commands used for router startup

▶ Managing configuration files in Privileged Exec mode

▶ Maintaining the IOS software image

▶ Listing commands used to load IOS software

▶ Copying and manipulating configuration files

· ·

*A*ccording to Cisco, a Cisco network administrator spends the majority of his or her time working at the router configuring, updating, and administering router stuff. Fortunately, this is only partially true and the part that is true is that you only work at the router intermittently once it is set up. To do so, also according to Cisco, you must know, in nitpicky detail, most of the major commands used to start, configure, maintain, and manage the router's software.

This chapter focuses only on the router commands, configuration, and setup topics that any self-respecting Cisco network administrator should know or at least know about. Pay attention to the command syntax and the mode in which each command is executed. Someone in the past said that the devil is in the details. It's our guess that whoever said this did so immediately after configuring a Cisco router for the first time. If you have a router handy — one that you can reset, reconfigure, and generally muck about with — practice the commands in this chapter as you read. If you don't have a router available, we recommend that you visit the Mentor Labs Virtual Lab Web site at www.mentorlabs.com/vlab/access, where you can practice on a virtual router on the Web.

Setting Up and Configuring a Router

Arguably, the thrill of being the first person to open the box and unpack a new router is one of the top three thrills a person can experience in life. We'll leave it to you to supply your version of what the other two might be. Nothing else is quite like that new router smell to get your heart pumping. However, as joyful as this experience may be, it soon fades when you plug it in, fire it up for the first time, and realize that you're in setup mode. If you hear the *Twilight Zone* theme about now, then you've experienced what we're describing. In this section, we provide you with information on the following setup and configuration activities for a brand new router:

✔ Setting up a router powered on for the first time

✔ Setting and using passwords

✔ Initializing an interface

✔ Saving the setup

Watch out, it's a setup!

The first time a router is powered up, it automatically enters setup mode, and the router display should look something like this:

```
Router#setup
--- System Configuration Dialog ---
At any point you may enter a question mark '?' for help.
Use ctrl-c to abort configuration dialog at any prompt.
Default settings are in square brackets '[]'.
Continue with configuration dialog? [yes]:
```

If you want to continue with the setup dialog — and you do! — setup displays its default answer in square brackets ([...]). You need only press the Enter key to accept the default value or response. Beyond the first time you power on the router, you can access setup mode in two other ways and both are entered in the Enable Exec (Privileged) mode:

✔ Enter the **setup** command at the # prompt to display the command sequence shown earlier in this section.

✔ Enter the **erase startup-config,** or **erase start** command with the network administrator's permission of course and then power the router off and back on to begin again just like when the router was brand new. What's the password?

Setup shows an initial interface summary that shows the default values assigned to the router interfaces and then prompts you to accept the current

Enable versus Enable Secret Passwords

Cisco routers and switches are administered through the command interpreter of the Cisco IOS. In order to perform administrator functions on the router, you must log into the Exec mode. The Exec mode has two levels: the user Exec mode and the Privileged Exec mode. The EXEC mode provides access to commands to set and modify the general configuration of the router. However, the Privileged EXEC mode provides access to commands that are used to configure the operating parameters of the router. Because of its sensitive nature, a second and protected password is used to prevent unauthorized access to this level of authority.

Since Cisco IOS release 10.2(3), the **enable secret** command has been available to set a password for access to the Privileged Exec mode. The **enable password** command is still available for protecting access to the user Exec mode. The enable secret password is a secure password that is stored in an encrypted form. The enable password is much less secure and is stored in clear text form. If an enable secret password is configured, an enable password is not required, but if one is configured, it must be used. These passwords should be different. The IOS will accept them as the same, but it will warn you about using the same password for both.

values, if any, for the hostname, Enable Secret, Enable, and Virtual Terminal passwords. Alternatively, you can change them. This sequence looks like this:

```
The enable secret is a one-way cryptographic secret used
        instead of the enable password when it exists.

Enter enable secret [<Use current secret>]:

The enable password is used when there is no enable secret
        and when using older software and some boot
        images.

Enter enable password [gilster]:
Enter virtual terminal password [ulstad]: maddox
```

As the first line indicates, when the Enable Secret password is used, you don't need to set an Enable password for most of the newer Cisco routers. When in doubt, set it to a value that you can remember, just in case. The virtual terminal password is used to gain access to the router through a telnet session from a remote host. See Chapter 14 for information on the virtual terminal interface and telnet sessions.

Setting up the interface

After you finish setting the passwords, the setup process continues by configuring the router's interfaces. Here's a sample of what should be displayed by setup at this point:

```
Configure IP? [yes]:
    Configure IGRP routing? [no]:
        Your IGRP autonomous system number [1]:

Configuring interface parameters:

Configuring interface Ethernet0:
  Is this interface in use? [yes]:
  Configure IP on this interface? [yes]:
    IP address for this interface [192.168.1.6]:
```

Notice that the setup process first asks you if you want to configure and enable the IP routing, and then this question repeats for each of the individual interfaces.

The word or value contained in the brackets following the command interpreter's prompt is the default value. If you press the Enter key, the default value is what is assigned to that particular parameter. Generally, at this level you are merely indicating whether or not an interface is in use and whether or not the interface is a local interface or an internetworking interface connected to other routers or the outside world (or both). The information entered here should come from your network planning diagrams that should include the information needed to configure each of the interfaces installed on the router. See Chapters 9 and 19 for information on how to plan and configure a network. Understand that if you respond no (with the word "no" or the letter *N*) to any of the higher level questions, none of its configuration questions will appear. Here is what the display shown earlier in this section would look like, had a "no" response been entered:

```
Configure IP? [yes]: n

Configuring interface parameters:

Configuring interface Ethernet0: n
```

If you do wish to configure an interface for IP routing, you enter the correct IP address information for each interface. See Chapter 7 for information on IP addressing.

IP routing is enabled as the default. If you wish to turn off IP routing for all interfaces, then you must enter the command **no ip routing.** To turn it back on again at some future point, enter the command **ip routing.** The "yes" is implied.

Summarizing configuration After you respond to all of setup's enable and configuration requests, the setup command displays a summary of the router's configuration as you just defined it and asks whether you want to accept the configuration shown. As a safety against a default value being accidentally entered, no default value appears and you must enter either Yes or No. If you answer yes, the router's configuration as defined is then built and stored in NVRAM, and the router is ready to be put into service.

If you answer no, the configuration you have just defined is discarded and the default configuration continues as the active configuration and you will be returned to the router's default prompt. If you wish to rerun the configuration program, enter the **setup** command.

The configuration running in the router's RAM is the *running-configuration,* and the configuration saved in the router's NVRAM is the *startup-configuration.* Restarting the router loads the startup-configuration into RAM, where it becomes the running-configuration. Copying the running-configuration to flash (NVRAM) overwrites the startup-configuration previously stored there. See Chapter 10 for more information on RAM and NVRAM.

If You Start It Up, It Never Stops

After the router receives its initial configuration, the next time you power it on, the router goes through a five-step startup process:

1. A hardware check is performed by running the POST (Power On Self Test), and the bootstrap program is loaded to RAM from ROM.

2. The router uses the configuration register to locate the IOS software.

3. After the IOS is located, it's loaded to RAM and started.

4. The source of the configuration file is located.

5. The configuration file is copied into RAM from NVRAM or another source.

We discuss each of these steps in more detail in the following sections.

POST it up

The POST (Power On Self Test) on a Cisco router is similar to the POST that runs at startup on a personal computer. The router's POST checks its CPU, memory, and all interface ports to make sure that they're present and operational, just as the PC's POST checks its CPU, memory, and peripheral devices.

If all is well, the bootstrap (also called the boot) program is read from ROM and begins the process of locating and loading the IOS operating system.

Is your IOS registered?

The primary purpose of the bootstrap program is to find a valid Cisco IOS configuration image (see "Setting Up and Configuring a Router" earlier in the chapter) from a location specified by the router's configuration-register. The *configuration-register* contains the location from which the IOS software is to be loaded. The value representing the location of the IOS software can be changed using the **config-register** command from the global configuration mode. The hyphen between *config* and *register* should be there.

Typically, the Cisco IOS is loaded from flash memory (see Chapter 10), and that's the default value found in the configuration-register. The router looks for the IOS software to be in one of three places:

- Flash memory
- ROM
- TFTP server

The router knows where to look based on the value in the configuration-register. The configuration-register holds a hexadecimal value that designates the location of the IOS software. The value in the configuration-register actually supplies a bit pattern in the same pattern that can be configured with a hardware jumper block, as was used on very old routers.

Three configuration-register settings determine where the router should look for the boot system:

- **0x02 through 0x0F:** When the configuration-register has the hexadecimal value 0x02 through 0x0F (which represents 0010 and 1111 in binary), the router will look for boot system commands in startup-configuration to tell it where to find IOS. If no boot system commands are in the startup-configuration, the router searches in the default places: flash, then ROM, then a TFTP server.
- **0x00:** If the configuration-register value ends in 0x00 (binary 0000), the router will enter ROM Monitor Mode (see Chapter 8).
- **0x01:** If the configuration register value ends in 0x01, the router boots from ROM.

Changing your boots

If you want to change the source location from which you want the router to load the IOS system files, you can use these two things together:

- The command **boot system**
- The hexadecimal parameter that directs the router to the IOS source that you wish to use

It is the **boot system** command that the router looks for when the configuration-register tells it that the boot system commands are included in the startup-configuration.

If no **boot system** commands are in the startup-config, the router will search in the default places (flash, then ROM, and then a TFTP server). If the configuration-register value ends in 0x00, the router enters ROM monitor mode. If the configuration-register value ends in 0x01, the router boots from ROM.

The following **help** (?) command display shows the various parameters that can be used to tell the router where to look for the IOS.

```
Cisco_Network(config)#boot system ?
  WORD    System image filename
  flash   Boot from flash memory
  mop     Boot from a Decnet MOP server
  rcp     Boot from a server via rcp
  rom     Boot from rom
  tftp    Boot from a tftp server
```

The current setting of the configuration-register is displayed using the **show version** command.

Finding and loading the configuration

The startup-configuration file, like the IOS, can be loaded from other sources besides the NVRAM, such as a host or server on the network, or in cases where the configuration files are not where the IOS expected to find it, the configuration file can be loaded manually from a range of sources.

For example, to set the IOS to load the configuration file from a host on the network named "ws1," the following commands are used:

```
CNFD1# configure terminal
CNFD1(config)# boot host wk1
CNFD1(config)# service config
CNFD1(config)# ^Z
CNFD1# write memory
```

Otherwise, the startup-configuration file is located in NVRAM and loaded to RAM as the running-configuration file. Any changes made to the configuration after the router has booted are made to the running-configuration and must be saved to the startup-configuration to become permanent, if that is the desire.

It's not a trivial matter

Configuration files can also be stored outside the router itself. Using the Trivial File Transfer Protocol (TFTP), configuration files can be copied and stored on a TFTP server (any computer running the TFTP server software). In fact, after you've backed up a copy of the configuration files to the TFTP server, the configuration copy on the TFTP server can be used as the configuration source during the boot sequence.

Backing up to a TFTP host

The primary reason you would back up the configuration to an outside server is to ensure that the router has a source for its configuration even in the event that the configuration file on the router gets corrupted or accidentally (or possibly, quite intentionally) erased. If the router's configuration is corrupted or removed, the router's boot system can be directed via the configuration-register to look for a TFTP server. And yes, you may actually have reasons to erase the startup-configuration on purpose.

Hosting a TFTP party

A TFTP host can be any computer on a TCP/IP network that has the TFTP server software installed and is able to store files. Almost any computer on a Cisco network can be the TFTP host. Cisco has a shareware version of TFTP that can be downloaded from its Web site (www.cisco.com).

You should check for a few conditions before setting up a TFTP host:

- The IP (Internet Protocol) must be enabled, loaded, and running.
- You must be able to PING the router from the TFTP host.
- The TFTP host must have room for the downloaded configuration file.

Checking ahead for room

The **show flash** command can be used to determine the size of the startup-configuration file stored in flash. It looks like this:

```
Cisco_Networking>sh flash

System flash directory:
FileLength      Name/status
  1 6844384c3200-d-7_122-15.bin
[6844448 bytes used, 1544160 available, 8388608 total]
8192K bytes of processor board System flash (Read ONLY)
```

If you have more than one IOS version in flash, then you should use the **show version** command to display all the IOS files in flash. But beware that this command will not indicate which of the files represents the running-configuration.

Backing up the flash

You should have a backup copy of the router's flash memory on a TFTP server just in case the configuration file on the router gets corrupted or erased. Read over this sample of the code used and the results displayed by the router:

```
Cisco_Network(boot)#copy flash tftp
PCMCIA flash directory:
File  Length    Name/status
  1   3070408   c1600-y-1.111-12.AA
[3070472 bytes used, 1123832 available, 4194304 total]
Address or name of remote host [255.255.255.255]? 192.168.1.2
Source file name?  c1600-y-1.111-12.AA
Destination file name [c1600-y-1.111-12.AA]?
Verifying checksum for 'c1600-y-1.111-12.AA'
        (file # 1)...  OK
Copy 'c1600-y-1.111-12.AA' from Flash to server
  as 'c1600-y-1.111-12.AA'? [yes/no]yes
!!!!!!!!!!!!!!!!!!!!!!!!!!!!!!!!!!!!!!!!!!!!!!!!!!!!!!!!!!!!!!!!
           !!!!!!!!!!!!!!!!!!!!!
Upload to server done
Flash device copy took 00:00:52 [hh:mm:ss]
```

You can upgrade flash memory using the TFTP server. After you obtain an upgraded IOS image from Cisco, store it on the TFTP server and use the **copy TFTP flash** command to move it to the router's flash memory.

Saving your work

Two types of configuration files are stored on a router: startup and running. Both files can be copied to and from each other, as well as to and from the TFTP server. Why, you ask, would you copy these files to one another? Here's are the primary reasons why you would do so:

✔ **Running-configuration to startup configuration:** If you make changes to the configuration of a running router, those changes are made to the running-configuration. If you wish to save these changes and make them permanent, the running-configuration must be saved to the startup-configuration. Otherwise, the next time the router is booted, and the startup-configuration is loaded, all our your changes will be lost. Remember that at boot time, the startup configuration is loaded to RAM to become the running-configuration.

✔ **Startup-configuration to running-configuration:** You would copy the startup-configuration to the running-configuration to reset any changes you have made and did not save by copying the running-configuration to the startup-configuration. These changes could be configuration tests or mistakes. Rebooting the router causes the stored version of the system's configuration to be loaded to RAM as the running-configuration.

Use these commands to copy the files:

✔ **copy start tftp** — copies the startup-configuration to the TFTP server.

✔ **copy run tftp** — copies the running-configuration to the TFTP server.

✔ **copy tftp run** — copies the configuration stored on the TFTP server to the running-configuration file on the router.

✔ **copy tftp start** — copies the configuration stored on the TFTP server to the startup-configuration file on the router.

✔ **copy start run** — copies the startup-configuration from flash to the running-configuration in RAM.

✔ **copy run start** — saves the running-configuration to flash over-writing the previous version of the startup-configuration.

To use them, you must be in Privileged Exec mode — the one with the # character prompt.

This example code shows these commands as you would enter them on the router:

```
Cisco_Networking#copy start tftp
Cisco_Networking#copy run tftp
Cisco_Networking#copy tftp run
Cisco_Networking#copy tftp start
Cisco_Networking#copy start run
Cisco_Networking#copy run start
```

Using the command-completion help files that are built into the command line interface, you can simply type only the word "start" or "run" to indicate startup-configuration and running-configuration.

This sample code shows the console output that results from the command to copy the startup-configuration to a TFTP server:

```
Cisco_Network#copy star tftp
Remote host []? 192.168.1.5
Name of configuration file to write [Cisco_Network-confg]?
Write file Cisco_Network-confg on host 192.168.1.5? [confirm]
Writing Cisco_Network-confg !! [OK]
```

Covering your tracks

After updating the running-configuration, you should make sure that the startup-configuration is also updated. Probably the best way to do this is to simply copy the running-configuration to the startup-configuration. Use this command to accomplish that task:

```
Cisco_Network#copy run star
Building configuration...
```

If you forget to update the startup-configuration, or if you decide not to, the router will revert to its previous configuration the next time you boot, which could be actually what you planned all along.

A command performance

Table 11-1 includes a list of commands that you should know — and you should know when to use and why.

Table 11-1	Configuration Startup and Save Commands	
Command	*Action*	*When to Use*
show version	Displays the current software version	To verify the current software version and the name of the system image file
show config	Displays the startup-configuration, which includes the current passwords assigned, and information on the interfaces and routing protocols configured	To verify the overall configuration
show startup-config	Displays the startup-configuration	To verify the startup-configuration
show running-config	Displays the running-configuration, which is the configuration in use	To verify the running-configuration
setup	Begins the manual configuration prompting sequence	To enter or modify all or part of the router's configuration
write mem	Used in IOS versions 10.3 and earlier to save changes made to the running-configuration	Saves the running-configuration to the startup-configuration; performs the same action as **copy running-config startup-config**
reload	Copies the startup-configuration into RAM	To reset the running-configuration to the startup-configuration
erase startup-config	Deletes the startup-configuration in NVRAM	Probably never, unless you want to reset the router back into its initial startup and configuration states

You can store multiple IOS versions in NVRAM (flash). One way to free up space in NVRAM is to erase unused versions and buffers.

Approaching Configuration Manually

An alternative approach to setting up the configuration on a router is to do it through a manual configuration, which is what Cisco calls *completing the setup one step at a time,* as opposed to using the **setup** command. While requiring more time and attention to detail, it provides you with greater control over the resulting configuration. Using the **setup** command, as shown earlier in this chapter (see "Watch out, it's a setup!"), only a very basic configuration is enabled.

1. **Get in global configuration mode.**

2. **Begin entering each of the specific interfaces that you want to configure.**

   Interface means the ports and connection points on the router. Depending on the router model in use, this could include an Ethernet port, one or more serial ports, and others. Ethernet ports are designated by either the word Ethernet or the letter "e," followed by a sequence number, beginning with zero. Serial ports follow a similar pattern: the word serial or the letter "s" and an integer port number. For example, to designate the first Ethernet port, the code e0 can be used and for two serial ports, s1 and s2 can be used.

3. **Enter the IP address and subnet mask for each interface.**

   Remember that router interfaces are used by network nodes to address the router over a certain type of interface media and port. The subnet mask is used by the router to determine if additional routing is needed for traffic from the interface.

The following is a sample of the commands used to manually configure an Ethernet port on a router:

```
Cisco_Network#config t
Enter configuration commands, one per line.
          End with CNTL/Z.
Cisco_Network(config)#int e0
Cisco_Network(config-if)#
Cisco_Network(config-if)#IP address ?
  A.B.C.D  IP address
Cisco_Network(config-if)#IP address 192.168.1.6
% Incomplete command.
Cisco_Network(config-if)#IP address 192.168.1.6 255.255.255.0
```

To properly configure an Ethernet port, you must enter *both* the IP address and its subnet mask. For more information on IP addressing and subnet masks, see Chapter 7.

Chapter 12

Going the Full Route

The world of Cisco networking is a world built around routing. In a nutshell, routing is deciding the best path that a message should take to its destination and then sending the message out on that path. Some subtle distinctions should be made between the different variations of route, including routes, routing, and routed, and you should understand these distinctions.

Getting There Is All the Fun!

The most basic of all concepts to routing is that of a route. Routes on a network, such as the Internet, are similar to the interstate and local highway system around the United States. Just as you can choose any one of several routes to get from your house to Aunt Sally's on Sunday, a network can also provide several routes to a destination. And just like road construction and other obstacles can change the desirability of one route over another, the path from one computer to another over the network can also change. The core purpose of routing is deciding which of the available routes is the best route for each message. The key words to the preceding statement are *available* and *each*. Each message (or message segment) can be sent out over a different route. Because networks are dynamic environments, routes can change, and come and go.

Keeping it static and simple

Suppose that you have a favorite route you use when you drive over to Aunt Sally's. You know, the one where you can really let the old Pacer do its stuff. If you were to invariably use the same route every time you make this trip, you would be, if effect, using a static route. In this context, as well as most others, static means never changing, or fixed in place.

On a network, you (as the administrator) may want packets from one specific router to use a particular route to reach another specific router. Such a route, in the parlance of Cisco networking, is called a *static route*. The network administrator can enter static routes directly into the router (see Chapter 14) to specify that messages being sent to a particular destination address must use a single route.

A static route is a very simple instruction to the router. It essentially consists of only the address (usually the IP address) of the router that should be used to send messages to a certain network. In very simple terms, to send a message from a workstation on one network to a workstation on another network, the router on network A routes the message to the router on network B. (You can find more detail in Chapter 7.) The destination router takes care of getting the message to the destination workstation. A static route is used when there is only one choice available to get to a particular routing destination.

Dynamically speaking

Suppose that, during the summer, your favorite route to Aunt Sally's is under construction and as such loses its road-race appeal; you may need to look for other available routes. Your choice will likely be based on the distance, the sites along the way, and the time it takes to get to your destination. When you use this type of analysis to determine the most desirable route to take, you are performing dynamic routing.

An administrator can also configure a network router to use *dynamic routes*. The router can use information that it receives from other routers on the network to learn about and make judgments on the possible routes that it can use to destinations on the network.

Choosing the best route

Routers determine the best route for a packet to take to reach its destination. For some destinations there is only one way and one way only, other destinations have myriad routes that could be used to reach them. Because of these two situations, the network administrator must choose between using static or a dynamic routing as the means of choosing the best route.

Static routing

When a router is configured for static routing only, the administrator must manually update the router whenever a topology change occurs on the network. The change may be a new network segment, a new router added to a nearby network, or even a new neighboring network. These types of changes are topology changes. Using only static routing is probably not the best of choices on a network of any significant size because of the amount of maintenance that the administrator must do to keep the network routes up to date. Static routing may be preferable when you need to keep routing information private. Dynamic routing passes information about your network between routers, which are used to determine available routes. If you don't want to share routing information with other networks, use a static route.

Static routing is useful for certain networking situations. If only one route is available between networks A and B, a static route works nicely. Other examples are a *stub network,* a network with only one possible path, or a dial-on-demand network. In each of these cases, static routes provide the single route required and eliminate the operating overhead of dynamic routing. Default routes are also configured as static routes. When a router cannot determine the route to use for a particular packet destination, the traffic is forwarded along a static default route.

Later in this chapter, we will discuss routing algorithms (see "Routing to the Algorithm") and how they determine the best route for a packet to take. However, static routing algorithms aren't really algorithms at all. They are tables of route mappings that have been established manually by the network administrator. These tables do not change (meaning that they are static) until the administrator changes them.

Static routing systems are unable to react to topology changes in the network. As a result, they are generally not suited for use on a large, dynamic network. Static routes work best for network environments where the traffic is predictable and the network design is relatively simple.

Dynamic routing

In a dynamic routing environment, routers make decisions based on information they acquire from other routers about changes in the internetwork. Dynamic information in a router is updated automatically whenever information is received from the network about changes in the topology. This information is also passed on to other routers on the network in the form of routing updates.

Because of the rapid growth of networking, especially those connected to the Internet, most of the more commonly used routing algorithms are dynamic routing algorithms. Dynamic routing algorithms adjust to changes in the network by analyzing incoming routing update messages sent by other routers. If the routing update indicates that a topology change has occurred, the routing algorithm recalculates its routes and passes along this new routing information. As the routing update messages are passed around the network, each router dynamically recalculates its routing tables accordingly and the routing environment of the whole network may change. This is why you should use dynamic routing on networks connected to other networks, including the Internet, which it is safe to say is definitely a dynamic network.

Although dynamic routing will work in virtually all routing situations, it is especially useful in certain environments. For example, in situations where links go up and down frequently, no matter the reason, or where a destination has a number of possible paths, dynamic routing is a better choice over static routing because it eliminates the need for the constant reconfiguration that static routes would require.

Dynamically static routing

Cases exist where a dynamic routing algorithm can be given one or more static routes to use. An example of this is the *router of last resort* (a router to which all unroutable packets are sent), which is used when no other route can be determined for a packet's destination address so that all messages are at least handled in some way.

When a router does not know how to reach a destination network addressed by a message, it must somehow decide where to send the message. In cases such as this, the router uses its *default route.* By definition, a default route is the route used for a message when no specific information is available about the destination network. There isn't a great deal of difference between the router of last resort and the default route.

Another usage for a static route in a dynamic environment is for routing paths that you wish to keep private. Static routes are not included in the dynamic routing updates sent out to other routes. By using a static route, a routing path that rarely changes or is secure remains virtually unknown to the internetwork.

Are You Routing or Merely Routed?

Before we get too far into our discussion on dynamic routing, we should review the differences between *routed* protocols and *routing* protocols.

- **Routed protocol:** Using a *routed protocol,* a router examines the addressing of any incoming messages, makes a determination on how best to forward it to its destination, and then forwards the message to that destination.

- **Routing protocol:** *Routing protocols* are used by a router to learn about neighboring networks to which it has access and which of its ports it should use to reach each network.

Using a routed protocol, such as IP and IPX (see Chapters 7 and 8 for more information on the IP and IPX protocols), the router examines the data packet looking for the destination address and then cross-checks the destination address with its internal table to determine from which path it should forward the data packet.

However, when multiple paths exist to a network, the router must decide which path is the best route to that network. The details of how this happens depend on the routing protocol being used. (We cover this in some detail later in this chapter.) Examples of routing protocols include Routing Information Protocol (RIP), Interior Gateway Routing Protocol (IGRP), Open Shortest Path First (OSPF), NetWare Link Services Protocol (NLSP), Intermediate System to Intermediate System (IS-IS), and Enhanced Interior Gateway Routing Protocol (EIGRP).

Routers keep all their static routes and information about all their dynamic routes in the routing table. The routing table, which is an interior table to the router, is maintained by the network administrator and dynamically updated by routing protocols through routing updates. This ensures the best and latest information regarding possible routes on the network that are or aren't available to the router.

Unless the routing table is completely full of static routes and no routing protocol is in use, which is a true waste of a good router, the routing table is constantly being updated. As networks appear and disappear, the routing information for each of the router's ports is upgraded to reflect the true status of the network. Remember that a network is seen only through its router to other routers. Should a router fail or someone trip over its power cord, all other networks showing it as a possible route will be updated to show that its network is unavailable until the problem is fixed.

The *routing table* contains entries that match up destination addresses or ranges to information that helps the router determine the best available (or only) route to get a packet to a destination address, including the IP address of the destination host or network, the gateway or next upstream router (hop) used to reach each destination address, the router interface through which the packet must be sent to reach the gateway, plus metrics used in the route calculations. The routing table's contents are determined by the routing protocol in use. Most Cisco routers use RIP, but there are others commonly used as well. See "Routing to the Algorithm," later in this chapter, for more information on routing protocols.

Here is an example of the information found in a router's routing table:

Destination	Next Hop	Metric	Interface	Protocol
63.23.104.232	63.23.104.2	1	e1	static
192.63.0.0	162.23.145.11	3	e0	rip
202.0.0.0	202.11.124.2	1	e0	rip
203.98.123.0	192.87.34.2	2	s1	local

Worldly routers are multiprotocol

In general, Cisco routers offer *multiprotocol rout-ing*, the ability to support more than one routing protocol at a time. A router that supports multi-protocol routing maintains separate routing tables for each routing protocol. Depending on the routed protocol in use, the router looks at the associated table and makes its routing decisions accordingly.

Here is a brief description of the router table entries:

- **Destination:** The IP address of a remote host or a router to which pack-ets are to be sent. On the third line of this example, notice that any packet addressed to any node on the network under 202.0.0.0 will be for-warded using that router table entry.

- **Next Hop:** This is the address of the next router (gateway) to which the packet will be sent to reach the destination address.

- **Metric:** This is usually how many hops (routers) the packet will traverse to reach its destination's network.

- **Interface:** The port on the router that the packet should use to reach its destination.

- **Protocol:** Which routing protocol is used to maintain the information on this route.

The Dynamics of Routing

One thing about networks, especially those that are connected to other net-works, is that keeping up with the neighbors can be a very dynamic exercise. As other networks come and go, the number and permutations of available routes from one network to another is very dynamic. This is why dynamic routing should be used on networks connected to other networks, including the Internet. In fact, networks that are interconnected to form a larger net-work, create what is called the internetwork. An *internetwork* is a network of networks interconnected by routers so that it operates as one large dynamic network. The Internet is an example of a very large (the largest) internetwork. In fact, the Internet gets its name from the word internetwork. A local net-work may not be a part of an internetwork if it has no connection to an out-side network or its routers are used only for internal purposes. But, if that local network were to connect to the Internet or to any other WAN through a router, it then becomes a part of an internetwork.

Using multiprotocol routing with dynamically assigned routes is an effective solution when a router must forward different routed protocols to different destination networks based on the protocol being routed. Figures 12-1 and 12-2 illustrate how dynamic routing increases the deliverability of data packets across an internetwork. When Host A sends a packet destined for Host B with a static route from Router 1 to Router 2 to Router 3, the packet will arrive if both links, Router 1 to Router 2 and Router 2 to Router 3, are up (Figure 12-1). But if the link between either is down, the packet cannot be delivered (Figure 12-2). This would require that the administrator reconfigure the router with a new static route through Router 1 to Router 4 to Router 3.

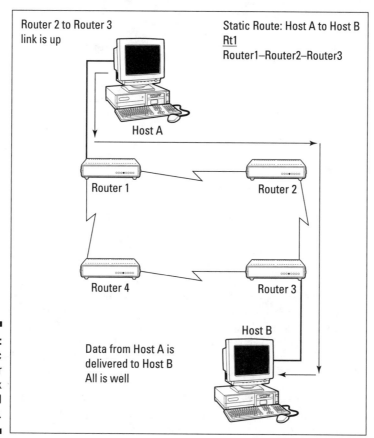

Figure 12-1:
Static
routes over
a network
with all
links intact.

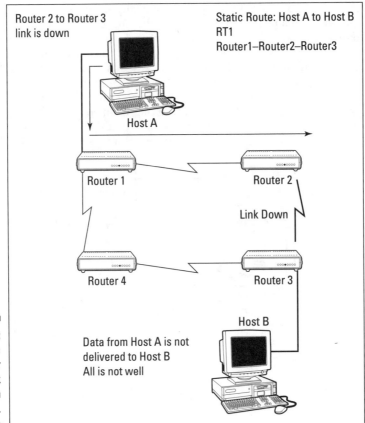

Router 2 to Router 3
link is down

Static Route: Host A to Host B
RT1
Router1–Router2–Router3

Host A

Router 1

Router 2

Link Down

Router 4

Router 3

Host B

Data from Host A is not
delivered to Host B
All is not well

Figure 12-2:
Static
routes over
a network
with broken
links.

When Host A sends a packet destined for Host B, assuming that dynamic routing is in use from Host A to Host B, the packet arrives if either route is available — Router 1 to Router 2 and Router 2 to Router 3, or Router 1 to Router 4 to Router 3 (Figure 12-3). If any one link in either route is down, the packet is delivered (Figure 12-4) through the alternative route without intervention by the administrator.

We are sorry to scare you by invoking the word *mathematics* into this, but dynamic routing involves the use of a number of calculations and algorithms to determine the best available route for a packet. Don't worry, the router does all of the calculating and such.

Two functions are necessary for dynamic routing to be successful:

✔ **Well-maintained routing tables:** How well-maintained the routing tables are is determined by a combination of the efforts of the network administrator staying on top of things within his or her own network and the quality of the information provided the router through dynamic routing updates.

✔ **Timely delivery of network topology changes between routers:** The delivery of network topology information between routers is carried out by routing protocols. The maintenance of the routing tables is the primary mission of a group of algorithms, which determine the best available routes and update the routing table.

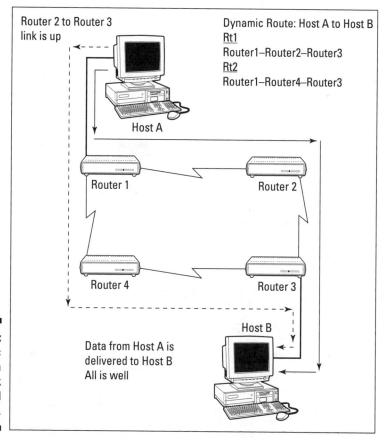

Figure 12-3:
Dynamic routing on a network with all links up.

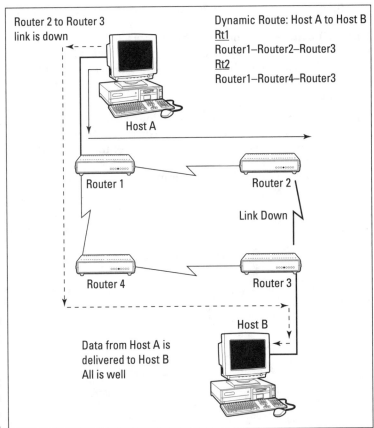

Router 2 to Router 3
link is down

Dynamic Route: Host A to Host B
<u>Rt1</u>
Router1–Router2–Router3
<u>Rt2</u>
Router1–Router4–Router3

Host A

Router 1   Router 2

Link Down

Router 4   Router 3

Host B

Data from Host A is
delivered to Host B
All is well

Figure 12-4:
Dynamic
routing on a
network
with broken
links.

Routing to the Algorithm

You'll find three basic types of routing algorithms:

- ✓ **Distance vector:** RIP and IGRP are distance vector routing protocols commonly used on a Cisco network. See "Hopping to the RIP" for more information on the RIP.

- ✓ **Link-state:** As a group, link-state protocols, which pass information about neighbors and path costs, are called *shortest path first* (SPF) protocols. OSPF is the link-state protocol most commonly used on Cisco network. See "Putting the Router into a Link-State" for more information on link-state routing protocols.

✔ **Balanced hybrid:** This type of routing protocol uses a combination of link-state and distance vector protocols to learn the network topology and to resolve issues associated with convergence. Examples of a balanced hybrid protocol are IS-IS and EIGRP. See "Striking a Balance with Hybrid Protocols" for more information on balanced hybrid protocols.

Adding up the metrics

Each algorithm defines just what is a best route in its own way, but it does produce a number, called a *metric,* that is used to evaluate the routes. The metrics produced by the routing algorithms measure some time element in the route. Each metric may measure a single characteristic of a route, or it may be a combination of weighted characteristics. Typically, the lower a route's metric, the better the route.

Some standard routing metrics are used in Cisco routers:

✔ **Hop count:** Each router through which a packet must pass is considered a hop. Counting the hops on a route gives an indication of the path's length. The lower the path length, the better the route.

✔ **Ticks:** Each tick represents one-eighteenth of a second and represents a delay across a route.

✔ **Cost:** The cost of a path is an arbitrary value associated with each link crossed on the path. Slower links typically have a higher cost associated with them than do faster links. The route with the lowest total path cost is typically the route selected as the fastest.

✔ **Bandwidth:** The maximum throughput of a link, in terms of bits per second, is considered its bandwidth. The route with the highest bandwidth is considered to be the fasted route possible. This is not always the case, because a high-bandwidth link may already have too many users sending data across the link, effectively slowing the link. A link with a lower bandwidth may not have as many users and be able to send the data instantly.

✔ **Delay:** The summation of many factors results in a delay rating, a commonly used metric. These factors include link bandwidth, router queue length, network congestion, and physical distance.

✔ **Load:** This is a dynamic factor that is based on such items as router processor utilization and packets processed per second. Although it's an effective metric, the monitoring of these items may require high resource demand.

✔ **Reliability:** This is a combination of how often a link fails and how long it takes to bring the link back up. Other measures may be included in the overall reliability rating. Typically, the administrator assigns this rating, although some protocols can dynamically calculate the rating for you.

✔ **Expense:** For some operations, it is more important to consider operating costs than performance for a network. Including an expense metric allows the administrator to factor in the monetary cost of a route so that it will be considered in routing decisions. Don't confuse this with the cost metric (which refers to the number of hops and the cost to transfer speed of each hop). The expense metric refers to the actually dollar value of a link.

✔ **MTU (maximum transmission unit):** This metric relates to the maximum length of a message across the entire path measured in octets (8 bits).

Determining the distance vector

You know how you have to decide which store to go to for chips and drinks so that you miss the least amount of the game? In much the same way, distance vector protocols determine the distance and direction to an address on an internetwork. It isn't important how the streets are laid out, only that one store is six blocks and the other is across town.

A router that uses a distance vector protocol periodically passes a copy of its entire routing table to its neighboring routers. A distance vector routing protocol only knows how far it is from to an individual destination, but it doesn't know the actual topology of the internetwork. When the topology of an internetwork changes, all the routers affected pass copies of their routing tables to the all adjoining routers.

Figure 12-5 graphically depicts how these routing table updates occur. Router 1 is directly connected to both Router 2 and Router 6; Router 2 is connected to Routers 1 and 3; Router 3 is connected to Routers 2 and 4; Router 4 is connected to Routers 3 and 5; and Router 5 is connected to Routers 4 and 6. Router 1 sends a periodic update of its routing table to Routers 2 and 6, the routers to which it is directly connected. Likewise, Router 2 sends its updates to Routers 1 and 3; Router 5 sends its updates to Routers 6 and 4, and so on. As you look at Figure 12-5, also remember that routers know each other only by their IP addresses and not the names given to them by administrators.

Using hop count as the distance metric, the routing tables of each router would resemble those depicted in Figure 12-6. As illustrated in Figure 12-5, quite a bit of information is being passed back and forth between routers in order to maintain their routing tables.

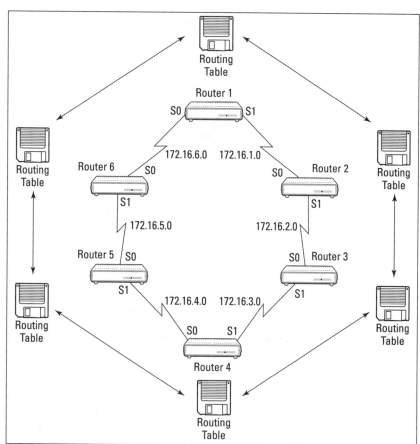

Figure 12-5:
An inter-
network.

Router 1		
Network	Port	Disc
172.16.6.0	S0	0
172.16.1.0	S1	0
172.16.5.0	S0	1
172.16.2.0	S1	1
172.16.4.0	S0	2
172.16.3.0	S1	2

Router 2		
Network	Port	Disc
172.16.1.0	S0	0
172.16.2.0	S1	0
172.16.6.0	S0	1
172.16.3.0	S1	1
172.16.5.0	S0	2
172.16.4.0	S1	2

Router 3		
Network	Port	Disc
172.16.2.0	S0	0
172.16.3.0	S1	0
172.16.1.0	S0	1
172.16.4.0	S1	1
172.16.6.0	S0	2
172.16.5.0	S1	2

Router 4		
Network	Port	Disc
172.16.4.0	S0	0
172.16.3.0	S1	0
172.16.5.0	S0	1
172.16.2.0	S1	1
172.16.6.0	S0	2
172.16.1.0	S1	2

Router 5		
Network	Port	Disc
172.16.5.0	S0	0
172.16.4.0	S1	0
172.16.6.0	S0	1
172.16.3.0	S1	1
172.16.1.0	S0	2
172.16.2.0	S1	2

Router 6		
Network	Port	Disc
172.16.6.0	S0	0
172.16.5.0	S1	0
172.16.1.0	S0	1
172.16.4.0	S1	1
172.16.2.0	S0	2
172.16.3 .0	S1	2

Figure 12-6:
Sample
routing
tables using
a distance
vector
metric.

Neverending Hops on Distance Vector Protocols

When all of the routers on an internetwork are up to date on the current topology of the internetwork, a state of *convergence* exists. Convergence is good. You may ask yourself, and you should, "What happens if the routers don't contain current information about the internetwork?" Good question, self. The answer is simple: *routing loops.* Routing loops, which are bad, exist when a packet is allowed an unlimited number of hops to reach its destination. For example, if the packet is trying to reach an unknown and non-existent address, the packet could hop around forever. This condition is known as a *counting to infinity* loop. These loops happen because no limits are set for the number of hops that a packet can take. The solutions, and there must be some, involve setting a hop limit on a packet. You know, we think you're really picking this stuff up.

Solving the infinite loop problem

Several solutions are available to solve counting to infinity loop problems for distance vector routing protocols:

- **Maximum hops:** Only in routing can infinity actually be less than 15. One solution for counting to infinity loops is to set a maximum number of hops as being equal to infinity. Routing protocols have maximum loop counts. For example, RIP (Routing Information Protocol) has a default maximum hop count of 16. If the hop count is greater than 15, the router assumes that the destination network is unreachable.

- **Time To Live (TTL):** This parameter is contained in some routing protocol packets. A TTL factor is a countdown parameter that is reduced by one each time its packet is examined by a router. If the resulting TTL is equal to 0, meaning it has no time to live, the router discards the packet without forwarding it.

- **Split horizon:** In addition to eliminating routing loops, the split horizon technique also helps speed an internetwork's time to convergence. Essentially, the split horizon technique instructs a router to only send information about a route to the originator of the information if the new information is better than that already received. This means that if Router A sends a routing update to Router B about a certain routing destination, Router B will only inform Router A of updates to that destination should its update information contain a lower metric than what Router A included in its original route information. Complicated? Not really, but it sure sounds like it.

✔ **Poison reverse:** A derivative of the split horizon technique, poison reverse helps solve routing loops by simply making an entry in its routing table that a given route is unreachable. When a router receives an update from a neighboring router indicating that the poisoned route is reachable through it, the router simply ignores the update for that route until a certain amount of time has passed. The poison reverse technique is implemented in conjunction with hold-down timers.

✔ **Hold-down timers:** This routing mechanism is used to block regular update messages that incorrectly indicate that a link is available when, in fact, it isn't. Hold-down timers instruct a router not to accept regular updates on a particular route until a specified time period has expired. The specific time is calculated to be just a bit more than the time needed for the internetwork to reach convergence.

Removing the restraint

Three situations can remove a hold-down timer on a router. First, we'll create a situation in which a hold-down timer would be implemented, and then we'll list the situations in which the hold-down timer would be removed. Refer to Figure 12-7 when reading the hold-down timer scenario and the removal situations.

A state of convergence exists on the internetwork depicted in Figure 12-7, and the world is at peace. Suddenly, a series of events turns this peace into madness. Network 172.16.1.0 goes down. The hop count in Router 3's routing table indicates that Network 172.16.1.0 is 1 hop away. Router D notifies Router C through a triggered update that network 172.16.1.0 is now unreachable. Router C poisons the route and starts a hold-down timer on updates about Network 172.16.1.0. Regular updates are sent from Router A to Router B indicating that it has access to network 172.16.1.0 with a hop count of 3 and Router B forwards a regular update on to Router 3 indicating that it has access to network 172.16.1.0 with a hop count of 4 via Router A. Of course, because it has a hold-down time on a poisoned route, Router C ignores the information from Router B.

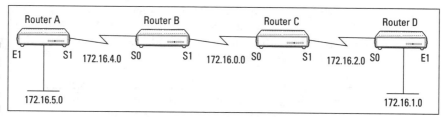

Figure 12-7:
An inter-
network.

In the following situations, the hold-down timer would be removed prior to its expiration, allowing the internetwork to reach convergence:

- ✔ If Router D, the original messenger, sends a new update indicating that Network 172.16.1.0 is once again available, the hold-down timer is removed from Router C.

- ✔ If Router C receives an update from an adjoining router (say, Router B) that indicates that it (Router B) has access to Network 172.16.1.0 and that its (Router B's) hop count is less than the hop count Router C has in its router table, the hold-down timer is removed from Router C. This system ignores any updates received while a hold-down timer is active that contain a poorer (meaning higher) metric than exists for the poisoned route, which allows additional time for convergence to occur.

- ✔ When the hold-down timer expires, the route to Network 172.16.1.0 remains poisoned in Router C's routing table, but Router C will now at least accept any updates regarding routes to Network 172.16.1.0.

Be careful with that trigger, please

Triggered updates are critical to resolving routing loops. A *triggered update* results when a router senses that a link to which it is directly connected has changed from available to unavailable or the reverse. (In the situation described in the preceding section, Router 4 sent a triggered update to Router 3 to notify it that Network 172.16.1.0 was no longer available.) This discovery triggers an update event in which the router immediately notifies its neighbors. Unfortunately, some time passes before a chain reaction of triggered updates can be spread across an internetwork, and during the propagation time, regular updates can be sent across the network with erroneous information.

Hopping to the RIP

RIP (Routing Information Protocol) is a distance vector protocol that uses hop count as its metric for selecting the best path to a destination address. RIP has a usable hop count of 15. A maximum of 16 hops, RIP's version of infinity, indicates that a destination address is unreachable. RIP routing updates are broadcast every 30 seconds by default.

One of the benefits of RIP is its ability to perform load balancing when multiple paths exist. Load balancing is the ability to use multiple equal distance paths to deliver data to a destination. By default load balancing with RIP is enabled with four parallel paths.

RIP is the most basic routing protocol and is best applied to a small internetwork. Virtually every router supports a common implementation of RIP, which allows routers from different manufacturers to co-exist on an internetwork.

RIPing up the router

RIP is configured with the command **router rip** in the global configuration mode (see Chapter 14), which is indicated by the prompt

```
IDG_Books(config)#
```

In this example, IDG_Books represents the name that has been assigned to the router (see Chapter 14).

After entering the **router rip** command, the attached network must be defined with the **network network-number** command.

```
IDG_Books (config)#router rip
```

Given a network number (in other words, an IP address) of 10.1.0.0, the command to define the attached network is

```
IDG_Books(config-router)#network 10.1.0.0
```

If the router is connected to more than one network, the additional networks also need to be entered. Each network is entered in the same format as the first network. After all networks have been configured, the router is configured and has permission to send routing updates (called *advertisements*) to other RIP routers associated with each attached network.

Showing off your RIP

To view a router's RIP information, you can use any of the following three commands:

- ✔ **show ip protocol:** This command displays information about routing timers and the network information associated with the entire router. This is a valuable command when attempting to identify a router sending faulty routing information.

- ✔ **show ip route:** This command displays the entire contents of the IP routing table in the RIP router, including codes that indicate how the router learned about each path.

- ✔ **debug ip rip:** This command displays RIP routing updates as they come into and are sent out of the router, including information about the interface through which an update arrives. You must be in Privileged Exec mode to use the debug command.

Each of these commands is entered from the user mode on a router, which is indicated by the *router_name>* prompt, such as

```
IDG_Books>
```

We discuss these commands in more detail in Chapters 13 and 14.

Using IGRP for Advanced Routing

IGRP (Interior Gateway Routing Protocol) is a more advanced distance vector routing protocol originally developed by Cisco Systems in the mid-1980s. Because of its advanced features, which include scalability, rapid response to topology changes, sophisticated metrics, and multi-path support, nearly all router manufacturers now support it.

In contrast to RIP's default update time of 30 seconds, IGRP broadcasts periodic updates every 90 seconds, whether it needs to or not. Flash updates (IGRP's version of triggered updates) are sent out when an IGRP router detects a network topology change, such as a route becoming inactive or a new route being added to the internetwork.

IGRP is a distance vector protocol that does not use up lots of system resources and, as a result, can operate on large internetworks on less expensive routers than other protocols. For example, unlike RIP, IGRP does not use a maximum hop count to limit routing loops. Instead, IGRP uses flash updates which really speeds up the time to convergence. Most distance vector protocols, including RIP, have longer convergence times.

By default, IGRP considers only a network's bandwidth and the amount of network delay in its metric. The network administrator can configure other options to create a composite metric that can include such other metrics as reliability and network load. This provides the administrator with greater flexibility in setting up a router's path determination scheme. IGRP by default supports four paths, but can be configured for six paths, to a destination network, providing for both increased bandwidth and route diversity.

When the timer goes off, take the poison and split

IGRP uses the same routing loop control techniques found in RIP (see "Hopping to the RIP," earlier in this chapter), including poison reverse, hold-down timers, and split horizon. However, IGRP has slightly different rules for the use of each technique. This section provides a brief description of how IGRP uses each technique:

 ✔ **Poison reverse:** IGRP sends out poison reverse updates when a route metric increases by a factor of 1.1.

 ✔ **Hold-down timer:** The IGRP hold-down timer is set to three times the periodic update interval, plus 10 seconds. This means that because the default update interval is 90 seconds, the hold-down timer setting is 280 seconds.

 ✔ **Split horizon:** Using the split horizon technique increases the speed of convergence on an IGRP internetwork because route updates are not sent back across the same route. If a router does not receive an update about a route for three consecutive update periods, that route is marked as unreachable. If seven update periods pass without a route update, that route is removed from the routing table, which helps to reduce the size of routing tables stored in the router's memory.

Setting up IGRP

To configure IGRP on a router, you must be in the global configuration mode, the one with a prompt like the following:

```
IDG_Books(config)#
```

To configure the router, enter the command **router igrp autonomous-system-number**, where the *autonomous system number* (ASN) is a globally unique number used to identify your internetwork.

```
IDG_Books(config)#router igrp 232
```

After entering this command, you must associate the network number (IP address) of all connected networks to the router using the **network network-number** command:

```
IDG_Books(config-router)#network 10.1.0.0
```

This command must be repeated for each network connected to the router for which you want to establish an IGRP link.

Checking out the IGRP status

After your router is configured for IGRP, you can view the information associated with IGRP functions, through the following commands:

 ✔ **show ip protocols:** The **show ip protocols** command displays parameters, filters, and network information for all networks configured on the router.

✔ **show ip interfaces:** The **show ip interfaces** command displays the status and global parameters associated with available interfaces.

✔ **show ip route:** The **show ip route** command displays the entire contents of the IP routing table contained in the IGRP or RIP router, including codes that indicate how the router learned about each path.

✔ **debug ip igrp transaction** and **debug ip igrp events:** The **debug** commands display similar information about transactions and events occurring on the specified networks.

The **show** commands can be entered from the user Exec mode, but the **debug** commands must be entered from the Privileged Exec mode. See Chapters 11 and 13 for more information on user Exec and Privileged Exec modes. You may also want check out the Glossary at the back of the book.

Putting the Router into a Link-State

Link-state protocols, also known as Shortest Path First (SPF) algorithms, maintain a complex database about an internetwork's topology, including information about other routers and how those routers interconnect, inside each router. This database provides each link-state router with a common view of the entire internetwork. Link-state routing protocols commonly used on Cisco networks include NLSP, OSPF, and IS-IS, which are described in this section.

A link-state router uses more processing power and memory than a distance-vector router because it is storing more information in memory and executing algorithms to calculate SPF trees and routing tables. Initially, link-state routers flood the network with LSPs ("Hello's") to learn who their neighbors are. After the initial flooding, link-state routers use only a little bandwidth for their periodic or topology-change triggered LSP updates.

Getting to know the internetwork

Link-state protocols use a complex five-step process to learn about the internetwork of which they are a part (see Figure 12-8):

1. A link-state router learns from all the other routers in the autonomous system the status of any adjoining routers and keeps track of those routers in its routing table.

2. The router transmits link-state packets (LSPs), which are also known as "Hello" packets to all the other routers in the autonomous system.

   Each friendly LSP contains all the information the router knows about the networks to which it is directly connected.

3. Using the information provided by the LSPs from all the other routers in the autonomous system, the router builds its topological database.

4. The router processes this information through the SPF algorithm to determine the shortest possible path to every reachable network on the link-state protocol internetwork.

   This results in the creation of an SPF tree with the router at its root.

5. The router then uses the SPF tree to enter the best path to each network into its routing table.

As changes occur in a link-state internetwork, the routers that initially become aware of the change send out notifications to other routers or to a designated master update router that makes sure that all other routers become aware of the changes. Each router then proceeds through the five-step process to recalculate its individual routing tables with the new shortest routes to each network.

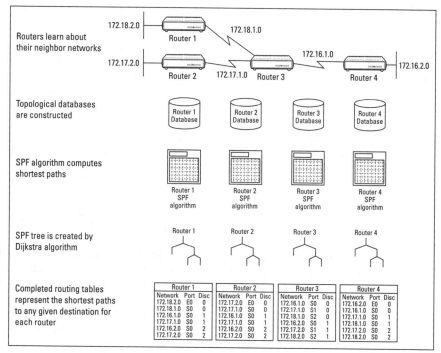

Figure 12-8:
The five steps in link-state routing.

Living in the link-state world

It is essential that all routers on a link-state internetwork view the internetwork topology with a common point-of-view, which is no easy task, to say the least. Because each router calculates its routing table entries from the LSP information that it receives, some routers on the internetwork can do so using different LSP information. This can result in the internetwork being split into two or more routing segments, which can result in slower connections between some routers, LSP updates being improperly synchronized, and insufficient processing power to keep up with all the tasks being performed.

To solve the various faulty LSP transmission problems, the well-read administrator will implement one or a combination of the following solutions:

✔ **Configure the router to send LSPs at larger intervals.** This increases the time for convergence to occur and does not interfere with triggered updates caused by a change in the internetwork topology.

✔ **Configure the router to use a multicast approach to sending LSPs, instead of the flood approach typically used.** This allows a small group of routers to act as masters of the internetwork's topology data.

✔ **Segment the internetwork into LSP domains with a master topology router for each domain.** This effectively reduces the size of the internetwork, reducing the chance of inconsistent LSP information because of synchronization or transmission speed issues.

✔ **Tag the LSPs with link-state enabled internetworks.** Tagging allows the LSPs to be flagged with time stamps, sequence numbers, aging schemes, and other mechanisms that help to verify that the most current topology data is used by the routers.

IS-IS spelled backwards is SI-SI

IS-IS (Intermediate System to Intermediate System) routing exchange protocol was developed by ANSI (American National Standards Association) as a link-state routing protocol. Based on an SPF routing algorithm, IS-IS shares all the advantages common to other link-state protocols. It also routes both IP packets and pure OSI packets in their natural state, with no extra encapsulation because IS-IS is able to handle both packet types by design. IS-IS supports type of service (TOS) identifiers, IP subnetting, variable subnet masks, external routing, and authentication.

IS-IS routing decisions are based on a two-level scheme. Level 1 routers know only the topology of their local network. Level 2 routers know of other level 2 routers on the internetwork and the addresses that are reachable. If a level 1 router has no knowledge of a specific destination address, it passes the traffic to a level 2 router.

The best place to use the IS-IS protocol is on an internetwork router that must transport both IP packets and pure OSI packets. You should make sure that all IS-IS routers are interoperable. Some manufacturers have proprietary implementations of IS-IS that will not communicate with other manufacturers' equipment.

Routing in the NetWare world with NLSP

NLSP (NetWare Link Services Protocol) is the Novell derivative of the IS-IS standard that was developed as a link-state replacement for Novell's IPX RIP and SAP (Service Advertising Protocol), which were designed to primarily handle small, local networks and are not well-suited to large, global networks. NLSP is backward-compatible with both IPX RIP and SAP, so migrating a Novell network to a link-state routing protocol is easy.

NLSP routers use three databases to make routing decisions:

- **Adjacency database:** This database contains information taken from responses to Hello (LSP) broadcasts sent out by each NLSP router, which could actually be a NetWare server with NLSP enabled.
- **Link-state database:** This is the common database on all routers in the area. It is also built using the information in the Hello responses.
- **Forwarding database:** This database contains the best path from a specific router to each possible destination. Each router has different paths to each destination and thus the forwarding databases on each router are different.

After all the routers have learned about each other, they hold an election to designate one router per LAN segment as the designated router responsible for communicating the topological information about its segment to all other areas of the internetwork.

NLSP also uses a three-level hierarchy for communications:

- **Level 1** consists of communications between routers within a single area.
- **Level 2** consists of communications between routers across two areas.
- **Level 3** consists of communications between routing domains (groups of areas).

NLSP should only be enabled on a Novell NetWare network running IPX. Remember that starting with Novell Netware 5.0, IPX is only an option because Novell has finally embraced TCP/IP as its standard protocol for network communications.

Finding the shortest path, first

The OSPF (Open Shortest Path First) routing protocol is a creation of the IETF (Internet Engineering Task Force), and it too is a derivative of the OSI IS-IS standard. OSPF is an *open standard,* which means that it is available to all manufacturers of routing equipment to help to ensure interoperability.

Similar to NLSP, OSPF utilizes three databases to make routing decisions:

- ✔ **Adjacency:** The adjacency database contains information about OSPF neighbors.

- ✔ **Topology:** The topology database is based on the adjacency database and maintains information about all available routes.

- ✔ **Route:** The route database stores the best route to each known destination.

An OSPF router uses Hello packets to announce its existence to any other OSPF routers in its local area. After neighboring routers have sent back hello responses and adjacency database entries are created, a router and a backup router are designated to control communications with other autonomous systems. The primary routing metric used with OSPF is bandwidth.

OSPF is best applied to growing networks consisting of routers from multiple manufacturers or in medium to large networks consisting of routers from multiple manufacturers.

Striking a Balance with Hybrid Protocols

Balanced hybrid protocols use a combination of the features available from link-state protocols and distance vector protocols to learn the network topology and to resolve issues associated with convergence. The best example of a balanced hybrid protocol used on a Cisco network is EIGRP. Although technically a link-state protocol, IS-IS (see the section "IS-IS spelled backwards is SI-SI" earlier in the chapter) can be categorized as a balanced hybrid protocol as well. Balanced hybrid protocols use distance vectors to determine the best paths to destination networks, but they use more sophisticated metrics in their determinations. Convergence occurs quickly using the balanced hybrid approach similarly to link-state protocols. Balanced hybrid protocols, however, focus on the economy of resource requirements, including bandwidth, memory, and processor utilization.

EIGRP (Enhanced Interior Gateway Routing Protocol), a proprietary protocol developed by Cisco, is a very stable and scalable protocol. However, if you mix router manufacturers on your internetwork, you must also enable a secondary routing protocol, because EIGRP will function only between Cisco routers.

EIGRP utilizes three databases to determine the best path selection for reaching a destination:

- ✔ **Route:** The route database contains information about the best routes to destinations.

- ✔ **Topology:** The topology database contains information about all routes to destinations.

- ✔ **Neighbor:** The neighbor database contains information about other neighboring EIGRP.

EIGRP is capable of routing three different protocols: IP, IPX, and AppleTalk, and when a router is enabled for all three protocols, EIGRP creates a total of nine databases, three for each protocol.

EIGRP uses a process called *route tagging,* which identifies the source (internal or external) of a new route during a session. The Hello protocol is used to establish formal neighbor relationships, which is called *peering.* EIGRP sends routing updates only for the changes and not for the entire routing table. EIGRP also supports IP subnets, variable length subnet masking, and equal path load balancing, and it allows the administrator to select the metric used to calculate the best path.

Verification of proper EIGRP performance is completed with any combination of the following six parameters, which are placed after the **show ip** command:

- ✔ **route eigrp:** Displays the routing table's EIGRP entries

- ✔ **eigrp neighbors:** Displays all the neighboring EIGRP routers

- ✔ **eigrp topology:** Displays all the topology table's EIGRP entries

- ✔ **eigrp traffic:** Displays a count for both sent and received EIGRP packets

- ✔ **protocols:** Displays active protocols session information

- ✔ **eigrp events:** Displays log entries of EIGRP events such as route additions

EIGRP is an excellent choice for a network of any size that will be growing with Cisco equipment. When non-Cisco routers are included with Cisco routers, a second routing protocol is necessary, because EIGRP communicates only between Cisco equipment.

Running for the border gateway protocol

BGP (Border Gateway Protocol) is used by all network entities that make up the Internet. Unless you are the system administrator at a regional ISP or the Layer 3 engineer in a large corporation with a large private WAN, you may never need to use BGP.

BGP is used in two situations. One: connecting to two or more ISPs and attempting to balance the load over multiple connections. Two: connecting an enterprise network to multiple ISPs and attempting to load balance over multiple links.

BGP comes in two flavors:

✔ **Internal BGP (iBGP)** is used between routers within an autonomous system. Route information from one iBGP router is not shared with other iBGP peer routers.

✔ **External BGP (eBGP)** is used between routers located in different autonomous systems to inject routes owned by one autonomous system into another autonomous system.

BGP utilizes several metrics in determining the best route to a destination, including those listed below:

✔ **Weight:** This metric allows a system administrator to manually assign values to learned paths.

✔ **Local preference:** This metric is used by system administrators to assign values to routes when multiple paths exist.

✔ **MED (Multi-Exit Discriminator):** This metric identifies which path to use when separate autonomous systems are connected with multiple paths.

Part IV
Managing a Cisco Network

The 5th Wave   By Rich Tennant

"You the guy having trouble staying connected to the network?"

In this part . . .

This part could just as easily have been titled "Working with a Cisco Network" or "Administrating a Cisco Network," but the title we ended up choosing better reflected the nature of the administrator's job. Cisco networks must be managed, which includes administration, configuration, monitoring, and in most situations, cussing, stomping, praying, pouting, and sacrificing network segments to the gods.

This part of the book provides an overview of how the network administrator works with a Cisco router, including working with the command line interface, muddling through the configuration processes, providing for security, and delving into the "s-words" — subnet, subnet mask, and subnetting. See, we told you there was cussing involved.

Chapter 13

Working at the Command Line

*T*his chapter covers only the most basic router commands and operations, so nothing in it is especially mentally taxing. However, you should have a steel-trap grasp on these commands, concepts, and operations because this is the stuff you work with day-in and day-out. We guide you through the processes used to log into a router from a variety of different sources. Although you can use more than 17 different operating modes after you have logged in, you should only use about 6 of them in real day-to-day life.

This may not be the most important chapter in the book, but it's certainly among the top 30. If you've had some good hands-on experience with Cisco routers, chances are good that you already know this stuff. However, if you're just getting started, this is very important foundation knowledge.

Oh Phooey, There's No GUI

Success in operating a Cisco router is accomplished through the router's Command Line Interface (CLI). Those of you who remember the DOS command line, that paragon of user-friendliness, will have little or no problem with the CLI. However, if your technical life has been spent in the warm and safe cocoon of GUI (graphical user interface) screens and mouse clicks, then this may present a challenge to you.

Depending on your background, the CLI can be like an old friend that you use every day, or it can be a cursed multi-headed monster that's constantly attempting to turn your life into sheer misery. If the latter is the case, remember that practice and perseverance are the virtues to conquer the monster and win the day. Feel better now? You will.

As an introduction to the command line interpreter, you need to have an overview of the various rules, procedures, and actions you must, may, and can take to setup, configure, and work with your router from the start. Here are the things we think you need:

- ✔ **Syntax:** You must have a basic understanding of the structure of the various commands and what the most common abbreviations mean.

- ✔ **Access:** You can access the router in only a handful of ways, and you should know the procedure used to enter the router through each.

- ✔ **Logging in:** The router should be secured through a series of passwords and you must know which of the five passwords you use to gain the level of access you need.

- ✔ **Mode:** You use different command line modes to enter the various commands of the Cisco IOS (the router's operating system — see Appendix A for a list of the more common IOS router commands) and you do need to know which mode you need to be in to take certain actions.

Spelling and syntax: Getting it right

Without sounding too much like your high school English teacher, spelling and syntax are crucial elements of the CLI and its successful use. You want a command to be successfully executed? Make sure that you do these things:

- ✔ Spell it correctly.
- ✔ Get all of the command's parameters and components in their right places.
- ✔ Correctly spell the command's parameters and components.

The world of Cisco internetworking is rampant with abbreviations. Fortunately, most of the abbreviations are what I call TLAs (three (or two) letter acronyms), such as RIP, OSI, ARP, TCP, IP, and the like, but you will also encounter FLAs (yes, four-letter acronyms) and the dreaded EFLAs (the extended four-letter acronyms). TLAs and FLAs are commonly used as abbreviations for names and descriptors of networking protocols and technologies.

Speaking of abbreviations, you should know that Cisco IOS commands and parameters can be abbreviated to any length that still uniquely identifies the command or parameter. For example, the command **configure terminal** can be abbreviated to **conf t,** which contains enough of the original command to avoid being ambiguous. The shortest unique abbreviation for configure is **conf.** The abbreviation "con" wouldn't work because of the **connect** command; how would your router know which command you actually wanted. On the other hand, **terminal** is the only parameter of the **configure** command that starts with the letter *t,* so you only need that much to have it recognized. You'll find other examples of abbreviated commands and parameters throughout this chapter.

At any time, you can enter as much of a command as you remember followed by a space and a ? (question mark) and the IOS will display the syntax and command structure of the command you've entered. This is one way to verify that you're using the correct command before you use it for real. See "Getting By with a Little Help" later in this chapter for information on getting help on the command line.

Accessing the router

You can access the router for configuration via one of several routes:

✔ Asynchronous serial port

✔ Auxiliary port

✔ Virtual terminal connection with the TCP/IP Telnet protocol

✔ TFTP (Trivial File Transfer Protocol) server

✔ SNMP (Simple Network Management Protocol) network management station

All Cisco routers have a console port — an asynchronous serial port — located on the back of the router and aptly labeled CONSOLE. The *console port* is used to connect a computer to the router and, through a *terminal emulator* (such as Windows' HyperTerminal, SecureCRT from Van Dyke Technologies, or the like), to create an interactive control console on the router.

Most Cisco routers also have an auxiliary port, labeled cleverly as AUX, located just to the right of the console port. The *auxiliary port* allows a dial-up modem to be attached, and asynchronous remote dialup access can be used along with a terminal emulator to configure or control the router.

In addition to using the console and auxiliary ports, you can also access the router via a virtual terminal connection with the TCP/IP Telnet protocol. *Telnet* is used to connect to remote devices, including routers, over a network. Cisco routers can support up to five Telnet sessions at one time.

A couple of less popular, but nonetheless available, ways you can access a router for configuration purposes is from a TFTP (Trivial File Transfer Protocol) server or from a network management station using the SNMP (Simple Network Management Protocol).

TFTP differs from FTP (File Transfer Protocol) in that TFTP does not verify each packet of data transferred, which makes it very fast, but sometimes unreliable. It is commonly used as a means to store and restore a router's IOS configuration files (see Chapter 11) on a remote host. Because the size of these files is not all that large and because you are generally connecting over a local network, any risk is virtually removed. Any host running the TFTP software is a TFTP server. You can also access a router from a network management station, which is any workstation running network management system that supports SNMP, such as HP OpenView or What's Up Gold, or the like. Cisco routers (and most of their other networking devices for that matter) are SNMP-compatible, which means that they can be accessed and managed remotely.

Logging into the router

To gain access to a Cisco router, you must know the password for the type of access you want to gain. A single router can have up to five different passwords, one for each type of access, but having only one password set for all login types is not uncommon.

However, Cisco warns that the encrypted password created with the **enable secret** command should never be same as any of the other passwords. The secret password is the system administrator's edge in router security. It is encrypted when created and stored in the configuration files, so it cannot be discovered. All other passwords are stored in clear text in the configuration data.

Figure 13-1 illustrates the action of logging into a router. In general, whether you log in from the console port or the auxiliary port, or over one of the other access methods, you must know a password to gain access to the Exec command interpreter. Using the command line interpreter (CLI), you may access User and Enable (also called Privileged) mode commands and actions, some of which may require an additional password. Use the Glossary in Appendix B or see "Oh Phooey, There's No GUI" earlier in this chapter for information on the CLI.

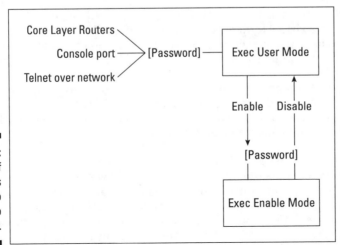

Figure 13-1:
The levels of passwords used to log into the router.

Working with the Exec command interpreter

The working name for the CLI is the Exec command interpreter. The Exec command interpreter has two Exec modes, or command groups, that can be used to perform a variety of functions:

- **User Exec:** After you successfully log into the router, meaning that you entered the appropriate password correctly, you automatically enter User Exec mode. In this mode, you can connect to other devices (such as another router) to perform simple tests and display system information. You'll know that you're in User Exec mode if the prompt displayed on your screen looks like this:

```
RouterHostname>
```

In this example, the RouterHostname represents the assigned name of the router. It's the greater than sign (>) that's significant here. When this symbol appears in the prompt, it means you're in User Exec mode.

- **Enable Exec:** Also known as Privileged or Privileged Exec, this mode is accessed from User Exec mode through the **enable** command and a password. If an Enable Exec mode password has not been set, this mode can be accessed only from the router console port. You can perform all User Exec mode functions from within Enable Exec mode. Plus, you have access to higher-level testing and debugging, detailed probing of the router functions, and the ability to update or change configuration files. The prompt that indicates this mode is

```
RouterHostname#
```

The pound or number sign (#) at the end of the prompt indicates Enable Exec mode.

Running into other command modes

Most of the time your work on the Cisco router is through either the User Exec mode or Enable Exec mode, but you may have occasion to use a few other command line modes. You can use these command modes on your router.

ROM Monitor mode

The ROM Monitor mode is displayed during the boot process if no operating system is loaded in the flash memory (see Chapter 11). From this mode, the router's configuration can be completed. After configuring the router so that it may complete the startup process, the continue command moves you into User Exec mode. The prompt that indicates this mode is either just a greater than sign or the prompt

```
rommon>
```

However, the ROM Monitor mode can be avoided by booting the system from an alternative source, such as a TFTP server.

Setup mode

When a router is first configured from the console port, Setup mode is invoked. Setup mode can also be invoked from the Enable Exec mode prompt with the **setup** command, or by rebooting the router after deleting its startup-config file through the **erase startup-config** command.

The **setup** command is a prompted dialog that guides you through the setup process to configure the router. This action has no special prompt. You should know that after you erase the startup-config file, which is stored in the flash memory, the router will be in Setup mode when it is restarted.

Another way to restart the router is to issue the **reload** command.

Configuration mode

Like the Setup mode, you enter the Configuration mode through a command, in this case the **config** command.

To move into what is called the Global Configuration mode, enter the following **config** command at the Enable Exec prompt (the one with the # symbol):

```
Cisco_Networking#config terminal
```

The parameter **terminal** or its abbreviation **t** is absolutely necessary. The **config** command can be used to configure the network settings and memory with the **config net** and **config mem** commands, respectively.

Configuration mode (also known as Global Configuration mode) allows you to manually configure the router or make changes to the router's status. You may also move to another mode within Configuration mode — the Configuration Interface mode — to make changes to individual interfaces. Take a look at Table 13-1 for a peek at mode prompts.

Table 13-1	Mode Prompts
Mode	*Prompt*
Configuration Mode	RouterA#(config)#
Configuration Interface Mode	RouterA#(config-if)#

This should be fairly easy to remember. The word config without any other additions indicates plain ol' Configuration mode. The word config-if indicates that you are in Configuration Interface mode. The suffix *-if* means Interface.

Ready set, start running

Two basic configurations are stored in each router. Table 13-2 shows you which command displays which configuration.

Table 13-2	Configuration Commands
Configuration	*Command*
Startup	**show startup-config** or **sh star**
Running	**show running-config** or **sh run**

We want to be sure that you understand the shortcut commands used in this example. The unique abbreviation for **show** is *sh,* and in either form, this command can be used to display the contents of a configuration file. The abbreviations *star* and *run* indicate the **startup-configuration** and the **running-configuration** commands, respectively. The Tab key is used to complete a shortcut command line.

To exit Configuration mode, you press Ctrl+Z.

For now, don't worry about the commands and parameters used to create the router's configuration. The various commands used for this purpose are detailed in Chapter 14.

Getting By with a Little Help

Getting help on a Cisco router is actually fairly easy. Two levels of context-sensitive help are available to assist you with IOS commands. In fact, Cisco IOS tries to guess what you are trying to do and provides you with help in both the User Exec and Enable Exec modes.

The two levels of context-sensitive help available on the command line from the IOS are:

- ✔ **Word help:** The IOS tries to recognize the command you are entering from as few keystrokes as possible — sometimes even from a single keystroke

- ✔ **Command syntax help:** If you are unsure of a command's syntax or required or optional parameters, the IOS will provide you with the command structure and parameter list if you forget

What's a four-letter word beginning with an h?

Suppose, for example, that you know Cisco has a specific command to perform a task, but you can't remember its command word. By typing its first letter (or as many letters as you feel are needed) and a question mark without a space in between, the router displays a list of the available commands that begin with that letter. If multiple commands meet your criteria, they are all displayed. For example, entering *cl?* on the command line interface produces the following results:

```
Cisco_Networking#cl?
clear clock
```

The display indicates that two commands begin with *cl:* the **clear** command and the **clock** command.

In this example, the name of the router, Cisco Networking, is displayed along with the #, indicating Enable Exec mode.

The location of the question mark in the command line entry is very important. If you include no space before the question mark, as in *cl?,* the command line interface lists all the commands that begin with *cl.* If you include a space before the question mark, as in *cl ?,* the command line interpreter attempts to display the next element of syntax for the command.

However, entering the letter *c* followed by a space and then a question mark *(c ?)* will not get you a list of all the commands that begin with *c.* Instead, you will get the response "Ambiguous Command Request." Remember that the space in the command line indicates you wish the CLI to complete the command line for you, if it can. Because it can't, it tells you that it doesn't have a clue as to what command you want.

Choosing from a list

To see all the commands available for a command mode, simply enter a question mark at the command prompt. If the list being displayed requires more than one screen, only the first screen of information is displayed followed by the - - more - - prompt.

For you UNIX, Linux, and DOS buffs, you probably know the **more** command very well. For those of you not of those persuasions, you can advance the display by either pressing the spacebar to advance to the next screen of information or by pressing the Enter key to move the display up one line at a time.

Helping the terminally lazy

Another gee-whiz feature built into the user interface of the Cisco router is really great for people who don't like to type. For example, suppose that late at night, you've just finished configuring a distant router through a Telnet session. You're so tired that you can barely keep your eyes open, much less type. So, to end the telnet session, you type **disc** and then press the Tab key. Lo and behold, the word "disconnect" is magically completed for you.

Try this quick quiz: Which key do you press to complete a word or a shortcut command? Open up a can of *Tab,* and think about the correct answer.

Okay, now show me the rest

Another level of context-sensitive help available from the Cisco IOS is *command syntax help* that displays the remaining command elements for a partially entered command string. If you enter the command, or at least enough of the command so that it can be recognized, followed by a space and a question mark, the command line interpreter displays the next parameter of the command. For example, Figure 13-2 illustrates a portion of what is displayed when the command string *show ?* is entered in Enable Exec mode.

Figure 13-2:
The results
of the *show*
? entry.

```
CCNA_For_Dummies#show?
WORD                  Flash device information-format<dev:>[partition]
access-expression     List access expression
access-lists          List access lists
accounting            Accounting data for active sessions
aliases              Display alias commands
arp                   Arp Table
async                 Information on terminal lines used as router interfaces
.
.
.
```

Controlling the Present through the Past

The user interface of the Cisco IOS includes some features to allow you to review and re-use commands you've entered in the past, to move the cursor around the command line or its history, or both. In this section, we will provide you with an overview of:

✔ **Working with the command history:** The Cisco IOS allows you to scroll back through all previously entered commands to review what you've already entered.

✔ **Command line shortcuts:** The Cisco IOS includes a variety of keyboard commands, called *enhanced editing,* that allow you to control the cursor position and move it directly to certain points on the command line or its history.

✔ **Combining the editing features:** When used together, the ability to access the command history and the enhanced editing features, you can move back into the command history to edit and re-use long or complicated commands instead of re-entering them again.

Editing history

Another feature of the Cisco router IOS user interface is access to the command history. If you are of the UNIX/Linux persuasion, this kind of feature is old hat to you, but if you are a DOS/Windows person, this feature will seem like a gift from the gods.

The command history is a chronological listing of the commands that have been entered or displayed on the router in the current session. Depending on the Cisco device, you may have by default 10 to 20 of the previous commands available for review or re-use. On most Cisco devices, you have the ability to set the size of the command history buffer through the **terminal history** command.

The command history is a very handy feature because during a logged in session, you can recall previously entered commands — especially those long or complex commands — and access lists you sweated bullets over and finally got right. Any of the entries in the command history buffer can be edited, copied, or removed. This gives you flexibility and saves you time because you don't have to reenter a long command string that really only needs some minor editing or a new IP address to be used again. The ability to edit the IOS command history allows you to copy these long sequences for reuse, or to check back on an earlier action that may need correcting. Remember that the history is only the short-term past — actually, only the history from the current session is available and then only to the limit of the buffer size set for your device. After you save the running-configuration and log off, poof — it's all gone.

The Cisco IOS uses a special set of keyboard commands, which are included in the enhanced editing commands (see "Living the good life with enhanced editing," later in this section) to recall the command history. Some devices, such as the Catalyst switches and high-end routers, have their own set of commands, called the *history substitution* commands, that can be used to access, retrieve, and replace entries in the command history. Table 13-3 lists a few of the history substitution commands available to some Cisco internetworking devices.

Table 13-3	History Substitution Commands
Keyboard Entries	*Action*
Repeating recent commands:	
!!	Repeat the most recent command
!-nn	Repeat the nnth most recent command (where nn is the number of commands prior to the current command)
!n	Repeat command number n
!aaa	Repeat the command beginning with the string aaa (where aaa is a text string)
!?aaa	Repeat the command containing the string aaa anywhere in the command
To modify and then repeat the most recent command:	
^aaa^bbb	Replace the string aaa with the string bbb in the most recent (immediately preceding) command
To add a string at the end of a previous command and repeat it:	
!!aaa	Add string aaa to the end of the most recent command
!n aaa	Add string aaa to the end of command n
!aaa bbb	Add string bbb to the end of the command beginning with string aaa
!?aaa bbb	Add string bbb to the end of the command containing the string aaa

Living the good life with enhanced editing

Enhanced editing mode is designed to make your life with routers easier. It provides you with such time savers as the ability to quickly enter one or more commands by repeating one or more entries. Enhanced editing is actually a series of keystroke combinations that move the command line cursor about, recall recent commands, or complete entries for you automatically.

To use enhanced editing commands, you press the key combinations together to cause the associated action. For example, to move to the end of the current command line, press Ctrl+E (uppercase or lowercase; it doesn't matter). The cursor moves to the end of the current command line.

To show how truly enhanced it is, enhanced editing is automatically enabled in either User Exec mode or Enable Exec mode. (See "Working with the Exec command interpreter" earlier in this chapter for more information.) To disable it, enter the command line **terminal no editing.** To turn it back on, enter **terminal editing.** Some of the other important enhanced editing keyboard commands that you will find handy are listed in Table 13-4.

Table 13-4	Enhanced Editing Keyboard Commands
Key(s)	*Action*
Ctrl+A	Move to the beginning of the current line
Ctrl+E	Move to the end of the current line
Ctrl+B (or ←)	Move back one character
Ctrl+F (or →)	Move forward one character
Ctrl+N (or ↓)	Recall most recent command
Ctrl+P (or ↑)	Recall previous command
Esc+B	Move back to beginning of previous word (or beginning of current word)
Esc+F	Move forward one word
Tab	Complete the current word

Changing history

By combining Cisco IOS's ability to edit the command history with the enhanced editing feature, you have the complete toolset to really do some serious editing.

Remember, the ↑ or the key combination Ctrl+P can be used to scroll back up through the recent history of commands and actions on the router. These two interchangeable commands, along with the Ctrl+A (move to the beginning of the current line) command, are the most commonly used editing commands.

You can use these configuration commands in editing the command history:

- **show history:** This command displays the contents of the command history.

- **terminal history size:** This command is used to change the default value of how many lines of the command history are to be displayed by a show history command. The default is set to show the last 10 commands.

✔ **terminal no editing:** This command turns off the enhanced editing feature and is used to exit enhanced editing.

✔ **terminal editing:** This command turns the enhanced editing feature on. Enhanced editing is on by default and must be turned off with the **terminal no editing** command.

Let's Play Password

Passwords play an important role in the security of your router, protecting its configuration and access lists from evildoers. In the same way that passwords are used to protect data networking elements by verifying that someone logging in has authorization to do so, passwords protect your network's routers as well. Earlier in this chapter, we discussed when you need a password to log into the router (see "Logging into the router"). A Cisco router can have up to five different passwords, each on a different level. You will find that knowing the processes used to manage and modify router passwords is very helpful.

Don't be so sensitive

Cisco router passwords are case sensitive, which means that it really does matter whether an alphabetic character is uppercase or lowercase in a password. In the ASCII (American Standard Code for Information Interchange) character set, every displayable character has a different hexadecimal and binary value. An uppercase *A* has a different numerical value than a lowercase *a*. So when you create a password, remember that it will be stored exactly how you enter it — in other words, case SenSiTiVe. Also remember that when you use it to access the router, you must enter it exactly as it was stored — again, case SenSiTiVe.

Getting into Configuration mode

The first step in the procedure used to change (which includes setting it for the first time) a password on a Cisco router is to be in Terminal Configuration mode, (also known as Global Configuration mode). To get to Terminal Configuration mode, use the following series of prompts and commands:

```
Cisco Networking#config t
Enter configuration commands, one per line. End with CNTL/Z.
```

After you're in Terminal Configuration mode, the router name will be followed by the word *config* in parentheses — *(config)* — indicating that you are in Terminal Configuration mode.

Changing the locks

You can set and use five different passwords in a Cisco router:

- ✔ Enable Secret
- ✔ Enable
- ✔ Virtual Terminal
- ✔ Console
- ✔ Auxiliary

We put the passwords in this sequence to indicate their importance to gaining access to the router and having the most access to critical configuration settings. If you are concerned with the security of your router, pay attention to the passwords in this order. The following sections show the commands used to set each password.

Cisco router passwords are divided into two groups with different security policies applied to the groups. The first group, Enable Secret and Enable passwords is much more secure than the other group — the User passwords — which includes the Virtual Terminal, Console, and Auxiliary Passwords.

Setting the Enable Secret password

The Enable Secret password adds a level of security over and above the Enable password. When set, this password, which is one-way encrypted, has precedence over the Enable password.

Without sounding like the CIA, one-way encryption is a hashing algorithm that converts the password into a 128-bit or 160-bit value, depending on the device. This encryption scheme is based on a security process called the *Secure Hash Algorithm.* Cisco claims that it is impossible to decode an Enable Secret password using the contents of a router's configuration file.

The following statements show the commands used to set the Enable Secret password:

```
Cisco Networking(config)#enable secret gilster
Cisco_Networking(config)#^Z
```

The ^Z entry is what's displayed when you press Ctrl+Z, which is the enhanced editing command for ending a command entry. (See "Living the good life with enhanced editing" earlier in this chapter.) If you enter a carat (^) followed by a Z, as is displayed in the preceding example, the command line interpreter won't have a clue what you're trying to do.

Setting the Enable password

Your best bet is to set the Enable Secret password and not use the Enable password. The only difference between these two passwords is the level of encryption (see "Setting the Enable Secret password"). The Enable password uses a very lightweight encryption, compared to the IPSec (IP Security Standard) level encryption used for the Enable Secret password. No claims of invulnerability are made for the simple algorithm used for the Enable password.

The Enable password is also used for older router software versions. The router uses the Enable password only when no Enable Secret password has been created.

The following statements are used to set the Enable password:

```
Cisco_Networking(config)#enable password gilster
The enable password that you have chosen is the same as your
          enable secret.
This is not recommended. Re-enter the enable password.
Cisco Networking(config)#enable password cup0soup
Cisco_Networking(config)#^Z
```

Cisco recommends that the **enable password** command no longer be used in favor of the **enable secret** command. They feel this provides for better router security. However, the one time that the **enable password** might be used is when the router is running in boot mode, which doesn't support the **enable secret** command.

Setting the Virtual Terminal password

The Virtual Terminal password is used to gain access to the router using a Telnet session. Unless this password, also known as the *vty password,* is set, you cannot Telnet into the router.

The following statements show the commands used to set the Virtual Terminal password:

```
Cisco_Networking(config)#line vty 0 4
Cisco_Networking(config-line)#login
Cisco Networking(config-line)#password kevin
Cisco_Networking(config-line)#^Z
```

The **line** command enters Line Configuration mode, which is used to configure physical access points, such as Telnet, and the console and aux ports. The **vty 0 4** part of the command line specifies that the password entered will apply to vty (virtual terminal) lines 0 through 4. It is possible to set a different password for each different vty line.

In order to set a password on the vty lines, you must first indicate the lines to be affected. In this case, the command **line vty 0 4** is the first line of the commands and indicates that the actions that follow it should affect the login password for all five virtual terminal lines.

Setting the Console password

The Console password is used to gain access to the router through the console port. To set the console password, use the following commands (changing the password, of course):

```
Cisco_Networking(config)#line con 0
Cisco_Networking(config-line)#login
Cisco_Networking(config-line)#password tur7le
Cisco_Networking(config-line)#^Z
```

Setting the Auxiliary password

The auxiliary password controls access to any auxiliary ports on the router. To set the password for this interface, use the following commands:

```
Cisco_Networking(config)#line aux 0
Cisco_Networking(config-line)#login
Cisco_Networking(config-line)#password pi22a
Cisco_Networking(config-line)#^Z
```

Giving the Router an Identity

Do nothing. That is, do nothing if you want the generic name "Router" to display on every prompt line, and you don't plan to update or access your router from another router or other SNMP device. Your router is perfectly happy and functional with the router name "Router." But, if you have more than one router in your network or you do plan to interact with other nearby routers on the WAN, then it might be a good idea to give your router an identifying name, even if it is only "RouterA."

Not naming your router would be like not giving a baby a name when it is born. This poor child would have to go through life as "Child," "Kid," "Boy," "Girl," or some other unidentifying nondescript name. To avoid an identity crisis for your router, we believe that you will want to give your router its own unique name, or its own *hostname*. If fact, we highly recommend that you assign a hostname for the router.

Follow just two simple rules to assign a hostname to your router:

✔ The router must be in Enable Exec (Privileged) mode. (See "Working with the Exec command interpreter," earlier in the chapter). When you're trying to remember all the details of configuring a router, it can seem that all configuration actions are carried out under Configuration mode. That's why we're making such a big deal out of this.

✔ The command used to assign the hostname is **hostname.** What did you expect? The command you'd use to assign a hostname to your router would be much like this sample:

```
Router(config)#hostname Cisco_Networking
```

So, okay, what's wrong with this prompt?

```
Router>
```

Hostnames can't be duplicated within a LAN. Which is what's wrong with the generic hostname "Router." If you have more than one router on a LAN, you absolutely must assign a hostname to at least one of them, and preferably both. They can't both have the name Router.

Throughout this chapter, and the rest of the book, you will see the hostname "Cisco_Networking" assigned to our router. You may not want to use a name quite this clever, ingenious, or descriptive, but whatever naming scheme you choose, the hostnames that you assign should be somewhat meaningful. The hostnames must identify each specific router on the network uniquely. If your network has only one router, then the name is less important, of course. In which case, have some fun and use something like "Cisco Networking For Dummies." Shameless, aren't we?

Remember these two key things when assigning a hostname to a router:

✔ The router must be in Global Configuration mode (see "Getting into Configuration mode," earlier in this chapter).

✔ The command **hostname** is one word with no space between host and name.

Set a hostname this way:

```
Router#config t
Enter configuration commands, one per line. End with CNTL/Z.
Router(config)#hostname Cisco_Networking
Cisco_Networking(config)#
```

Waving the Banner

Each router can be configured with a banner message to be displayed whenever someone logs into the router. The banner message is a text display that is sent to the display device of anyone logging onto the router. It can be virtually anything the administrator wishes to have displayed. The message part of the banner is called the *message of the day* (MOTD), a term borrowed from our UNIX/Linux friends. The MOTD banner is displayed at login and is a good way to get the word out about scheduled network downtime or any other endearments that the administrator wants to share with his or her loyal users.

Follow these steps to create an MOTD banner:

1. **Put yourself in Global Configuration mode (see "Getting into Configuration mode," earlier in this chapter).**

2. **Follow the** banner motd **command with a delimiting character.**

   Entering the delimiting character at this point declares to the IOS which character you will be using to delimit your message. The choice of the delimiting character that you will use to indicate the end of your message is totally up to you. The delimiting character is entered as a part of the **banner motd #** command string, where # represents the character you've chosen.

3. **Enter the message.**

   Your message cannot contain the delimiting character you've chosen. The command line interpreter knows that the message is ended when you enter your delimiting character. For this reason, this character should normally be a special character not likely to be used in the MOTD message.

Use commands such as the following to create or modify the MOTD banner:

```
Cisco_Networking(config)#banner motd $
Enter TEXT message. End with the character '$'.
IOS upgrade scheduled for next Thursday.
   $
Cisco_Networking(config)#
```

In this example, you need to press the Enter key after entering the delimiting character *($)* to end the message. Actually, any character not included in the message can be used as a delimiter.

Many administrators routinely use the pound sign character *(#)* as the delimiter.

The result of this would be that the next time anyone logs into the router, the following would be displayed:

```
IOS upgrade scheduled for next Thursday.
User Access Verification
Password:
```

The MOTD banner message is the first line displayed in the login display.

Naming Names

You may also add descriptions to lines, interfaces, and other configured elements of your router. To do so, the command **description** is used to apply a name, circuit number, or other nomenclature to whatever element is being edited. The **description** command is very simple in that it contains only two elements, the command and the description. Look at this example:

```
Cisco_Networking(config)#int e0
Enter configuration commands, one per line. End with CNTL/Z.
Cisco_Networking(config-if)#description Ethernet link to Web
          Host
Cisco_Networking(config-if)#^Z
```

These statements apply the description "Ethernet link to Web Host" to the Ethernet 0 interface (see Chapter 14 for information on router Ethernet ports).

Chapter 14

Making It Do What You Want

*R*outers are great networking tools. They connect network segments together and they connect you to other networks, which extend the value of all of the networks involved, and they connect you to the wide world of the Internet (the big internetwork). They have more benefits for sure, but you can't realize any of them if your router's interfaces aren't configured to support these connections.

Beyond setting its basic operating configuration, most of an administrator's work on a router is in configuring the router's interfaces. Exactly which interfaces must be configured depends on your network and to whom it connects. Even routers on simple networks, which are used only for interconnecting to the Internet or a lesser WAN, have at least standard ports (for example, serial, virtual terminal, or console) and very likely an Ethernet interface or two. To this end, this chapter provides you with a look at what's involved with configuring a router's interfaces, defining the parameters that define the nature of an interface's connections, and using SNMP (Simple Network Management Protocol) to manage interfaces, routers, and other remote devices.

Configuring the Router and Its Protocols

Assuming that the router has been set up with its running configuration (see Chapter 11), you next want to configure the router protocols, which really means that you need to configure its interfaces. Basically, a router applies its form of intelligence to the question of where a network data packet should be forwarded so that it most efficiently reaches its destination. The "where" in this case refers to which of its interfaces should be used. The decision as to which interface to use is really the hardest part of this process, but it is all for nothing if the port (interface) it wants to use is not properly configured.

If a router isn't told which interfaces it has, which are in use, and the protocols supported by each; it can't include them in the routing decision. So, obviously, the router needs to know just how you intend to use each of its interfaces, if at all, and some specific things about each port, such as the addresses that can be reached, any security considerations, data speeds, and so on.

Setting up the routing protocol

The first task in configuring the router-to-router traffic is to assign a routing protocol. A *routing protocol* moves data traffic over the network from router to router. Don't confuse this with a *routed protocol,* which is the protocol used by routers to communicate information about the network to other routers. Cisco routers support a wide variety of routing protocols. Table 14-1 lists the routing protocols that you can set up on your router. Each of the routing protocols in Table 14-1 requires additional information to complete its setup on the router.

Table 14-1	Routing Protocols Supported on Cisco Routers
Protocol	*Configuration keyword*
Border Gateway Protocol (BGP)	bgp
Exterior Gateway Protocol (EGP)	egp
Enhanced Interior Gateway Routing Protocol (EIGRP)	eigrp
Interior Gateway Routing Protocol (IGRP)	igrp
ISO IS-IS	isis
IGRP for OSI Networks	iso-igrp
Mobile routes	mobile
On demand stub routes	odr
Open Shortest Path First (OSPF)	ospf
Routing Information Protocol (RIP)	rip
Static routes	static
Traffic-engineered routes	traffic-engineering

The most common protocol you will use is RIP. However, in some specific situations you may need to use static routes.

Building the router's configuration

To begin the process of building the router's configuration, you must first be in the global configuration mode. With that out of the way, you can begin entering each of the specific interfaces that you want to configure. Remember that "interface" means the ports and connection points on the router. Depending on the router model in use, this could include an Ethernet port, one or more serial ports, and more. Ethernet ports are designated by either the word Ethernet or the letter "e," followed by its sequence number, beginning with zero. Serial ports follow a similar pattern: the word serial or the letter "s" and an integer port number. For example, to designate the first Ethernet port, the code *e0* can be used and for two serial ports, *s1* and *s2* can be used. Look at this sample of the commands used to manually configure an Ethernet port on a router:

```
CISCO_Networking#config t
Enter configuration commands, one per line. End with CNTL/Z.
CISCO_Networking(config)#int e0
CISCO_Networking(config-if)#
CISCO_Networking(config-if)#IP address ?
  A.B.C.D  IP address
CISCO_Networking(config-if)#IP address 192.168.1.6
% Incomplete command.
CISCO_Networking(config-if)#IP address 192.168.1.6
        255.255.255.0
```

Remember that to properly configure an Ethernet port, you must enter both — that's right, both — the IP address and its subnet mask.

Configuring Interface Parameters

If you have additional interface modules or WAN interface cards installed on your router, you'll likely need to configure additional parameters. These configurations may include the following:

- ✔ Ethernet interface
- ✔ Fast Ethernet interface
- ✔ Token ring interface
- ✔ Serial interface
- ✔ Asynchronous/synchronous serial interface
- ✔ ISDN BRI interface
- ✔ E1/T1/ISDN PRI interface
- ✔ 1-port, 4-wire 56kbps DSU/CSU interface

You will need to be in the configuration mode of the Privileged Exec mode to configure these interfaces. For more information on the Privileged Exec mode of the command interpreter, take a look at Chapter 11.

Moving to the mode

To work on the configuration of an individual router interface, you must first get to the right mode level of the command line interpreter (CLI). Table 14-2 lists the **command line interpreter** commands used to move down to the interface configuration mode.

Table 14-2	Commands Used to Configure an Interface	
CLI Prompt	*Command*	*Purpose*
Router>	**enable**	Moves to privileged Exec mode
Router#	**configure terminal**	Moves to global configuration mode
Router(config)#	**interface ethernet0**	Opens the configuration of the ethernet0 interface port
Router(config-if)#	**exit**	Exits to Global configuration mode
Router#	**copy running-config startup-config**	Saves the modified configuration to NVRAM for IOS versions 11.0 and after
Router#	**write memory**	Used on IOS versions prior to 11.0
Router#	**disable**	Returns to user Exec mode
Router>	**Prompt**	Shows CLI is in user Exec mode

Your best bet for configuring the interfaces on your router is to do it during the initial configuration sequence that runs when you first power up the router for the first time or after you erase the startup configuration.

The **setup** command that runs automatically during the initialization sequence is your first, and perhaps your best, chance to configure each interface. For each interface on the router, a series of prompts is displayed to guide you through its configuration. You only need to enter the specific information needed or accept the default or current value to complete the configuration appropriate for your router and network.

In each of the following sections, we have listed the prompts displayed by the **setup** command for each of the interfaces possibly included on your router. Depending on the IOS version and router you are using, the configuration message that you see may vary.

Ethernet interface

An Ethernet interface or port connects the router into a network using Ethernet 10BaseT, 10Base2, or 10Base5 technologies and protocols. This interface assumes a data transfer rate of 10Mbps on the network. Here is a sample configuration for an Ethernet interface from the **setup** command:

```
Do you want to configure Ethernet0/0 interface [yes]:
  Configure IP on this interface? [yes]:
IP address for this interface: 192.168.1.6
Subnet mask for this interface [255.255.255.0]:
Class C network is 192.168.1.0, 24 subnet bits, mask is /24
  Configure IPX on this interface? [no]: y
IPX network number [1]:
Need to select encapsulation type
[0] sap (IEEE 802.2)
[1] snap (IEEE 802.2 SNAP)
[2] arpa (Ethernet_II)
[3] novell-ether (Novell Ethernet_802.3)
Enter the encapsulation type [2]:
```

Fast Ethernet interface

A Fast Ethernet interface connects the router to a network running Ethernet 100BaseTX technologies and supports data speeds up to 100Mbps. Here is a sample of the configuration prompts displayed by the **setup** command for a Fast Ethernet interface. You may not see much difference between this configuration and that shown for a not-fast Ethernet port in the preceding section, other than the inclusion of the word "Fast," that is. But, if you look real close, you will see a couple of additional prompts that deal with duplexing and the connector used.

```
Do you want to configure FastEthernet0/0 interface [yes]:
  Use the 100 Base-TX (RJ-45) connector? [yes]:
  Operate in full-duplex mode? [no]:
  Configure IP on this interface? [no]: yes
  IP address for this interface: 192.168.1.1
  Number of bits in subnet field [24]:
  Class C network is 192.168.1.0, 24 subnet bits, mask is /24
Configure IPX on this interface? [yes]:
IPX network number [1]:
Need to select encapsulation type
```

(continued)

```
[0] sap (IEEE 802.2)
[1] snap (IEEE 802.2 SNAP)
[2] arpa (Ethernet_II)
[3] novell-ether (Novell Ethernet_802.3)
Enter the encapsulation type [2]:
```

Token ring interface

This interface type connects the router into a network running on token ring structures. The network data speeds supported are 4Mbps or 16Mbps. Here is a sample of the configuration prompts displayed for a token ring interface by the **setup** command.

```
Do you want to configure TokenRing0/0 interface? [yes]:
 Tokenring ring speed (4 or 16)? [16]:
 Configure IP on this interface? [yes]:
IP address for this interface: 6.0.0.1
Subnet mask for this interface [255.0.0.0]:
Class A network is 6.0.0.0, 8 subnet bits; mask is /8
 Configure IPX on this interface? [no]: y
IPX network number [1]:
Need to select encapsulation type
[0] sap (IEEE 802.2)
[1] snap (IEEE 802.2 SNAP)
Enter the encapsulation type [0]:
```

Serial interface

A serial interface offers more access method options than any other interface type of a Cisco router. The most common of options supported on a serial port are:

- HDLC (High-level Data Link Control)

- HSSI (High-Speed Serial Interface — pronounced "hissy")

- L2F (Level 2 Forwarding)

- PPP (Point-to-Point Protocol)

- PPTP (Point-to-Point Tunneling Protocol)

- SLIP (Serial Line Interface Protocol)

- STUN (serial tunnel)

Choosing between DCE and DTE

Serial interfaces designated as one of the synchronous serial interfaces, which is nearly all serial protocols, must be designated as either DCE (data circuit-terminating equipment) or DTE (data terminal equipment). The documentation that comes with your interface card or the router includes information on whether it is by default a DTE or DCE device or can be configured as either. Table 14-3 lists some examples of DCE and DTE devices.

Table 14-3	DCE/DTE Devices
Type	*Typical Devices*
DTE	Terminal, PC, Router interface
DCE	Modem, CSU/DSU (Channel Service Unit/Data Service Unit), Multiplexer

Here are brief descriptions of the DCE and DTE designations:

✔ DCE (data circuit-terminating equipment) — A DCE device is the network end of a user-to-network connection. The DCE provides a DTE device with a physical connection to the network and a clock signal for timing communications.

✔ DTE (data terminal equipment) — A DTE is typically a user workstation on a network. A DTE connects to the network and receives its clock signal through a DCE device.

Configuring a serial interface

Here is a sample of the prompts displayed by the **setup** command to configure a serial interface.

```
Do you want to configure Serial0/0 interface? [yes]:
Some encapsulations supported are
ppp/hdlc/frame-relay/lapb/atm-dxi/smds/x25
Choose encapsulation type [ppp]:
```

The router will attempt to determine if the serial port is to be DCE or DTE using the cable attached to the port and the device attached to the other end of the cable. If a serial cable is not attached, which is usually the case during the initial configuration, the router will remind you and ask you to designate the port as either DCE or DTE, with DTE as the default (see "Choosing between DCE and DTE" earlier in this section).

```
No serial cable seen
Choose mode from (dce/dte) [dte]:
```

If a cable is attached, and the interface is DCE, then you will be asked to set the clock rate for the interface. Otherwise, if the interface is to be DTE, the serial cable and the DCE attached to it will set the clock rate.

You will need to know the clock rate of the DTE equipment you are supporting to set the clock rate for a DCE designation. When in doubt, choose the default rate.

```
Serial interface needs clock rate to be set in dce mode.
The following clock rates are supported on the serial interface.
0
1200, 2400, 4800, 9600, 19200, 38400
56000, 64000, 72000, 125000, 148000, 500000
800000, 1000000, 1300000, 2000000, 4000000, 8000000
 Choose clock rate from above: [2000000]:
 Configure IP on this interface? [yes]:
IP address for this interface: 8.0.0.1
Subnet mask for this interface [255.0.0.0]:
Class A network is 8.0.0.0, 8 subnet bits; mask is /8
 Configure IPX on this interface? [no]: yes
IPX network number [6]:
```

If you were to configure a DCE device manually, here is an example of the commands you would enter (in interface configuration mode):

```
interface Serial0/0
encapsulation ppp
clock rate 2000000
ip address 27.0.0.1 255.0.0.0
```

Designating the encapsulation

A serial interface must also be configured for the type of data encapsulation it should expect. The encapsulation types that can be configured to a Cisco router serial interface are with the **encapsulation** command parameter of each in parentheses:

- Asynchronous Transfer Mode-Data Exchange Interface (**amt-dxi**)
- Frame Relay (**frame-relay**)
- High-Level Data Link Control (**hdlc**)
- Point-to-Point Protocol (**ppp**)
- Switched Multimegabit Data Services (**smds**)
- Synchronous Data Link Control (**sdlc-primary/sdlc-secondary**)
- X.25 (**x25**)

See Chapter 17 for more information on these encapsulation formats.

Completing a Frame Relay definition

If the interface is being configured for Frame Relay, then some additional configuration information must be entered. Beyond the normal interface configuration data, the LMI (Local Management Interface) and DLCI (data-link connection identifier) information is required. See Chapter 17 for more information on these two Frame Relay technologies.

If you have designated the interface to be **frame-relay**, then the prompts (remember we are using the configuration prompts from the **setup** command for our examples) request the following information:

```
The following lmi-types are available to be set,
 when connected to a frame relay switch
[0] none
[1] ansi
[2] cisco
[3] q933a
Enter lmi-type [2]:
Enter the DLCI number for this interface [16]:
Do you want to map a remote machine's IP address to dlci?
          [yes]:
IP address for the remote interface: 7.0.0.1
Do you want to map a remote machine's IPX address to dlci?
          [yes]:
IPX address for the remote interface: 38.2468.1357
Serial interface needs clock rate to be set in dce mode.
The following clock rates are supported on the serial interface.
0
1200, 2400, 4800, 9600, 19200, 38400
56000, 64000, 72000, 125000, 148000, 500000
800000, 1000000, 1300000, 2000000, 4000000, 8000000
Choose speed from above: [2000000]: 1200
Configure IP on this interface? [yes]:
IP address for this interface: 7.0.0.10
Subnet mask for this interface [255.0.0.0]:
Class A network is 7.0.0.0, 8 subnet bits; mask is /8
```

If you specify none for the DLCI (data-link connection identifier), the router asks for the actual DLCI (see Chapter 17 for more information on DLCI and LMI). If you specify another LMI type or accept the default, then the protocol chosen determines the DLCI.

If your are configuring IPX on this Frame Relay interface, you are prompted as follows:

```
Do you want to map a remote machine's IPX address to dlci?
          [yes]:
IPX address for the remote interface: 2e.45.3bce.df2
```

Configuring for other encapsulations

Each encapsulation type you choose to assign to an interface has its own series of prompts. Here are examples of the prompts you see if you choose one of the more common encapsulation types:

ATM-DXI

```
Enter VPI number [1]:
Enter VCI number [1]:
Do you want to map the remote machine's IP address to vpi and
          vci's?
[yes]:
IP address for the remote interface: 6.0.0.1
Do you want to map the remote machine's IPX address to vpi
          and vci's?
[yes]:
IPX address for the remote interface: 2e.45.3bce.df2
```

SMDS

```
Enter smds address for the local interface: b232.4365.0247
We will need to map the remote smds station's address
 to the remote stations IP/IPX address
Enter smds address for the remote interface: b232.4365.0146
Do you want to map the remote machine's smds address to IP
          address?
[yes]:
IP address for the remote interface: 7.0.0.1
Do you want to map the remote machine's smds address to IPX
          address?
[yes]:
IPX address for the remote interface: 2e.45.3bce.df2
```

X25

```
x25 circuit can be either in dce/dte mode.
 Choose from either dce/dte [dte]:
 Enter local x25 address: 2468
We will need to map the remote x.25 station's x25 address
 to the remote stations IP/IPX address
Enter remote x25 address: 1357
Do you want to map the remote machine's x25 address to IP
          address?
[yes]:
IP address for the remote interface: 2.0.0.2
Do you want to map the remote machine's x25 address to IPX
          address?
[yes]:
IPX address for the remote interface: 2e.45.3bce.df2
Enter lowest 2-way channel [1]:
Enter highest 2-way channel [64]:
Enter frame window (K) [7]:
Enter Packet window (W) [2]:
Enter Packet size (must be powers of 2) [128]:
```

Asynchronous/synchronous serial interface

Serial ports can also be configured as asynchronous and synchronous. *Asynchronous,* which is Greek (isn't it all) for "not at the same time," supports those access methods and protocols operate without regard to the clock rate or a formalized communications structure. In general, asynchronous communications proceed until one of the communicating devices needs to interrupt the process. *Synchronous,* which loosely translates to "at the same time," communications are dependent on a clock rate from a single reference clock and usually require a formalized structure between the two communicating devices.

Chapter 17 can provide you with some information on why you would choose one type of interface configuration over the other. In general, this is dictated by the protocol assigned to the port.

Here is a sample of the asynchronous/synchronous configuration prompts you see when configuring a serial interface during the initial configuration of the router. You need to enter the appropriate information for your router and network.

Depending on the IOS version and router you are using, the configuration message that you see may vary.

```
Do you want to configure Serial1/0 interface? [yes]:
Enter mode (async/sync) [sync]:
```

If you choose the default (synchronous), the router responds with the following:

```
Do you want to configure Serial1/0 interface? [yes]:
Enter mode (async/sync) [sync]:
Some supported encapsulations are
ppp/hdlc/frame-relay/lapb/x25/atm-dxi/smds
 Choose encapsulation type [hdlc]:
```

If you choose `ppp` or `hdlc`, no additional configuration is necessary. To configure the other encapsulation types, refer to the sections earlier in this chapter pertaining to the configuration of the specific encapsulation type.

If you choose to configure the interface for asynchronous timing, the router responds with the following:

```
Do you want to configure Serial1/1 interface? [yes]:
Enter mode (async/sync) [sync]: async
Configure IP on this interface? [yes]:
Configure IP unnumbered on this interface? [no]:
IP address for this interface: 23.0.0.0
Subnet mask for this interface [255.0.0.0]:
Class A network is 2.0.0.0, 0 subnet bits; mask is /8
Configure LAT on this interface? [no]:
```

(continued)

```
Configure AppleTalk on this interface? [no]:
Configure DECnet on this interface? [no]:
Configure CLNS on this interface? [no]:
Configure IPX on this interface? [no]: yes
  IPX network number [8]:
Configure Vines on this interface? [no]:
Configure XNS on this interface? [no]:
Configure Apollo on this interface? [no]:
```

In this example, notice that in most cases, the default value was accepted and only where we chose to designate the interface for async mode, enter the IP address, and to configure IPX did we enter new data. The information we supplied came from the network planning documents (see Chapter 19 for more information). You don't want to do any guessing at this point in the process.

ISDN BRI interface

To enter configuration data for an ISDN BRI (Integrated Services Digital Network Basic Rate Interface) connection, you need to know the type of ISDN switch to which you are connecting. If you don't have this information, check with the provider of the ISDN service. You can use Table 14-4 to help determine the proper switch type to enter.

Table 14-4	ISDN Switch Type	
Description	*Country*	*IDSN Switch Type*
Australian TS013 switches	Australia	Basic-ts013
German 1TR6 ISDN switches	Europe	Basic-1tr6
Norwegian NET3 ISDN switches (phase 1)	Europe	Basic-nwnet3
NET3 ISDN switches (UK and others)	Europe	Basic-net3
NET5 switches (UK and others)	Europe	Basic-net5
French VN2 ISDN switches	Europe	Vn2
French VN3 ISDN switches	Europe	Vn3
Japanese NTT ISDN switches	Japan	Ntt
New Zealand NET3 switches	New Zealand	Basic-nznet3

Description	Country	IDSN Switch Type
AT&T basic rate switches	North America	Basic-5ess
NT DMS-100 basic rate switches	North America	Basic-dms 100
National ISDN-1 switches	North America	Basic-ni1

Here is a sample configuration for an ISDN BRI interface that is displayed during the initial configuration setup of the router. If you are configuring a BRI port, you must supply the data requested or accept the default value. Depending on the IOS version and the router you are using, the configuration message that you see may vary slightly. During the configuration, if you choose HDLC, no additional configuration is necessary. For PPP, we will show you the additional configuration items. The additional encapsulation options are configured as shown earlier in this chapter (see "Configuring for other encapsulations"). Review Chapter 17 for more information on HDLC and PPP.

```
BRI interface needs isdn switch-type to be configured
Valid switch types are:
[0] none..........Only if you don't want to configure BRI.
[1] basic-1tr6....1TR6 switch type for Germany
[2] basic-5ess....AT&T 5ESS switch type for the US/Canada
[3] basic-dms100..Northern DMS-100 switch type for US/Canada
[4] basic-net3....NET3 switch type for UK and Europe
[5] basic-ni......National ISDN switch type
[6] basic-ts013...TS013 switch type for Australia
[7] ntt...........NTT switch type for Japan
[8] vn3...........VN3 and VN4 switch types for France
Choose ISDN BRI Switch Type [2]:
Do you want to configure BRI0/0 interface? [yes]:
Some encapsulations supported are
ppp/hdlc/frame-relay/lapb/x25
Choose encapsulation type [ppp]:

Do you have a service profile identifiers (SPIDs) assigned?
          [no]: y
Enter SPID1: 12345
Enter SPID2: 12345
Do you want to map the remote machine's IP address in dialer
          map? [yes]:
IP address for the remote interface: 23.0.0.1
Do you want to map the remote machine's IP address in dialer
          map? [yes]:
IPX address of the remote interface: 2e.45.3bce.df2
To get to 2.0.0.1 we will need to make a phone call.
Please enter the phone number to call: 55555555555
Configure IP on this interface? [yes]:
Configure IP unnumbered on this interface? [no]: y
Assign to which interface [Ethernet0/0]:
IP address for this interface: 23.0.0.0.1
Enter the subnet mask [255.0.0.0]:
```

Had you accepted the default or responded with PPP when prompted with:

```
Choose encapsulation type [ppp]:
```

In the above series of prompts, you would also be prompted with the following items:

```
Would you like to enable multilink PPP [yes]:
Enter a remote hostname for PPP authentication [Router]:
Enter a password for PPP authentication:
```

E1/T1/ISDN PRI interface

E1, T1, and ISDN PRI (ISDN Primary Rate Interface) modes provide channelized (clusters of DS0 (64K) circuits) that can be separated in to distinct channels for voice and data transmission. See Chapter 17 for more information on these carrier types.

Here is a sample of the E1/T1/ISDN PRI interface prompts displayed during the initial configuration run of a router. The information you provide to configure the interface is available from ILEC (incumbent local exchange carrier) or CLEC (competitive local exchange carrier) from whom you are receiving the service. E1, which is a European standard, and T1, the North American standard, are roughly equivalent services.

```
The following ISDN switch types are available:
[0] none...........If you do not want to configure ISDN
[1] primary-4ess....AT&T 4ESS switch type for US and Canada
[2] primary-5ess....AT&T 5ESS switch type for US and Canada
[3] primary-dms100..Northern Telecom switch type for US and
          Canada
[4] primary-net5....European switch type for NET5
[5] primary-ni......National ISDN Switch type for the U.S
[6] primary-ntt.....Japan switch type
[7] primary-ts014...Australian switch type
Choose ISDN PRI Switch Type [2]:
Configuring controller T1 1/0 in pri or channelized mode
Do you want to configure this interface controller? [no]:
Will you be using PRI on this controller? [yes]:
```

If the answer to this last prompt is "no," then you are finished with this configuration step. However, if you are using PRI mode for E1/T1, the following or similar script will be displayed:

```
The following framing types are available:
esf | sf
Enter the framing type [esf]:
The following linecode types are available:
ami | b8zs
```

```
Enter the line code type [b8zs]:
Enter number of time slots [24]:
Do you want to configure Serial1/0:23 interface? [yes]:
Configuring the PRI D-channel
Would you like to enable multilink PPP? [yes]:
Configure IP on this interface? [no]: y
Configure IP unnumbered on this interface? [no]: y
Assign to which interface [Ethernet0/0]:
All users dialing in through the PRI will need to be authen-
        ticated using CHAP. The username and password are
        case sensitive.
Enter more username and passwords for PPP authentication?
        [no]: y
Enter the username used for dial-in CHAP authentication
        [Router]:
Enter the PPP password of the user dialing in on PRI:
Enter more username and passwords for PPP authentication?
        [no]:
```

If you are configuring the interface for a T1 channelized mode, which is the other option to the PRI mode option, the following or similar script will be displayed:

```
The following framing types are available:
esf | sf
Enter the framing type [esf]:
The following linecode types are available:
ami | b8zs
Enter the line code type [b8zs]:
T1 is capable of being configured for channel 1-24
Enter number of time slots [24]: 3
Configure more channel groups? [no]: y
Enter number of time slots [21]: 3
Configure more channel groups? [no]: y
Enter number of time slots [18]: 3
Configure more channel groups? [no]: y
Enter number of time slots [15]:
Configure more channel groups? [no]:
```

If you are using E1 channelized mode, because you indicated the primary ISDN switch type as [4] primary-net5 – European switch type for NET5 early in this process, the following or similar script will be displayed:

```
The following framing types are available:
no-crc4 | crc4
Enter the framing type [crc4]:
The following linecode types are available:
ami | hdb3
Enter the line code type [hdb3]:
Do you want to configure Serial1/1:0 interface?: [Yes]:
Configuring the Channelized E1/T1 serial channels
Some encapsulations supported are
```

(continued)

```
ppp/hdlc/frame-relay/lapb/atm-dxi/smds/x25
Choose encapsulation type [ppp]:
Configure IP on this interface? [no]: y
Configure IP unnumbered on this interface? [no]:
IP address for this interface: 129.40.0.1
Subnet mask for this interface [255.255.0.0]:
Class B network is 129.40.0.0, 16 subnet bits; mask is /16
```

1-port, 4-wire 56kbps DSU/CSU interface

Some interface connections, such as a ISDN PRI or fractionalized T1 (single channel), require a DSU/CSU (data service unit/channel service unit), also called a CSU/DSU. The two halves of this combined service perform the following services:

✔ **Data Service Unit:** A device used in digital data transmissions to adapt a DTE device to a T1 or E1 line. A DSU also provides as signal timing.

✔ **Channel Service Unit:** A digital interface device that connects a DTE to the local digital telephone service.

The name of this interface type describes exactly what is being connected and supported to the port. A single port connection to a 4-wire carrier supporting 56Kbps through a CSU/DSU to the digital telephone system.

Here is a sample of the prompts that are displayed during the configuration sequence of the **setup** command for a 1-port, 4-wire 56kbps DSU/CSU interface. You need to enter the appropriate information for your router and network. Depending on the IOS version and router you are using, the configuration message that you see may vary. This WAN card can be configured to be used on either a circuit-switched or a dedicated-line service and examples of both configurations is provided.

Which type of connection you have depends on the service provided to you by your provider. *Circuit-switched* refers to the good old everyday telephone system and would be used primarily for voice traffic. *Dedicated-line* service (also called DDS — dedicated digital service) covers data lines provisioned by the telephone company to carry digital data.

Circuit-switched service

```
Do you want to configure Serial0/0 interface? [yes]:
Some encapsulations supported are
ppp/hdlc/frame-relay/lapb/atm-dxi/smds/x25
Choose encapsulation type [ppp]:
Switched 56k interface may either be in switched/Dedicated
        mode
Choose from either (switched/dedicated) [switched]:
```

```
The following switched carrier types are to be set when in
        switched mode
(at&t, sprint or other)
Choose carrier (at&t/sprint/other) [other]:
Do you want to map the remote machine's ip address in dialer
        map? [yes]:
IP address for the remote interface : 117.0.0.2
Do you want to map the remote machine's ipx address in dialer
        map?
[yes]:
IPX address for the remote interface : 2e.45.3bce.df2
Please enter the phone number to call : 55555555555
Configure IP on this interface? [yes]:
IP address for this interface: 117.0.0.1
Subnet mask for this interface [255.0.0.0] :
Class A network is 117.0.0.0, 8 subnet bits; mask is /8
```

Dedicated-line service

```
Do you want to configure Serial0/0 interface? [yes]:
Some encapsulations supported are
ppp/hdlc/frame-relay/lapb/atm-dxi/smds/x25
Choose encapsulation type [ppp]:
Switched 56k interface may either be in switched/Dedicated
        mode
Choose from either (switched/dedicated) [switched]: dedi
When in dds mode, the clock for sw56 module can be from
        line/internal.
Choose clock from (line/internal) [line]: internal
Warning: internal can be choose only when connected back to
        back.
Serial interface needs clock rate to be set in dce mode.
The following clock rates are supported on the serial inter-
        face.
auto, 2.4, 4.8, 9.6, 19.2, 38.4 56, 64
choose clock rate from above [56]:
Configure IP on this interface? [yes]:
IP address for this interface: 117.0.0.1
Subnet mask for this interface [255.0.0.0] :
Class A network is 117.0.0.0, 8 subnet bits; mask is /8
```

Setting up the SNMP Network Management

This part of the chapter doesn't directly deal with interface configuration, but after SNMP (Simple Network Management Protocol) services are set up on the router, they are available for use in monitoring and managing the interfaces you configure on the router.

SNMP is a widely-used network monitoring, control, and management protocol that is part of the TCP/IP protocol suite (see Chapter 2). SNMP devices, called agents (routers, bridges, switches, hubs, and so on), on a network report data on their activities to an SNMP server that collects, stores, and analyzes the data. A MIB (Management Information Base) is maintained for each agent that contains data on what information the agent provides and how it is managed. If the router and its interfaces are to be SNMP agents, they must be configured as such.

During the initial configuration process of the **setup** command and right after you set the router's passwords, you will be asked to configure the SNMP network management. The sequence of prompts you see look something like this:

```
Configure SNMP Network Management? [yes]:
    Community string [public]:

Current interface summary

Any interface listed with OK? value "NO" does not have a
        valid configuration

Interface              IP-Address       OK? Method Status
            Protocol

Ethernet0              unassigned       NO  unset  up
            down

Serial0                unassigned       NO  unset  down
            down


Enter interface name used to connect to the management net-
        work from the above interface summary: Serial0

Configuring interface Serial0:
    Configure IP on this interface? [yes]:
        IP address for this interface: 172.16.10.1
        Subnet mask for this interface [255.255.0.0] :
        Class B network is 172.16.0.0, 16 subnet bits; mask is
            /16

The following configuration command script was created:

hostname CISCO_Networking
enable secret 5 $1$MYXQ$ZgAdF.GO9XME./GGEfbwo/
enable password networking
line vty 0 4
password cisco
snmp-server community public
!
no ip routing
```

```
!
interface Ethernet0
shutdown
no ip address
!
interface Serial0
no shutdown
ip address 172.16.10.1 255.255.0.0
!
end

[0] Go to the IOS command prompt without saving this config.
[1] Return back to the setup without saving this config.
[2] Save this configuration to nvram and exit.

Enter your selection [2]:
Building configuration...
Use the enabled mode 'configure' command to modify this con-
          figuration.
```

Chapter 15

Guarding the Doors

. . . .

. . . .

*E*very network administrator has at least one horror story to tell about breaches in security, a hacker that got in and then got away, corrupted files, and other bits of nastiness. That's why security is always a hot topic when administrators of networks of all sizes and levels get together. If network security isn't on your list of important issues, it should be, and if it is, it should be near the top of the list.

Security on routers is something with which that all network administrators should be very familiar. When it comes to routers, security means access lists and SAP (Service Advertising Protocol) filters. This can be a very tricky subject and one you will be challenged with daily.

We have structured this chapter much like a Cisco training course, with some lecture and some practice. You will benefit from working through the examples on a router. Nothing is quite like doing it to learn it. In other words, if you really want to understand access lists, you really should get on the router and get some practice working with them.

Making Up the Guest List

In the context of a Cisco router, the purpose of an access list is to allow or deny traffic through a router. An access list consists of formally structured statements that provide the criteria with which a router can decide what it is to do with any packet that enters the router.

Cisco routers have two types of access lists:

- ✔ IP (Internet Protocol)
- ✔ IPX (Novell NetWare)

Both work like packet filters, in that incoming packets are compared to the rules and conditions in the access list, and depending on the results of the comparison, those packets are acted upon.

Configuring an IP Access List

You'll find two types of IP access lists:

✔ **Standard IP access lists:** This type of access list analyzes the source IP address in a TCP/IP packet and then takes action to permit or deny the packet to pass through the router based on the outcome of its analysis. Standard IP access lists rely on the source IP address contained in the IP packet.

✔ **Extended IP access lists:** This type of access list permits or denies a packet using a variety of factors, which are collectively known as the Layer 4 header, including:

- Source address

- Destination address

- IP protocol (TCP, UDP, ICMP)

- Specific port (HTTP, FTP, Telnet)

Examining the packet and its port

As shown in Figure 15-1, the information contained in an IP packet includes the destination IP address and a protocol field that contains the specific well-known port to be used for the data in the packet.

Figure 15-1:
The contents
of an IP
packet.

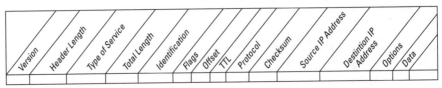

Extended IP access lists allow the router to filter packets based on the information contained in the Layer 4 header. The content of the protocol field tells the router the type of Layer 4 header to look for. The starting point here is whether the protocol is connection-oriented or connectionless. A connection-oriented protocol uses TCP as its Layer 4 protocol. The TCP header is shown in Figure 15-2. A connectionless protocol uses UDP for the Layer 4 protocol. The UDP header is shown in Figure 15-3. See Chapter 2 for more information on the OSI Model's Layer 4 and the TCP/IP protocols.

Figure 15-2: The fields of a TCP header.

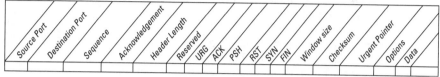

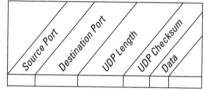

Figure 15-3: The contents of a UDP header.

In both connection-oriented (TCP) and connectionless (UDP) transmissions, you are interested in the source and destination port numbers. The port number identifies the server or application software to which the data payload in the packet is to be delivered for processing. Through the port number, the receiving host knows that the incoming data is to be sent to the software that handles HTTP (Hypertext Transfer Protocol), FTP (File Transfer Protocol), or SMTP (Simple Mail Transfer Protocol), for example. See Chapter 5 for more information these protocols and "Knowing the Better-Known Ports" later in this chapter for information on TCP port numbers.

Extended IP access lists include the information needed to filter traffic based on the higher layer protocols in use, including TCP, UDP, or the like, along with the corresponding port. As with a standard access list, the TCP/UDP port number determines the application or server software that will process the data.

Standard access lists are fine and work well in situations where only the IP address is enough to determine who can or can't have access through the router to the network.

Extended lists provide the ability to determine access to the network based on the type of activity an IP address is requesting. You may want to allow a particular network segment (IP address range) general access to the network, but disallow all telnet requests, all FTP requests, and allow only SMTP e-mail traffic. This level of security is virtually impossible for a standard access list, but it is exactly what the extended access list is meant to do.

Access list rules and conditions

When an access list is created, a unique number is assigned so that the router knows which list to check for a particular protocol and interface. Like everything else in the router, certain rules govern how access list numbers are assigned.

Each type of access list has a block of numbers assigned to it. When an access list is created, the number it is assigned specifies its type to the operating system. Beginning with Cisco IOS release 11.2, standard and extended IP access lists can be given an alphanumeric name. Prior to that, access lists were designated only with a number, and the number had to come from the block of numbers for that type of access list. Table 15-1 lists the access list types with the block of numbers assigned to each block within the Cisco IOS.

Table 15-1	Access List Types
Access List Type	*Number Block*
IP Standard	1 – 99
IP Extended	100 – 199
Protocol type-code	200 – 299
48-bit MAC address	700 – 799
IPX Standard	800 – 899
IPX Extended	900 – 999
IPX SAP	1000 – 1099

An implied **deny any** command is at the end of any access list. This command serves the purpose of denying all traffic not specifically meeting the conditions in the filter statements in the access list.

Knowing The Better-Known Ports

In your role as a Cisco network administrator, you will learn quite a few of these port numbers because you work with them frequently, but you don't need to know the complete list by heart. The entire list of designated port numbers, known as the well-known port numbers, contains a long list of ports representing a wide variety of specific upper-layer protocols.

TIP

Another thing you need to remember is that TCP and UDP both use port numbers, and fortunately their port numbers are the same for each application.

Table 15-2 contains only a small sample of some of the more commonly used well-known ports for TCP and UDP.

Table 15-2	Well-Known TCP Port Numbers	
TCP Port Number	*UDP Port Number*	*Application*
21	21	FTP
23	23	TELNET
25	25	SMTP
53	53	DNS
69	69	TFTP
80	80	HTTP
161	161	SNMP

Officially, port assignments fall into three categories:

✔ **Well-known ports** — Ports 0 to 1023

✔ **Vendor-specific** — Ports 1024 to 2047

✔ **Client ports** — Ports 2048 and up

For a complete and detailed list, use an Internet search engine to search for RFC 1700 or go to the Internet Assigned Numbers Authority (IANA) Web site at www.iana.org. IANA is the authority for most of the world for the registration and assignment of certain Internet-related numbers, including TCP and UDP port numbers, Class D (multi-cast) addresses, SNMP (simple network management protocol) private enterprise numbers, PPP (point-to-point protocol) numbers, and MIME (Multi-Purpose Internet Mail Extensions) media type numbers.

Applying the Access List

Access lists can contain more than one filtering statement, which are evaluated in physical sequence. Creating an effective access list requires that a certain amount of algorithmic logic be applied. If not carefully constructed, the actual results of an access list may be quite different from what you intended.

An access list works like this:

1. An incoming packet is compared to each line of the access list in sequence until a match is found.

2. After a match is made, the action of the access list entry is acted upon and any remaining access list lines are ignored. However, if no match is found, no action is taken.

Like a safety net, all access lists should end with a statement that denies all access. The catchall statement is called an "implicit deny any," which means that if a packet hasn't matched any lines of the access list to that point, it will be discarded. For both standard and extended access lists (see "Configuring an IP access list" earlier in this chapter), a two-step process is used to activate them.

1. In global configuration mode, you define the access list by entering its lines one at a time, one after the other in sequence.

2. In interface configuration mode, the access list is applied to a specific interface (e0, s1, and so on). One more thing: You are allowed only one access list per protocol per interface.

If your access list contains multiple lines, maintenance can be a little tricky. With numbered (not named) access lists, you cannot simply add a line in the middle of the list. If you want to change an existing access list, you must first remove any and all preceding access list lines, line by line, and then re-enter them with the new line in its proper sequence.

Standard access lists

The general syntax of a standard access list is:

```
Access-list [number][permit or deny][source address]
```

After the access list is built, is it activated using the **protocol** configuration command. The option at the end of the command is used to indicate whether this access list entry is controlling incoming or outbound traffic (*out* is the default setting). The syntax of this command is:

```
protocol access-group access-list number {in|out}
```

A sample session yields this result:

```
Cisco_Networking(config)#access list 1 deny 172.30.16.0
Cisco_Networking(config)#int e0
Cisco_Networking(config-if)#IP access-group 1
```

The first command creates access list 1 with an entry to deny access to 172.30.16.0. Next, configuration mode is entered, and e0 (Ethernet0) is selected. Finally, the **IP access-group** command is used to assign access list 1 to e0 as an IP outbound access list. Remember that *out* is the default value.

The effect of these commands is to deny any traffic from IP address 172.30.16.0 from going out from the Cisco Networking router interface e0. Traffic from that network comes in on interface s0, but it will not be permitted to go out to interface e0, even if that was the route it wanted to take.

Extended access lists

Extended access lists filter packets using data other than just the source address. They also use the following data as filters:

- ✔ Destination address
- ✔ Source port
- ✔ Destination port
- ✔ Specific protocol in use (UDP, ICMP, or TCP)

As with a standard access list, applying an extended access list is a two-step process: Create the list and then apply it to an interface.

The command syntax for the Extended IP access list statement is

```
access-list [number] [permit or deny] [protocol] [source]
            [mask] [destination] [mask]
```

Here is the result from a sample session creating an extended IP access list on interface E0 (Ethernet interface 0) that permits IP traffic from the specific host 172.16.0.1 to any host on 192.168.1.0:

```
Cisco_Networking(config)#access-list 101 permit ip host
            172.16.0.1 192.168.1.0 0.0.0.255
Cisco_Networking(config)#int e0
Cisco_Networking(config-if)#access-group 101 in
Cisco_Networking(config-if)#^Z
```

In this example, notice that the next-to-last line uses the **access-group** command to assign access list 101 to the interface. The **access-list** command is used enter the access list, but the **access-group** command is used to link the access list to the interface.

Extended access lists can also deny (or permit) traffic by port number. A common error made when setting up an access list statement to permit or deny a specific port is that the port number cannot be denied by IP. It must be done with TCP or UDP.

Well-known ports are also called *TCP ports,* and that may help you tie the two together. When specifying a specific port to deny, remember that the protocol must be either TCP or UDP and that the port must be the correct TCP or UDP port number. (See "Knowing the Better-Known Ports," earlier in this chapter.)

The command structure used to permit or deny traffic using the port number adds the port, the operator operand, and the established parameters to the extended access list command:

```
access-list [number][permit or deny] [protocol] [source]
            [mask] [destination] [mask] [port] [operator
            operand] [established]
```

The **port** parameter indicates the port number to be permitted or denied. The **established** option permits TCP traffic to pass only if the packet is using an established connection. The **operator operand** options are

- ✔ lt = less than
- ✔ gt = greater than
- ✔ eq = equals
- ✔ neq = not equal

Here is a sample command that denies Telnet (port 23) access from IP address 10.1.1.1 into 10.1.1.2:

```
Cisco_Networking(config)#access-list 102 deny tcp host
            10.1.1.1 host 10.1.1.2 eq 23
```

Remember that extended access lists must be numbered in the range of 100 to 199. (See Table 15-1 earlier in the chapter.)

Named access lists

Beginning with Cisco IOS version 11.2, IP access lists can be assigned an alphanumeric name instead of the number required on all previous IOS releases. Using a named access list has two primary advantages over unnamed (numbered) lists:

- ✔ The limitation of only 99 standard access lists and 100 extended access lists is removed.
- ✔ Named access lists can be edited.

Two general rules concern using named IP access lists in place of numbered access lists:

> ✔ A name can only be used once, which means the same name cannot be used for multiple access lists or different types (an extended access list and a standard access list can't have the same name).
>
> ✔ Cisco IOS releases before 11.2 cannot use named IP access lists.

The name is entered in place of the number in the **access-list** command syntax:

```
Cisco_Networking(config)#access-list notelnet deny tcp host
        10.1.1.1 host 10.1.1.2 eq 23
```

Verifying the access list

After an access list has been configured and attached to an interface, you should always verify what has actually been put into operation. The **show ip interface** command lists all the active access lists. The following sample router display would be generated by the **show ip interface** command (this display has been modified from its original format; we have edited this display to fit your book):

```
Cisco_Networking#show ip interface
Ethernet0 is up, line protocol is up
...
Outgoing access list is 1
Inbound access list is not set
```

The command **show run,** which displays the running-configuration, also displays the interfaces that have access-groups assigned to them.

The **show-access list** command, which can be executed from user exec mode, displays all the access lists currently active on a router and how many times (since the last clear counter command) the access list has been enforced. You can modify this command by adding the specific access list that you want to see. For example, you could use **show access list 101.** Here's a sample display from this command:

```
Cisco_Networking>show access list
Standard IP access list 1
    deny    172.130.16.0
    (10 matches)
Extended IP access list 101
    permit ip host 172.130.0.1 192.168.1.0 0.0.0.255
    (22 matches)
```

Removing an access list

Removing an access list uses essentially the same procedures used to create it, only in reverse.

1. Remove the access list from the interface with the **no ip access-group** command.

2. The access list itself is removed with the **no access list** command.

The following results from a router session that removes the standard access list entered earlier in the chapter. (See "Extended access lists" earlier in this chapter.)

```
Cisco_Networking#config t
Enter configuration commands, one per line. End with CNTL/Z.
Cisco_Networking(config)#int e0
Cisco_Networking(config-if)#no ip access-group 101
Cisco_Networking(config)#no access-list 101
Cisco_Networking(config)#^Z
```

In configuration mode, the **no ip access-group 101** command removes the assignment of access list 101 from the Ethernet0 interface. Then the **no access-list 101** command removes access list 101 from the running-configuration on the router.

One word of caution for removing the access list from an interface: Any packets attempting to cross that interface will be passed along unchallenged. The effect of having no access list is to **permit any.** So, before removing an access list, be very sure that's what you want to do or that you are going to immediately replace it.

Wildcard Masking

Wildcard masks are used to permit or deny traffic based upon a specific IP address or group of IP addresses. Think of a wildcard mask as the exact opposite of the subnet mask (see Chapter 7). Binary numbers are still used, but now the 0s mean "check the number to see if it is valid" and the 1s mean "ignore the number." It's not true that Cisco did this only to confuse you; it is actually logical if you really think about it.

These examples should help you understand this new twist:

Example 1: You wish to deny all traffic from IP address 192.168.1.6, but only from it. What wildcard mask would you use?

```
              Decimal                    Binary
IP Address    192.168.1.6  11000000 10101000 00000001 00000110
Wildcard Mask 0.0.0.0      00000000 00000000 00000000 00000000
```

A wildcard mask of all zeroes (0.0.0.0) tells the router to check every bit in the incoming IP address to make sure that it is an exact match to the address in the access list statement.

Example 2: What if you want to deny traffic from the specific network of 192.168.0?

```
              Decimal                    Binary
IP Address    192.168.1.0  11000000 10101000 00000001 00000000
Wildcard Mask 0.0.0.255    00000000 00000000 00000000 11111111
```

The effect of this wildcard mask (0.0.0.255) is that the router checks each of the first three octets, and if they match the network address, it is denied (in this case) no matter what value the last octet may be.

A secret for figuring out what the wildcard mask should be to determine the subnet mask and then subtract it from 255.255.255.255. This will give you the appropriate wildcard mask. In that preceding example, if you subtract the subnet mask 255.255.255.0 from 255.255.255.255, you get the wildcard mask of 0.0.0.255.

```
  255.255.255.255
 +255.255.255.000     subnet mask
    0.  0.  0.255     wildcard mask
```

Another way to look at this is that the sum of every octet in both the subnet mask and the wildcard mask must total 255.

```
  255.255.224.000     subnet mask
 +  0.  0. 31.255     wildcard mask
  255.255.255.255
```

Moving in a different direction

Wildcard masks are applied in the opposite direction of a subnet mask. An IP subnet mask uses the bits covered by the binary 1s as the network ID and those corresponding to the 0s as the host ID. Remember that a subnet mask is trying to extract the network ID.

In wildcard masking, the portion of the IP address covered by the 0 bits is the part extracted to match the IP address in the access list criteria exactly. Any bit in the IP address covered by a 1 bit in the wildcard mask automatically is a match, because they are ignored.

This is an example of an **access list** command, followed by the syntax of the access list entry, and yes, you must enter the hyphen:

```
access-list 2 deny 172.16.10.196 0.0.0.0
access-list number {deny|permit} source [source-wildcard]
```

In this example, the source IP address is 172.16.10.196 and the wildcard mask is 0.0.0.0. The effect of this **access-list** command is that all traffic from the source IP address 172.16.10.196 will be denied. This is the affect of the all zeroes wildcard mask.

Take a look at the following access list. What traffic will this line permit?

```
access-list 3 permit 172.16.0.0 0.0.255.255
```

If your answer is that all traffic from any node on the 172.16 network will be allowed, you are correct! The wildcard mask of 0.0.255.255 instructs the router to match on the first two octets only. So, any source IP address with 172.16 in the first two octets is a match. The 172.16 of the source is covered by the 0.0 of the wildcard, thus these bits must mach exactly in order for this line to permit the traffic. The remaining two octets can have any value at all. Because of the 255.255 in the wildcard mask, they automatically match.

Remember that IP addresses, subnet masks, and wildcard masks have only four octets each. This will help you to separate those 0s that the router displays so closely together. If you think it is hard to separate them in our printed examples, it's worse when you are working on an actual router.

Discerning wildcard word meanings

Every time you type in a number, you have a one in ten chance of making a mistake. A typo in an access list can cause major problems for your users. The wrong number in either the IP address or the wildcard mask can permit all the wrong people or deny all the right people from your network. In case you're not sure, both of these conditions are bad.

The developers of the Cisco IOS must be as fumble-fingered as the rest of us, because they included a couple of features that help avoid making number entry mistakes when entering an access list entry. The access list wildcard words **any** and **host** can be used when building an access list.

The parameter **any** is the equivalent of the 255.255.255.255 wildcard mask, which says that you aren't concerned about the IP address. A good use for this option is to limit access by port number instead of the IP address (see "Extended access lists" later in this section). This line

```
access-list 4 permit 0.0.0.0 255.255.255.255
```

has the same effect as this line

```
access-list 4 permit any
```

This command, which you may or not want to use, would permit any traffic that had not been otherwise permitted or denied in an earlier statement. This may be either good or bad, so use it wisely and carefully, if at all.

The wildcard parameter **host** is the equivalent of assigning the wildcard mask 0.0.0.0 to an IP address, which means that the router is to check for a specific address. You would use this parameter like this:

```
access-list 111 permit tcp host 192.240.16.3
```

Working with IPX Access Lists

IPX access lists, like IP access lists, can be either standard or extended. However, standard IPX access lists, unlike standard IP access lists, can deny or permit based upon both source and destination addresses. Table 15-3 shows the access list numbers used for IPX access lists.

Table 15-3	IPX Access List Numbers
Access List Type	*Number Range*
Standard IPX access lists	800-899
Extended IPX access lists	900-999
IPX SAP access lists	1000-1099

The named access list option is not available on IPX.

You're in denial

A good access list statement to know and use is

```
deny any
```

This command is pretty darn arbitrary. It denies all traffic that was not permitted or denied by a preceding access list criteria. This command is implicitly added to the access list automatically by the router. You may include it if you wish, just as a reminder, but you really don't need to.

Remember that an access list is evaluated sequentially from the first line to the last. After the criteria is met, that action is taken on that packet and any remaining statements are ignored. If a packet does not match any of the criteria in the access list, then the packet is tossed aside by the implicit **deny any** command.

Applying the standard model

The syntax and structure of the IPX standard **access list** command is

```
Access list [number]{permit|deny} source network[network-
            node] destination network [network-node]
```

A couple of shortcuts are available in the IPX **access list** commands. In place of the local network number, you can substitute the number 0 and the number −1 (minus 1) to match all networks. Here are the results of some sample command entries:

```
Cisco_Networking(config)#access-list 801 deny FF 0
Cisco_Networking(config)#access-list 801 permit -1 -1
```

The first entry denies traffic from network FF to the local network; the second entry permits all other traffic.

Using the extended form

In addition to the abilities of the IPX standard access list, the IPX extended access list can filter traffic based on the IPX protocol (SAP, SPX, and so on) and the source and destination socket (address plus port) numbers.

The command structure and syntax for creating an IPX extended access list is

```
Access-list {number} {permit/deny} {protocol} {source}
            {socket} {destination} {socket}
```

The codes that can be used for the common protocols and sockets are listed in Tables 15-4 and 15-5, respectively.

Table 15-4	IPX Protocol Type Numbers
Protocol	*Code*
Any	−1
Undefined	0
RIP	1
SAP	4
SPX	5
NCP	17

Table 15-5	IPX Socket Numbers
Socket	*Code*
All	0
NCP	451
SAP	452
RIP	453

The syntax and structure of the command used to activate an IPX access list is

```
ipx access-group access-list number [in|out]
```

These are sample commands used to create an IPX access list:

```
Cisco_Networking#config t
Enter configuration commands, one per line. End with CNTL/Z.
Cisco_Networking(config)#access-list 801 deny 35 5
Cisco_Networking(config)#access-list 801 permit -1 -1
Cisco_Networking(config)#int e0
Cisco_Networking(config-if)#ipx access-group 801 out
Cisco_Networking(config-if)#^Z
```

The first entry in IPX access list 801 denies access to network 5 from network 35. The second entry permits anything not already denied or permitted and is roughly the equivalent of the **permit any** of the IP access list. The next-to-last command assigns the access list to Ethernet0 for outbound traffic.

Using SAP filters

No, this isn't some new device to keep your brother-in-law away! IPX informs clients and neighboring routers of changes in network resources and services availability though SAP (Service Advertising Protocol) advertisements. Routers don't forward these SAP broadcasts (advertisements). Instead, they build SAP tables, which are broadcast every 60 seconds. By setting up an SAP filter, you can limit the amount of information that is sent out in the SAP updates, and you can limit who can access them as well. SAP filters can be either input or output.

- ✔ **Input SAP filters** reduce the number of services entered into the SAP table, which results in a reduction in the size of the SAP table itself.

- ✔ **Output SAP filters** reduce the number of services transmitted from the SAP table.

To configure an SAP filter to an interface, the **ipx input-sap-filter** and the **ipx output-sap-filter** commands are entered in interface-configuration mode. Each SAP filter, regardless of input or output, must be assigned an **access list number** command in the range of 1000–1099.

This is a sample of the commands used to configure a SAP filter:

```
Cisco_Networking(config)#access-list 1050 permit
            15.0000.0100.0001 0
Cisco_Networking(config)#int e0
Cisco_Networking(config-if)#ipx input-sap-filter 1050
Cisco_Networking(config-if)#^Z
```

These commands create an access list with the number 1050. This filter is reserved for IPX SAP filters that let the outside world see only the network specified in the command over the Ethernet0 interface. Any packets entering this port will be included in SAP updates.

Part V
LANs and WANs

The 5th Wave   By Rich Tennant

"This part of the test tells us whether you're personally suited to the job of network administrator."

In this part . . .

*I*f we could put an icon on this part, it would be the "Technical Stuff" icon. This part of the book covers the ways in which a switch can be used to improve the operations of a LAN and takes a look at bridging as a network option.

The use of a Cisco router on a network usually means the network is connecting to a WAN. Well, many different types of transport models can be used to move data from a LAN out into the wide world of the Internet. This part of the book takes a look at many of the more common transport technologies in use and how your router can be configured to work with them.

A network is a wonderful thing, if it just wasn't for those darn users. Well, as bad as your LAN's users may be, they're nothing compared to the nasties lurking out on the WAN. This part of the book also provides an overview to the ways in which a firewall, proxy server, or cache server can be used to add another layer of security.

Finally, we finish up with a step-by-step guide to the processes and considerations of designing a Cisco-based network.

Chapter 16

Switching Around the LAN

. . . .

In This Chapter

▶ Listing the advantages of LAN segmentation

▶ Segmenting a LAN with a switch

▶ Describing switching methods

▶ Defining a virtual LAN

. . . .

*I*f this book had a subtitle, it would be "Routing and Switching," because that's really what a Cisco network is all about and routing and switching deals primarily with local area networks (LANs). Routing is the primary focus of a Cisco network administrator's duties, but network switching isn't that far behind. Routing is a very important element of Cisco's overall networking strategy, but anyone working on a Cisco network should also be well versed in the other major Cisco products, especially switches, and their applications. We won't be surprised if, in the not-too-distant future, separate jobs pop up around the community with titles like "Cisco routing administrator" and "Cisco LAN switching administrator."

In an attempt to provide some fairness and the semblance of equal time, this chapter focuses on Cisco switches, including LAN segmentation with a switch and why you would want to do it. There's more to switching than just segmenting LANs, and we include information on the other important switching areas.

Switching Around the Network

A switch is a Data Link layer (Layer 2) connectivity device used in networks to help move data to its destination. A switch's capability ranges from not much more than a smart hub to functions that are virtually the same as a router. But by and large, a *switch* is used to select the path that a data packet should use to reach its destination address on a local area network.

In comparison to a router, a switch is simpler in construction and logic and, as a result, is a much faster device than a router. A router must have knowledge of the network and the routes through the network to be effective. To do its job, a switch needs to know only one thing: whether a destination address can be found on a network segment attached to the switch.

Talking about switches

You may find that some of the same terms used to describe routers are used for switches as well. When data moves from one switch to another, it takes a *hop*. A switch also has *latency,* which is the time it takes the switch to determine where to send a packet.

This is as good a place as any to discuss the types of switching:

- ✔ Port switching
- ✔ Circuit switching
- ✔ Packet switching

You need to know how these switching types differ, because it can really have an impact on your network's performance and efficiency if you try to use the wrong ones.

Switching IP packets

First of all, when only the word *switching* is used, it refers to LAN switching. *Packet switching* is the type of switching used on LANs and most WANs. Packets are switched between parts of the network, depending on the source and destination addresses. Cisco switches are packet-switching switches; they are also referred to as IP switches. An IP switch uses the Internet Protocol (IP) addressing in each packet to determine the best route the packet should use, which is exactly what packet switching devices do.

Switching circuits

Circuit switching involves creating a circuit or connection for the exclusive use of two or more parties for a period of time, at which point the circuit is switched and assigned to another set of parties. If this sounds something like the telephone system, it is. Circuit switching is used for standard voice traffic, but it's also used for broadband technologies like ATM (Asynchronous Transfer Mode), a cell-switching technology.

Switching from port to port

A *port-switching device* is an intelligent network device, meaning a network device that includes some processing capability, that can be attached to multiple LAN segments. Using software, a port-switching device connects one of its station ports to one particular LAN segment to create a sort of virtual LAN (VLAN). (See "Virtually Segmenting the LAN," later in this chapter, for more information on VLANs.) The most common port-switching devices are called hubs, but Catalyst (a Cisco brand name) switches also include port-switching capabilities.

Switches and LANs

A LAN can be segmented for performance purposes using a switch, in the same way that it can be segmented using a router or a bridge. (See the next section, "Segmenting a LAN.") Because routers are so expensive and bridges are harder to find and are much more specialized, Cisco networks are most commonly segmented using a switch.

A switch provides the following services to a LAN:

- Full-duplex networking
- Multiple simultaneous connections
- High-speed networking support featuring low latency and high data rates
- Dedicated and adaptable bandwidth per port

The switch's ability to connect to and support virtual LANs (VLANs) using different bandwidths on separate port connections is its most valuable feature, not to mention its value in LAN segmentation.

Segmenting a LAN

Depending on how LAN segmentation is implemented, several benefits can result. The primary benefits of segmentation are

- Increased bandwidth per user
- Creating smaller collision domains
- Overcoming the maximum node and distance limitations associated with shared media networks, such as Ethernet

Probably the first thing we should establish for you is why would you want to segment a LAN in the first place. Just because the Cisco Web site contains lots of white papers on this subject doesn't mean that it's like a real thing, does it? Well, yes and no. Not every LAN needs to be segmented, but it is a technique that can be applied to ensure a network's performance as it grows. Think of it this way: When too many cars try to occupy the highways and freeways around cities, the roadways get congested. Networks don't have gawker blocks, thank goodness, but when too many users are demanding too much bandwidth from a network, it can become congested. On the roads, other factors can contribute to the problem besides too many cars. Perhaps a slow traffic light or a stalled car is the problem, much like a slow server or too little RAM can slow the throughput on a network.

Whatever the cause of the congestion, one of the best and most efficient ways to solve the problem is to break up the network into smaller subnetworks, called segments, which maximizes network resources over smaller groups, usually of common or compatible resource needs.

You can segment a network in two ways:

- **Physical segmentation:** A router or bridge is used to create more, but smaller, collision domains. This action minimizes the number of workstations on the same network segment and reduces the demand for bandwidth by simply limiting the nodes on a segment. See Chapter 10 for more information on segmenting a LAN with a router.

- **Network switching:** You can use a switch to further divide a physical segment by providing packet switching, which relieves bandwidth congestion on the network segments attached to it.

Segmenting a LAN with a bridge

Using a bridge to segment a network is one of the physical segmentation techniques. You can use a bridge, which operates on the Data Link layer (Layer 2) of the OSI model, to create two or more physical or logical segments. The network nodes on a bridged network segment are on the same subnet (logical network), and any broadcast messages generated on a bridged network segment are sent only to the nodes on the same network segment. This serves to keep local traffic local and relieves other segments of unnecessary traffic.

However — and this is one of the bad things about using a bridge to segment a LAN — if a destination node is unknown to the bridge, the message is broadcast to all connected segments. Only a single path exists between bridged networks, and usually no provision is made for redundancy in the bridge. You can bridge a LAN using two major methods:

- ✔ Transparent
- ✔ Source-route

Crossing the transparent bridge

Transparent bridging occurs primarily on Ethernet networks, where the bridge is responsible for determining the path from the source node to the destination node. A *transparent bridge* examines the incoming frame and reads the destination MAC address. It then looks in its bridging table and, if it finds the address, sends the packet to the appropriate port. Otherwise, the frame is sent to all ports except the one that it came in on.

Bridging from the source

Token ring networks use source-route bridging (SRB). In this bridging method, the responsibility of determining the path to the destination node is placed on the sending node, not on the bridge.

In an SRB environment, these steps are taken:

1. Token ring devices send out a test frame to determine whether the destination node is on the local ring.

2. If no answer is forthcoming, which means the destination node is not on the local ring, the sending node sends out a broadcast message, which is called an *explorer frame.*

3. The bridge forwards the explorer frame across the network through the network's bridges.

   Each bridge adds its ring number and bridge number to the frame's routing information field (RIF), which is a sort of Hansel and Gretel breadcrumb trail, so it can retrace its route later.

4. The destination device, if it exists, receives and responds to the explorer frame. The sending node gets this response.

5. The sending node initiates communications between the two devices, with each intermediate bridge using the RIF value to determine the path between the two nodes.

Because SRB uses RIF information to determine its routes, no bridging table is created.

Segmenting the LAN with a router

Routers, which operate on the Network layer (Layer 3) of the OSI model, allow you to create and connect several logical networks, including those using different topologies or technologies, such as Token ring and Ethernet (see Chapter 2 for information on these networking technologies), into a single internetwork. Inserting a router into a network, which is a physical segmentation, creates separate network segments, which the router manages independently. Routers provide multiple paths between segments and map the nodes on the segments and the connecting paths with a routing protocol and internal routing tables (see Chapter 10).

Routing over a segmented network is no different than routing over any internetwork.

1. When the router receives a frame, it looks at the destination network address.

2. One of three things happens:

   • If the destination is on a network segment directly connected to the router, the router forwards the frame over the appropriate port interfacing to that segment.

   • Otherwise, the routing table is searched to determine whether the router has a forwarding address for the packet or if the default route should be used.

   • If multiple segments are attached to the router, chances are the frame will remain in the physical and logical structure connected to the router and will not be broadcast throughout the entire network.

Segmenting a LAN with a switch

Using a switch to segment a LAN increases the chances that a message will be forwarded to the right segment without the need for network-wide broadcasts. Fewer broadcast messages means more bandwidth for other traffic, which translates to more bandwidth for everyone.

A switch, which operates on the Data Link layer (Layer 2) of the OSI model, typically has a high-capacity back plane (commonly in the gigabit range). The *back plane* serves as a buffer to temporarily store message frames. A switch's back plane provides an additional pool of available bandwidth to each node on each segment attached to the switch.

When a data frame enters a port, the switch reads the source MAC address of the frame and stores it along with the TCP port ID (see Chapter 5) in the CAM (content-addressable memory) table — assuming, of course, that this information isn't already in the table. Using the CAM table, a switch can readily look up a node by its MAC address, should anything come into the switch addressed to it. In this way, the switch keeps track of which nodes are on which segments. The CAM table is stored in volatile RAM, which means that the CAM table must be rebuilt if the power is interrupted.

The ports on a switch can be configured to support a virtual LAN (VLAN). A *VLAN* is a logical network segment with a unique configuration to that of the segments on the other ports of the switch. Simply put, a VLAN is a way to flock birds of a feather together. Each port on the switch can be uniquely configured to provide adjustments for data speed, transmission mode, and any other special LAN characteristics used by the logical network segment represented by the VLAN.

Applying Three Methods to Switching Success

The three most common methods used to forward data packets through a switch are cut-through (a.k.a. real-time), store-and-forward, and fragment-free.

- **Cut-through switching:** This type of switching method has lower latency (the additional time required for switching the packet) because it begins to forward a frame as soon as the source and destination MAC addresses are read, which is typically within the first 12 bytes of an Ethernet frame.

- **Store-and-forward switching:** This type of switching has higher latency because it reads the entire frame into its buffer before beginning to forward the frame out to another port. The benefits of the increased latency are filtering, management, and traffic control. In addition, a store-and-forward switch can recognize and discard runts (frames missing segments), giants (frames with extra segments), and damaged frames. Discarding these defective frames reduces traffic on the network.

- **Fragment-free switching:** This switching method is a hybrid of cut-through switching that receives just a little more of the frame before beginning to forward the frame. The amount of the frame received is called the *collision window.* The frame isn't sent out until 64 bytes have been received. Frames shorter than 64 bytes, which may be mistaken for collision fragments — the damaged flotsam of frames that have collided on the network — aren't transmitted.

Virtually Segmenting the LAN

A VLAN (virtual LAN) is a logical grouping of networked nodes that communicate directly with each other on Layers 2 and 3. When you use switches to segment a LAN, you will need to create at least two VLANs across two or more switches. VLANs are also called logical LANs because they aren't created physically using Layer 1 media and devices. Instead, they're created logically or virtually through the configuration on a router or switch. A VLAN is not geographically or functionally fixed in place (such as within a single department of a company or for all account representatives). It's created and managed on either a router or a switch, which serves as the VLAN controller.

VLANs are created usually in the process of segmenting a network with the objective of load-balancing traffic over the network and managing bandwidth allocations more easily than with the physical management of a LAN. Each station port on a switch can host a separate VLAN with its own data speeds, modes, technologies, and other characteristics.

The primary benefits offered by VLANs are

- ✔ Functional workgroups
- ✔ Broadcast control
- ✔ Enhanced security

Building workgroups

Study Figure 16-1 and follow this scenario to help you understand VLAN implementation.

- ✔ Switch A is located in the MDF (Main Distribution Frame).
- ✔ Switches B and C are located in IDFs (Intermediate Distribution Frame) on two different floors, connected by fiber optic media through a trunking protocol.

The alpha character on the workstation represents the switch to which each node is connected, and the numeral indicates a workgroup. Because members of workgroups tend to communicate more with other members of the workgroup than with outsiders, grouping them logically into VLAN1, VLAN2, and VLAN3 makes sense, despite the fact that they're physically located on different floors.

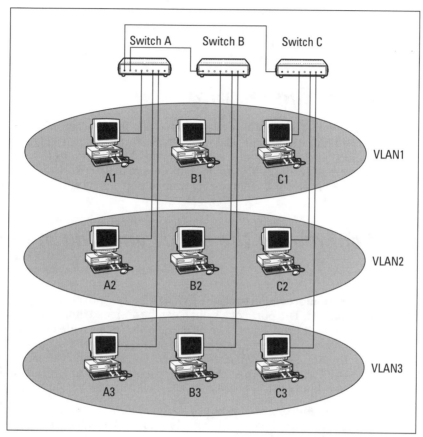

Figure 16-1:
A VLAN
workgroup
created
across three
physical
LAN
segments.

The point at which the physical wiring from multiple network components is concentrated is called a *distribution frame*. A *main distribution frame* is the central wiring location for a network, such as the telephone closet in a building. An *intermediate distribution frame* is a connecting point located between the main distribution frame and network workstations.

Broadcasting to smaller domains

You can think of a VLAN as a broadcast domain with logically defined perimeters that are unconstrained by physical location, media, addressing, or transmission rates. The virtual broadcast domain created by the VLAN may contain workstations with different characteristics, including location, network medium, a MAC addressing scheme (IP versus IPX), and bandwidth. By limiting broadcast messages to smaller and more manageable logical broad-cast domains or virtual workgroups (VLANs), the performance of the entire non-virtual network is improved.

Improving security

Implementing a VLAN improves a network's security automatically. Members of one VLAN can't access data being transmitted on other VLANs or on any circuits outside the VLAN. This means that back in Figure 16-1, the users of the workgroup on VLAN3 are in their own virtual network and are prevented from seeing any of the data being transmitted across either VLAN1 or VLAN2.

Configuring the VLAN one way or another

The assignment of a VLAN can be made in four different ways on the switch:

- **Port address:** Port-assigned VLANs are the most commonly imple-mented. The ports of a switch can be assigned individually, in groups, in rows, or even across two or more switches, provided the switches are properly connected through a trunking protocol. Port-based VLANs are the simplest to implement and are typically used in situations where DHCP (Dynamic Host Control Protocol) is used to assign IP addresses to network hosts.

- **MAC address:** MAC address-assigned VLANs are rare, primarily due to the increased popularity and use of DHCP on networks. MAC-based VLANs enable a user to belong to the same VLAN at all times, even when connecting to the network with a different MAC address or through a dif-ferent port on the switch. The MAC addresses in a MAC-based VLAN must be entered into the switch and configured as a part of a specific VLAN. Although this is great for users who may move about, this type of VLAN can be very complex and difficult for the administrator to manage and troubleshoot.

- **User ID:** User ID-assigned VLANs are also quite rare because they are complex to set up, administer, and troubleshoot. All VLAN users must be identified and entered into the switch and configured as a part of a spe-cific VLAN. On a user-based VLAN, the user remains a part of the same VLAN regardless of where on the network or on which host they log onto the network.

✔ **Network address:** Network address-assigned VLANs are configured much like MAC-based VLANs, with the exception that nodes are registered using their logical or IP addresses. Network address-based VLANs are uncommon primary because of the use of DHCP to assign workstation IP addresses. Like the MAC-based VLAN, this type of VLAN allows the user to remain part of the same VLAN even when he relocates to a different physical port connection to the network, provided, of course, that he keeps the same IP address.

Trunking together VLANs

Normally, segmenting a LAN with switches involves the creation of at least two VLANs across two or more switches. After the VLANs are created, any information about them is shared between the switches using a trunking protocol. Sharing information allows all the switches involved in a VLAN to be fully aware of the VLAN, its hosts, and the locations of the hosts so that each switch is ready to support it. By default, trunking protocols, which are used to pass information between switches, are disabled on all ports.

Before a VLAN can be configured between two switches, trunking be must enabled on the ports to be used to connect the switches together. A trunk line carries the combined traffic of one or more VLANs to another switch or router. Trunking services allow VLANs to be extended across the network and over other switches or routers.

The two most commonly used trunking methods are:

✔ **Inter-Switch Link (ISL):** ISL is a proprietary Cisco protocol that's supported only between Cisco devices. ISL supports transportation across Ethernet, FDDI, or token ring environments. A physical router interface to each VLAN is unnecessary with a Cisco router running ISL.

✔ **IEEE 802.1Q:** The 802.1 subcommittee defines this as an industry standard protocol that allows VLAN information exchange between dissimilar manufacturers' equipment.

Two other trunking methods are used on Cisco networks — IEEE 802.10 and an ATM-based protocol called LANE (LAN Emulation), but they are advanced topics not commonly found on most LANs. We mention them here just so you have heard of them.

Picking the Right Switch for the Job

Cisco has more than 10 different series of switches available, one of which will provide an appropriate type of switching to any network. And this doesn't include the hubs and smart hubs that Cisco lists in the switching products family.

These are the most popular switching equipment items offered by Cisco:

- **Catalyst 1900 series:** The switches in this series represent the best combination of value and power in the Cisco Catalyst switch line. These switches provide both 10Mbps and 100Mbps, powering both the desktop and workgroup connectivity over UTP wire or fiber-optic cable (see Chapter 4 for more information on network cabling).

- **Catalyst 2900 series:** This switch family delivers the same power as larger Cisco switches, but in a smaller package. The Catalyst 2926 is a single configuration 10Mpbs/100Mbps auto-sensing switch that uses the same architecture and software as the larger Catalyst 5000. The Cisco Catalyst 2900 XL switches are 10/100 auto-sensing switches that offer a wide range of different port densities, configuration options, and pricing. The Cisco 2912 and 2924 switches are very common on LANs.

- **Catalyst 3500 series:** The 12-, 24-, and 48-port switches in this series are 10/100 and gigabit Ethernet switches that offer very fast switching. The 3500 series is an excellent choice for high-performance LANs, including such features as Cisco Switch Clustering multi-device management architecture, and VoIP (Voice over IP).

- **Catalyst 3900:** This switch offers a stackable, flexible switching solution to token ring networks.

- **Catalyst 5000 series:** This switch series provides large intranets and high-performance switched LANs with media-independent support for all LAN switching technologies over Ethernet, Fast Ethernet, FDDI, ATM, token ring, and gigabit Ethernet (see Chapter 2 for more information on network technologies). This switch group is capable of handling more than 10 million packets per second.

Get another book

Cisco does have larger, more sophisticated switching solutions above the Catalyst 5000 series, such as the 6000 and 8500 series, but these switches are normally found only in LAN/WAN integration and CAN (Campus Area Network) situations. If you find yourself in one of these situations, you need much more information than this book can provide.

Chapter 17

Making a WAN Work

*W*elcome to acronym land! The wacky world of WAN, itself a TLA, is chocked full of abbreviations and acronyms. You may find more TLAs (three-letter acronyms) and FLAs (four-letter acronyms) in this chapter than perhaps any other in this book. Acronyms just come with the territory. We're not sure that we believe it, but we hear that after Alexander Graham Bell made his first voice connection with Mr. Watson (and no this is not the same guy who founded IBM), he wrote in his notes, "poor SVC; investigate PPP or ISDN."

Data communications and especially WAN services are the domain of protocols, and protocols are the domain of funny sounding acronyms. In this chapter, we look at the protocols and services used to connect a network to the outside world, whether it is only to another segment of the same network or to the global network.

Differentiating WAN Services

WAN services are the various protocols and technologies that you can use to connect your LAN to the Internet or to interconnect LAN networks within a single enterprise. Nearly all LANs use at least one WAN service, which is why you don't need to be an expert on every WAN service to manage your network or to manage the people who manage your network. However, you should have a good understanding of the various WAN services available in order to make the best choices for your network and to know the right way to configure your routers.

Deciphering WAN services

To really be prepared to make the best choices for your network and to impress your friends and associates with the girth of your knowledge, we believe that you should know about the following WAN services:

- **ATM (Asynchronous Transfer Mode):** ATM is a connection-oriented, packet-switched network architecture, loosely based on ISDN that delivers very high bandwidth, up to 2.488 gigabits per second.

- **Frame-Relay:** This WAN service creates permanent virtual circuits (PVCs) between points on the network to provide fast packet switching and very fast throughput.

- **HDLC (High-Level Data-Link Control):** This bit-oriented, synchronous protocol is used for high-level connections to X.25 packet-switching networks. HDLC uses variable-length packets to gain throughput efficiency.

- **ISDN (Integrated Systems Digital Network):** Some people that say that ISDN stands for "It still doesn't network." Actually, ISDN has been around for a while and is still somewhat popular for both home and office use. ISDN sends digital signals over the PSTN (public switched telephone network — you know, the regular telephone system) to carry as much as 1.536Mbps.

- **PPP (Point-to-Point Protocol):** This is the industry standard, the veritable workhorse, of WAN communications. It should be no surprise that PPP is designed to carry data from router to router, from host to host, or from one network workstation to another; in other words, from point to point.

- **X.25:** Despite the fact that it sounds like a secret government project, which they deny of course, X.25 is one of a series of *X* communications standards. The X.25 standard covers how a message is formatted for transmission over a common carrier between networks of dissimilar hardware and software.

Learning the lingo

Okay, so we threw around a few phrases such as ". . . high-level connections to X.25 packet-switching networks," and we will again in the remainder of this chapter. We try to be as gentle as we can, but WAN services have their very own language and you just can't get around it.

So, in the interest of your continued reading and understanding pleasure, we present these definitions of the more important WAN terms that you should know:

✔ **Bit-oriented:** Services oriented to transferring data in bit streams without regard to packets or cells are called bit-oriented.

✔ **Cell-switching:** Services that move data in fixed-length packets over pathways between end nodes called virtual circuits are referred to as cell-switching services. ATM (Asynchronous Transfer Mode) is a cell-switching service.

✔ **Circuit-switching:** Networks, including the PSTN (public switched telephone network), that create (or "nail up") a circuit that exists only to handle a single communications session, such as a telephone conversation, are circuit-switched networks.

✔ **Local exchange carrier (LEC):** The company that provides telephone services to your home or business (including dial tone) is your local exchange carrier. The company occupying the central office (CO) where your telephone circuits terminate is the incumbent LEC (ILEC). Any competing company that arranges with the ILEC to provide services from the CO (such as most DSL providers) is a competing LEC (CLEC).

✔ **DCE (Data Communication Equipment):** In data communications, this is the device that physically exchanges the data with a computer (the DTE) and transmits the data over the communications media.

✔ **DTE (Data Terminal Equipment):** In data communications, this is the device or interface used by a computer to exchange data with a modem or other serial device (the DCE).

✔ **Encapsulation:** The inclusion of one data structure in another data structure that results in the first data structure being hidden or masked during data transmission is called encapsulation.

✔ **Packet switching:** Small units of data, called packets, are transferred over the network based on the destination address of the packet. Routed networks are packet-switched networks.

✔ **PVC (permanent virtual circuit):** A software-defined logical connection in a Frame-Relay network that defines the connections and bandwidth between two end points is called a PVC. A PVC is permanently defined and remains defined between the two end points before and after communications sessions.

✔ **SVC (switched virtual circuit):** A virtual circuit that exists only for the duration of a communications session is called an SVC.

✔ **VC (virtual circuit):** A circuit or path between two points on a network that is allocated as needed to meet traffic requirements is called a VC. Two types of VCs exist: PVCs and SVCs.

Connecting with the Mysterious X.25

Way back in the 1970s, many so-called public data networks were actually owned by private companies and government agencies. In most cases, the wide area network of one company or agency was unique and often incompatible with the network of another company or agency. Naturally, when it became necessary for these networks to interconnect, some form of common network interface protocol became necessary.

In 1976, the International Consultative Committee for Telegraphy and Telephony (CCITT), which by the way is now called the ITU (International Telecommunication Union), thank goodness, recommended a protocol it called X.25. This protocol defined a packet-switched networking protocol for exchanging data over a connection-oriented service.

X.25 also defines the control information that is passed between these two things:

- **Data Terminal Equipment (DTE):** A user device. DTE equipment typically consists of terminals, PCs, routers, and bridges that are owned by the customer.
- **Data Circuit-Terminating Equipment (DCE):** DCE equipment are typically carrier-owned internetworking devices.

In the following sections, we cover a range of X.25 topics that are definitely of interest to you if you plan to incorporate X.25 services into your network, including:

- X.25 addressing schemes
- Virtual circuits
- X.25 router interfaces
- The layers of X.25 communications.

Addressing the X.25 world

On both the X.25 and LAPB layers (see "The layers of the X.25 cake" later in this section), an emphasis is placed on flow control and error checking (see Chapter 5 for more information on these two concepts), which reduces the need for these services to be performed by protocols or services outside of X.25, such as TCP. This is very important over connections using an unreliable service, such as analog (cell-switching) dialup access to a modem (see "Getting from Point-to-Point" later in the chapter). However, when X.25 is used over more reliable digital connections, such as Frame-Relay or dedicated digital telephone lines, X.25's insistence on performing flow control and error checking can be a drawback, because these actions aren't really necessary and add additional overhead.

Each X.25 link consists of a DTE at one end and a DCE at the other. The DTE is typically a router or PAD (Packet Assembler/Disassembler), while the DCE is a switch or concentrator on the public data network.

The X.25 addressing scheme consists of a four-decimal-digit DNIC (Data Network Identification Code) and a NTN (Network Terminal Number) that consists of up to 11 decimal digits. The DNIC ("dee-nick") includes the country code and a provider number that is assigned by the ITU. But wait, there's more! The combination of the last digit of the DNIC and the first eight digits of the NTN makeup the unique address that is allocated to a specific X.25 network.

Now for the bad news: X.25 does not include a protocol like TCP/IP's Address Resolution Protocol (ARP) (see Chapter 5 for information on TCP/IP protocols), which means that if you want to connect a router to an X.25 service, you must manually map all X.25 addresses to their associated IP addresses in the router. We don't need to tell you how much fun that can be!

Working with virtual circuits

X.25 uses a virtual circuit (VC). The VC has many aliases, including:

- ✔ Virtual circuit number (VCN)
- ✔ Logical channel number (LCN)
- ✔ Virtual channel identifier (VCI)

A VC may consist of a permanent virtual circuit (PVC) or a switched virtual circuit (SVC).

- ✔ A PVC, which is called a "nailed up" circuit, is a permanent, dedicated, and continuous VC. A PVC is permanently defined

- ✔ An SVC is a temporary virtual circuit that is created especially for and exists only for the duration of a particular data communications session. An SVC, the one you care about, exists only for a single communications session.

Three steps are associated with creating, using, and clearing an SVC:

- ✔ **Call setup:** Before any of the data is sent, the sending DTE sends a circuit request packet to its local PSE (packet-switching equipment, usually at the phone company) that contains, in addition to the network address of the destination DTE, a VCI reference number. The PSE forwards the packet through the network. At the destination PSE, a second VCI is assigned to the request, which is forwarded to the destination DTE. When the destination DTE connects, in effect accepting the call, a virtual circuit exists between the two DTEs

- ✔ **Information transfer:** After the SVC is created, the information transfer phase assigns each packet the same VCI numbers as were used to create the circuit. This allows the DTEs to differentiate packets from multiple sessions arriving on the same link. Because error and flow control are provided at the packet level, data reliability is very high.

- ✔ **Call CLEAR:** At the end of the session, the circuit is cleared by the source DTE sending a clearing request to the PSE, which relays it on to the destination PSE and DTE. If the circuit is a permanent virtual circuit (PVC), this step is not performed.

Routers and X.25

A single X.25 interface on a router can be configured to support up to 4,095 (your lucky number) SVCs. By combining multiple SVCs for a single specific protocol the throughput can be increased assuming that the protocol provides its own packet resequencing. A maximum of eight SVCs may be combined into one path for a protocol.

When implementing X.25 on a Cisco router, you must configure three interface items. You use these commands to do that:

```
encapsulation x25 dte or dce (dte is the default)
x25 address x.121-address
x25 map protocol address x.121-address [options]
```

Using a tunneling process, almost any Network layer protocol (see the next section) can be transmitted across X.25 virtual circuits. *Tunneling* is a process in which packets are encapsulated within an X.25 packet for transmission over a virtual circuit.

The following data communications protocols and services support X.25 WAN services:

- ✔ IP (Internet Protocol)
- ✔ AppleTalk
- ✔ Novell IPX

✔ Banyan Vines

✔ XNS (Xerox Network Systems)

✔ DECnet

✔ ISO-CLNS (Connectionless Mode Network Service)

✔ Apollo

✔ Compressed TCP (Transmission Control Protocol)

✔ Bridging

The layers of the X.25 cake

X.25 has three layers that track to the lower three layers of the OSI model (Network, Data Link, and Physical). See Chapter 5 for information on the OSI model and its layers. The three layers of X.25 services are

✔ **X.25** (Layer 3), which is also called the Packet Level, describes the data transfer protocol in the packet switched network. It is similar to the OSI Network layer (Layer 3) model and similarly creates network data units called packets, which contain both control information and user data. The packet level also includes procedures for establishing virtual circuits (temporary associations) and permanent virtual circuits (PVC) which is a permanent association between two DTEs, and defines datagrams — self-contained data units that include the information needed to route the unit to its destination.

✔ **LAPB** (Layer 2), which is also called the Link level, ensures the reliable transfer of data between the DTE and the DCE using a sequence of frames that contain address, control, and data fields. The functions performed by the Link level also include link synchronization, error detection, and recovery. These protocols used on this level of X.25 protocols:

  • **LAPB (Link Access Protocol, Balanced)** is a derivative of HDLC (High-Level Data Link Control) that is the most commonly used X.25 Link level protocol.

  • **LAPD (Link Access Procedure, D Channel)** is an ISDN protocol (not to be confused with the Los Angeles Police Department).

  • **LLC (Logical Link Control)** is an IEEE 802 protocol used to transmit X.25 packets over a LAN.

  • **LAP (Link Access Protocol)** is the precursor to LAPB and is no longer commonly used.

✔ **Physical level** (Layer 1) describes interfaces with the physical environment much like the OSI model's Physical layer.

Connecting Up with Frame-Relay

Compared to X.25 (see "Connecting with the Mysterious X.25" earlier in this chapter), Frame-Relay is a next-generation protocol that is optimized for better performance and more efficient frame transmission. You should know these key characteristics of Frame-Relay:

- **Encapsulation:** Rather than a specific interface type, Frame-Relay is an encapsulation method that operates over virtually all serial interfaces.

- **Error-checking and flow control:** Frame-Relay depends on upper-layer protocols to provide flow control and error correction.

- **Media:** Frame-Relay was designed specifically for use on fiber-optic cables and digital networks.

Frame-Relay operates on Layers 1 and 2 (the Physical and Data Link layers) of the OSI reference model (see Chapter 5). Although originally designed to operate on ISDN networks, it is frequently implemented on numerous other network interfaces. (See "Deciphering WAN services" earlier in this chapter for more Frame-Relay information.) The Cisco implementation of Frame-Relay supports the following protocols:

- IP
- DECnet
- AppleTalk
- XNS (Xerox Network Services)
- Novell IPX
- CLNS (Connectionless Network Service)
- ISO (International Organization for Standards)
- Banyan Vines
- Transparent Bridging

Framing the frame

Like most WAN services, Frame-Relay provides a communications interface between the DTE and DCE devices. And like X.25, Frame-Relay provides connection-oriented Layer 2 communications over a packet-switched network, although Frame-Relay is faster and more efficient than X.25.

This is an excellent opportunity to discuss encapsulation. Although briefly mentioned in Chapter 2, *encapsulation* is the process that allows a data packet to move through the various protocols and services to reach its destination. At various stages on its way out of the source network, the original data bundle has additional information added to it, in the form of headers and trailers, that is used at the destination network to ensure it gets to its destination with its contents intact. Before all of this information is sent out over a WAN service, it is placed in what amounts to a Physical layer shipping container, a process called encapsulation.

The encapsulation container for Frame-Relay is the frame. The format of the Frame-Relay frame is shown in Figure 17-1. Data transmitted over a Frame-Relay line is encapsulated in frames that are in this format. The information field segment of the frame is where the original data bundle, along with any added headers or trailers, is placed. You don't really need to know the format of a Frame-Relay frame, you should at least be aware of parts of the Frame-Relay header, as they can impact the performance of the system, as we discuss in the next few sections.

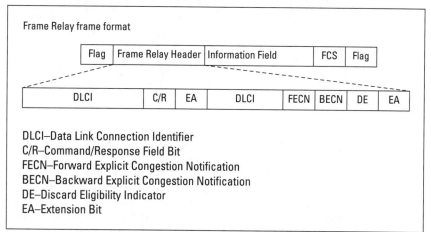

Figure 17-1:
The Frame-Relay frame format.

Framing the DLCI

Frame-Relay has two key players:

- ✔ The DTE (also called customer premises equipment or CPE), which is typically a router.

- ✔ The PSE (packet-switching equipment), which is located at the network service provider (commonly the phone company or a CLEC), that takes the form of the DCE.

Frame-Relay also has the following characteristics:

- ✔ Frame-Relay uses statistical multiplexing to combine multiple virtual circuits and transmit them over a single transmission circuit. *Statistical multiplexing* involves interleaving the data from two or more devices onto a single line (DLCI or data-link connection identifier) for transmission over a Frame-Relay network.

- ✔ Each set of DTEs, which is one or more of sending and receiving CPEs, is assigned a DLCI (pronounced as "delcie"). The DLCI identifies the link that carries the combined (multiplexed) data from all of the linked DTEs.

- ✔ The DLCI is mapped to a specific permanent virtual circuit (PVC) path through the DCE/PSE equipment. With the DLCI in place, the entire path from source to destination is known even before the first frame is sent.

Because all the VCs (virtual circuits) on a circuit may not belong to the same customer, such as on a shared media circuit, the customer is assigned a committed information rate (CIR) on their circuit. The CIR is the minimum bandwidth the customer will receive, although additional bandwidth is available to handle periodic bursts of data above the CIR, if necessary. In most instances, the CIR is about one-half of the data transfer rate of the line. In other words, if the circuit is a T1 line (1.54Mbps), then the CIR is likely to be 768Kbps.

Handling Frame-Relay traffic jams

Network congestion is caused by too much data being sent over too little bandwidth. In the Frame-Relay world, this means that when users on a Frame-Relay circuit with a total CIR of 64K send a combined 96K of data, the extra 32K of data causes network congestion and must dealt with it somehow. See "Framing the DLCI" in the preceding section for more information on how a CIR works.

A Frame-Relay circuit has two options when a jam occurs. Each has its own funky side effects:

- ✔ The data creating the congestion must be delayed (retransmitted), but retransmitted data can cause even more congestion.

- ✔ The data creating the congestion must be discarded (not forwarded). Discarding packets can create data reliability problems between the sender and receiver.

Frame-Relay operates on a kind of honor system that depends on the constraint of its users to avoid problems. But, when the honor code breaks down and users send more data than they have bandwidth commitments for, which they do on occasion, Frame-Relay is ready for them with some built-in mechanisms it uses to solve the problem.

As shown back in Figure 17-1, the Frame-Relay frame includes two mechanisms that are used to reduce network congestion:

🖛 The Explicit Congestion Notification (ECN) fields:

- The Forward Explicit Congestion Notification (FECN)

- The Backward Explicit Congestion Notification (BECN)

🖛 The Discard Eligibility (DE) field

Here is how Frame-Relay attempts to reduce network congestion. For this next trick, we need you to divert your full and undivided attention to Figure 17-2 (ignore the man behind the curtain), which depicts a Frame-Relay network with three nodes: A, B and C. You can see two things:

🖛 Node B is located between nodes A and C.

🖛 Network congestion is occurring in the direction of node A to node C.

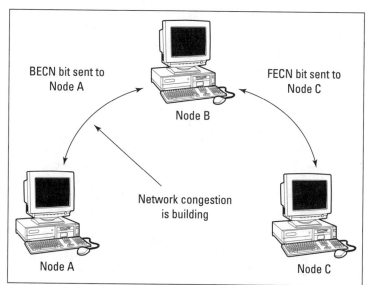

Figure 17-2:
Frame-Relay
network
with
congestion.

BECN bit sent to Node A

FECN bit sent to Node C

Node B

Network congestion is building

Node A

Node C

FECN

FECN and BECN are used to alert Frame-Relay nodes to problems with transmission over the network usually caused by network congestion. In the ECN method of congestion notification, the key point to remember is that if the FECN or BECN bit is set to 1, congestion exists on the network.

The Forward Explicit Congestion Notification (FECN) is an Explicit Congestion Notification (ECN) field used when frames are sent by Node A to Node C. *FECN*, as its name implies, is a bit set by a Frame-Relay network in a message frame intended to notify an a receiving DTE that it should take steps to avoid an apparent congestion on the network. Node A notifies the stations to which it forwards messages.

- Frames are sent from Node A and pass over the PVC that connects Node A to Node B.

- Node B examines the frames and determines they need to be passed along to Node C over the PVC connecting it to Node C.

However, should Node B detect a problem, such as network congestion, the ECNs are put into play, as follows:

- Node B detects that congestion is beginning and signals Node C by changing the FECN (Forward Explicit Congestion Notification) bit from 0 to 1 on those frames addressed for Node C.

- Node C, and any other nodes between B and C, learn from the FECN bit (set to 1) that congestion exists on the affected DLCIs.

In this way, Node B sends notice to all upstream DLCIs that there is congestion on the network and an alternate route should be found until the congestion is eased.

BECN

What if network congestion is detected between nodes B and A? Node B can't use the FECN to notify A because A is behind B, but through the use of the BECN, node B can notify node A (and any nodes between B and A) that there is a problem. The *Backward Explicit Congestion Notification (BECN)* is a bit set by a Frame-Relay network in a message frame intended to notify a receiving DTE that it (the sending device) will be taking steps to avoid some apparent network congestion.

- Node B also detects congestion on the circuit between C and A.

- Node B begins watching for frames coming from C toward Node A.

- Node B signals Node A of the congestion by setting the BECN (Backward Explicit Congestion Notification) bit in those frames from 0 to 1.

- Node A, and any other devices between A and Node B, know from the BECN bit (set to 1) that congestion is building on the affected DLCIs.

Please see the FECN section that precedes for more information about BECN.

Throwing out everything over the limit

When a Frame-Relay circuit becomes congested and frames must be discarded as a way to solve the congestion, it is better to have the sending device decide which frames can be discarded instead of having a router pick frames at random to throw out. The idea is that the sending device probably knows which frames are critical and which aren't.

The mechanism used to control which frames are discarded is the Discard Eligibility (DE) bit. When the sending device is aware that congestion may exist in the direction in which it is sending frames, it uses the DE bit to designate the expendable frames. The DE bit is set to 1 (or "turned on") in those frames that are knowingly being sent in excess of the CIR (Committed Information Rate) and can be discarded.

If the network is congested, those frames that have their DE bit turned on, are discarded until the congestion is relieved. However, if discarding DE frames does not clear up the congestion, then all bets are off, and frames are discarded regardless of their DE bit setting. When no congestion exists, the DE bits of all frames are ignored.

Switching Frame-Relay around on a router

Remember that Cisco routers can be configured to perform Frame-Relay switching and that doing so involves a series of things in pairs. There are two parts to Frame-Relay switching:

- ✔ The Frame-Relay DTE (router)
- ✔ The Frame-Relay DCE (switch)

A Cisco router can be configured for two types of switching:

- ✔ **Local Frame-Relay switching:** Enables it to forward frames based on the DLCI number found in the frames header. See "Framing the DLCI" earlier in the chapter for information on the DLCI.
- ✔ **Remote Frame-Relay switching:** Enables it to encapsulate frames into an IP packet and tunnel them across an IP backbone (see Chapter 3 for more information on network and IP backbones).

Routing Frame-Relay

Configuring a Frame-Relay connection on a Cisco router is done through a simple six-step process. Here are the steps used to configure a Frame-Relay interface on a Cisco router:

1. **Select the interface to be configured.**

```
Cisco_Networking(config)#int s0
```

This command selects serial interface 0 and selects configuration interface mode on the Cisco_Networking router.

2. **Configure a DLCI number to the interface.**

```
Cisco_Networking(config-if)#frame-relay interface-dlci 13
```

3. **Select the encapsulation type — cisco or ietf (cisco is the default).**

```
Cisco_Networking(config-if)#encapsulation frame-relay
     ietf
```

Cisco encapsulation is the default type; *ietf* encapsulation is used only when creating an interface that will be used to connect two routers from different manufacturers.

4. **Specify the LMI type (Cisco IOS 11.1 and earlier).**

```
Cisco_Networking(config-if)#frame-relay lmi-type cisco
```

In Cisco IOS versions 11.2 and later, the LMI type is auto detected by the router. Otherwise, LMI type "cisco" is the default value.

5. **Configure a subinterface.**

```
Cisco_Networking(config)#int s0.13 point-to-point
```

Create a subinterface number 13 that is a point-to-point link. Remember that subinterfaces are specified as s0.n or e0.n, where n is the subinterface number.

6. **Map the Frame-Relay interface using Inverse ARP**

```
Cisco_Networking(config-if)#ip address 192.168.1.1
     255.255.255.0
```

Using Inverse ARP (see Chapter 5), which is enabled by default, allows you to avoid entering mapping commands for each virtual circuit and use the dynamic mapping functions of the **inverse-arp** function. Inverse ARP automatically enables dynamic mapping, which continuously updates the mapping of IP addresses to physical addresses. You can choose not to enable Inverse ARP, in which case you must manually manage the ARP with static mapping entries, which is not something you want to do on a large network with several Frame-Relay connections.

Mapping IPs to DLCIs

In order for IP devices to communicate with each other over a Frame-Relay network, their IP addresses must be mapped to their DLCIs. Two methods ensure that this mapping occurs: manual and automatic.

The manual method, also known as *static mapping,* uses the **frame-relay map** command to enter the static IP mappings one by one. Static mapping is required when OSPF is used over Frame-Relay, when Inverse ARP is not supported on the remote router, or when you want to control broadcast traffic.

The command used to manually map the IP addresses to the DLCI is:

```
Router(config-if)#frame-relay map protocol protocol-address
        dlci broadcast][ietf|cisco|payload compress
        packet-by-packet]
```

Here is an example of what might be entered to map a DLCI manually:

```
Cisco_Networking(config-if)#frame-relay map ip 192.168.1.1
        255.255.255.0 dlci cisco
```

The way to automatically map IP addresses to their DLCIs is by using the inverse ARP (IARP) function. IARP is enabled by default on an interface, but it's disabled automatically on a DLCI when the **frame-relay map** command is used. The IARP approach is much easier to configure than the static map approach. However, because configuration errors can occur when a virtual circuit is mapped to an unknown device, the static approach is more stable and less prone to configuration errors.

The steps in "Routing Frame-Relay," listed earlier in this section, include an example of the command used to automatically map an IP address to a DLCI.

So what is the LMI?

LMI (Local Management Interface) is an interface type that was created in 1990 by a consortium of four internetworking companies (Cisco, StrataCom, Northern Telecom, and Digital Equipment Corp). This group (called the "Gang of Four") enhanced the existing Frame-Relay protocol by allowing routers to communicate with a Frame-Relay network. LMI messages include information about the network's current DLCI values, whether the DLCIs are local or global, and the status of virtual circuits.

To configure the LMI interface type, you need to set two values. You also have an option to set the LMI polling and timer intervals.

✔ LMI type — defines the standard to be used to configure the Frame-Relay interface.

✔ LMI "keepalive" interval — defines the interval between packets sent over the circuit to keep the circuit open.

In Cisco IOS versions 11.2 or later, the LMI interface is detected automatically. If you choose not to use the auto-sensing feature, you must configure the interface manually. The type you use depends on the type in use at the remote device. The default LMI type is Cisco, which is the Gang of Four LMI, and the default keepalive period is 10 seconds. Use one of these three types:

✔ Cisco

✔ ANSI

✔ Q933A

Connecting to subinterfaces

When multiple virtual circuits are created on a single Frame-Relay or serial interface, each of the VCs is considered a *subinterface*. Using subinterfaces has several advantages, most importantly the ability to implement different network layer characteristics on each virtual circuit. For example, one subinterface could be running IP routing while another (on the same Frame-Relay interface) could be running IPX.

Subinterfaces are defined with the command

```
int s0.subinterface number
```

where the subinterface number can be any number in the range from 0 to 4,292,967,295. Typically, the DLCI number is assigned to an interface as the subinterface number. There are two types of subinterfaces:

✔ Point-to-point is used when connecting two routers over a single virtual circuit.

✔ Multipoint is specified on the center router in a star topology of virtual circuits.

Keeping watch on the Frame-Relay

You can use several commands to monitor the various activities of a Frame-Relay network, including dynamic mappings, LMI statistics, ECN statistics, and more (see "Handling Frame-Relay traffic jams" earlier in the chapter). The commands used to monitor Frame-Relay activities are:

✔ **frame-relay-inarp:** Dynamically clears any IP-to-DLCI mappings created through the inverse ARP function.

✔ **sh int type [number]:** Displays DLCI and LMI information.

✔ **sh frame-relay lmi [type number]:** Displays LMI statistics.

✔ **sh frame-relay map:** Displays the current map entries.

✔ **sh frame-relay pvc [type number [dlci]]:** Displays the current PVC statistics.

✔ **sh frame-relay traffic:** Display statistics about the Frame-Relay traffic.

✔ **sh frame-relay route:** Displays the static routes configured in a Cisco router.

✔ **sh frame-relay svc maplist:** Displays all the SVCs under a specific map list.

Communicating on a High-Level

HDLC is the default serial encapsulation method on Cisco routers. HDLC (High-Level Data Link Control) is an ISO (International Standards Organization, you know — the OSI folks) standard. A problem with HDLC is that it may not be totally compatible between devices from different manufacturers, depending on the way each vendor chose to implement it. HDLC provides support for both point-to-point and multipoint services over synchronous serial data links and ISDN interfaces.

HDLC supports four different transfer modes:

✔ **NRM (Normal Response Mode)** allows a secondary device to communicate with a primary device, but only when the primary device initiates the request.

✔ **ARM (Asynchronous Response Mode)** allows either the primary or the secondary device to initiate communications.

✔ **ABM (Asynchronous Balance Mode)** allows a device to work in what is called "combined" mode, which means it can work as either a primary or secondary device.

✔ **LAPB (Link Access Protocol, Balanced)** is an extension of the ABM transfer mode, but this one allows circuit establishment with both DTE (data terminal equipment) and DCE (data communications equipment).

Getting from Point-to-Point

On a Cisco network, PPP (Point-to-Point Protocol) is used for router-to-router and host-to-network communications over synchronous and asynchronous circuits, including HSSI (High-Speed Serial Interface, pronounced "hissy") and ISDN interfaces. PPP is an industry standard protocol that enables point-to-point data transmissions of routed data. It is largely protocol independent and allows you to connect a network over data lines. PPP works with several network protocols including IP, IPX, and ARA (AppleTalk Remote Access).

PPP uses two internal protocols to perform its functions:

- ✔ **LCP (Link Control Protocol)** includes the procedures for creating, configuring, testing, and terminating data-link connections, as well as managing serial links for bridges and routers over a WAN.
- ✔ **NCP (Network Control Protocol)** provides routing, error control, testing, and addressing for SNA (Systems Network Architecture) devices.

Passwords are part of PPP

You are most likely familiar with PPP from using it on a dialup connection to your ISP (Internet Service Provider). One of the features of PPP is security, including

- ✔ PAP (Password Authentication Protocol)
- ✔ CHAP (Challenge Handshake Authentication Protocol)

The first step in establishing a PPP connection is *authentication,* which is performed through PAP. This is what happens:

- ✔ The device requesting the connection sends an authentication request that includes the username and password of the requesting party to the processing router.
- ✔ If the router recognizes the username and password as a valid combination, it returns an authentication acknowledgment.

Although PAP offers very basic authentication security, CHAP offers a more robust authentication process. *CHAP* is a procedure used to authenticate requests by users to connect to the network. CHAP, operating as the receiving device, initiates a challenge sequence that the user must verify before the connection can be established.

Here's how CHAP works:

✔ A connection is made and the receiving device transmits a challenge message to the requesting device. The requesting device responds with an encrypted value calculated using a one-way math function.

✔ The receiving device checks the response by comparing the response to its calculation of what should be the same calculated value.

✔ If the two values match, authentication is acknowledged. If the values do not match, the connection is usually broken.

Connecting to the WAN with PPP

A router's serial port can be configured to support a PPP interface. This configuration enables the port to emulate PPP data encapsulation, which allows Cisco devices to communicate with non-Cisco devices across a WAN link. PPP is probably the best tool to use when you need to connect devices from different manufacturers over a WAN. This is in spite of the fact that PPP can be more complex to use than the default protocol, HDLC. Of course, Cisco's solution to this problem is to have all Cisco gear.

A serial port must be configured to use PPP before it supports PPP encapsulation over a serial connection. Once the port is enabled for PPP, the interface subcommand **encapsulation ppp** is used to complete the configuration, where s0 is the subinterface number being configured:

```
CISCO Networking(config)# interface s0
CISCO_Networking (config-if)# encapsulation ppp
```

Presenting the ISDN Twins

ISDN service operates over multiple 64Kbps B channels, which carry payload (voice and data), and either a 16Kbps or 64Kbps D channel that carries command signals. It may sound like the names assigned to the channels were accidentally switched somewhere along the way, but they weren't.

✔ The bearer channel (B) bears the payload.

✔ The data channel (D) carries the data about the payload.

The number and combination of B and D channels differentiates the two available types of ISDN services.

There are two ISDN twins, and they are definitely fraternal twins.

✔ Primary Rate Interface (PRI)

✔ Basic Rate Interface (BRI)

FYI: ISDN PRI is for WANs

Don't confuse the data channel for something that carries data. The D channel carries command and control signals used to manage the data transmitted over the B channels. This chapter is about WAN services and ISDN PRI is definitely a WAN service.

Both use B and D channels in the same way, but beyond that these "twins" are very different. Primarily the differences lie in their construction, but the way in which they are used is also a major difference. Which service you choose, providing either is available to you, depends on the access level that your network needs.

Parading along with PRI

One of the best uses for ISDN PRI services on a WAN is providing RAS (Remote Access Service) access to your network. ISDN PRI provides you with 23 dialup access lines that can be used by remote workers, customers, or whoever, to gain dialup access to your network.

How does one ISDN PRI service line provide 23 access lines? PRI service consists of 23 B channels (30 in Europe) and one D channel, each of which carries 64Kbps (the same bandwidth for a telephone system DS0 line). Okay, with some simple arithmetic, this adds up to 24 channels, the same number of channels available on a T1 or DS1 circuit, which provides 1.544Mbps of bandwidth and 24 times 64Kbps equals 1.536Mbps. Where did the missing 8Kbps go? When a T1 line is channelized, 8Kbps are lost to the channelization and cannot be used for either data or control signaling. Here is a summary of PRI service:

24 (23 B & 1 D Channels) x 64Kbps (DS1) + 8Kbps = 1.54Mbps (T1 or DS1)

Each of the 23 B channels can have a separate telephone number assigned to it. This allows you to terminate 23 different dialup access connections at your network's router. An ISDN PRI line can be terminated in an RJ-45 connector and directly connected to an ISDN PRI interface on a Cisco 7000 series router. This simplifies the deployment of dialup RAS connections by reducing what would be multiple phone lines, modems, and connecting cables into a single interface.

Unfortunately, ISDN PRI is not available everywhere, so if it is something you wan to incorporate into your network, check with your Local Exchange Carriers (Incumbent or Competitive).

Bringing on the BRI

ISDN BRI service consists of two B channels of 64Kbps each and one D channel with 16Kbps. The arithmetic is much simpler for BRI than that of PRI. A BRI line has a combined bandwidth of 144Kbps, consisting of the two B channels and one D channel (128Kbps for the actual data and 16Kbps used for control signaling). Here is an arithmetic look at the BRI service:

(2 B Channels x 64Kbps [DS1]) + (1 D Channel x 16Kbps) = 144Kbps

Connecting ISDN BRI to your network requires some special setup and configuration; it's a true case of less requiring more. BRI is usually configured on a Cisco router as a dial-on-demand routing (DDR) link. DDR is a Cisco IOS interface configuration type that provides several functions, including creating the illusion that the router has full-time connectivity over dial-up interface.

In order for calls to be made or received on an ISDN network through the router, specific network-wide configuration information is needed:

- **Directory numbers (one for each B channel):** Each channel must have a regular telephone number assigned.

- **Encapsulation type:** Typically PPP (point-to-point) encapsulation is used which also sets the authentication type, preferably CHAP.

- **SPIDs (one for each B channel):** Service profile identifiers (SPIDs, pronounced "spids", of course) are assigned by the ISDN service provider to each B channel.

- **Switch type:** Table 17-1 lists the common switch types used on Cisco routers and their configuration keywords. This information should come from your service provider or LEC.

Table 17-1	ISDN Switch Types
Switch Type	*Configuration Keyword*
AT&T 5ess	primary-5ess
AT&T 4ess	primary-4ess
AT&T basic rate	basic-5ess
ISDN PRI	primary-dms100
National ISDN-1	basic-ni1
Nortel DMS-100 basic rate	basic-dms100

Defining some ISDN basics

Several characteristics are used to define and describe ISDN services, including the terminal type, reference points, protocols, channelization, and the type of service (BRI versus PRI; see the preceding section).

Are you my terminal type?

Two types of terminals or CPEs can connect to an ISDN network:

- **TE1:** Terminal equipment type 1 complies with the ISDN standards. TE1 devices are designated as ISDN compatible devices and usually quite obviously. This includes such things as an ISDN telephone or fax machine, or less obvious, a computer with internal ISDN terminal adapter.

- **TE2:** Terminal equipment type 2 can only be used when a terminal adapter is applied because they were around before the ISDN standards were developed. This is stuff like an analog telephone or any interfacing device used to connect to an analog line.

If you are looking to connect your network to an ISDN service, you must know the ISDN terminal type of your terminating devices (usually a router or multiplexer). In most instances, this is a no-brainer, because any Cisco equipment with an ISDN interface is a TE1 type terminal. However, if you have equipment from other manufacturers or equipment a few years old, check with the manufacturer's Web site or your reseller for the ISDN terminal type.

Be sure that you ask your service provider for the "ISDN terminal type," which is information you will need for your router interface.

In order to connect your TE1 or TE2 equipment to an ISDN service, you must also use the correct network termination. Network terminating devices connect four-wire network cabling to two-wire service provided by the ISDN provider (usually a LEC). You can use two types of network termination:

- **Network termination type 1 (NT1):** In North America, NT1 equipment is the customer's CPE device. In most other parts of the world, NT1 devices are included in the network services provided by the ISDN carrier.

- **Network termination type 2 (NT2):** This type of network termination is used for digital private branch exchanges (PBXs).

In most cases, if you are connecting your LAN to an ISDN service, you will be using a NT1 network termination type to connect your TE1 or TE2 to the ISDN service.

A terminal adapter (TA) is a device that connects a computer to an ISDN line, or any other type of digital communications line. A terminal adapter is like a digital modem that only passes digital signals between the computer and the ISDN service. Basically, a TA connects your TE2 equipment (see the preceding section) to your ISDN service. Terminal adapters are available as either internal expansion cards or as external devices that connect to a serial port.

Knowing your points of ISDN reference

Another defining characteristic of ISDN interfaces, and yes, there are more, are four reference points or interfaces. A *reference point* designates the logical interface type and configuration of an ISDN connection. Four reference points are used to define ISDN logical interfaces:

- ✔ **R** — The interface type between a non-ISDN device and a terminal adapter (TA).
- ✔ **S** — The interface between a user terminal and an NT2 device.
- ✔ **T** — The interface between an NT1 device and an NT2 device.
- ✔ **S/T** — A common hybrid interface type used to connect terminal equipment to the NT1.
- ✔ **U** — The interface between NT1 or NT2 devices and the line-termination equipment on the carrier's network. The connection between the two-wire service provided by the LEC and your NT1 device is the U interface.

Just a little more about the S/T interface: It's the ISDN network inside your building. It begins at the NT1 device and ends with a bus termination, which is a terminating device placed at the end of your internal ISDN network. You can run ISDN throughout your network providing that the network's total length is 200 meters or less and that you connect eight or fewer devices. The cable connecting each network node can be up to 10 meters in length.

ISDN protocols

One last bit of ISDN definition — one that you may run into in your reading or troubleshooting. There are three basic types of ISDN protocols, which are designated with the letters E, I, or Q in their first letter:

- ✔ **E protocols** support ISDN on the PSTN (Public Switched Telephone Network)
- ✔ **I protocols** define ISDN concepts, terminology, and services
- ✔ **Q protocols** define signaling and switching

Reading the palm of S/T ISDN

The S/T ISDN network may be the home network of the future. It can be used to control your microwave, alarm system, lighting, stereo, and more, provided that the total number of devices in use at any one time does not exceed the number of the channels of your ISDN service.

Figure 17-3 illustrates how all of the termination types, interfaces, and protocols are used together to create an ISDN network.

If you are planning to install an ISDN network, you will need more information than we have provided you here. Usually, the interfaces shown between the network terminations in Figure 17-3 are provided by the connecting devices. What you need to provide is caution and interoperable devices.

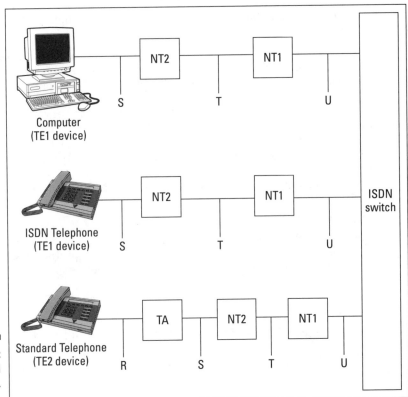

Figure 17-3: An ISDN network.

Sneaking In Some ATM

Most higher-end Cisco routers, switches, and access concentrators provide ATM connections in either T1 or T3 (DS3) rates that support both Frame-Relay and clear-channel (dedicated digital service).

As the Internet backbone grows, and LMDS (local multipoint distribution service) and other wireless and faster transfer services, such as ATM (asynchronous transfer mode) are becoming available directly to end-user networks for WAN connections.

ATM is a dedicated-connection switching technology that transmits data in fixed length 53-byte cells. The cells are transmitted over the physical medium, fiber or copper, in digital signals using hardware technologies. Because no analysis, from software is typically involved, data is processed and switched much faster. ATM operates by definition at 155.520 Mbps or 622.080 Mbps, but some ATM networks now reach gigabit speeds.

Chapter 18

Implementing Firewalls, Proxies, and Safety Measures

In This Chapter

▶ Reviewing firewall and proxy server concepts

▶ Looking at Cisco firewalls and cache servers

▶ Examining the functions of firewalls and proxy and cache servers

▶ Integrating firewalls and proxy and cache servers into a network

▶ Supporting e-commerce

Contrary to common belief, most damage to networks happens from within rather than from outside. Protecting the network from harm, inside or out, is a major part of any network administrator's job, and not always the easy part of the job either.

The primary networking devices used to provide security, beyond that of the router, are firewalls (of the hardware kind) and proxy servers. Cisco Systems produces some of its own hardware. We don't want to alarm you, but every two or three seconds, a LAN is violated by some evil nasty person lurking on the internetwork. Actually, we made up the two or three seconds part, but we wouldn't be at all surprised to find out that's true. What is true is that mean, evil, and nasty people are waiting to infiltrate your network to do their dirtiest and most heinous work. This stuff would make an excellent horror movie.

Reviewing the Arsenal

We want you to have a general understanding of what firewalls, proxy servers, and cache servers are and aren't. The latter part is the easiest, so we'll start there. These devices are not intelligent and cannot, by themselves, tell who is a good guy and who is a bad guy. They have no special analyzing capabilities and do not use artificial intelligence to determine who should or shouldn't have access to a system, a network, or a particular site. No magic is involved, and everything a firewall and a proxy or cache server do is by definition, configuration, and plan.

Keeping the fire from spreading

A *firewall* is a device that runs software developed to specifically to separate the internal network from the external network and to protect the former from the latter. (Sometimes, the reverse is true as well.) This software's job is to inspect each data packet attempting to enter or leave the local network. This examination is made to determine whether the packet will be allowed into or out of the network. This activity is called *packet filtering*. Packet filtering is based on access control lists, very much like those used to permit and deny traffic to a router (see Chapter 15).

A firewall gets its name from the construction technique of building a wall completely to the roofline to prevent fire from jumping from one room to the next through the ceiling. Like a building's firewall, a network firewall prevents bad stuff, the equivalent of a network fire, from spreading from network to network.

A high-end firewall (a fully featured one like the Cisco Pix firewall) typically runs on a specialized operating system and not on a general-purpose operating system like UNIX or Microsoft Windows NT. This makes the firewall less likely to be accessed through operating system portals and tampered with or defeated. A firewall with a free-access side door would be like the building firewall with a big hole in the center — not much protection there.

Providing a proxy

A *proxy server* is a special purpose server that acts as a go-between for the internal network and the external network. Unlike the firewall, a proxy server has no real security responsibility, although most proxy servers also provide some level of security. The proxy server acts as an agent on behalf of network nodes to help shield them from the darkness outside the confines of the nice, safe LAN.

Proxy servers are especially helpful when non-public, internal IP addressing is used on a LAN. You may recall that blocks of IP addresses (10.xxx.xxx.xxx, 172.xxx.xxx.xxx, and 192.xxx.xxx.xxx) can be used on any internal network and are set aside in the IP addressing schemes for that purpose. For every network that uses these IP schemes, there are likely hundreds of others, so these addresses are not the best to use on the public network as source IP addresses. The network would have a hard time keeping straight just exactly which 10.0.0.34 is which. This is where the proxy server comes in. For more information on IP addressing, see Chapter 7.

Figure 18-1 illustrates the basic operation of a proxy server. Here's how it works:

1. **Each network node communicates its desire to access a destination on the external network.**

   For example, suppose that node 10.0.0.34 wants to access a remote server to retrieve a Web document and communicates this to the proxy server.

2. **The proxy server assigns a public IP address to the node.**

3. **The proxy server then places both the public and the private addresses in a table so they can be cross-referenced.**

   In Figure 18-1, the proxy server records that the assigned public IP address (200.106.2.25) is temporarily assigned to node 10.0.0.34.

4. **When the requested data returns, the proxy server looks up the public address and forwards the incoming data to the internal IP address associated with it.**

   In other words, the proxy server acts as the internal node's proxy to the outside network.

By using external network IP addresses, the proxy server hides the internal network from the view of the external network. This provides some security in that the addressing of the internal network is not known beyond the proxy server. Most proxy servers are not a separate piece of hardware, but rather is a piece of application software running on a general-purpose operating system, such as UNIX or Windows NT on a PC.

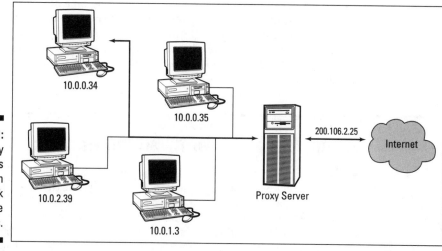

Figure 18-1:
The proxy server helps maintain network node aliases.

10.0.0.34

10.0.0.35

10.0.2.39

10.0.1.3

Proxy Server

200.106.2.25

Internet

Caching in on a good thing

In spite of the fact that millions of documents are available on the World Wide Web, about 20 percent of all the Web sites account for the vast majority of the internetwork traffic. What this means to you as a network administrator is that if you or another network user visits a Web site and downloads it, chances are very good that another user from your network will very soon download the same site. This may be great for the hit count and popularity indices for this site, but it unnecessarily ties up your bandwidth.

Wouldn't it be great if a server on your network could keep copies of the most frequently accessed Web pages or other downloaded files? Well, it is great, and it's called a cache server. A *cache server* is a server that saves frequently accessed Web pages, FTP files, or other files designated by the administrator.

The cache server has two primary benefits:

- ✔ **It reduces network latency.** A cache server creates the convenience of a much faster download to the requesting user because the file is being served from a local server and not the originating server across the internetwork.

- ✔ **It reduces bandwidth utilization.** A cache server reduces the amount of traffic flowing from an internal network out to the external network, which translates into a lower bandwidth utilization and perhaps even less bandwidth requirements altogether between the internal and external networks.

Cache servers can be software applications running on a standard server or PC hardware platform, but more often you'll find that a network cache server is a specialized device performing only caching. Cache servers have complex formulas that they use to determine which sites, pages, or objects should be cached. They also automatically update those pages or parts of pages that are frequently changed.

Caching the proxy or proxying the cache

Well, here's the twist: A proxy server, which is often set up to provide for firewall service, may also serve as a cache server. Cache servers are often capable of working as proxy servers, too. These double-duty devices are great for companies with a limited budget that want to gain the benefits of both services without spending the money for the dedicated devices.

Remember that the more you have a single computer do, the more powerful (and expensive) that machine must be to prevent its performance from suffering. When caching or proxy server performance suffers, the benefit of these timesavers evaporates and users spend more time waiting for their data. So, whether combining caching and proxy servers onto a single computer is a good idea for your network depends on your network and the nature of your users.

Looking Over the Cisco Catalog

Because this book is about using Cisco Systems' products in networks, we need to take a look at Cisco's firewall, proxy servers, and cache servers. Although we can't state that Cisco makes a product to fit each network and its needs, it does make a great range of products from which you may find one that meets your particular requirements. For information on Cisco Systems' products, visit its Web site at `www.cisco.com/public/products_prod.shtml`.

Firing up the firewall

Cisco's firewall series is called the Cisco Secure PIX (which as far as we can tell, doesn't stand for anything other than a product name) firewall. Currently, three levels of Cisco firewalls are available:

- **Cisco Secure PIX Firewall 520:** This firewall device is best-suited to large corporations (what Cisco calls an "enterprise") and network or Internet service providers. It is the largest of Cisco's firewall units and can connect to a variety of network technologies, including Ethernet, Token Ring, and FDDI (see Chapter 1). The PIX 520 can handle up to 385Mbps of throughput and as many as 250,000 simultaneous connections.

- **Cisco Secure PIX Firewall 515:** This Ethernet-only device is designed to support the needs of small and medium businesses. The PIX 515 can handle up to 125,000 simultaneous connections with a maximum of 120Mbps of throughput demand.

- **Cisco Secure PIX Firewall 506:** As more and more small businesses become connected to the outside world via the Internet, and with the emergence of the telecommuter, the COHO (company office/home office), and the SOHO (small office/home office), a need has arisen for increased security services for these smaller entities. The Cisco PIX 506 is the newest and smallest of the PIX firewalls. It is designed especially to meet the needs of the smaller (bandwidth-wise) users.

Just having a Cisco Secure PIX Firewall may not be quite enough to completely secure your network. Other tools may be required to complete the job, depending on the situation. Cisco has partnered with several other venders to provide additional solutions and utilities to extend the capabilities of the Secure PIX Firewall series. Here is a brief description, by category, of several of these programs.

Monitoring and reporting

Here are a few software products that will help you verify the configuration of your firewall, as well as list who has been trying to access your network:

- ✔ **Private I:** This utility from OpenSystems.com allows you to verify the configuration of your PIX firewall by translating the syslog data of the PIX. Its built-in reporting tool, ReportVU, turns the log data into easily understood information. You can access a demo or beta version of this tool at `www.opensystems.com`.

- ✔ **Telemate:** This utility from Telemate.net is only one of a suite of utilities available to report on how your network is being used and by whom. Another related utility available from this company is Netspective, which categorizes who has been accessing your network. For more information, visit `www.telemate.net`.

- ✔ **HP Openview:** This Hewlett-Packard product is probably the most widely used of the network node manager (NNM) utilities. HP Openview, which is available for a range of operating systems, provides in-depth graphical views of your network. Cisco provides a free software module, PIXView, to enhance HP Openview software for monitoring the PIX firewall. For more information, visit `www.openview.hp.com`.

Content filtering

This list of products includes applications that allow you to limit by site or content where on the Internet network users can visit:

- ✔ **Websense:** This application is used to restrict access to certain Internet sites and content, with the belief that this will make network users (meaning workers) more productive. It prohibits certain content from downloading to network nodes. Visit Websense, Inc.'s Web site at `www.websense.com`.

- ✔ **Tumbleweed Integrated Messaging Exchange:** This application is a policy-based e-mail content security system that enables businesses to create a secure, interactive communications channel to their customers and partners. Working with existing security measures, it allows network administrators to configure and enforce Internet mail policies for the entire enterprise. Visit `www.tumbleweed.com` for more information.

- ✔ **SurfinGate:** This security utility from Finjan Software performs gateway-level content inspection, including filtering of executable files, of Java, ActiveX, and JavaScript, VBScript, cookies, and browser plug-ins. SurfinGate allows network managers to selectively block specific files from being downloaded to end-user network computers and to allow access to specific files. For more information and a demo version, visit `www.finjan.com`.

Token and PKI authentication

Sometimes, regular passwords just aren't enough to protect your network security from being penetrated. These software products provide additional public key or token protection:

✔ **CRYPTOAdmin:** This product provides a more secure user authentication process using PKI (Public Key Infrastructure) to keep out unauthorized users. CRYPTOAdmin is from CRYPTOCard Corporation. Visit `www.cryptocard.com` for more information and a downloadable version.

✔ **CRYPTOCard:** This is a token-based product from the same company that produces CRYPTOAdmin. A *token* is a one-time use password or security code that is generated by a token-security device, such as a credit-card-sized or key-chain code calculator. This device is provided to authorized users who used them to log onto a network. The device is read directly like a credit card or it displays a changing number that is entered as a one-time password. Visit `www.cryptocard.com` for more information.

✔ **RSA SecurID:** This approach to token authentication is based on both a password or PIN and a token generated by what RSA Security calls an authenticator. Visit `www.rsasecurity.com/products/securid` for more information.

✔ **KyberPASS:** This product uses PKI to implement security policies and simplify security administration. This software authenticates users, provides access control to information, and secures applications. For more information visit KyberPass's Web site at `www.kyberpass.com`.

A Cisco tool and a great information site

This is the miscellaneous part of the list. Cisco provides a great tool for inventorying and analyzing your network for security holes, and an Australian company provides a great site for security information:

✔ **Cisco NetSonar:** This Cisco utility will scan your network looking for any security weak points. It automatically creates an inventory of all the devices and servers on your network, which it then uses to identify any point of vulnerability on the network. Any security weaknesses are then displayed in a grid. For information on this Cisco product, visit `www.cisco.com/univercd/cc/td/doc/product/iaabu/netsonar/`.

✔ **Computer and Network Security Reference Index:** This index site contains links to information sources on network security provided for education and application of computer security. Visit it at `www.telstra.com.au/info/security.html`.

Firing up the caching engine

Cisco makes a series of caching servers that can be used in conjunction with Cisco routers and switches to reduce the amount of traffic and demand placed on the Internet by a network and to provide a small level of increased security.

The Cisco Cache Engines work like this:

1. **A user requests a Web document from a remote Web server.**
2. **The router or switch redirects the user's request to the Cache Engine.**
3. **One of two things occurs:**
   - Should the cache server have the information, it supplies the requested document, eliminating the need to go on the Internet for it.
   - If the cache server doesn't have the user's document, it accesses the remote server for the information, stores a copy in its cache, and forwards a copy on to the user's workstation.
4. **Routers and switches work with the cache server through the WCCP (Web Cache Communications Protocol).**

   The WCCP is used to redirect HTTP (Hypertext Transfer Protocol) requests coming from the original site into the Cache Engine's cache.

Cisco offers four models of caching servers in its Cache Engine 500 Series: 505, 550, 570, and 590. Depending on the model of cache server, these caching appliances work in tandem with Cisco routers or switches. Table 18-1 indicates the router or switch with which each Cache Engine model can be combined.

This brief description of the Cisco Cache Engine models should help you make a choice for your network:

- ✔ **Cisco Cache Engine 590:** This is a high-end cache engine best suited to large enterprises and ISPs using large bandwidth (DS3 or better). This caching server has such high capacity that combining it with a Cisco Storage Array is required. The Cisco Storage Array (no model number or abbreviation at this time) is a high-capacity disk storage device that mounts separately in a rack. It holds up to 144GB in its six 18GB slots. Everything about the Cisco Cache Engine is big. Its standard configuration includes 1GB of RAM, two 10/100 NIC cards, two internal 18GB disk drives, and a SCSI interface for the Cisco Storage Array.

- ✔ **Cisco Cache Engine 570:** As you might suspect, this model is a mid-range cache engine designed for medium to large enterprises and mid-sized ISPs. The use of the Cisco Storage Array is optional but recommended to enhance its performance.

- ✔ **Cisco Cache Engine 550:** This is the smaller of the two mid-range cache engines. This one is designed for networks with connectivity of 10Mbps or less.

- ✔ **Cisco Cache Engine 505:** This is an entry-level cache engine well-suited for smaller offices with bandwidth around the level of a T1 (1.54Mbps).

Table 18-1	Cisco Cache Engine Models
Cisco Cache Engine Model#	*Cisco Router/Switch Series*
590	Cisco 7000, Catalyst 6000/MSFC, and 5800 Universal Access Server
570/550	Cisco 3600, Cisco 5300, Catalyst 4000
505	Cisco 1600, Cisco 2600

Building Up an E-Commerce Network

With the growth of many different commerce functions on the Internet and the advent of the extranet, the extension of the internal network to external, trusted, users, the need for security and access practices has become all the more complicated. Network administrators must know who needs access to network resources from the LAN and from the WAN as well.

Regardless of whether you are building up a network for e-commerce or just to serve the needs of your LAN and WAN users, the need for security remains the same. This section on e-commerce appears in this chapter primarily because letting outsiders into your network, just because they want to buy something, is still scary and wrought with danger. If you approach the security of the network from the point-of-view that nobody is to be trusted, then you already have the right security philosophy and the rest is just execution.

Explaining e-commerce

E-commerce is buying and selling goods and some services over an electronic medium such as the Internet or a direct dialup. E-commerce is also referred to as e-business, e-tailing, and e-sales (e-gad!). You will also hear about B2B (business-to-business), B2C (business-to-consumer), and B2E (business-to-employee).

✔ **B2B:** A rapidly growing segment of the commerce base of the Internet and Web is businesses transacting business to buy, sell, and transfer goods, services, and money between themselves. The need for security to both parties is very high. This type of Internet business is also called "click and mortar" (versus brick and mortar) to refer to its dual personality as both an electronic transaction and a physical shipping operation.

✔ **B2C:** This is what is now considered the common, everyday e-commerce of the Internet, the type you'll find at www.amazon.com, www.bn.com, and www.toysrus.com. The need for security is important to the buyer, who wishes to protect his credit card and other personal data, and to the seller, who wishes to protect its e-commerce site, customer data, and inventory records.

✔ **B2E:** Employees working at home — once called telecommuters, and now said to operate a SOHO (small office/home office) or COHO (company office/home office) — need to access company records and other private or sensitive information or messaging. This working arrangement is giving rise and development to virtual private network (VPN) technology (see "Creating a Virtually Private Network" later in the chapter), which creates a secure tunnel for data to move through from point to point.

Considering the e-security issues

Security is an issue in e-commerce because you are opening up your company's information to outsiders via the Internet. When putting an e-commerce site on the Web, you typically include product literature, photographs, pricing information, inventory availability, customer identification, shipping fees, tax collection, and payment processing. Much of this information is stored in a database for purposes of sharing it with customers, but it is still sensitive enough that it must not fall into the wrong hands. To provide the security needed, the system is typically set up with segregated services. It is common for a site to have an e-commerce server, a database server, and a secure transaction server, all of which are located behind a firewall (a Cisco Secure PIX Firewall, of course) as illustrated in Figure 18-2.

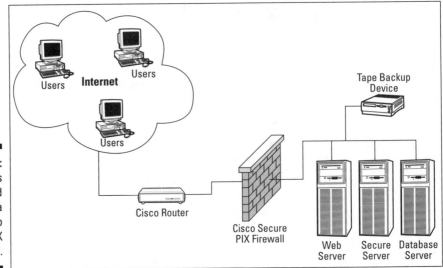

Figure 18-2:
Servers located behind a Cisco Secure PIX Firewall.

Most large e-commerce sites are not hosted on the servers of the company operating the site. Large Web-host services such as Concentric, HighSpeed.com, and HostPro provide fast, secure, and reliable hosting environments that relieve the operating company of much of the worry, concern, and expense of setting up the servers and security that this type of operation requires.

Several issues should be considered when evaluating e-commerce from the points of view of both the site provider and the business operating the site:

- ✔ Security
- ✔ Site availability
- ✔ Payment processing
- ✔ Product type
- ✔ Language
- ✔ Taxes
- ✔ Foreign currency conversion
- ✔ Scalability

Another important network security consideration is the issue of the integrity of the data itself. What must be considered and supported are both the server's reliability and accessibility, as well as the data itself being protected and archived (backed up) against the possibility of a catastrophic incident.

Transacting e-commerce

This section contains some tips on setting up an e-commerce business. If we knew a formula on how to succeed with an online business, we would not be writing this book. We'd be retired in the Cayman Islands. So take our advice with the spirit in which it is offered: You may want to consider this stuff before leaping too far.

Accepting cash

One of the most important features and services of an e-commerce site is payment processing. To be truly successful, you must be able to process multiple payment methods, such as credit cards or e-checks (electronic checks written over the Internet) and multiple currencies. One thing often overlooked by a merchant going online is that after your "store" is on the net, the whole world can see it, and if the business has something of interest to anyone in the world, someone will want to buy its products.

Most e-commerce payments are made with a credit card. Credit card processing is fairly straightforward on the Internet these days, and nearly all major credit card processors accept and convert currency types automatically. Exactly which cards are to be accepted is usually a choice of the merchants, but certainly if increased sales is the goal, the more cards you accept, the more potential buyers you qualify.

If the site operates as a B2B entity, another payment type that you may want to consider is direct invoicing (an invoice sent via email or directly inserted into a database online) — you know, the same type used every day for conducting non-Internet business-to-business dealings. This is great for existing customers, especially those who have credit established with your business. Other forms of payment that you may also want to accept are debit cards, wire transfers, and e-cash (money transferred from a trusted third-party who is acting on your behalf). Check into each, and be sure that you understand the strengths and weaknesses before signing on. Your web-hosting company should be able to help you understand how they work.

Speaking the language

Remember that the Internet world is not limited to the 10 square miles around your warehouse. The whole world is watching, and language can be a challenge for an e-commerce site, especially one with high hopes. The best advice is to start with the language of your primary market. English is virtually the language of the Web, but its hold is eroding as better language tools and more non-English users go online. If you do want to go international with your site, you would be wise to consider having your site translated into Spanish, German, Japanese, or Chinese.

Creating a Virtually Private Network

A *Virtual private network* (VPN) uses advanced encryption techniques and tunneling protocols to create a secure, end-to-end private network over the Internet. In effect, a VPN turns the public network into a private network. Don't misunderstand, the Internet is still a public non-exclusive network, but the VPN makes one small part of it extremely private.

Tunneling for gold

Using the Internet for a VPN eliminates expensive leased DDS or Frame Relay lines (see Chapter 17) to create a private network between two points. Not only can these be difficult to arrange, they can have long lead times and be difficult to arrange for some remote locations. A VPN exists between two connecting points only while it is in use. With the right equipment or software, a traveling user can connect to the corporate offices from anywhere he or she can get Internet access. The VPN provides the user with a secured, private network over the Internet from anywhere they may roam. A VPN can also be used to secure access with suppliers and partnering companies to allow them to use applications running on the company servers. But, the overriding reason for a VPN is its advanced security features.

Cisco has a wide range of VPN products, that range from VPN-enabled routers and firewalls to dedicated VPN routers and access concentrators. Cisco divides its VPN products into two primary groups:

- ✔ **Site-to-Site VPN:** This group of products extend a company's WAN by creating secured, encrypted links between two or more fixed sites, such as a branch office and the corporate headquarters, over the Internet.

- ✔ **Remote Access VPN:** This product group supports secured, encrypted remote connections between mobile or remote users and the corporate network using Internet access from an ISP or other third-party network service provider.

Tunneling over the Internet

While it may sound like it involves digging or boring holes in the Internet, tunneling could very well be called smuggling. Tunneling protocols, which are the mainstay of VPNs, create packets into which packets from other protocols are placed. This is the way that protocols like IPX or AppleTalk can be connected over the Internet, a process called *IP tunneling.* The tunneling protocol (TP) places the entire packet from the host protocol inside a transport packet before sending it over the network. At the other end, the TP extracts the host protocol packet and sends it on its way. In many respects, TPs are more like transport services than protocols.

Tunneling from point to point

Probably the most common tunneling protocol is Microsoft's *Point-to-Point Tunneling Protocol (PPTP).* This TP encapsulates the packets from other protocols for transmission over an IP network. Because it supports various encryption techniques, such as RSA (Rivest-Shamir-Adleman) encryption, PPTP is used for VPNs. *RSA encryption* is a very secure encryption technique developed by RSA Data Security, Inc. (www.rsa.com) that uses a two-part key. One part, the private key, is kept by the originator and the other part, the public key, is published with the message. Another tunneling protocol gaining popularity is the L2TP (Layer 2 Tunneling Protocol), developed by the IETF (Internet Engineering Task Force) as a combination of Microsoft's PPTP and Cisco's Layer 2 Forwarding (L2F). The L2TP was developed specifically for VPNs created over the Internet. L2TP supports non-IP protocols, such as AppleTalk and IPX, and incorporates the IPSec protocol.

Tunneling with security

The growing use of the Internet for secure transmissions has prompted the IETF to develop and publish a security protocol standard called *IPSec,* or IP Security, to provide authentication and encryption services over the Internet. IPSec works at Layer 3 (see Chapter 2) to secure everything sent over the network. IPSec was designed specifically for use with TCP/IP protocols and is likely to become the standard protocol for VPNs on the Internet.

For more information on VPNs

Here are some Web sites and our favorite VPN book that you can use to find more information on VPNs:

- Cisco's VPN Website: `www.cisco.com/warp/public/779/largeent/learn/technologies/VPNs.html`.

- The Internet Engineering Task Force (IETF) Web site: `www.ietf.org`.

- Tina Bird's VPN Information on the World Wide Web: `kubarb.phsx.ukans.edu/~tbird/vpn.html`.

- SoftFX's VPN Insider: `www.vpninsider.com`.

- Our favorite VPN book: *Virtual Private Networks For Dummies* (IDG Books Worldwide) by Mark Merkow.

Chapter 19

Designing Your Network

· ·

In This Chapter

▶ Listing the design tools you need

▶ Incorporating all of the design considerations

▶ Looking at the layers of the Cisco network model

· ·

You really shouldn't let the process of designing your network come last on your to-do list, as we have in this book. However, it is something that you can't do, or at least you can't do well, without some knowledge of networking and internetworking fundamentals, media, software, and hardware. For that reason, we have placed this chapter last in the book. We wanted to give you the chance to gain some understanding of Cisco networking before we addressed the considerations and process steps of network design.

Designing a Cisco network really involves matching the physical and logical components available to the needs of the organization. The easiest way by far to fit the best Cisco tools to your network needs is to work directly with your Cisco reseller or the fine folks at your local Cisco office.

Cisco also provides their version of the design processes and considerations we've described in this chapter. You can find all the internetworking design tips you'd ever want at www.cisco.com/univercd/cc/td/doc/cisintwk/idg4/.

Regardless of the specific design steps we recommend in this chapter, you must remember that every network is unique in some way. Gilster's Law of Network Design says that "You never can tell; and it all depends," which means that you won't find one sure-fire or pat network design, and the best design for your network really depends on the needs of your organization, its existing hardware and software, and you.

Gathering the Tools

Before you can begin doing the work of network design, you will need to measure and collect some technical performance data about your existing network, assuming that you have one. You'll need to measure the planned network path collecting the data that will help you to determine the distances over which your network will be stretched. This data must be analyzed to ensure that you aren't exceeding the limitations or capabilities of your physical media or planned networking devices.

If you don't have an existing network, then read this section with an eye to the near future when you will need to upgrade your network. No network configuration lasts forever.

Analyzing the analysis tools

You'll need some application software to generate performance data on your network. These tools can help (you can find the Cisco tools by searching the Cisco Web site at www.cisco.com):

✔ **CiscoWorks Windows:** This is a very handy tool for displaying in GUI form the status and configuration of Cisco internetworking devices on a network, as well as performing some troubleshooting and diagnostics and configuration activities. Versions of this product are available for the different versions of Windows NT and Windows 2000.

✔ **CiscoWorks Blue:** This version of CW is an IBM mainframe application that provides SNA (Systems Network Architecture) resource information to the two CW client-side workstation applications: CW Blue Maps and SNA View. CW Blue itself doesn't have any end-user interface or functions.

✔ **Cisco Routed WAN Management Solution:** This is actually a group of WAN management tools that extends the capabilities of CiscoWorks2000, a bundle of network management software tools that includes Cisco WAN Manager, Equipment Manager, and CiscoView, among other tools. These tools allow you to view, monitor, and analyze the functions of a network, end to end. This bundle includes applications that can be used for configuring, administering, monitoring, and troubleshooting the routers on a WAN.

✔ **Cisco NetFlow:** This product, which is officially named the Cisco NetFlow FlowCollector with Network Data Analyzer (NDA), works with the IOS of most Cisco switches and routers to analyze network traffic. Data from the NetFlow NDA tools are collected and filtered and then passed back to the NetFlow-enabled devices on the network. This data provides information used for traffic analysis, network planning, and network monitoring. The Network Data Analyzer application can also be used to graphically display the NetFlow data.

✔ **Cisco Netsys Service-Level Management Suite (Cisco NSM):** This application suite provides tools to help you manage, monitor, and maintain a Cisco internetwork (a network that interconnects through a router or switch to other networks). The two primary modules of the NSM are the Connectivity Service Manager and the Performance Service Manager.

✔ **Cisco Netsys Baseliner:** Although it sounds like the economy version of the Cisco NSM, the Netsys Baseliner is a distinct and separate application that displays, debugs, and validates a network's configuration by creating a working and offline model of your network. This allows you to test and debug over 100 common network problems and simulate any configuration or topology changes before they are implemented. The Baseliner also provides you with a graphical view of your network's configuration. It checks for many common network configuration problems.

✔ **CiscoView**: This is one of the many applications in the CiscoWorks 2000 suite. CiscoView is a GUI-based management tool that can be used to view the status, activities, and configuration of either local or remote Cisco routers and switches.

✔ **Network Associate's Sniffer:** Several different Sniffer products exist, ranging from the Basic Analyzer model to the Sniffer Pro Packet over SONET. Sniffer applications perform fault and performance management for networks, capturing data, monitoring network traffic, and collecting network statistics. Visit `www.sniffer.com` for more information on Sniffer products.

✔ **NetSCARF (Network Statistics Collection And Reporting Facility):** This tool, developed by the members of Project SCION, is a set of standalone utility programs that collects and reports statistics on TCP/IP networks. NetSCARF is available free and can be downloaded from `ccuftp.ccu.edu.tw/pub2/packages/net-research/netscarf/`.

You may want to take the time to evaluate each of these tools, especially the ones that you have to buy, to determine which of the tools is best suited for gathering network data on your network. These applications should provide you with two things:

✔ A graphic of a network's existing components

✔ The identification of any existing network bottlenecks or performance problems

Checking out the drawing tools

After you have some information on a network, you will probably want to depict your solution to its problems, or if you don't have an existing network, you may want to graphically represent what your networking masterpiece will look like. Despite the fact that your picture is worth at least a thousand words, you will still need to write out the justification and application of the network design for your boss, yourself, or posterity. Everyone will need to know next week, next month, or next year just what you were thinking when you designed the network.

You may want to consider these tools for use in documenting the network and your new design:

- **Microsoft Visio 2000:** This is perhaps the most popular diagramming tool among network administrators. It has a wide assortment of stencils, including network elements, connectors, and other drawing and charting objects that you can apply to create professional looking diagrams. Information on this product is available at www.microsoft.com/office/visio/.

- **Cisco ConfigMaker:** This is a free (downloadable from Cisco Systems' Web site) and easy-to-use Windows-based software tool that allows you to configure a network of Cisco networking devices (routers, switches, hub, and so on) and generate the bill of materials of the network components. To find more information and to download a copy of this tool, visit www.cisco.com/warp/public/cc/cisco/mkt/enm/config/.

- **Word processing and other personal productivity software:** You will definitely need a word processor and maybe even an electronic spreadsheet or another application software package for use in documenting your network completely. You probably already have the software found in the Microsoft, IBM (Lotus), or Corel suites.

We can't overly emphasize the importance of documenting the design of any new network or changes to an existing network. Trust us: A few months from now, you won't remember why you needed to make any changes that you are making or why you laid out the network the way you have.

Gathering the Facts

Any network that you design must meet one primary objective in order to be considered an effective network: It must support the objectives of the organization. Beyond that, its speed, its size, its complexity, its efficiency, and so on, all are meaningless if the network just doesn't work in its environment.

In order to design a network that can fulfill this lofty goal now and especially into the future, you need to understand where the company or organization is at present, as well as where they plan to be (sales, employees, locations) in three to five years. How far into the future your network plan may extend will vary depending on your situation or the company's goals and objectives. Some network plans require little or no change for even the next ten years; others will be hard pressed to predict next quarter.

It may also be helpful to understand a little about the organization and its environmental influences. This includes such things as products, services, competitors, staffing, and technical infrastructure. At minimum, you need to know the organization's business goals for the near and long-term future.

The organization chart is a good place to begin your topology analysis. The network must support the implied requirements of the organization structure. The organization chart can be the key to such network characteristics and services as security, segmentation, WAN issues, and remote access. A study of the organization structure should reveal any geographical considerations of the network.

Profiling the Network

You should gather a good amount of technical information before beginning the design of a new network or before making major modifications to an existing network. Using a structured approach to gather the information needed is your best bet to accomplish two things:

- ✔ No data is missed — all the information that you need is collected and available for analysis.

- ✔ The data is automatically documented to show just what it was you had in mind when you designed the network.

We recommend an eight-step process. We recommend that you not skip a step, even if you are redesigning an existing network that you know quite well. You'd be surprised how unfamiliar you can be with your own network.

The tools you need to gather the information, at the level required, are described earlier in the chapter in the section titled, "Gathering the Tools." You should also have a good understanding of the goals and objectives of the company, some information on the history and evolution of the network, and a very good idea of the requirements of the network's users. This information provides a context for the data you will gather as you work through our eight-step information gathering process.

Taking inventory of the network applications

Figure 19-1 shows a sample form that can be used to document the applications supported on the network. This doesn't mean that you should document all the applications on each network workstation. This step focuses on just the major applications that have a specific impact on the performance and perhaps the structure of the network.

The inventory of the applications should also attempt to document any new applications that are likely to be added to the network in the foreseeable future. Again, you are looking only for the major applications that may have an impact on the network's performance.

Making a list of the network protocols

Document the protocols operating on the network using a form similar to that shown in Figure 19-2. The list of protocols should include all the protocols being supported on the network, including those of the workstations, peripherals, and WAN interfaces. This list should be inclusive so that you don't overlook any network activity that is dependent on a particular protocol.

	Customer Name: _____ Site Address: _____ City, State, ZIP: _____ Contact Person: _____			Date of Inventory: _____ Sheet number _____ of _____ Phone #: _____	
	Application Name	Application Type	Number of User	Number of Hosts/Servers	Comments
1					
2					
3					
4					
5					
6					

Figure 19-1: A sample form used to inventory the applications supported on a network.

Network Protocol Inventory

Customer Name: _____   Date of Inventory: _____
Site Address: _____   Sheet number _____ of _____
City, State, ZIP: _____
Contact Person: _____   Phone #: _____

	Protocol Name	Protocol Type	Number of User	Number of Hosts/Servers	Comments
1					
2					
3					
4					
5					
6					

Figure 19-2:
A sample form for documenting the protocols used on a network.

Recording the network design

Assuming that you have an existing network to document, this step of the design process creates a comprehensive documentation of the network's topology, structure, and naming, among other characteristics. If you have been doing your job all along, and maintaining the network log and journal, this step of the process shouldn't be too strenuous. If you have an up-to-date record of the network and its maintenance activity, verify the documentation, correcting it where necessary.

However, if the network has never been documented or if you have been shirking your administrator duties, you need to compile a complete documentation of the network as it exists today. In fact, that wouldn't be such a bad title for the data compilation you'll end up with: "The Network Today." Whether you collect your data into a single document, or into separate documents for each step of the process, you will want to organize it for easy access and analysis. Follow these steps to create the documentation of the network's design:

1. **Diagram the network topology.**

2. **On the topology diagram created in the previous step, document the data transfer speed rating of the hubs, switches, routers, and workstation NICs of each network segment.**

3. Identify each of the major networking devices (servers, routers, switches, and so on) by name and address. Each device has a network name, ID, and IP address assigned to it. Add this information to the topology diagram for each node.

4. Write down the network media used throughout the network. Identify the type of cable used for each network segment, such as UTP, Thinnet, fiber optic, and so on.

5. Document all the network's addressing schemes, including the subnet masks (see Chapter 7) in use and the source of and to whom routable IP addresses are assigned and by whom.

Record any ongoing network problems or concerns expressed by network users regarding the topology, security, performance, and so on, and any design issues to be addressed in the new design. This could involve the use of the network analysis software, such as the tools listed in "Analyzing the analysis tools," earlier in the chapter, or a protocol analyzer — a piece of equipment used to analyze the bits sent over the networking cable.

Dear Diary: Keeping a network journal

Every network has a past. Regardless of how good, bad, or indifferent that past may be, it should be documented in a written history. Far too many networks have only an oral history that has been passed on from administrator to administrator, and as you might guess, the story gets more vague each time it is told. The answer to this problem is to steadfastly maintain a written network log and a network journal.

A network log contains dated entries that detail each maintenance, upgrade, or configuration change made to the network. It can exist in electronic form, in a text document, a worksheet, or database, or it can be on a clipboard, or in a binder. Its form really doesn't matter. Because nearly all networks will have multiple administrators over its life, the value of this information store to each new succeeding administrator is immense. It should be kept where anyone working on the network can access it for information or to add an entry.

A network journal provides some of the philosophy and reasoning behind the network and its evolution. It is like the ship's log maintained by a sea captain. It addresses the who, what, when, why, and how of toplogy, configuration, and design issues of the network. Each change, modification, or upgrade to the network should be documented with a signed and dated entry that explains just what you were thinking so that those who follow you don't have to wonder.

Accounting for network availability

You should focus on two indicators to determine how available the network has been to its users:

🗸 **The network's average MTBF (mean time between failure):** You may need to determine this value as an average of the MTBF of each of the network's segments. The MTBF is calculated as the amount of time between failures, meaning the network or a segment is not available to users. Use a form similar to that shown in Figure 19-3 to determine the MTBF.

🗸 **The financial impact of a network or segment failure:** It is not unusual for financial data to be unavailable, but in some instances, such as in a call center or inside sales department, the downtime of the network can translate directly into money. This is typically expressed as a per-hour amount.

Figure 19-3:
A sample form used to record information on a network's availability.

Network Ability

Customer Name: _____ Date of Inventory: _____
Site Address: _____ Sheet number _____ of _____
City, State, ZIP: _____
Contact Person: _____ Phone #: _____

	Segment Identity	MTBF	Date of Incident	Durabin	Cause
1					
2					
3					
4					
5					

Auditing the network's reliability

Not to be confused with availability, the network's *reliability* is determined using the tools discussed earlier in this chapter (see "Gathering the Tools"). You can use a network monitor or network management tool on each segment to gather the data needed to make a determination about its reliability. A form like that of the sample shown in Figure 19-4 can be used to gather:

- Total megabytes
- Total number of frames
- Total number of CRC errors
- Total number of MAC errors
- Total number of broadcast/multicast frames

Noting the network's utilization

About the best way to gather statistics on a network's utilization is to apply the network-monitoring tool you have selected and configure it to collect network utilization stats about once every hour. If the network is saturated (carrying data traffic equal to or greater than its bandwidth) or heavily used, you may want to gather data as often as every minute. Remember that usage peaks — which are spikes of bandwidth demand — of 40 percent or more above normal traffic levels that last more than one minute indicate high utilization and potential performance problems.

Figure 19-4: A sample form used to gather raw data about a network.

Raw Network Reliability

Customer Name: _____ Date of Inventory: _____
Site Address: _____ Sheet number ____ of ____
City, State, ZIP: _____
Contact Person: _____ Phone #: _____

	Segment Identity	Total Megabytes	Total Number of Frames	Total Number of CRC Errors	Total Number of MAC Errors	Total Number of Broadcast/ Multicast Frames
1						
2						
3						
4						
5						

Evaluating the router

The real story of a network, especially one with a connection to a WAN or with more than one router, is gained by evaluating the status of the existing routers. The configuration of a router that is working well has a wealth of information about the network to which the router is connected, including

- **The number and type of interfaces on the router:** The interface types installed and configured on the router indicate the transport or network technologies included in the network, such as Frame Relay, Ethernet, Token Ring, ISDN, and more. Use the **show interfaces** command to list the interfaces on the router.

- **The processes running on the router:** The **show processes** command displays the active processes running on the router and its resource utilization over the past five seconds, one minute, or five minutes. This command displays a matrix that includes the process ID, name, status, runtime, and other information. The types of processes and their recurrence let you to categorize the actions of the router and its network.

- **The number of available buffers:** Included in the display produced by the **show buffers** command is an analysis of the buffers assigned to specific interfaces. *Buffers* are blocks of memory used to hold network packets during I/O operations. Five buffer types exist: small, middle, big, large, and huge. Buffers are either temporary, created and destroyed as needed, or permanently allocated. One of the key indicators that the router may be experiencing high traffic on a certain interface is the number of times the interface's buffer pool was depleted.

You can choose from virtually dozens of different versions of the **show** command for use in analyzing the actions, configurations, and connections of a Cisco router or switch. The documentation or CD-ROM that came with your Cisco equipment contains a "Command Reference" section that lists the show commands available on your particular device.

Use a form similar to the one shown in Figure 19-5 to document the information you learn about each router.

Creating a scorecard

After completing the preceding steps, you should have a fairly good understanding of your network, new or old. With your newfound network knowledge, you should be able to grade the network using a scorecard like that shown in Figure 19-6. Clearly mark those areas in which the network passes or fails.

Router Status

Customer Name: _____   Date of Inventory: _____
Site Address: _____   Sheet number _____ of _____
City, State, ZIP: _____
Contact Person: _____   Phone #: _____

	Router Name	5 Minute CPU Utilization	Output Queue Drops/Hr	Input Queue Drops/Hr	Missed Packets per Hr	Ignored Packets per Hr	Comments
1							
2							
3							
4							
5							

Figure 19-5: A sample form for documenting a network's routers.

Network Report Card

Grade	Criteria	Exceptions
☐	All Ethernet segments are at 40% or less utilization	_____
☐	All Toke Rings are at 70% or less utilization	_____
☐	All WAN links are at 70% or less utilization	_____
☐	The average and mean response times are less than 100 milliseconds.	_____
☐	All segments have less than 20% broadcasts/multicasts.	_____
☐	All segments have less than one CRC error per million bytes of data.	_____
☐	Ethernet, less than 0.1% of the packets result in a collision.	_____
☐	Token Ring, less than 0.1% of the packets result in a collision.	_____
☐	FDDI, one or fewer operations per hour are not related to ring insertion.	_____
☐	All Cisco routers have a 75% or lower "5–minute CPU utilization rate.	_____
☐	All Cisco routers have less than 100 output queue drops per hour.	_____
☐	All Cisco routers have less than 50 input queue drops per hour.	_____
☐	All Cisco routers have less than 25 buffer misses per hour.	_____
☐	All Cisco routers have less than 10 ignored packets in an hour on any interface.	_____

Additional comments: _____
_____
_____
_____
_____

Figure 19-6: A network report card.

Classifying the Network

Networks can be classified into one of three general types of networks:

✓ **Hierarchical networks:** Cisco uses a three-tier network model that creates a hierarchy of network layers:

- **Core layer** — The Core layer is where the biggest, fastest, and not surprisingly, most expensive routers (the ones with the highest model numbers) are found. Core layer routers merge geographically separated networks and move data as fast as possible, commonly over dedicated, leased lines. Dedicated lines are usually a part of a private network and aren't shared with other users. You won't find anything but servers on this layer. The Cisco 7000 router series are typical of the devices found on this layer.

- **Distribution layer** — Routers on the Distribution layer connect what Cisco calls "large functional groups," such as the accounting department or sales department, or buildings. Distribution routers filter network packets and forward them either up or down to the next router layer. The bulk of your routing policy decisions are made on this layer. Distribution layer routers are in the Cisco 3600 series.

- **Access layer** — It is on this layer that host computers access a network and most network traffic finds its destination. Access layer routers are used to segment LANs. Access layer routers are in the 2500/2600 series.

✓ **Redundant networks:** These robust, high-availability networks have *secondary pathing* (redundant routing), as well as redundant routers, switches, or servers, and even cable media. See "Building a redundant, redundant network" later in this section.

✓ **Secure networks:** A secure internetworking design contains hardware, software, or both to implement security services. An example would be a network with a firewall included. See "Securing the secure internetwork" later in this section.

Building a redundant, redundant network

A redundant network is usually designed to provide support for mission-critical systems, services, applications, or network paths. The ultimate in redundancy is that every possible single point of failure is eliminated. Depending on the reliability and availability needs of the network, you may want to adjust the design-level of the network from one that is fully redundant to one where you back up only those individual network components that must not fail. For example, if only the server and router on a network are deemed to be critical, then they may be the only devices with redundancy. Typically, the redundancy in a network is handled by the addition of a redundant (secondary) routing path between two points.

Four types of redundancy can be designed into a network:

- ✔ **Node-to-router redundancy:** A node on a routed network can learn the address of and get data to another network node located beyond its local router in several ways. This can be accomplished through ARP, RIP, IPX, or AppleTalk, each of which can be designed into the network to provide alternative pathing solutions.

- ✔ **Server redundancy:** If a server must be available at all times, the best solution is to include a mirrored server on the network. The mirrored server should be located on separate network segments and be powered from completely separate power sources. If this is overkill for your needs, then consider using some form of fault tolerant hard disk system, such as a RAID (Redundant Arrays of Inexpensive Disk) solution. Probably the least expensive and most easily implemented data redundancy technique is to simply use a tape backup to protect the data.

- ✔ **Route redundancy:** Providing redundancy over a WAN can be challenging, but when two critical networks are geographically separated, having redundant routes between them is important. A technique called *load balancing* can be applied to provide consistent loading that should translate into reduced network downtime. Load balancing is supported by most IP routing protocols for up to six paths over which network traffic can be balanced. Load balancing also helps smooth over the loss of any one of the servers to which traffic is being forwarded.

- ✔ **Media redundancy:** Designing two (or more) completely different media types into a network, especially a WAN, provides the assurance that should one type of media fail, the other, which should not be affected, can continue to carry the network's traffic. For example, if a WAN is linked by a fiber-optic landline and a wireless LMDS link and the fiber-optic line suffers *back-hoe fade,* the wireless link can keep the network alive. Of course, this works only if the two media types are not routed back to the same source, which means that true media redundancy requires the addition of route redundancy as well. On a LAN, multiple lines can be placed between switches to provide for redundant links.

Back-hoe fade: Can you dig it?

Fade, in the telecommunications world, is a loss of service quality or connectivity. A connection may fade for several reasons. If you've ever had a cell phone, you understand the concept of fade.

A very common cause of service interruptions is what is referred to, with tongue-in-cheek, as *back-hoe fade*. This phenomenon is the result of somebody digging in the area of a buried cable, which never fails to be the main service fiber bundle. Back-hoe fade is usually the cause when your entire town suddenly loses its Internet backbone connection. Back-hoe fade is why you see those signs posted that say, "Call before you dig!"

Securing the secure internetwork

A secure internetworking design is commonly implemented with a firewall, such as the Cisco Secure PIX Firewall. However, a firewall can be any device or software that has the responsibility to protect a network from any outside untrusted network, such as the Internet and its gangs of nasties.

Creating a design for a secure network involves the inclusion of a security device not only to keep bad things out, but also to keep the bad things inside from doing any harm as well. You can do this in several ways. You can do these things to design your network to make it more secure:

- **Packet filtering on a router** — You should place packet-filtering services used as a part of a security scheme on the routers before or after bastion hosts on the network, as depicted in Figure 19-7. A *bastion host* is a secure host, in this case buffeted by the packet filtering routers, supporting limited applications that can be accessed by outsiders.

- **Firewall appliances** — Some network hardware appliances, such as the Cisco Secure PIX Firewall, are specifically designed to operate as firewalls. When these are included in a network, bastion host servers, to which you wish to provide access to outside users, are placed in a DMZ (demilitarized zone). The DMZ logically separates these devices from all other parts of the network, so that access to this part of the network does not provide access to any other network resources. Figure 19-8 illustrates this setup. See Chapter 15 for more information of firewalls in general and the Cisco Secure PIX in particular.

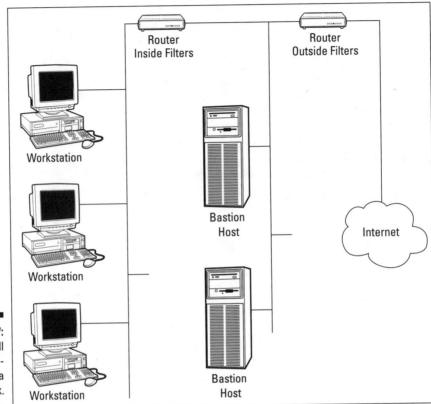

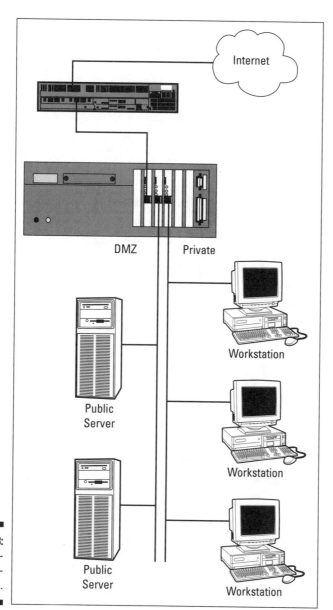

Figure 19-8:
A PIX fire-
wall imple-
mentation.

Part VI
The Part of Tens

"It's okay. One of the routers must have gone down and we had a brief broadcast storm."

In this part. . .

This part of the book provides you with four lists of ten pieces of valuable information: ten really great sites for information on Cisco routers, switches, and other networking equipment; ten network design tips that will help you create a better network; ten tips for a safe and trouble-free installation; and ten things you should pay attention to when configuring a Cisco router.

Use them or not, they are for your information and later reference.

Chapter 20

Ten Really Great Sites for More Information

*O*ther than the fact that a Cisco network is a complex undertaking, nothing could be more true than the fact that you can never have too many references or resources. The best site on the Web for information is Cisco Systems' own Web site, but others can provide you with a wealth of information, experiences, and even products to help you as you build and administer your Cisco network.

The Web sites and other resources listed in this chapter are sites that we believe you'll find helpful. Please understand that all of these sites actually did exist at the time we wrote this book. If any of these sites has disappeared, you should search for others with the search criteria "Cisco networks."

Cisco Systems, Inc.

www.cisco.com

This Web site actually should count as the first twenty or so of the really great sites to get information on Cisco networking, but because you really want ten different sites for this information, we'll only count it as one.

The Cisco Connection Online (CCO) site should be your first stop for information on any Cisco device, program, technology, or concept. Cisco has product documentation, catalogs, design aids, utility software, and white papers on a wide range of Cisco networking topics. This is the proverbial "horse's mouth" for Cisco information. Cisco Systems keeps the information on this site up to date with information on technical support, training, industry news, and other networking information.

Cisco Faxback Server

www.ciscofax.com/

Okay, so this is another Cisco site, but what do you expect? Cisco, Inc., has all the best Cisco sites. This particular site is a good one for having information about Cisco products and white papers faxed directly to you.

From this Web site, you can request a fax from several information libraries. You can request product information, compliance documentation, or information on training or certification programs to be faxed directly to you within one hour.

Cisco World Magazine

www.pcinews.com/cisco/

This site, hosted by Publications & Communications Inc., advertises that it is the "independent journal for networking professionals." This online version of a print magazine allows you to read the featured articles of the latest edition, search back through previous editions, and even get a free trial subscription.

Cisco Small Business Resource Center

www.cisco.com/warp/public/779/smbiz/resource_net/

Okay, we're sneaking in another Cisco.com site, but we wanted to be sure that you knew about this one. Chances are good that you work for a small or medium business or you will someday, and you should know about the information available from this part of the Cisco Web site.

On the Small Business Resource Center page, you can find networking solutions tips, an array of Cisco networking tools and tutorials, some networking case studies and suggestions for next steps, and a list of software and information resources to help you plan, design, and administer your network. (Cisco also has a Medium Business Resource Center page, in case you work for a "bigger" small business.)

The Information Technology Professional's Resource Center

www.itprc.com

This site provides access to a wide range of information on IT topics, including career choices, technologies, operations, humor, links to other IT sites, and an open forum on IT subjects. Topics of special interest to networking administrators highlighted on this site include training and certification, TCP/IP, OS and NOS, QoS, IP routing, voice and data integration, VPN, and more.

Use this site as a general reference for all types of IT information, including a very thorough section on IP routing that includes tutorials on BGP and other protocols; Cisco (and other manufacturer) resources; and a host of configuration, design, and installation tips.

File Watch

www.filewatch.com

Keeping up on the latest developments in IT and networking is difficult, especially if you are a busy network administrator. Staying current requires time, often time you don't have, to seek out information from hardware and software vendors about new fixes, patches, updates, service packs, and product enhancements. You can spend way too much time wading through trade magazines looking for nuggets of information that relate to your situation or interests. And in spite of the fact that much of the information, files, or data you need is available in a downloadable file, finding them takes time. That's where this Web site can help you.

File Watch is like that technology-aware assistant you don't have to keep you up to date on all the latest developments in hardware and software, especially those that you support. Best of all, it works for free. On this site, you find product updates, including drivers, patches, fixes, and white papers for many of the most popular manufacturers and software publishers, including the likes of Hewlett-Packard, 3Com, Microsoft, and others.

MentorLabs

www.mentorlabs.com/vlab/access

MentorLabs' first offering is vLab, which is a learning environment offering hands-on experience over the Web to state-of-the-art equipment. MentorLabs teams up with Cisco Systems to create the vLab's first application, a Cisco routing and switching laboratory. This method is especially useful if you want to gain some experience on Cisco equipment without screwing up your own network in the process or if don't have access to Cisco equipment and want to try before you buy in a virtual environment.

The Network Analysis Institute

www.netanalysis.org

Formed in 1998 as a source for network troubleshooting information, the Network Analysis Institute provides information for network administrators new to packet-level analysis or to networking in general, as well as to experienced network admins. A wide array of support information and links are aimed at making your life a little easier and, according to the Institute, "perhaps more interesting."

Planet IT Networking

www.planetit.com/techcenters/networking

This Web site, which is part of CMP Media, Inc.'s TechWeb site, is an excellent source of networking news, tips, and new product information. You'll also find case studies, white papers, and specific information on LANs, VPNs, network management and administration, NOSs, security, and more to browse through.

Network Magazine

www.networkmagazine.com

If you don't subscribe to this magazine in print, then you should visit this site often for newly published information on a variety of networking topics. You can search current and past issues for articles on Cisco networking topics.

The TechWeb Encyclopedia

www.techweb.com/encyclopedia

This site, another operated by CMP Media, Inc., is a great site to look up information on specific terms or concepts to get a well-worded definition, as well as a few reference links that you can use to further your understanding. This is one of the best general reference sites on the Web.

Whatis.com

www.whatis.com

Perhaps the best all-around reference available on the Internet for computing and networking terms and concepts, the Whatis.com site enables you to select from a list of terms at the top of the frameset. Use this site when all other sources for a definition fail you.

Online Booksellers

www.amazon.com

www.barnesandnoble.com

www.borders.com

www.dummies.com

www.fatbrain.com

www.idgbooks.com

www.iuniverse.com

www.mightywords.com

What are booksellers doing in a list of Cisco networking sites, you ask? Well, whether you use the bookstore at Dummies.com or fatbrain, these sites can provide a list of the very latest Cisco networking guides, how-to's, reference books, and tutorials available in print.

Online publishers, such as iUniverse.com and MightyWords.com, also offer booklets, pamphlets, and self-published papers from some of the most respected networking authorities in the world. These materials, which are available for a small fee usually, are not available from other sources.

Online materials are fine, but sometimes nothing is better that a printed book, especially when you're away from your PC — on an airplane, in the bath, or out on a date (this is important stuff!).

Visit these sites and search for "Cisco Networking."

A Few More Good Sites to Visit

These sites have a wide array of information, services, products, certification references, and more that you may find useful:

- ✔ The Network Buyers Guide lists places to buy networking stuff: www.networkbuyersguide.com

- ✔ Learntosubnet.com offers a step-by-step tutorial on learning to subnet a network: www.learntosubnet.com/

- ✔ NetSys.com has information and tips for UNIX/Linux network administrators: www.netsys.com

- ✔ The Network Startup Resource Center offers global networking information for local network administrators: www.nsrc.org

- ✔ TechnoTips.com has web-based tools and resources for networking professionals, with an occasional one for Cisco network administrators: www.technotips.com

- ✔ Protocols.com offers information on networking and data communications protocols: www.protocols.com

- ✔ RAD Communications, Inc., has a site for definitions and tutorials on many key protocol, media, and transport types used in networking: www.rad.com/networks/tutorial.htm

- ✔ PC Help Online is a site devoted to helping you find information, utilities, and tools for diagnosing and troubleshooting PC problems: www.pchelponline.com

- ✔ The RFC (Request For Comments) Index lists all of the RFC's that have been accepted and implemented to date. In case, you don't know, RFC's are the mechanism that cause changes to the protocols and standards used on the Internet: ftp://ftpeng.cisco.com/fred/rfc-index/rfc.html

✔ The RFC Editor's Page is another site that catalogs and allows searches of accepted RFC's: www.rfc-editor.org/

✔ Although, we've not discussed certification, if you are interested here are some sites with good information about Cisco (and other) certifications:

- www.certification.net/it/

- www.cisco.com/warp/public/10/wwtraining/

Chapter 21

Ten Things You Should Remember When Designing Your Network

S hould you ever be so lucky as to have the opportunity to design your very own Cisco network, you have our condolences. Yes, we are ambivalent about this task. Designing your very own network allows you to put into use all you ideas for how a network really should be put together. On the other hand, when you are the designer of the network, you must shoulder the blame (and credit) for how the network performs in real life. Often, the creative and brilliant design that looked so wonderful on paper could use just a little more design work, in reality.

In this chapter, we have included ten areas, considerations, or issues that we believe must be a part of a successful network design. If you have never designed, or redesigned a network, then hopefully the information in this chapter will help you. If you are an old hand at this, your reaction after you've read this chapter may be, "I knew that!" And that's great! We are just glad we could remind you.

Ten Steps to Include When Designing a Network

Here are ten steps that you really should include when designing your network:

Determine the users' needs

If you think you know more about your users' needs than they do, think again! Regardless of how you feel about it or what you believe to be their true requirements, the users definitely know what they need the network to do. Ask and document; then design.

Document the existing network

If you have an existing network, it likely will be the basis of any future network. So make sure that the existing network is well documented — good and bad. The good is what it does well, and the bad is what it could do better. The bad is often why you are redesigning the network in the first place, but make sure that you include the good stuff in the new, redesigned network, as well.

Determine the appropriate structure

Using what you've learned in the preceding steps, you should now be able to decide the arrangement, topology, and technology that best supports the needs of the users and addresses the best of the existing network. If you can't, then you must repeat these steps until you can. Chances are if you had an Ethernet network with departmental segmentation before and that wasn't the problem causing a redesign, then that's what you should have moving forward. You likely are not replacing a functioning Fast Ethernet network with a Token Ring, but it could happen.

If you are designing a new network, the physical arrangement of the organization and the users will be a major consideration in designing the layout of the network, as well as its topology. If the organization is all in one building, it may be spread over separate floors. If the organization is in many buildings on a campus, then that will definitely impact your decision on both structure and topology.

Create a network drawing

This is the perfect time to convert your vision to a drawing. This will help you to visualize what you had in mind and perform your first reality check. This drawing will be the visual reference for your network design as you go forward. As you complete each subsequent step, you should update the drawing and include an increasing amount of detail about the elements depicted. Even if you aren't much of an artist or draftsperson, tools such as Microsoft's Vision 2000 are available to bring out the artist in anyone.

Choose the hardware and media

Okay, now that you have laid out the network and have chosen the topology that you're going to use, you must choose the network hardware and data transmission media best suited to the demands of the network. This is actually a fairly big phase of the design process.

> ✔ **First, you must choose the network media best suited to the performance requirements established by the users.**
>
>   For example, if the consensus is that the network must be Fast Ethernet, then you know right away that you can no longer use the Cat 3 wiring in the wall and must replace it with Cat 5. Some things are just obvious. If the network is to be Ethernet with a data speed of 10 Mbps or faster, the wiring is Cat 5 or better.
>
> ✔ **Set the physical distance limitations of the network.**
>
>   This nails down the switching and routing devices to be used. These devices must also be fitted to the functions, topology, and speeds planned for the network. Cisco includes a number of tools and guides on their Web site (www.cisco.com) to assist you in this activity.
>
> ✔ **Redraw the network layout, this time to scale.**
>
>   Make sure that all the segments are properly served with adequate bandwidth and that the media runs do not exceed the distance limitations. This is also an excellent time to apply your naming convention and assign network names to the switches and routers on the net.

Select routing and switching protocols

Each of the Cisco routers and switches that you have included in the design of the network most likely has a range of routing, bridging, and switching protocols from which you can choose. Use caution to ensure that the protocols you choose are interoperable with all equipment on the network. Remember that some protocols may be best suited for LANs and others to WANs.

Determining which is best in which situations may require some research. Again, the Cisco Systems' Web site is an excellent source for information. For a list of the protocols available on a particular device, consult the *Cisco Product Guide.*

Choose the operating system

The network operating system (NOS), see Chapter 8, that will operate the network from the main network server must be chosen or reconfirmed. However, this isn't the only operating system that will operate on the network. In addition to determining the features of the NOS that must be installed, you should also determine the features (and version) of the Cisco IOS that your network will require.

Document the new design

If you have been updating your network design drawing as you went along, you now need only to write a narrative that describes what you have included on the network diagram. If you have been skipping that part of the design process, you will unfortunately now need to create both a detailed network drawing and an explanation of the network details depicted.

It would be valuable at this point if you met again with your users to explain to them, in non-technical terms, just what the network has been designed to provide to them. A review with the technical or Information Technology (IT) staff of your organization would be an excellent idea at this point as well. Remember that these peer review sessions are also called "turkey shoots" for a reason.

Verify the network's design

Verify your network's design with a tool, such as the Cisco Interactive Mentor (CIM), or a 3rd party network simulator. Simulation tools enable you to build a virtual prototype of your network to test its functionality and, if desired, to probe for security weaknesses as well. For information on the Cisco Interactive Mentor, visit www.cisco.com/warp/public/710/cim/.

Test the network

Remember that nothing is quite like real life for providing the ultimate test. If it is at all possible, you need to build up the network design using the actual routers and switches to test their interoperability and compatibility prior to deploying them around the network. Of course, this is only feasible with completely new networks, or in very wealthy companies.

At minimum, test the network under as many peak use conditions as possible. Try to simulate every operating condition you identified way back in the step that identified the users' needs. Don't be too surprised if a user discovers the one weakness that you forgot to test the minute he logs onto the network.

Designing around Network Congestion

In much the same way that highways become congested at rush hour, networks can become congested when too much network traffic tries to move along too little bandwidth. Congestion is a common reason for network redesign, or at least adjustment.

Common causes for network congestion are

- Segments or collision domains with too many users for the available bandwidth

- Too many users vying for the same networked applications, such as bandwidth hogs like desktop publishing or multimedia, or too many large files moving across the network

- A large percentage of workstations accessing the Internet

- Network workstations' processing power that has increased faster than the network's capabilities

Congestion can be avoided or minimized by including some basic design considerations:

- Place network clients on the same logical network as the servers that they use most. Logical networks are defined in the network's NOS. This reduces the amount of traffic moving over the network's backbone from segment to segment.

- Move applications and files from one server to another to help balance traffic and contain it to one segment. If you can't move software and files, then try moving the user workstations to balance the demand.

- Design the network around the 80/20 rule, which requires that 80 percent of the network traffic remains local to its segment and only 20 percent of the network traffic ever moves across the network backbone.

- Increase the number of servers supporting user client/server activities, so that more servers are providing resources to more local segments.

- When all else fails, you should apply what is perhaps the most commonly used solution to network congestion: Increase the number of network segments by inserting a switch or a router into the network. This step may require a quick design review of the network, though.

A Checklist of Network Must-Haves

The items in the checklists in the following sections may seem like "no-brainers," but sometimes the simplest (and most obvious) things can be overlooked in a design.

Don't forget these in a small LAN

These items are essential for a small LAN:

- ✔ You need at least two network workstations (clients).
- ✔ The workstations must each have at least one NIC installed.
- ✔ A client/server network must have at least one server.
- ✔ The workstations must be connected to the network via a hub.
- ✔ Some form of network compatible cabling must be used to connect the workstation NICs and the server to the hub.
- ✔ The server requires a NOS.
- ✔ If the network is connecting to the outside world, it will need a modem or a small router.

You'll need these to connect offices

In addition to the items required for the small LAN, you'll need to add the following to your network to connect geographically dispersed offices:

- ✔ If the offices are just on different floors of the same building, then one or more switches can be used to connect them.
- ✔ If the offices are in different geographical locations, you may need to use routers to interconnect the LAN of each office to the WAN.
- ✔ Assuming the WAN is also connected to the Internet, you will need a router for that purpose as well.
- ✔ You can't have a WAN without some form of WAN service. This could be in the form of ISDN, Frame Relay, or a leased-line from the ILEC.
- ✔ If users are allowed to access the network via a dial-up connection, you will need to provide an access server.

Chapter 22

Ten Network Installation Tips

*I*nstalling a network requires the same analysis, planning, and attention to detail, regardless of its size or complexity. Whether you are building a simple network with one segment or a complex network with hundreds of segments on a corporate campus or WAN, you need to know the network's objectives and how it must meet the needs of the organization. For any installation to be successful, the planning is the same. The only question is one of degree.

In this chapter, we have listed ten steps to take in any network installation project. How much time each takes depends on how much detail is required for your network, but one thing is for sure: You must give each step all the time that it requires and not rush the planning to save time. Any shortcuts taken in the preinstallation processes may very well show up later as problems on the network.

Chapter 19 contains some additional information on the processes that are used to develop the requirements, design the network, and plan for its installation.

Using a Site Preparation Checklist

Cisco includes several preinstallation, site preparation, and safety checklists in the documentation of nearly all of its products and definitely for all of its router and Catalyst switch products. You can also get these checklists online at the Cisco Web site (www.cisco.com). These checklists are general guides that list what you should consider when preparing a site for networking equipment.

You should locate and apply these two specific guides:

- ✔ The Preinstallation Checklist
- ✔ The Site Preparation and Safety Guide

Checking out the Preinstallation Checklist

With Cisco routers, you should be given a Preinstallation Checklist to complete. This checklist serves two purposes. First, it lets Cisco know who your contact person is to be for the installation, how to contact him or her, and where and when you would like to install the router. It also provides a list of preparation questions that, when answered, will provide you with virtually every consideration for preparing to install the router. These questions are included in the Preinstallation Checklist:

- ✔ Will the equipment be installed in a rack or a table?

- ✔ Is the appropriate power source available?

- ✔ If required, are the WAN circuit components (CSU/DSU, Frame-Relay circuit, and so on) installed and ready to be connected?

- ✔ Is the LAN connection installed and ready to be connected?

- ✔ Is an RJ-11 connection for an active analog phone line (to be used for dial-up access) available within 50 feet of the installation location?

- ✔ Are all required LAN and WAN cables in the appropriate length and with the proper connectors ready and available?

- ✔ What is the Cisco IOS version to be installed on the router?

- ✔ What tests are to be performed, and who is to perform them, to prove that the installation is successful?

Studying the Site Preparation and Safety Guide

Right off the bat, you will get the feeling that if you don't know what you are doing, you should leave the installation of your router or switch to a trained professional. In fact, the first words in this guide — right after it tells you that you should read the guide before installing or servicing your system — are that only trained and qualified personnel should ever install, replace, or repair your Cisco equipment.

Next it tells you that the guide is designed to keep you from electrocuting yourself and to prevent other accidents that may cause bodily injury. We're definitely all for that!

These things are highlighted in the Site Preparation and Safety Guide:

✔ Choosing the best possible site for installation

✔ Protecting the system from electrical problems

✔ Properly grounding the system

✔ Keeping the area around the system safe during and after installation

✔ Properly installing the system in a rack-mounting

✔ Lifting the system without injuring yourself

✔ Providing the proper electrical power source

✔ Preventing ESD (electrostatic discharge) damage to your system

✔ Installing and servicing the system safely to avoid electrical, laser, and EMI (electromechanical interference) problems

Preparing the Site's Environment

A Site Environmental Guideline is included in the installation materials that come as a part of your Cisco system's documentation. This document contains the minimums and maximum for each of the environmental characteristics that you need to address as a part of your installation preparations.

For example, the environmental characteristics required for the Cisco 6400, listed in its environmental guidelines, are summarized in Table 22-1.

Table 22-1	Environmental Guidelines for the Cisco 6400	
Characteristic	*Minimum*	*Maximum*
Ambient operating temperature	25° Fahrenheit (–4° Celsius)	104°F (40° Celsius)
Relative humidity	5%	95%
Operating altitude	-200 feet (-61 meters)	10,000 ft (3,048 m)
Operating vibration	-	5 to 200 Hertz

Racking It Up

One topic that Cisco installation guides cover in extreme detail is how to properly install your system in a rack-mount. However, the one point we want to make about rack-mount installations is that you must plan this type of installation very carefully, taking into consideration the equipment already installed in the rack or the equipment that you plan to install in the rack at some later time.

You must provide for proper airflow and wire management, as well as common-sense weight distribution, when installing any equipment into an existing or a new rack-mount. Probably the most important of these, not that any are really unimportant, is the weight distribution. Don't forget that two-rail rack systems must be bolted to the floor and that you want to put the really heavy stuff on the bottom and the lightest equipment at the top.

Planning the rack according to its functional mates (switches with punch-downs, or routers with firewalls) may not actually provide you with the safest installation, when you consider the weight of the devices. And never arrange your rack by color or any other non-technical or whimsical way. Not only is it likely to hurt you or a co-worker, but it may well damage your very expensive equipment, should a top-heavy rack topple over.

Flooring the Load

Along with the considerations of weight distribution of a rack-mount system (see the preceding section), you should at least consider the weight distribution and floor loading of the entire networking system. Many buildings, especially high-rise buildings and older buildings, have floor loading specifications or codes with which you must comply.

No one piece of networking equipment, including servers, routers, firewalls, switches, racks, and so on, is all that heavy by itself. However, when you add up all the equipment that is stacked in one or two rack-mount bays, then you may have a great deal of weight sitting on a small piece of flooring. You may need to space apart rack bays or locate the rack on a part of the floor supported by a weight-bearing beam or joist.

Table 22-2 contains a sample of the device weight information included in the installation guidelines for the Cisco 6400 switch. Not every component is listed, but you can see how the weight of devices can add up.

Table 22-2	Component Weights for the Cisco 6400	
Component	*Weight/lbs*	*Weight/kg*
Empty chassis	37.80	17.20
AC Power Entry Module	10.90	4.95
DC Power Entry Module	6.20	2.80
Blower/Fan module	10.95	4.97
Totally populated chassis	130.00	59.02

Powering the System

Not all Cisco gear is powered by 110 AC electrical power. In fact, much of the higher-end equipment is available in either AC-powered or DC-powered models. Each piece of Cisco equipment has a very definite power requirement. You can find the power considerations for your system in the Site Preparation and Safety Guide, as well as in the documentation of the system.

The power considerations of a Cisco router includes the wattage of the internal power supply (AC or DC), the operating range allowable for the power source, and any wiring recommendations. For example, Cisco 7500 series routers have the following power specifications:

- ✔ **600-watt internal power supply:** Either an AC-input power supply or a DC-input supply
- ✔ **AC voltage and current range:** 100 to 240 VAC and 50 to 60 Hz
- ✔ **DC voltage range:** –40 and –52 VDC (–48 VDC nominal)
- ✔ **AC wire specification:** 12 AWG with three leads, an IEC-320 plug (router end), country-dependent plug (power-source end)

In addition to ensuring that you have adequate and appropriate power sources for your system, you also need to make sure that you have protected your system against low-voltage, over-voltage, and surge conditions on the power source. You should also provide an ample UPS (uninterruptible power supply) power backup to power the system until your generator kicks in. You do have a generator, don't you?

Many of these considerations may seem a bit over the top if all you are planning to install is a Cisco 805 router and an 8-port hub. Remember, you still need to address the power requirements of the system, just not as in-depth as you would with the 7505 router.

Clearing the Cable Path

Before you get too carried away with all the nice new green toys from Cisco, you absolutely must do one thing before you can hook it all up. We mentioned in the section "Using a Site Preparation Checklist," earlier in the chapter, that you must have the LAN cabling and connections ready to connect to the router or switch when installing that device. However, you must take care of a few steps involving your cabling before you get to that point.

Critical to installing a network is installing its cable media. In many cases, cabling was installed by the electricians that helped build the building even before you were hired. Or it was installed when the building was remodeled, or you yourself just finished pulling the network cable into place. If the cabling issue has not be resolved, then you'll need to complete this job before you can complete the installation of your network.

Perhaps the most critical aspect of this part of the installation is making sure that you have a clear path for the cable. The cable needs to run cleanly without bends and kinks from one connector to the next. If you have chosen to install a wireless system, which is becoming more common lately, then make sure nothing obstructs or interferes with the devices you want to connect. In either case, wire or wireless, your network will perform better with no problems along the media path.

Sweeping the Cable Path

This section may seem like it belongs in the preceding section, but we feel so strongly about it, we've chosen to eat up one of your ten installation tips with it.

Even with the network media placed into the best possible pathways available, the whole network can be brought to its electronic knees by a electrically noisy pop machine, or that nearby radio tower, or that radioactive waste dump under your building. The cable path may be like a wide open four-lane highway, but if it must pass through interference for radio frequency (RF), electromechanical interference (EMI), or other electrical or magnetic noise hazards, it is all for naught.

In short, you really should check the network path for potential EMI, RF, and other hazards to your network cable media as a part of your installation preparations.

Tooling Up for the Job

Unfortunately for you frustrated Tim "the Toolman" Taylor wannabees, few specialized tools are required for the installation of a network. Largely, the tools you need for installing a network are a screwdriver, a pair of wire cutters, and a crimper suited to the connector that you are using. You could use a lifting device to raise a high-end router, firewall, or switch into place so you can attach it to the rack-mount rails. You could also use a digital multimeter, or a fox-and-hound style cable tone tester to verify electrical and cable connections. But, beyond that, you shouldn't need special tools.

Of course, the easiest way to make sure that you have all the right tools needed for the cable and system installation is to hire installers. Cisco will contract for the installation of your system, as will most Cisco value-added resellers (VARs).

Scheduling Downtime to Test

If you are adding or updating equipment in an existing network, you will need to schedule some downtime to fully test the new configuration of the network. If you work in an environment like ours, then this time will come after midnight, when the logged in subscriber base is smaller. If you work in a small office environment, then you may be able to employ network users in the test.

In most test situations, though, schedule network downtime for a time that is the least disruptive for the users of the network. Keep in mind why and for whom the network exists. Unfortunately, unless you own a large software company in the Seattle area, the network does not exist for you.

Training, Training, Training

If you are a network administrator or are working at becoming one, you have our permission to reproduce this section and give it to your supervisor.

Perhaps the most important, and often most overlooked, part of preparing for a network installation is the training of the key individuals who will be charged with the efficient, reliable, and secure operation of the network. Companies will spend thousands, even hundreds of thousands, of dollars to purchase the routers, switches, cabling, workstations, and software used to build the network, but will scrimp on the training of the people who are expected to make it all work. If keeping the network running were all magic, then it would be no problem. If Cisco were able to manufacture a system that fit perfectly in every situation, just by plugging it in, then training wouldn't even be needed. But training is needed. So train the network administrators. The investment in training always pays dividends, if not in operational efficiency, then at least in employee morale.

Best of luck with your new network.

Chapter 23

Ten Things to Check When Configuring a Cisco Router

*T*en actions that you should make absolutely sure to include in the procedure you use to control the configuration process of your routers, and a few helpful hints about some of these actions, are included in this chapter. Although others actions may be necessary in setting up your network, these are the ten that we believe you must include in your router configuration process.

Your Equipment

You're probably in one of two situations: You have ordered the specific equipment that you need, and you have been working with Cisco routers and switches for some time now. Or you are brand new to all this, and you really do want our help in defining the steps that you should take to configure a router. In either case, these steps provide a good checklist against forgetting a very valuable step in this critical activity.

Follows these tips to get started:

✔ Make sure that you have your router's documentation and locate any information about the router on the Cisco Web site (www.cisco.com). You need this information whether or not you have configured a router before.

✔ Make sure that you have all the appropriate cables, adapters, and connectors. Nothing is more frustrating than stopping the work because you don't have a vital piece of equipment.

✔ Test to be sure that your PC or notebook computer has the applications you'll need, such as HyperTerminal and Notepad, and that you know how to operate them. If you are using a notebook or laptop computer, check that you have a power supply and, if you will be working where no AC power is available, that the battery is adequate for the job.

✔ Make sure that the IOS version is the one you need for the network project. With some network implementations, you may also need more than the standard memory that was shipped with your router.

The Configuration Methodologies

How you configure your router today will impact how you, or your replacement, will configure it in the future. It is important to document exactly how you configure the router. Do you run the setup routine when you power the router up for the first time? (Although this is the common practice, you can use other options.) Do you use the automatic setup routine or do you manually enter the configuration one line at a time? Do you instead copy the initial configuration into the router in the global configuration mode?

Using a common router configuration from a previously configured router can be quite a timesaver. Remember that the configuration file is a text file and that you can use a text editor, such as Microsoft's Notepad, to create or modify a configuration, changing those items that are unique to a particular router, such as its hostname, banner, IP address, and any interface information. The file can then be copied to the router.

Regardless of how you configure the router, the configuration will affect how you modify the configuration in the future. Of course, what you do today does not mean that you can't use a different manner in the future, but it may affect how the configuration process is documented today. And documenting the configuration and the process used are the most important parts of these decisions.

Network Management

How are the network, and especially the routers and switches, to be managed? If the network is a simple affair with a small office router and a small number of nodes, management may be easily performed without the need for sophisticated management tools. However, if the network is very large, you need to decide which SNMP traps you want to see. As a part of the router's configuration, you must decide which traps are to be sent and where this information is to be sent.

LAN Addressing Scheme

Before you place your router into service on the network, you should check, and then check again, the IP addresses used in its configurations. Verify that, if you have decided to use an internal IP addressing scheme, you have consistently done so throughout the configuration. If you have used a specific numbering scheme to designate routers, switches, servers, and even printers and workstations on the network, check to see that it has also been consistently applied.

Be sure to check the access list wildcard masks and the application of subnet masks in the configuration. In case we haven't mentioned it, you should document the IP addressing scheme used on the network.

LAN Protocols

Be sure that all the LAN protocols required for all network nodes to talk with all other parts of the network are installed and enabled. Also be sure that any unneeded LAN protocols are removed or disabled, so that your network performance is not affected. Too many LAN protocols can hurt the network's performance just as much as too few.

WAN Addressing Scheme

Remember that you can't use an internal IP addressing scheme to communicate with the outside world over the Internet. You must be sure that the IP addressing scheme to be applied to WAN interfaces is a public scheme that is routable and built to conserve IP addresses. For example, link interfaces should use a 255.255.255.252 subnet mask when possible. This yields a network ID, one IP address for each WAN interface, and a broadcast address, conserving other IP addresses for other uses.

If you are working with Frame-Relay in your WAN configuration, you will also need to know the DLCI for your end of the Frame-Relay connection. For ATM, FDDI, SONET, or SMDS connections, you will need the specific information needed to configure the network beyond its IP addressing.

Be sure to document the structure of the WAN connections and the IP addressing scheme used.

WAN Protocols

You must make several decisions when configuring a router to work in a WAN environment. These include the decision of whether to enable NAT, and if so, whether to use a one-to-one or one-to-many IP addressing pool. Another decision is whether the security needs of the network require static IP addressing. And yet another is which routing protocols are to be configured for use.

In the WAN environment, you must look beyond your network in making these choices. Using proprietary Cisco protocols, such as EIGRP, is a bad choice if the next upstream hop is not a Cisco router.

Router Security

Two elements affect the security of the router itself. The first is its physical location and how accessible it is to non-administrators. You should follow your instincts that tell you to lock the router away, not only from prying eyes but the fingers and hands associated with them as well.

The second element of router security is the passwords on the router that screen access to the router's configuration. Be sure that every open access interface has a password associated with it. Make sure that each of the passwords you want to use, including the console, the virtual terminal (vty), enable, and enable secret passwords, are properly set and active.

Access List Verification

If you have included access lists as a part of your router's configuration, you absolutely must test them, test them, and test them again. If you have forgotten that an implicit deny is automatically placed at the end of any permit list, your testing should identify this for you when the one entry you forgot to include gains access.

Your testing should also address that the access lists are processed in sequence, and that after a condition is met, the appropriate action is taken, and all other conditions are ignored.

The Configuration Archive

If you do not have a backup copy of the current configuration, you must make one before anyone notices and way before you begin making changes. Never assume that you won't make mistakes.

After you have made all your changes, make another copy (not over the other one, please) to capture the new configuration. Name the files appropriately, use good media (such as Zip disks or CD-ROMs), and store them in a safe and secure place.

Perhaps the biggest single reason for these backups is that days or weeks may pass before the big error in the configuration shows up, and you may want to restore to the last working configuration quickly and easily.

Don't forget to save your configuration changes to the router as well. If you change the running configuration files and then fail to copy it to the flash RAM, it will be all for naught if the router ever needs or happens to restart.

Part VII
Appendixes

The 5th Wave   By Rich Tennant

"...and Bobby here found a way to extend our data transmission an additional 3000 meters using coax cable. How'd you do that, Bobby—repeaters?"

In this part . . .

We include two references that may come in handy: one for now and one for later. The one you can probably use now is the Glossary in Appendix B. We have included most of the technical terms used in the book and provided a non-technical (as much as we are able) definition for each. If nothing else, you could use the Glossary much like a foreign language dictionary to help you learn the language of the network.

Appendix A provides a reference of the more common IOS commands you may use as a Cisco network administrator. This is by no means a comprehensive Cisco IOS reference, but we do give you a look at the command, its options and parameters, and a brief description of when and why it would be used.

Appendix A
Cisco IOS Commands

••

*H*ere are many of the IOS commands found in Cisco IOS release 12.0, that you may encounter working on a Cisco network.

This Command...	Does This
**access-list access-list-number {permit	deny} address mask**	Establishes MAC address access lists
**access-list access-list-number {permit	deny} type-code wild-mask**	Builds type-code access lists
no access-list access-list-number	Removes a single access list entry
bandwidth	Sets a bandwidth value for an interface
channel-group channel-number	Assigns a Fast Ethernet interface to a Fast EtherChannel group
clear counters [type number]	Clears the interface counters
clear interface type number	Resets the hardware logic on an interface
clear rif-cache	Clears entries from the Routing Information Field (RIF) cache
clock rate bps	Configures the clock rate for the hardware connections on serial interfaces
**cmt connect [interface-name [phy-a	phy-b]]**	Starts the processes that perform the CMT function
**compress {predictor	stac}**	Configures compression for LAPB, PPP, and HDLC encapsulations
copy flash lex number	Downloads an executable image from Flash memory on the core router to the LAN Extender chassis
crc size	Sets the length of the cyclic redundancy check (CRC)

dce-terminal-timing enable	Prevents phase shifting of the data with respect to the clock
description string	Adds a description to a T1 controller
down-when-looped	Informs the system that it is down when a loopback is detected
**duplex {full	half	auto}**	Configures the duplex operation on an interface
encapsulation encapsulation-type	Sets the encapsulation method used by the interface
**framing {sf	esf}**	Selects the frame type for a T1 data line
full-duplex	Specifies full-duplex mode on full-duplex single- and multi-mode port adapters
half-duplex	Specifies half-duplex mode on an interface
**hold-queue length {in	out}**	Specifies the hold-queue limit of an interface
interface type number	Configures an interface type and enters interface configuration mode
interface dialer interface-number	Designates a dialer rotary group leader
invert txclock	Inverts the transmit clock signal
keepalive [seconds]	Sets the keepalive timer for a specific interface
**linecode {ami	b8zs	hdb3}**	Selects the line code type for a T1 line
loopback	Diagnoses equipment malfunctions between interface and device
**media-type {aui	10baset	100baset	mii}**	Specifies the physical connection on an interface
mop enabled	Enables an interface to support the Maintenance Operation Protocol (MOP)
mtu bytes	Adjusts the maximum packet size or maximum transmission unit (MTU) size
**physical-layer {sync	async}**	Specifies the mode of a slow-speed serial interface on a router
port	Enables an interface to operate as a concentrator port

show bridge group	Displays all bridge groups in the system
show controllers serial [slot/port]	Displays information specific to serial interfaces
show interfaces [type number] [first] [last] [accounting]	Displays statistics for all interfaces configured on the router
show interfaces ethernet	Displays information about an Ethernet interface
show interfaces ip-brief	Displays a brief summary of an IP interface's information and status
show interfaces serial	Displays information about a serial interface
show ip interface [brief] [type] [number]	Lists a summary of an interface's IP information and status
show rif	Displays the current contents of the RIF cache
shutdown	Disables an interface
**speed {10	100	auto}**	Configures the speed for a Fast Ethernet interface
**squelch {normal	reduced}**	Extends the distance limit on a 10BaseT beyond the standard 100 meters

Appendix B

A Glossary of Networking Terms

• •

*I*n this appendix, we include the terms that a Cisco networking administrator should know.

A

access layer router — Routers on the access layer direct network traffic to its destination and are used to segment LANs.

access list — An access list is a table of entries used to permit or deny traffic through a router that consists of structured statements outlining what a router is to do with an incoming packet.

ACL (Access Control List) — An ACL is maintained by virtually every operating system and network operating system. It lists the available services on a system, the users or nodes that have been granted access, and what kind of access has been granted to those services. After a user is authenticated on a system, the ACL controls what the user can and cannot access.

active hub — Active hubs re-energize the signal before sending it on to its ports. Smart active hubs intelligently direct a signal to the port on which its destination exists.

algorithm — The process used to determine the solution to a problem is called an algorithm. In routing, algorithms are used to determine the best route for traffic to take to get to its intended destination.

antivirus software — Antivirus software is used to detect the presence of and to remove computer viruses. Although not always thought of as a security issue, viruses pose a serious threat to the integrity of a system, which is why antivirus software is considered a security measure.

Application layer — Layer 7 of the OSI Model, this layer defines services to application software.

ARP (Address Resolution Protocol) — This protocol is used to resolve physical addresses into network addresses.

ATM (Asynchronous Transfer Mode) — This is a cell-switching broadband technology that transmits digital data in 53- cells on dedicated circuits. This is a Layer 2 technology, which is implemented by hardware that gives faster processing and switching speeds. ATM rates are 155Mbps 10Gbps.

ATP/NBP (AppleTalk Transaction Protocol/Name Binding Protocol) — These are AppleTalk's data transport protocols.

attenuation — The distance limit at which the electrical signal transmitted on a wire begins to weakens and is no longer recognizable is called attenuation.

authentication — Authentication is the process that verifies that a user, node, or workstation has the authority or permission to gain access to a system. The most common form of authentication is through the use of a user account name and a password.

autonomous system — An autonomous system is a network that operates under a single set of rules that may include one or more routing protocols.

auxiliary password — This password is set to control access to the router on an auxiliary port.

B

bandwidth — The maximum amount of data that can be transmitted over a network medium is expressed in bits-per-second and is referred to as bandwidth.

binary — A number system that uses two values (0 and 1) to represent numbers in positions representing increasing powers of 2 is a binary system.

bootstrap — The bootstrap program finds a valid Cisco IOS image in the location specified by the router's configuration register and loads it to RAM.

BRI ISDN — This type of ISDN service consists of two 64Kbps bearer (B) channels and one 15Kbps data (D) channel, for a combined bandwidth of 144Kbps.

bridge — A bridge, which is a Data Link layer (Layer 2) device, works with Layer 2 protocols and Layer 2 MAC sublayer addresses to forward messages within and outside of a network segment.

bus topology — The bus topology is a fundamental network topology. Using this topology, network nodes are connected to a central cable, called a backbone, which runs the length of the network.

C

Cat 3 — Cat 3 is a four-pair cable supporting bandwidth up to 10Mbps and is the minimum standard for 10BaseT networks. Wire category (cat) standards are developed by IEEE.

Cat 5 — Cat 5 is a four-wire cable with bandwidth up to 100Mbps and is used for 100BaseTX and ATM (asynchronous transfer mode) networking.

CDP (Cisco Discovery Protocol) — This proprietary Cisco protocol is used to update information on a router about directly-connected Cisco routers, bridges, and switches.

cell — This is a 53-byte digital data unit into which data transmitted over ATM circuits is divided for transmission. See *ATM*.

CHAP (Challenge Handshake Authentication Protocol) — This inbound authentication method allows a receiving device to initiate a challenge sequence, which is then modified by the requesting device before the connection can be established.

checksum — In this form of error-checking, the one's complement is summed for all of the 16-bit words that make up a TCP segment or UDP datagram.

CIR (Committed Information Rate) — The minimum bandwidth committed to a customer on a circuit is referred to as CIR.

classful — This is a term used to describe IP addressing schemes that are based on the Ipv4 address classes: Class A, Class B, Class C, Class D, and Class E.

classless interdomain routing (CIDR) — This is an addressing scheme that expresses the subnet network address in the form $/n$, where n represents the number of bits in the network address.

client — Workstations that make requests on the server for a function that it fulfills are clients of that server. Clients do not share their own resources with the network.

collision domain — A collision domain is a network segment on which networked devices share the same bandwidth and on which message collisions may occur.

command line interface (CLI) — CLI is the DOS-like user interface and prompt of Cisco routers.

configuration mode — This command line mode is used to manually configure a router or make changes to a router's status.

configuration-register — The location from which the IOS software is to be loaded during the boot process is a hexadecimal value in the configuration-register.

connectionless protocol — A connectionless protocol does not use a virtual circuit, or connection-oriented conduit, and no error-recovery functions are included.

connection-oriented protocol — A protocol is considered connection-oriented if it meets one of two criteria: Data is transmitted over a negotiated path, a virtual circuit, or between two nodes; or the protocol includes a process for error-recovery.

console password — This password is set to control access to the router through the console port.

convergence — When all routers on a network have the same knowledge of the network, the network is said to have convergence.

core layer router — Core layer routers are used to merge geographically separated networks. The focus of the core layer is on moving information as fast as possible, most often over dedicated or leased lines.

cost — An arbitrary routing metric value assigned by the administrator for the crossing and intersection of networks is called cost.

CPE (Customer Premise Equipment) — CPE is the equipment installed and operated from the customer end of a Frame-Relay circuit.

CRC (Cyclic Redundancy Check) — CRC is a calculated amount that's used for error detection. It is placed into the Data Link trailer added to the message frame before it's sent to the Physical layer.

cross-connect — This is the connection that interconnects the workstation cabling and the network cabling. A common method of creating network cross-connects is through a patch panel.

CSMA/CD (Carrier Sense Multiple Access/Collision Detection) — This access method is used on an Ethernet network.

cut-through switching — This switching method begins to forward a frame as soon as the source and destination MAC addresses are read, typically within the first 12 bytes of an Ethernet frame.

D

Data Link layer — Layer 2 of the OSI Model. This layer defines the mechanisms used to move data move about the network, including topology, such as Ethernet or Token Ring, and the ways in which data is reliably transmitted.

DCE (Data Communications Equipment) — In a communications connection, DCE equipment is typically carrier-owned internetworking devices.

default subnet mask — The default subnet mask for Class A IP addresses is 255.0.0.0. The default subnet mask for Class B IP addresses is 255.255.0.0. The default subnet mask for Class C IP addresses is 255.255.255.0.

DoS (Denial of Service Attack) — A DoS is a hostile action taken against a WAN server that causes the server to begin denying services normally provided to users because it is overloaded with bogus requests for service.

distance vector — A distance vector routing protocol uses hop counts to determine the best route, views the network from its neighbors' perspective, and copies its routing table to neighboring routers. Examples of distance vector protocols are RIP, IPX RIP, and IGRP.

distribution routers — These are routers on the intermediate level (distribution level). Distribution routers make most routing policy decisions, and they filter and forward packets to the other router layers.

DLCI (Data-Link Connection Identifier) — A DLCI is a single circuit mapped to an outbound port that combines multiple virtual circuits.

DSL (Digital Subscriber Line) — A broadband communications service delivered over telephone lines. DSL lines upload data at speeds ranging from 128Kbps to 6.1Mbps, with typical service offering from 512Kbps to 1.5Mbps download speeds and 128K upload speeds.

DTE (Data Terminal Equipment) — In a communications connection, DTE equipment typically consists of terminals, PCs, routers and bridges that are owned by the customer.

dynamic route — Dynamic routing enables a router to make route determinations using routing metrics and efficiencies. Any changes to the network are updated to the routing table automatically.

E

E1/E3: Carrier lines that are used in South America and Europe; they're similar to the T1 and T3 lines used in the U.S. The E1 is slightly larger than the T1 (2.048Mbps versus 1.54Mbps) and the E3 is slightly smaller than the T3 (34Mbps versus 44.736Mbps), but they are often referred to as equivalents.

EIA/TIA wiring standards — The EIA/TIA 568 and 568B standards are the wiring standards used for network media. These two standards are elements of LAN cabling, including telecommunications closets, equipment rooms, entrance facilities, work areas, backbone cabling, and horizontal cabling.

EMI (Electromagnetic Interference) — Interference generated by virtually all electrical devices that can cause interference and impair the signals of other devices. This is also called electrical noise.

Enable Exec mode — Also called Privileged Exec mode, this mode is used to perform high-level testing and debugging, and updating or changing configuration files.

Enable password — This password is used when an Enable Secret password has not been set. It's also used for older router software versions.

Enable Secret password — This password adds a level of security over and above the Enable password.

encapsulation — Also referred to as data encapsulation, this is the transformation process of data as it passes through the layers of the OSI model.

encryption — Encryption is the process that converts data into a form that cannot be deciphered by an unauthorized person. The encrypted data, called a cipher, must be converted back into an understandable form using a process called decryption.

error detection — This is the process of detecting errors that occur during the transmission of the bits across a wire.

Ethernet — An Ethernet is a network technology, defined in IEEE 802.3, that is the most popular networking technology for LANs. Ethernet networks are, by definition, built on a bus topology that operates on baseband rates of 10Mbps, 100Mbps, or 1,000Mbps (1Gbps).

extranet — This is actually an intranet that has been extended to included trusted external users or networks. In most cases, an extranet allows certain outside users, such as customers, suppliers, or other businesses, to gain access to part or all of an internal network's resources. See *intranet.*

F

FDDI (Fiber Distributed Data Interchange) — FDDI is an ANSI (American National Standards Institute) standard that defines a dual ring technology that operates at 100 Mbps over fiber optic cabling.

firewall — A firewall — commonly a combination of hardware and software — prevents unauthorized network traffic from entering a network. The firewall is a network's first level of security.

flash — Router memory that holds the image and microcode of the router's operating system, which can be upgraded under software control, is a process called *flashing.*

flow control — Flow control meters the flow of data between network devices that may not be running at the same speeds.

Frame Relay — This is a Layer 2 technology optimized for high performance and efficient frame transmission. Frame Relay operates across serial interfaces and was designed specifically for use on fiber optic cables and digital networks.

FTP (File Transfer Protocol) — FTP is a reliable, connection-oriented protocol used to copy files from one computer to another over a TCP/IP network.

full-duplex — This transmission mode allows communications to flow in two directions (from sender to receiver and from receiver to sender) of a session simultaneously. The PSTN (public switched telephone network) is an example of a full-duplex system.

H

half-duplex — This transmission mode transmits two directions (from sender to receiver and from receiver to sender), but only one way at a time. A citizens band (CB) radio is an example of a half-duplex system.

HDLC (High-Level Data Link Control) — HDLC is a standard that provides support for both point-to-point and multipoint services over synchronous serial data links and ISDN interfaces. HDLC is the default serial encapsulation method on Cisco routers.

hop count — The number of routers that a packet passes through to reach its destination is called the hop count.

host — A host is a server to which workstations are attached. A host server is usually a computer that is configured as a central controller to the rest of the network. The term *host* is usually applied to the computer that controls or coordinates resource access and usage by the network workstations.

hostname — Every router on a network should have a unique, identifying name. Cisco calls this name the hostname.

HSSI (High-Speed Serial Interface) — HSSI is a serial interface capable of transmitting data at more than 20 Kbps.

HTTP (Hypertext Transfer Protocol) — HTTP is the TCP/IP protocol used to transfer HTML documents on the World Wide Web. HTTP provides the rules under which any document can establish hyperlinks to any other document or location on the Internet.

hub — A hub is used to cluster workstations into a group. Hubs are either active or passive. When a hub receives a signal on one of its ports, it passes the signal on to all of its other ports.

I

ICMP (Internet Control Message Protocol) — This Network layer protocol is used for control and messaging services and carrying messages between systems regarding status, passing control codes, and delivering error codes.

IEEE 802.1Q — This 802.1 standard defines VLAN information exchange between dissimilar manufacturers' equipment.

IEEE 802.2 — This standard of the IEEE 802 Project defines logical link control (LLC) of the Data Link layer.

IEEE 802.3 — This standard of the IEEE 802 Project defines Ethernet and CSMA/CD.

IEEE 802.5 — This standard of the IEEE 802 Project defines logical ring topology, media, and interfaces (Token Ring).

IGRP (Interior Gateway Routing Protocol) — IGRP is a classful, distance-vector routing protocol very similar to RIP that must be identified to an autonomous system.

infrastructure — An infrastructure is all of a network's components, including its hardware, software, cabling, conceptual layout, and physical layout. The infrastructure of a network is its operating elements.

intranet — This is any internal private network that uses TCP/IP as its base protocol. On an intranet network, information is viewed by users with browsers. Most intranets are connected to the Internet, but they do not need to be.

IP access list — Two types of IP access lists exist: standard IP access lists that analyze the source IP address in a TCP/IP packet and then take action to permit or deny the packet to pass through the router based on the outcome of its analysis, and extended IP access lists that permit or deny a packet using a variety of factors, including Source address, destination address, protocol, and port.

IP address classes — Three IP address classes are usable: Class A, Class B, and Class C. Two other IP address classes do exist, but they're set aside for special purposes. Each IP address class (A, B, and C) has a finite number of bits assigned to hold each of the network and host IDs.

IPX — This Novell proprietary protocol is used by NetWare 4.*x* and earlier network operating systems.

IPX access list — This is used to deny or permit a packet to the router using both the source and destination addresses.

IPX address — This address consists of a 10-byte hexadecimal number that is made up of a 4-byte network number and a 6-byte node number.

IPX socket — This 16-bit number is added to the end of the network and node addresses in the IPX header in the format of *network.node.socket.*

ISDN (Integrated Services Digital Network) — ISDN is a digital service capable of transmitting voice, data and other source traffic over existing telephone lines. ISDN is available in two formats: PRI and BRI.

L

L2TP (Layer 2 Tunnel Protocol) — L2TP is a new tunneling protocol standard that extends the capability of PPTP. It is used to create private virtual circuits over the Internet. See *PPTP*.

LAN (Local Area Network) — A LAN supports data transfer on a physical infrastructure in a small, limited geographic area, such as within a single building or on a single floor of a building.

latency — Latency is the delay introduced by network devices, such as a bridge, switch, or router, as they process packets.

LDAP (Lightweight Directory Access Protocol) — LDAP is used to locate domains or an object located on a domain on the Internet. It allows you to search for the domain or an individual or file on the network.

link state — Link state protocols use the shortest path algorithm to determine the best route and update the routing table using event-triggered updates and LSPs (link state packets, which are also called "Hello" packets) sent to all neighboring network routers. Examples of link state protocols are NLSP, OSPF, and IS-IS.

LLC (Logical Link Control) sublayer — This sublayer of the Data Link layer creates connections between networked devices.

LMI (Local Management Interface) — This interface type enhances the Frame Relay protocol by adding the capability for internetworking devices to communicate with a Frame Relay network.

logical address — This address has a logical connection to all other addresses on its network, such as an IP address.

M

MAC (Media Access Control) address — A MAC address is a 48-bit address made up of two parts: the manufacturer's ID number and a unique serialized number assigned to the device by its manufacturer.

MAC sublayer — The MAC sublayer of the Data Link layer provides a range of network services, including controlling access to the network and physical addressing.

MOTD (Message Of The Day) banner — You can set up a banner message to be displayed when someone logs into the router.

N

NetBIOS/NetBEUI (Network Basic Input/Output System/NetBIOS Extended User Interface) — Microsoft's network protocols work together to manage communications and provide data transport services.

Netstat — Netstat is a utility program used to display protocol statistics and current active TCP/IP network connections.

NetWare link services protocol (NLSP) — This link state routing protocol is the default routing protocol on NetWare 4.11 and higher.

NetWare core protocol (NCP) — This Novell NetWare protocol provides client-to-server connections and applications.

Novell directory service (NDS) — This is Novell NetWare's directory services protocol.

Network layer — The Network layer (Layer 3 of the OSI Model) is the layer on which routing takes place and defines the processes used to route data across the network and the structure and use of logical addressing.

NVRAM — The startup configuration file is stored in this type of router memory.

O

OC (Optical Carrier) lines: The most commonly used OC (Optical carrier) lines are the OC-1, which transmits at 51.84Mbps, and the OC-3, which transmits at three times the base rate or 155.52Mbps.

OSI Model (Open Systems Interconnection Reference Model) — The OSI seven-layer model was developed by the ISO (International Standards Organization) and released in 1984. The OSI model describes how information moves from one network to another.

P

PAP (Password Authentication Protocol) — PAP is a challenge protocol used to verify username and password on a processing router.

parity — Parity is an error-detection method. Two types of parity are used — odd-parity and even-parity. In either case, an extra bit is used to set the number of bits in a data block to either an even or add number.

patch panel — A termination point for network cables, a patch cord is used to interconnect each port on the patch panel.

PDU (Protocol Data Unit) — A PDU is the package of data that moves through the OSI layers. A PDU has several forms as it moves. See *encapsulation*.

peer — Any workstation in a peer-to-peer network is a peer. Workstations are peers because they are equal.

physical address — This network address has no relationship to any other address on a network, such as a Layer 2 MAC address.

Physical layer — This is Layer 1 of the OSI Model. This layer defines the electrical and physical specifications for the networking media that carry the data bits across a network.

PING (Packet Internet Groper) — This command is used to verify Layer 3 connectivity. PING sends out ICMP messages to verify both the logical addresses and the physical connection.

POP3 (Post Office Protocol 3) — POP3, also known simply as POP mail, is an e-mail standard that collects user e-mail in a mailbox and then transfers the e-mail to the user's computer when he logs into the mail server.

port — A port is a logical connection that allows incoming data to be assigned to a particular application or service for processing. Each port is assigned a *port number,* which is a way to identify the specific process to which the message is to be passed. See also *well-known port.*

POTS (Plain Old Telephone System) — POTS is the common public telephone system. See also *PSTN.*

POST (Power-On Self-Test) — The router POST process checks the CPU, memory, and the interface ports to ensure that they are present and operational.

PPP (Point-To-Point Protocol) — This protocol is used for router-to-router and host-to-network communications over synchronous and asynchronous circuits, including HSSI and ISDN interfaces.

PPP/Multilink — This protocol combines two PPP links into a new virtual link with greater bandwidth of the two separate links. It is commonly used to distribute the bandwidth load of two links evenly over their combined capacity.

PPTP (Point-to-Point Tunneling Protocol) — This WAN protocol allows users to build virtual private networks (tunnels) through the Internet. PPTP, along with L2TP, is used to create a virtual private network (VPN).

Presentation layer — Layer 6 of the OSI Model, this layer is concerned with data representation and code formatting. Data formatting, such as ASCII, EBCDIC, and encryption are supported on this layer.

PRI ISDN — An ISDN PRI line consists of 23 64Kbps bearer (B) channels and one 16Kbps data (D) channel.

Privileged Exec mode — See *Enable Exec mode.*

protocol — A protocol is a set of rules that defines how two devices communicate with one another and the format of the packets used to transmit data over communications lines.

PSTN (Public Switched Telephone Network) — PSTN is the common telephone system.

PVC (Permanent Virtual Circuit) — This type of X.25 virtual circuit is permanent, dedicated, and continuous.

R

RAM (Random Access Memory) — RAM is router memory where active program and operating system instructions, the running configuration file, and routing tables are stored.

RARP (Reverse ARP) — This protocol is used to resolve network addresses into physical addresses.

repeater — A repeater is a device used on a network to solve attenuation problems in cable wire. A repeater cleans up the signal, gives it a boost, and sends it on its way.

RFI (Radio Frequency Interference) — Devices that broadcast wireless or radio signals can produce interference through radio wave transmissions picked up by other electrical devices, which is the cause of EMI.

ring topology — Using this fundamental topology, the primary network cable is installed as a loop, or ring, and the workstations are attached to the primary cable at points on the ring.

RIP (Routing Information Protocol) — RIP is a classful, distance-vector routing protocol that uses information provided by neighboring routers to maintain the cost, in terms of hops and other metrics, of a particular route.

ROM (Read-Only Memory) — The router's ROM is where the POST, bootstrap, and startup/power-up utilities, and a limited version of the Cisco IOS are stored.

route poisoning — Also known as poison reverse routing, this technique — which is used to avoid routing loops — assigns the maximum hop count plus one to the hop count metric of any route not available.

routed protocol — Routed protocols are used to carry end-user traffic across the internetwork. Examples of routed protocols are IP and IPX.

router — A router is a type of networking hardware or software that determines the best route that a packet should take to its destination. A router is connected to at least two networks, the internal (LAN) and the external (WAN). A router is typically used as the default gateway for a network.

routing — The process of moving data along a path from a source to a destination is called routing.

routing loop — A routing loop is a condition caused when routing tables are not updated accurately at the same time and erroneous route information is used. You may also hear them called count-to-infinity routing loops. A maximum hop count variable on the router is used to avoid routing loops.

routing protocol — A routing protocol is used to pass messages between routers for maintaining and updating routing tables. Examples of routing protocols are RIP, IGRP, OSPF, and EIGRP.

routing table — A routing table is stored in the RAM of a bridge or router, and stores message addresses for later use in forwarding messages to those addresses.

RTS/CTS (Ready To Send/Clear To Send) — RTS/CTS uses two wires in a cable, one for RTS and one for CTS. The sending device uses the RTS signal to indicate when it's ready to send. The receiving device uses the CTS to indicate it's ready to receive. When either is turned off, the flow is interrupted. This is also called "hardware flow control."

running configuration — The configuration in the router's RAM when it is operating is referred to as the running configuration.

S

SAP (Service Advertisement Protocol) — This Novell NetWare protocol is used to advertise (update) the services available over the network.

segment — A segment is a subnetwork on a network created by the insertion of a router, switch, or bridge. Segments are created to increase bandwidth efficiency, reduce congestion, and create smaller collision domains.

segmentation — Dividing a network into segments decreases congestion and reduces the chance of message collisions by creating smaller collision domains.

server — A specially designated computer in a network. It has been chosen to perform a special task to service the resource needs of the workstation (client) computers on the network.

session — A session is a series of related connection-oriented transmissions between network nodes.

Session layer — The Session layer (Layer 5 of the OSI Model) establishes, maintains, and manages the communication session between computers.

setup mode — The command line mode used to set the configuration of a router is called setup mode.

SLIP (Serial Line Internet Protocol) — SLIP is a point-to-point protocol for transmitting IP packets over a dial-up connection.

STP (Shielded Twisted-Pair) — STP has its wires wrapped in a copper or foil shield to help reduce EMI and RFI interference, which makes it more expensive than UTP wire. STP is common in Token Ring networks.

SMTP (Simple Mail Transport Protocol) — Where POP3 delivers e-mail to the end-user, SMTP is the TCP/IP protocol used to transmit e-mail over the Internet. SMTP has limited mailbox abilities, so it is not uncommon to use SMTP to send e-mail and POP3 to receive it. See *POP3*.

spanning tree protocol — A spanning tree protocol is a bridging protocol that designates interfaces to be in Forwarding or Blocking State. In Blocking State, only special packets reporting the status of other bridges on the network are allowed through. In Forwarding State, all packets are allowed to pass.

SPID (Service Profile Identifier) — An SPID is the number assigned by an ISDN service provider to each B channel of a BRI ISDN line.

split horizon — This technique is used to prevent bad routing information from being sent back to its source.

SPX (Sequence Package Exchange) — This Novell NetWare protocol provides connection-oriented packet delivery.

star topology — In this type of topology, each workstation connects directly to a central device with its own cable, creating a starburst-like pattern.

star-bus topology — In this topology, a hub or switch is used as a clustering device that is then attached to the network backbone. This is a common topology of Ethernet networks.

star-ring topology — A multistation access unit (MAU) clusters workstations and is connected to the next MAU on the network to create a ring structure.

startup configuration — The configuration file loaded from NVRAM during startup is called the startup configuration. Contrast this with *running configuration*.

static route — A static route is a router entry that is configured manually and by the network administrator for a network address for which only a single route is desired.

store-and-forward switching — This switching method reads the entire frame into its buffer before forwarding it. This type of switching results in variable-length latency.

subinterface — Each of the virtual circuits on a single serial interface is a subinterface. You'll encounter two types of subinterfaces: point-to-point and multipoint.

subnet mask — A binary bit pattern of 1s and 0s is applied to an IP address to extract the network ID and host ID portions of the address. These two items make up the subnet mask.

subnetting — The standard address class structure is expanded by borrowing bits from the host portion to provide more bits for the network portion of the address.

SVC (Switched Virtual Circuit) — A temporary virtual circuit is created especially for and exists only for the duration of a X.25 data communications session.

switch — A switch is a Layer 2 device that is used to move data to its destination with capabilities ranging from a smart hub to those virtually the same as a router.

T

T1 — A carrier line that transmits signals at the rate of 1.54Mbps and can transmit one megabyte of data in about 10 seconds.

T3 — A carrier line that is the equivalent of 28 T1 lines and can transmit signals at 44.736Mbps.

TCP/IP (Transmission Control Protocol/Internet Protocol) — This protocol suite of interconnected and interworking protocols provides for reliable and efficient data communications across an internetwork.

telnet — Telnet is a terminal emulation protocol used on TCP/IP-based networks to remotely log onto a remote device to run a program or manipulate data.

TFTP (Trivial File Transfer Protocol) — TFTP is a best-effort file transfer protocol used by Cisco routers to store and retrieve configuration files from a TFTP server.

Token Ring — Token Ring networks, defined in IEEE 802.5, are laid out in a loop that starts and ends at the same node, forming a ring network that operates at either 4Mbps or 16Mbps.

topology — The physical layout of the network is referred to as a topology.

trace — Also known as traceroute, this command tests the route from a source to a destination by sending out probe packets one at a time to each router or switch in the path and then displays the round-trip time for each packet.

Transport layer — Layer 4 of the OSI Model, this layer defines the functions that provide for the reliable transmission of data segments, as well as the disassembly and assembly of the data before and after transmission.

TTL (Time To Live) — This routing variable indicates the remaining number of hops that a packet can take before being expired.

twisted-pair (TP) wire — Twisted-pair wire comes in two types: unshielded (UTP) and shielded (STP).

U

UDP (User Datagram Protocol) — UDP is the TCP/IP best-effort protocol that isn't concerned with the reliable delivery of packets and doesn't bother with overhead such as acknowledgments.

User Exec mode — This command line mode is available immediately after logging into a router. It is used to connect to other devices, perform simple tests, and display system information.

UTP (Unshielded Twisted-Pair) — The most common type of cabling used in networks, UTP is commonly referred to as 10BaseT Ethernet cable.

V

virtual circuit (VC) — Also known as virtual circuit number (VCN), logical channel number (LCN), and virtual channel identifier (VCI), a VC can be a permanent virtual circuit (PVC) or a switched virtual circuit (SVC).

virtual terminal (vty) password — This password is set to restrict access to the router using a telnet session. Unless this password, also known as the "vty password", is set, you cannot telnet into the router.

VLAN (Virtual LAN) — A VLAN is a logical grouping of networked nodes that communicate directly with each other on Layers 2 and 3.

VPN (Virtual Private Network) — A VPN is the connection made between two computers using a tunneling protocol, usually the PPTP (Point-to-Point Tunneling Protocol), over which data can be transmitted privately. A VPN encrypts data and then encapsulates the encrypted data in a PPTP packet so that it is transmitted over the Internet without the danger of interception and misuse.

W

WAN (Wide Area Network) — A WAN is a network that interconnects LANs and across a broad geographic area and uses a data transmission technology provided by a common carrier.

well-known ports — Ports in the range of 0 through 1023 are used only by system processes or privileged programs. Well-known ports are generally TCP ports but can be registered to UDP services as well.

wildcard mask — This mask is used with access lists to filter specific IP addresses or groups of IP addresses by including a 0 in a position to be checked and a 1 in positions to be ignored.

windowing — Windowing is a flow control method that establishes a window that allows a certain number of packets to be transmitted before an acknowledgment must be sent.

workstation — Workstations and clients are synonymous. In some instances, the term *node* may also be interchanged with *workstation* as well, but technically, a node can be anything that is connected to a network. Unlike servers, they generally do not share their resources to the network.

X

X.25 — X.25 is a packet-switched networking protocol for exchanging data over a connection-oriented service.

XON/XOFF — This roughly stands for transmission on/transmission off, and is also called software flow control. The sending device sends data until the receiving device signals with a control character to stop so that the receiving device can catch up. When the receiving device is ready to go, it signals the sending device to restart the transmission.

Index

• *E* •

Notes

Notes

Notes

Notes

Notes

Notes

Notes

Notes

YOUR ONLINE RESOURCE

WWW.DUMMIES.COM

Discover Dummies Online!

The Dummies Web Site is your fun and friendly online resource for the latest information about *For Dummies*® books and your favorite topics. The Web site is the place to communicate with us, exchange ideas with other *For Dummies* readers, chat with authors, and have fun!

Ten Fun and Useful Things You Can Do at www.dummies.com

1. Win free *For Dummies* books and more!
2. Register your book and be entered in a prize drawing.
3. Meet your favorite authors through the IDG Books Worldwide Author Chat Series.
4. Exchange helpful information with other *For Dummies* readers.
5. Discover other great *For Dummies* books you must have!
6. Purchase Dummieswear® exclusively from our Web site.
7. Buy *For Dummies* books online.
8. Talk to us. Make comments, ask question get answers!
9. Download free software.
10. Find additional useful resources from authors.

WWW.DUMMIES.COM

For other technology titles from IDG Books Worldwide, go to
www.idgbooks.com

Link directly to these ten fun and useful things at
http://www.dummies.com/10useful

Not on the Web yet? It's easy to get started with *Dummies 101*®: *The Internet For Windows*® *98* or *The Internet For Dummies*® at local retailers everywhere.

Find other *For Dummies* books on these topics:

IDG BOOKS WORLDWIDE

Business • Career • Databases • Food & Beverage • Games • Gardening • Graphics • Hardware
Health & Fitness • Internet and the World Wide Web • Networking • Office Suites
Operating Systems • Personal Finance • Pets • Programming • Recreation • Sports
Spreadsheets • Teacher Resources • Test Prep • Word Processing

Register This Book and Win!

We want to hear from you!

Visit **http://my2cents.dummies.com** to register this book and tell us how you liked it!

- ✔ Get entered in our monthly prize giveaway.

- ✔ Give us feedback about this book — tell us what you like best, what you like least, or maybe what you'd like to ask the author and us to change!

- ✔ Let us know any other *For Dummies®* topics that interest you.

Your feedback helps us determine what books to publish, tells us what coverage to add as we revise our books, and lets us know whether we're meeting your needs as a *For Dummies* reader. You're our most valuable resource, and what you have to say is important to us!

Not on the Web yet? It's easy to get started with *Dummies 101®: The Internet For Windows® 98* or *The Internet For Dummies®* at local retailers everywhere.

Or let us know what you think by sending us a letter at the following address:

For Dummies Book Registration
Dummies Press
10475 Crosspoint Blvd.
Indianapolis, IN 46256

...FOR DUMMIES ™

BESTSELLING
BOOK SERIES